CONTENTS

W9-CEB-823

The *Michelin maps* you will need with this guide are

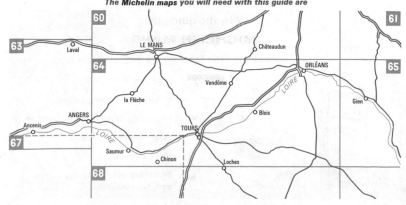

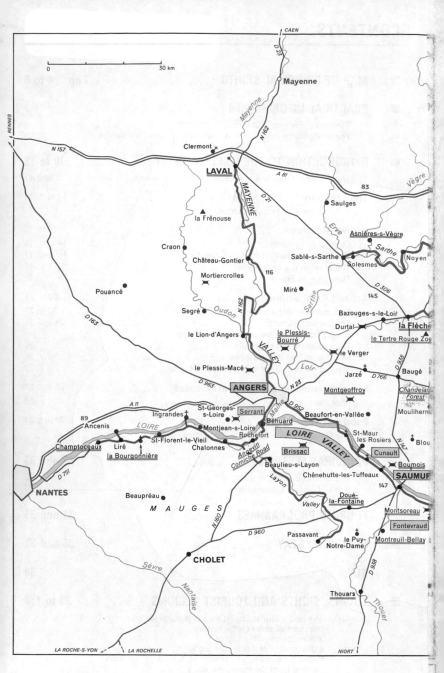

VISITING THE LOIRE COUNTRY?

The above map indicates a selection of sights described in the guide

Many others are to be found on pages 39 to 170

With the guide use

MICHELIN MAPS

Various touristic features are indicated

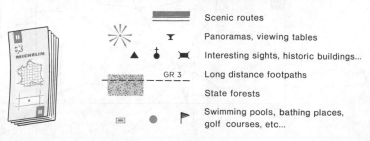

▬▬▬		Scenic routes
☀	⊤	Panoramas, viewing tables
▲ ✝ ✕		Interesting sights, historic buildings...
▬▬▬ GR 3		Long distance footpaths
		State forests
⬜ ● ▶		Swimming pools, bathing places, golf courses, etc...

4

PRINCIPAL SIGHTS

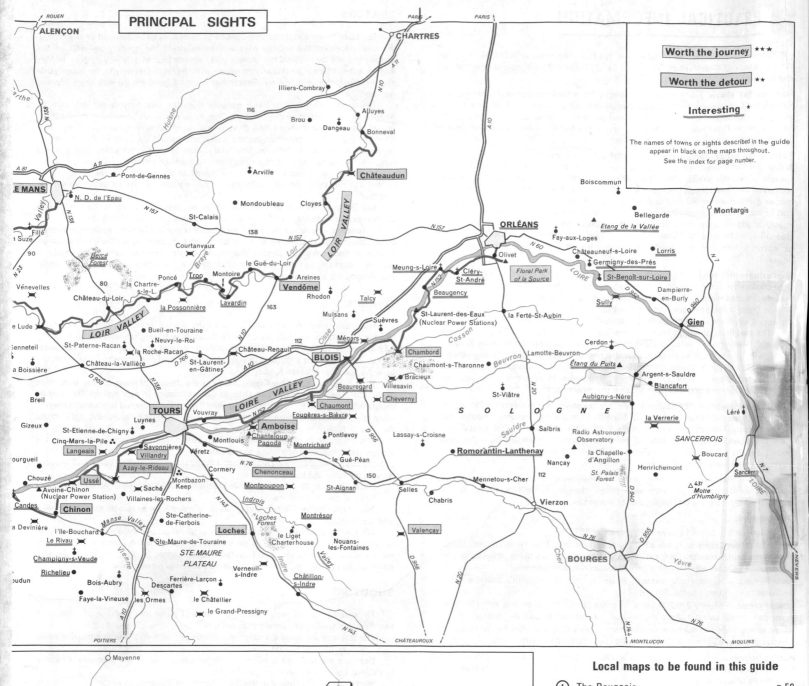

Worth the journey ★★★

Worth the detour ★★

Interesting ★

The names of towns or sights described in the guide appear in black on the maps throughout.
See the index for page number.

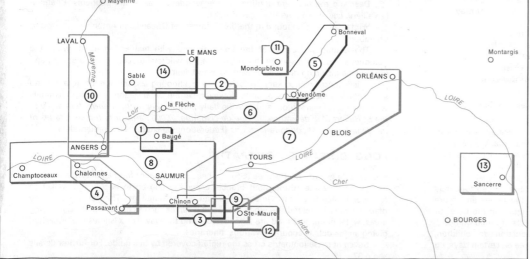

PRACTICAL INFORMATION

The French National Tourist Offices at 178 Piccadilly, London W1V OAL, Tel (01) 491 76 22 and 619 Fifth Avenue, New York, Tel (212) 757-1125 will provide information and literature.

How to get there. – You can go directly by scheduled national airlines, by commercial and package tour flights, possibly with a rail or coach link up, or you can go by cross Channel ferry or Hovercraft and on by car or train. Enquire at any good travel agent and remember, if you are going in the holiday season or at Christmas, Easter or Whitsun, to book well in advance.

Papers and other documents. – A valid national **passport** (or, in the case of the British a Visitor's Passport) is all that is required, for the car you need a valid **driving licence, international driving permit, car registration book** and a **nationality plate** of the approved size. Insurance cover is compulsory and although the Green Card is no longer a legal requirement for France it is the most effective proof of insurance cover and is internationally recognized by the police and other authorities. Caravan owners must, in addition, produce the caravan **logbook** and an inventory for customs clearance, green card endorsement for caravan and trailer. A **carnet** is required to import temporarily certain vehicles : pleasure craft over 5.5 m long and motor boats.

Motoring regulations. – Certain motoring organizations run accident insurance and breakdown service schemes for their members. Enquire before leaving. A **red warning triangle** or hazard warning lights are obligatory in case of a breakdown.

In France it is compulsory for the front passengers to wear **seat belts** if the car is equipped with them. Children under ten should be on the back seat.

The **speed limits**, although liable to modification, are motorways 130 kph - 80 mph (110 kph when raining); national trunk roads 110 kph - 68 mph; other roads 90 kph - 56 mph (80 kph - 50 mph when raining) and in towns 60 kph - 37 mph. The regulations on speeding and drinking and driving are strictly interpreted – usually by an on the spot fine and/or confiscation of the vehicle. Remember to cede priority to vehicles joining from the right and there are tolls on the motorways.

Medical treatment. – For EEC countries it is necessary to have Form E 111 which testifies to your entitlement to medical benefits from the Department of Health and Social Security. With this you can obtain medical treatment in an emergency and, after the necessary steps, a refund of part of the costs of treatment from the local Social Security offices (*Caisse Primaire de Sécurité Sociale*). It is, however, still advisable to take out comprehensive insurance cover.

Currency. – Your passport is necessary as identification when cashing cheques in banks. Commission charges vary with hotels charging more highly than banks especially when obliging on holidays or at weekends.

Duly arrived:

Consulates : British, 6 Rue La Fayette, Nantes. Tel 48 57 47.

Tourist Information Centres or *Syndicats d'Initiative* 🄱 are to be found in most large towns and many tourist resorts. They can supply large scale town plans, timetables and information on local entertainment facilities, sports and sightseeing.

Poste Restante. – Name, *Poste restante, Posto Centrale,* Department's postal number followed by the town's name, France.

Electric current. – Mostly 220-230 volts, in some places, however, it is still 110 volts. European circular two pin plugs are the rule – remember to take an adaptor.

Where to stay. – In the Michelin Guide France you will find a selection of hotels et various prices in all areas. It also lists local restaurants, again with prices.

Public holidays. – National museums and art galleries are closed on Tuesdays. The following are days when museums and other monuments may be closed or may vary their hours of admission :

New Year's Day	Whit Sunday and Monday
Palm Sunday	France's National Day **(14 July)**
Easter Sunday and Monday	Assumption **(15 August)**
May Day **(1 May)**	All Saints' Day **(1 November)**
Fête de la Libération **(8 May)**	Remembrance Day **(11 November)**
Ascension Day	Christmas Day.

In addition to the usual school holidays at Christmas, Easter and Summer there are week long breaks in February and early November.

Opening times and admission prices. – The **visiting times** indicate the hours of opening and closing and it is important to remember that many châteaux, museums, etc, refuse admittance from up to an hour before the actual closing time.

When **guided tours** are indicated, the departure time for the last tour of the morning or afternoon will once again be prior to given closing time. Most tours are conducted by French speaking guides but in some cases the term guided tour may cover group visiting with recorded commentaries. Some of the larger and more frequented châteaux offer guided tours in other languages. Enquire at the ticket or book stalls. Other aids for the foreign tourist are notes, pamphlets or audio guides.

The **admission prices** indicated are for adults, however reductions for children, students and parties are common. In some cases admission is free on certain days, eg Wednesdays, Sundays or public holidays.

SEASONS

The Loire Valley and its splendid series of châteaux can be admired at any time of the year. However the tourist who wishes to enjoy the scenery as well as the architecture will try to avoid the crowds and extreme heat of July and August. In May and June the region is particularly attractive with the fresh greenery of the countryside and a profusion of wild flowers. September is also a good month with relatively fine weather.

The climate of the Loire Basin benefits from the proximity of the sea and the Atlantic winds penetrate freely, clearing the air in winter and providing a refreshing breeze in summer. In former times these winds, which blow with trade wind regularity filled the sails of the boats plying the Loire and turned the sails of the numerous windmills perched on the hilltops. This mild climate has made the valley what it is – a region of vineyards, arable farms, nurseries and market gardening.

Upstream from Orléans the maritime influence is greatly diminished and a semi continental climate is the rule with very harsh winters and heavy summers on the plateaux.

The Orléans and Beauce are troubled by severely cold winds while the Blésois suffers occasional frosts – and even the Loire is sometimes full of drift ice.

In Touraine and Anjou the maritime climate is marked by hot summers tempered by sea breezes, mild autumns and benign winters, accounting for the Mediterranean type vegetation : palms, eucalyptus, magnolias, cedars, camellias, hydrangeas, medlars, monkey puzzle and fig trees. Spring is often damp but it is also warm and comes early, encouraging the early vegetables.

FISHING

The many rivers, streams and pools of the region teem with a wide variety of species. Blay, roach and dace are common throughout the region, with the Loire giving pike and even striped mullet, which in summer comes as far up river as Amboise. Catfish, tench and carp abound in the deeper pools of the Loire, Indre and Loir, while the Sologne pools are a haven for perch.

Trout fishing is best in the Creuse, Sauldre, the streams of Anjou and the tributaries of the Loir. The Berry, Briare and Orléans Canals abound in eels and crayfish can be caught with special nets. For salmon and shad fishing flat bottomed boats are necessary while the commercial salmon fishers use nets, supported by poles, strung right across the river *(p 104)*.

It is essential to obtain a membership card bearing the necessary fishing tax stamps. The latter vary according to the category of the waterway, the type of fishing and the region. Apply to the Departmental Federations for angling clubs and associations in the following towns.

28630 Chartres ; 37 Tours ; 41 Vallée Maillard ; 41000 Blois ; 45 Orléans ; 49 Angers ; 53 Laval and 72 Le Mans.

Tourist Information Centres and fishing tackle dealers may also be able to help with additional details.

Whatever type of fishing he chooses the angler must observe the federal and local regulations. For further particulars on such regulations, the close seasons and hours, the classification of waterways (first and second category and public or private), minimum size of fish, etc, apply to the same addresses given above.

SHOOTING

The diversity of the region offers a wealth of game and a choice of sport be it shooting, wildfowling or hunting with hounds.

The plains of the Beauce and meadowlands of Anjou and Touraine provide cover for partridges, pheasants, quails, thrushes, larks, hares and rabbits alike.

Deer and roe deer are confined to the wooded areas of the Baugeois, Château-la-Vallière, Loches and the Valençay district.

Wild boar are to be found in the dense forests of Orléans and Amboise and around Chambord.

The islands and banks of the Loire abound with teal and mallard, while the Sologne, a shooters' paradise, provides a bag of wildfowl (ducks, teal and snipe), and other game including pheasants, wild boar and deer.

It is generally necessary to belong to a shooting association be it a private syndicate or a local society or club. However, certain organizations and/or individuals welcome occasional visitors and provide daily permits. *For further information apply to the St-Hubert Club de France, 10 Rue de Lisbonne, 75008 Paris, or to the secretaries of the departmental shooting federations* (Fédérations de chasse départementales).

LONG DISTANCE FOOTPATHS

Sentiers de grande randonnée (GR). – These long distance footpaths form a network of marked itineraries throughout France, especially chosen to enable the walker to discover France in all the variety of its natural surroundings. The paths are clearly marked (with parallel red and white lines) and facilities such as hotels, shelters, camping areas, water points and food are signposted along the way. Topo Guides are published giving all the details about the various itineraries.

Seven of these footpaths cross the region covered by this guide. For further details see p 37.

THE CHÂTEAUX OF THE LOIRE

Between Sancerre and Nantes the banks of the Loire and the valleys of its tributaries offer an incomparable series of magnificent buildings rich alike in art and history and all in a harmonious setting.

The landscape. – The Loire landscape, with its simple, quiet lines, owes its charm to the subtle light that plays over it, displaying wide, pale blue skies, long stretches of often sluggish river, calm watercourses with soft reflections, sunny slopes with fertile vineyards, green valleys, smiling, flower decked villages and peaceful scenes. For these reasons it is also often referred to as the "Garden of France".

Castles and Châteaux. – The finest châteaux in the region were built in the Renaissance period (16C). Among these are Amboise, Azay-le-Rideau, Blois, Chambord, Chaumont, Château-dun, Chenonceau, Ussé, Villandry, etc. Also worthy of mention are the castles of Angers, Chinon, Langeais, Loches and Sully, which were built in the Middle Ages, and the châteaux of Cheverny, Valençay and Serrant dating from the Classical period (17 and 18C).

Their history. – In the 15 and 16C the châteaux were the favourite residences of the Valois. From Charles VII to Henri III, the kings of France often stayed in them. As the court moved from one to another in obedience to the sovereign's whim, life in these places was extremely lively.

Some of these buildings were the scenes of tragic or moving happenings which had a great effect on the history of France, such as the crushing of the Amboise Conspiracy in 1560, the murder of the duc de Guise at Blois in 1588 and, above all, the "recognising" of Charles VII by Joan of Arc at Chinon in 1429. This last was an essential step in the marvellous progress which was crowned, in the Loire country, by the relief of Orléans.

(After photo: Bertault-Foussemagne, Éd. Arthaud)

The Loire at Candes

The towns and abbeys. – The beautiful countryside and the historic châteaux are not the only attractions of this region.

Towns have long existed at the main bridging points of the great river: Gien, Orléans, Beaugency, Blois, Tours, Saumur and Angers. They have suffered much, especially in war, as a result of their strategic value as bridgeheads.

Happily almost all the finest buildings were spared and several towns such as Châteaudun, Laval, Loches and Vendôme have conserved older quarters with many picturesque houses in the traditional local styles while other towns have programmes of restoration for such quarters as in Blois, Chinon, Le Mans and Tours.

The Middle Ages with the upsurge in religious faith saw the establishment and growth of powerful abbeys. St-Benoît and Fontevraud still have today some magnificent examples of Romanesque architecture. Witness also to the mysticism of the mediaeval period are the Abbey at Vendôme, Candes Church and the Cathedrals of Le Mans and Tours.

The wines of the Loire. – A visit to the Loire country will not only offer the tourist pure artistic joys and moving reminders of French history. The slopes along the river and its tributaries produce excellent wines which will please gourmets: dry and aromatic Sancerre wines, fresh and fruity wines from the districts of Orléans and Blois, great vintages from Touraine – Vouvray, Montlouis, Azay-le-Rideau, Chinon, Bourgueil, St-Nicolas – sparkling wines from Saumur, the Loudun light reds and the sweet and heady wines of Anjou.

(After photo: Yvon)

Château de Chinon

The garden of France. – From whatever direction you approach the region be it across the immense plains of the Beauce, the harsher Berry countryside or the green *bocage,* wooded farmland, country of the Gâtine Mancelle, you will always be welcomed in the heart of the Loire country by the sight of vines, white houses and flowers.

For many foreigners this is perhaps one of the most typically French landscapes of them all with its peaceful, moderate and gentle countryside, a succession of blessed havens.

But make no mistake, the "Garden of France" is not a sort of Eden full of fruit and flowers. The historian Michelet once described it as a "homespun cloak with golden fringes", meaning that the valleys – the golden fringes – in all their wonderful fertility, bordered plateaux whose harshness was only tempered by occasional fine forests.

Geology. – Hemmed in by the ancient crystalline masses of the Morvan, Armorican Massif and Massif Central, the Loire region is actually part of the Paris Basin.

In the Secondary Era the area invaded by the sea was covered by a soft, chalky deposit known as the **tuffeau** or tufa. This is now exposed along the valley sides of the Loir, Cher, Indre and Vienne. Also deposited were the limestones of the **gâtines** (sterile marshlands) often interrupted by tracts of sands and clays supporting forests and heathlands. Once the sea had retreated, great freshwater lakes deposited more limestones, the surface of which is often covered with a topsoil of loess or silt. These areas are known as **champagnes** or *champeignes.*

During the Tertiary Era the folding of the Alpine mountain zone, created the Massif Central, and rivers descending from this new watershed were often laden with sandy clays which when deposited gave areas such as the Sologne and the Forest of Orléans. Later subsidence in the west permitted the invasion by the **Faluns Sea** or Mer des Faluns as far as Blois, Thouars and Preuilly-sur-Claise. The heritage of this marine incursion, are a series of *falunières,* or shell marl beds to be found on the borders of the Ste-Maure Plateau, and the hills edging the Loire to the north. Rivers originally flowing northwards were attracted in a westerly direction by the sea, thus explaining the great change of direction at Orléans. The sea finally retreated for good leaving an undulating countryside with the river network the most important geographical feature. The alluvial silts or **varennes** deposited by the Loire and its numerous tributaries were to add an extremely fertile element to this already rich and varied geological pattern.

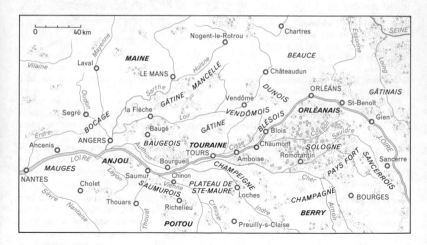

THE REGIONS

Physically very diverse the Loire region reaches from the Sancerre Hills in the east to the *bocage* landscapes of Maine and Anjou in the west.

Northern Berry. – This region lying between the Massif Central and the Loire country includes in the east the **Sancerrois** with its chalky, vineyard covered slopes overlooking the Loire and the **Pays Fort,** an area of clay soils sloping down towards the Sologne *(see Luçay-le-Mâle p 164).* This essentially *bocage* landscape is described by Alain Fournier in his novel *Le Grand Meaulnes.*

Between the Cher and Arnon and the Indre is the area known as the **Champagne.** Essentially an area of limestone soils but often silty, it has tracts of *mardelles.*

Orléanais and Blésois. – Below Gien the valley opens out, the hills are lower and a refreshing breeze makes the leaves tremble on the long lines of poplars and willows. This is the gateway to the Orléanais which covers the Beauce, the Loir Valley (ie the Dunois and Vendômois), the Sologne and Blésois or Blois region. Between Gien and Orléans the Loire meanders on the floor of a rich, wide valley. In the vicinity of St-Benoît the valley, commonly known as the **Val,** is a series of meadows, beyond which horticulture predominates with the growing of seedlings and rosebushes on the alluvial deposits known locally as *layes.* Orchards and vineyards flourish on the south facing slopes.

From Orléans to Chaumont the Loire cuts into, on its northern bank, the **Beauce** limestone and further downstream into the flinty chalklands and tufa. On the southern side the river laps the alluvial sands brought down by its own waters, and which, besides growing asparagus and early vegetables, are also covered in dense brushwood, through this the kings of France once used to hunt. The great châteaux then begin : Blois, Chambord, Cheverny, Chaumont...

The **Beauce,** the granary of France, a treeless plain covered with a thin layer (2 m - 6 ft maximum) of fertile silt or loess, is extended to the area between the Loire and Loir by the Petite Beauce. On the latter the *limon* gives way to clays : the Forest of Marchenoir. Villages, grouped round the pond and well, generally consist of a series of traditional closed courtyard type farms.

In the **Sologne** *(p 150)* and the **Forest of Orléans** patches of poor crops alternate with the woodland.

Touraine. – The **Val's** comfortable opulence delights the visitor already attracted by the luminous beauty of the light. The Loire, blue between golden sandbanks, flows slowly along its course hollowed out of the soft tufa chalk. Channels no longer occupied by the main river are divided into dead end reaches known as *boires* or occupied by tributary streams such as the Cher, Indre, Vienne *(p 76)* and Cisse *(p 58)*.

From Amboise to Tours the flinty chalk soils of the valley sides are clad with vineyards producing the well known Vouvray and Montlouis wines. **Troglodyte** houses have been carved out of the white tufa so that the passerby may well see plumes of smoke rising from amidst the vines.

The **Véron** *(p 73),* lying between the Loire and the Vienne, is a patchwork of small fields and gardens rising above the riverside osier beds, willows and poplars.

The plateaus of Touraine are not the harsh wastelands described by Michelet. The **Gâtine** of Touraine, between the Loir and Loire, was once a great forest : cut, cleared and improved the area is now agricultural land, although large tracts of heath and woodland still exist.

(After photo: Yvonne Sauvageot)

Vouvray — Troglodyte house

The sands and clays of the Touraine **Champeigne,** with its walnut studded fields, are covered with the Forests of Brouard and Loches and the Montrésor Gâtine. The plateaux of Montrichard and Ste-Maure *(p 140)* are similar in many ways to the Champeigne. The undulating landscapes of the **Richelais** and **Thouarsais** are dotted with red pantile roofed dwellings.

Anjou. – Anjou like the Touraine has little physical unity but is typified more easily by the gentleness of its countryside, so lovingly sung of by Du Bellay. The area includes the Maine-et-Loire Department and parts of the Mayenne and Sarthe in the north and Indre-et-Loire in the east.

The fertile **Bourgueil varenne,** or alluvial plain, extends along the north bank of the Loire. Spring vegetables flourish surrounded by the famous vineyards planted on the warm, dry gravels lying at the foot of the pine covered hills. Between the willow lined Authion and the Loire, green pasturelands, known locally as *prèe,* alternate with rich market gardens growing vegetables, flowers and fruit trees. Downstream from Angers are grown both vines, especially the famous vineyard coulée de Serrant, and hemp, in the vicinity of Béhuard.

The pleasant **Saumurois,** lying south of the Loire and extending from Fontevraud and Montsoreau to Doué-la-Fontaine and the Layon Valley *(p 91)* has three differing aspects : woods, plains and hillsides, the last often vine clad, which produce the white wine to which the town of Saumur has given its name. The many caves in the steep, tufa valley sides of the Loire around Chênehutte-les-Tuffeaux, are now used for mushroom growing *(p 103).*

North of the river the sandy **Baugeois** *(p 50)* is an area of woods (oak, pine and chestnut) and arable land.

(After photo: Yan)

Brissac — Wine harvest

Downstream from Angers is the schist countryside of Black Anjou which contrasts so sharply with the limestones of White Anjou. The countryside is greener heralding the *bocage* typical of the West and Armorican Massif. An area of wooded farmland or English hedgerow countryside it is characterized by a patchwork of small fields surrounded by hedge topped banks crisscrossed by deep lanes leading to small farmsteads. To the north is the Ségréen *bocage,* crossed by the Mayenne and Oudon while the **Mauges** *(p 115)* was the centre of Royalist insurrection, providing the perfect terrain for ambushing.

Around Angers nursery and market gardens specialize in flowers and seedlings.

Maine. – Only the southern part of this region is included in the guide.

The **Bas-Maine** otherwise known as Black Maine, watered by the Mayenne and Oudon is a region of sandstones, granites and schists, supporting a *bocage* type of vegetation. Geographically this area is part of the Breton Armorican Massif. The **Haut-Maine,** covering the Sarthe and Huisne basins, is known as the White Maine because of its limestone soils.

THE ECONOMY

The bountiful Loire Valley assures comfortable livelihood. Although basically an agricultural region, recent years have seen the establishing of numerous industries.

Activities of the past. – Many of the traditional local activities have disappeared : namely the growing of saffron in the Gâtinais ; of anise, coriander and liquorice in Bourgueil ; of madder ; and the silk industry based on the mulberries and silk worms introduced to Touraine by Louis XI. The once familiar fields of hemp around Bréhémont and Béhuard, have dwindled in number as have the dependent ropeworkers. Only occasionally does anyone now gather wild chicory or the unpalatable choke pears which were used to make perry.

Cottage industries have disappeared with the last of the local craftsmen although Villaines is still a centre for wickerwork, but coopers, cartwrights and sabot makers are now few and far between. The flints of Meusnes and Villentrois are no longer used for the firearms industry.

Gone also are the blacksmiths' forges which were once so numerous on the forest outskirts. The coal of the Layon Basin is no longer worked and the manufacture of *étamine,* the woollen fabric used to make ecclesiastical garments, in the Maine has been discontinued but there is a revival of silk manufacture at Tours.

The drastic decline in river traffic on the Loire has resulted in the closure of the boatyards at Angers and the sail making factories at Ancenis. However, there is still a demand for slates from Trélazé and the tiles and bricks made from Sologne clay but, rather astonishingly, the very fine white tufa stone from Bourré and Pontlevoy, which distinguishes the houses of Touraine, is no longer worked.

AGRICULTURE

Vines *(p 30),* cereals and fodder crops are to be found nearly everywhere but it is the great variety of fruit and vegetables which most astonishes the visitor.

Fruit. – Ripening well in the local climate the succulent fruits of the region are renowned throughout France. Many have a noble pedigree : the *Reine-Claude* plums are named after Claude de France the wife of François I, the *Bon-chrétien* pears originated from a cutting planted by St Francis of Paola in Louis XI's orchard at Plessis-lès-Tours. They were introduced into Anjou by Jean Bourré, Louis XI's Finance Minister. Rivalling the latter are the following varieties : *de Monsieur, William,* a speciality of Anjou, *Passe-Crassane* and *Beurré Hardy.*

Apples grow well throughout the region, the *Pomme de Madeleine* grows in the Val while the well known *Reinette* comes from Le Mans. The American Golden has in many cases superseded the local varieties.

In addition there are the strawberries of Saumur, the quince of Orléans, the clingstone apricots (or yellow fleshed peaches) of Touraine, blackcurrants, raspberries, redcurrants and gean or wild cherries which give the liqueur called *guignolet,* of Angers. Lemons, figs and pomegranates are also grown in the area.

Melons were introduced to the region by Charles VIII's Neapolitan gardener. Already in the 16C the variety and quality of the local fruit and vegetables was much praised by Ronsard among others. The walnut and chestnut trees of the plateaux yield oil and the much prized wood and the edible chestnuts, often roasted during evening gatherings.

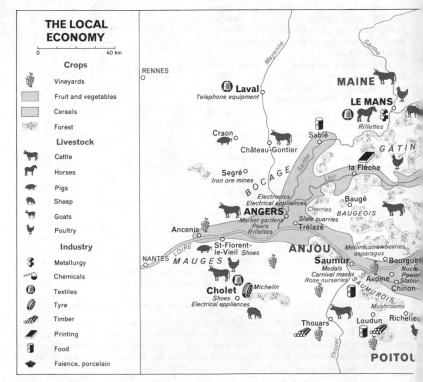

Early vegetables. – The main vegetable growing region is the Val de Loire and it has the supreme advantage in that its products, in general, are ready two weeks before those of the Paris region. Asparagus from Vineuil and Contres, potatoes from Saumur, French beans from Touraine and artichokes from Angers are despatched to Rungis, the main Paris market. Mushrooms are one of the region's more original crops. They are grown in the former tufa quarries situated near Montrichard, Montoire, Tours and particularly in the Saumur area.

The Orléans region grows great quantities of lettuce, cucumbers and tomatoes, all in massive greenhouses.

Flowers and nursery gardens. – Pots of geraniums or begonias, borders of nasturtiums and climbing wistaria with its pale mauve clusters adorn the houses of the region while the gardens are a profusion of camellias and hydrangeas. The region of Orléans-la-Source, Olivet and Doué-la-Fontaine is famous for its hydrangeas, geraniums and chrysanthemums grown under glass and rose nurseries. Tulips, gladioli and lilies are grown (for bulbs) near Soings.

Nursery gardens proliferate on the alluvial soils of the Loire, specializing in fruit trees, yew, cypress and cedar trees along with exotic shrubs. The lighter soils of Véron, Bourgueil and the Angers district are propitious to the growing of artichokes, onions and garlic for seed stock.

LIVESTOCK

Cattle, sheep and pigs. – In the fodder growing areas (champagnes and gâtines) young dairy stock are reared inside while elsewhere beef and dairy cattle feed on the pastures of the Maine and Anjou valleys and *bocages.* The most popular breeds are the Normandy *Maine-Anjou* and the *Pie noire.* Charolais cattle are fattened in the Mauges area. Milk production with the French Frisian *Pie noire* breed, is concentrated in the valleys of Touraine.

Sheep rearing is limited to the limestone plateaux of the Beauce and Haut-Maine where the black faced *Bleu du Maine* prospers. Pigs are to be found everywhere but especially in Touraine, Maine and Anjou where the popular pork meat specialities of *rillettes* and *rillons* are current in Vouvray, Tours, Le Mans and Angers. The ever growing demand for the well known goats' cheeses has resulted in an increase in goat keeping.

Market days in the west country are colourful occasions : the liveliest are the pig markets at Craon and the calf and goat sales at Château-Gontier, Chemillé and Cholet.

Horses. – Numerous studs continue to rear for breeding and racing purposes while the finer arts and traditions of horsemanship are perpetuated by the National Riding School and *Cadre Noir* of Saumur. Many a small town still has its racecourse and local riding clubs and schools keeping alive the local interest in horses and horseriding and its ancillary crafts.

INDUSTRY

Although the role of industry in the Val is far from predominant, a recent growth is noticeable in the main towns and in the development of ancillary industries based on the processing of agricultural produce. With the exception of Châteaudun and Vendôme, the main industrial centres are to be found along the Loire at Gien, Sully, St-Denis-de-l'Hôtel, Orléans, Beaugency, Mer, Blois, Amboise, Tours and Angers. Michelin tyre factories have been set up at Orléans, Tours and Cholet. Finally, nuclear power stations are in operation at Avoine-Chinon, Belleville-sur-Loire, Dampierre-en-Burly and St-Laurent-des-Eaux.

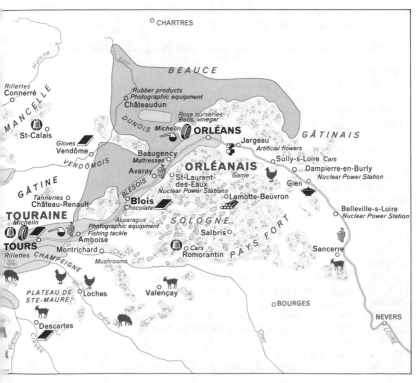

HISTORICAL NOTES

BC 59-51	Caesar conquers Gaul : four centuries of Roman occupation follow.
AD 313	Edict of Milan : Christians are granted freedom of worship.
4C	St Martin, the greatest Bishop of the Gauls and onetime legionary in the Roman army founds the first monastery on Gallic soil at Ligugé in Poitou and Marmoutier near Tours in 372.
397	St Martin died at Candes.
476	Decline of the Roman Empire because of the Barbarian invasions.
573	Gregory of Tours arrives from Clermont-Ferrand.
7C	Founding of the Benedictine Abbey of Fleury, later to be named St-Benoît.
late 8C	Alcuin of York formed a school for copyists at the behest of Charlemagne.
732	Charles Martel crushes the Saracens at Poitiers.
768-814	Charlemagne.
843-877	Charles the Bald.
9C	Norman invasions reach Angers, St Benoît and Tours.

THE CAPETS (987-1328)

996-1031	Robert II.
1010	Foundation of the Benedictine abbey at Solesmes.
1060-1108	Philippe I.
1066	William the Conqueror lands in England.
1104	First Council of Beaugency.
1137-1180	Louis VII.
1152	Second Council of Beaugency ; Eleanor of Aquitaine marries Henry Plantagenet.
1154	Henry Plantagenet becomes King of England as Henry II.
1164-1170	Thomas Becket in France during his exile (Chinon, Le Mans, Tours).
1172	Thomas Becket murdered in Canterbury Cathedral.
1174	Founding of the Hospital of St John (Angers).
1176	Foundation of the Carthusian charterhouse at Le Liget ; nuns from Fontevraud settled at Amesbury in expiation for the murder of Becket.
1180-1223	Philippe-Auguste.
1189	Death of Henry II Plantagenet at Chinon. Capets versus Plantagenets with the principal antagonists being Philippe-Auguste and Richard Lionheart (Chinon, Loches).
1199	Richard Lionheart dies at Chinon and is buried at Fontevraud.
1202	John Lackland loses Anjou (Chinon). Last of the Angevin kings he dies in 1216.
1215	Magna Carta.
1226-1270	St Louis or Louis IX.
1285-1314	Philippe IV, the Fair.
1307	Philippe the Fair dissolves the Order of the Knights Templars (Arville).

THE VALOIS (1328-1589)

1337-1453	Hundred Years War : 1346 Crécy ; 1348 Black Death ; 1356 Poitiers ; 1415 Agincourt.
1380-1422	Charles VI.
1418	The Massacre at Azay-le-Rideau.
1420	Treaty of Troyes : Henry V of England is recognized King of France.
1421	Battle of Vieil-Baugé : the Angevins and Scots mercenaries defeat the English.
1422-1461	Charles VII.
1427	The Dauphin Charles installs his court at Chinon.
1429	Joan of Arc delivers Orléans ; tried and burnt at the stake two years later (Chinon, Orléans).
1446	The Dauphin versus Agnès Sorel (Loches).
1453	Battle of Castillon : final defeat of the English on French soil.
1455-1485	Wars of the Roses : Margaret of Anjou leader of Lancastrian cause.
1461-1483	Louis XI.
1476	Unrest among the powerful feudal lords ; royal marriage at Montrichard.
1483-1498	Charles VIII.
1491	Marriage of Charles VIII and Anne of Brittany at Langeais.
1494-1559	The Campaigns in Italy.
1496	Early manifestations of Italian influence on local art (Amboise).
1498-1515	Louis XII ; he divorces and remarries Charles VIII's widow.
1515-1547	François I.
1519	French Renaissance : Chambord started ; Leonardo da Vinci dies at Clos-Lucé.
1539	The Emperor Charles V visits Amboise and Chambord.
1547-1559	Henri II.
1559-1560	François II.
1560	Amboise Conspiracy ; François II dies at Orléans.

1560-1574	Charles IX.
1562-1598	Wars of Religion.
1562	The Abbey of St-Benoît is pillaged by the Protestants; battles at Ponts-de-Cé, Beaugency and Sancerre.
1572	Massacre of St Bartholomew in Paris.
1574-1589	Henri III.
1576	Founding of the Catholic League by Henri, duc de Guise to combat Calvinism.
1588	The murder of Henri, duc de Guise and the Cardinal of Lorraine *(Blois)*.

THE BOURBONS (1589-1792)

1589-1610	Henri IV.
1589	Vendôme retaken by Henri IV from the Catholic Leaguers.
1598	Edict of Nantes; marriage of César de Vendôme *(Angers)*.
1600	Henri IV marries Marie de' Medici.
1602	Maximilien de Béthune buys Sully.
1610-1643	Louis XIII.
1619	Marie de' Medici flees Blois.
1620	Building of the college by the Jesuits at La Flèche.
1626	Gaston d'Orléans, brother of Louis XIII receives the County of Blois.
1643-1715	Louis XIV.
1651	During the Fronde – civil war directed against Mazarin – Anne of Austria, Mazarin and the young Louis XIV seek refuge at Gien.
1669	Première of Molière's play *Monsieur de Pourceaugnac* at Chambord.
1685	Revocation of the Edict of Nantes.
1715-1774	Louis XV.
1719	Voltaire exiled at Sully.
1756	Foundation of the Royal College of Surgeons at Tours.
1770	The duc de Choiseul in exile at Chanteloup.

THE REVOLUTION AND FIRST EMPIRE (1789-1815)

1789	Taking of the Bastille.
1793	Execution of Louis XVI; Local insurrection and ensuing strife between the Blues and the Whites *(Cholet, Laval, Les Mauges)*.
1795	Vendéen War; Proclamation of the Republic.
1803	Talleyrand purchased Valençay.
1804-1815	First Empire under Napoleon Bonaparte.
1808	Internment of Ferdinand VII, King of Spain, at Valençay.

THE RESTORATION AND SECOND REPUBLIC (1815-1852)

1815-1830	Restoration of the Bourbons: Louis XVIII, Charles X.
1830-1848	July Monarchy: Louis-Philippe.
1832	The first steamboat on the Loire.
1832-1848	Conquest of Algeria; 1848 internment of the Algerian leader *(Amboise)*.

THE SECOND EMPIRE (1852-1870)

1852-1870	Napoleon III as Emperor.
1870-1871	Franco-Prussian War.
1870	Proclamation of the Third Republic; following the encirclement of the Emperor and army at Sedan.
	Defence of Châteaudun; Tours was the headquarters of the Provisional Government.

THE THIRD REPUBLIC (1870-1940) TO 20C

1873	The Legitimist Pretender, comte de Chambord, wrecks his chances of success *(Chambord)*; Amédée Bollée completes his first car, *l'Obéissante (Le Mans)*.
1908	Wilbur Wright's early trials with his aeroplane.
1914-1918	First World War.
1919	Treaty of Versailles.
1923	The first Twenty-four hour race at Le Mans.
1939-1943	Second World War.
1940	Defence of Saumur; historic meeting at Montoire.
1945	Armistice of Reims.
1946	Fourth Republic.
1952	Inauguration of the *son et lumière* performances at Chambord.
1958	Fifth Republic.
1963	Opening of the Avoine-Chinon Nuclear Power Station, France's first nuclear power station.
1970	Founding of the University of Tours.
1974	The A 10 motorway links Tours and the capital.

THE LONG, RICH PAST OF THE LOIRE COUNTRY

Romans and Barbarians. — From the beginning of the conquest of Gaul by the Romans, the inhabitants of the Loire country showed their independent spirit. The "Carnutes", who lived between Chartres and Orléans, gave the first signal for resistance to Caesar's legions.

In the 3C, Christianity came in with St Gatian and triumphed in the following century with St Martin : at the end of the 4C the tomb of St Martin at Tours became the national sanctuary of the Merovingians *(p 155)*. The Saint's name is commemorated annually on 11 November — St Martin's Day.

For two centuries the Loire country suffered from invasions of Barbarians. Bishop St Aignan stopped the Huns, who had come from the shores of the Caspian Sea, from entering Orléans. Two centuries later Charles Martel prevented the Saracens, who were moving north from the Iberian Peninsula, from crossing the Loire. Fresh disaster followed one hundred years later : the Normans came up the river, killing, pillaging and desecrating from Nantes to St-Benoît-sur-Loire and looting the treasure of St Martin. Robert le Fort, Count of Blois and Tours stopped their advance but their depredations continued till 911 following the agreement of St-Clair-sur-Epte, creating the Duchy of Normandy.

Lords and castles. — The weakness of the last Carolingian kings encouraged the independence of turbulent and ambitious feudal lords. The Orléans region remained essentially a Capetian domain, its capital one of the sovereign's preferred residences but Touraine, Blésois, Anjou and Maine became so many separate States where the king's authority was hardly recognized. This was the age of powerful barons and every strategic point from Orléans to Angers was crowned by the stronghold of some warring feudal lord.

The counts of Blois had enemies in the counts of Anjou, the most famous of whom was **Foulques Nerra** *(p 42)*. Foulques was a formidable tactician, and as such he was the true precursor of Philippe-Auguste and Richard Lionheart. He slowly encircled his rival Eudes II's domain, the County of Blois, which was eventually to fall to his son, Geoffroi Martel.

The dynasty of the counts of Anjou reached its zenith with the Plantagenets *(p 42)*. In 1154 one of them became King Henry II of England. They now reigned over an Empire *(p 19)* which stretched from the north of England to the Pyrenees. Theirs was a formidable power facing the weaker Capet kings of France but the latter did not hesitate to resist their awesome neighbours. Fortunately for the Capets, quarrels between the Plantagenets helped them to success. In 1202 Philippe-Auguste confiscated all the provinces of John Lackland (the Bad King John of English schoolbooks). The Loire country became French again.

St Louis entrusted the territory to his brother, Charles of Anjou. This prince and his successors left their provinces to conquer the Kingdom of Naples. But the memory of the last of the dukes of Anjou, Good King René, has lingered in the minds of the people *(p 42)*.

Joan of Arc. — The Hundred Years War (1337-1453) brought back the English, who became masters of half the country. Then **Joan of Arc** appeared and persuaded Charles VII to give her a command *(p 73)*. With her little army she entered beleaguered Orléans, stormed the English strongholds and freed the city *(p 125)*. The fleeing enemy was beaten on the Loire, at Jargeau, and in the Beauce, at Patay. In spite of the betrayal of Compiègne and the stake at Rouen, the enemy's total defeat was now assured.

The decline. — The Wars of Religion (1562-1609) brought devastation and massacre : this was the time of the Amboise Conspiracy *(p 39)* and the bloody Massacre of St Bartholomew. Henri III connived at the assassination of the Guise brothers in the Château de Blois *(p 53)*. Churches and abbeys were sacked by the Huguenots. The accession of Henri IV (1589), which restored peace, marked the end of the most brilliant period for the Loire Valley. At the end of the 18C political decline was followed by a certain loss of prosperity.

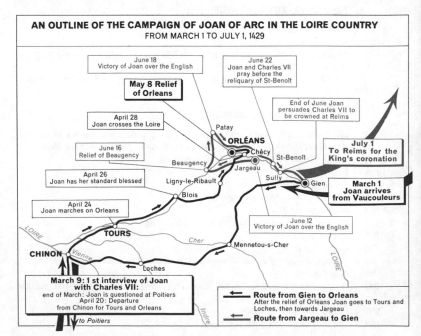

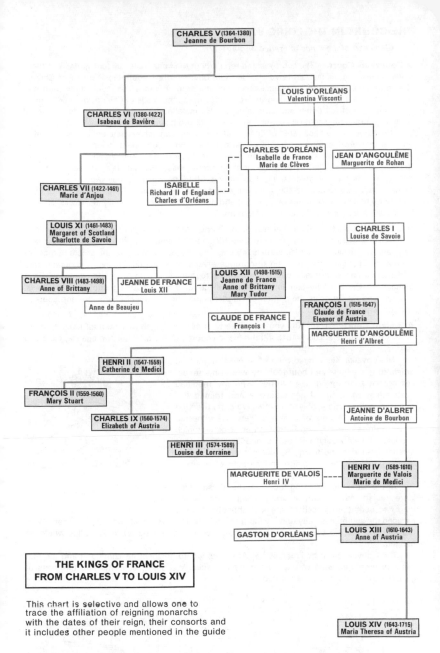

CHARLES V (1364-1380)
Jeanne de Bourbon

LOUIS D'ORLÉANS
Valentina Visconti

CHARLES VI (1380-1422)
Isabeau de Bavière

CHARLES D'ORLÉANS
Isabelle de France
Marie de Clèves

JEAN D'ANGOULÊME
Marguerite de Rohan

CHARLES VII (1422-1461)
Marie d'Anjou

ISABELLE
Richard II of England
Charles d'Orléans

CHARLES I
Louise de Savoie

LOUIS XI (1461-1483)
Margaret of Scotland
Charlotte de Savoie

CHARLES VIII (1483-1498)
Anne of Brittany

JEANNE DE FRANCE
Louis XII

LOUIS XII (1498-1515)
Jeanne de France
Anne of Brittany
Mary Tudor

FRANÇOIS I (1515-1547)
Claude de France
Eleanor of Austria

Anne de Beaujeu

CLAUDE DE FRANCE
François I

MARGUERITE D'ANGOULÊME
Henri d'Albret

HENRI II (1547-1559)
Catherine de Medici

FRANÇOIS II (1559-1560)
Mary Stuart

CHARLES IX (1560-1574)
Elizabeth of Austria

JEANNE D'ALBRET
Antoine de Bourbon

HENRI III (1574-1589)
Louise de Lorraine

MARGUERITE DE VALOIS
Henri IV

HENRI IV (1589-1610)
Marguerite de Valois
Marie de Medici

GASTON D'ORLÉANS

LOUIS XIII (1610-1643)
Anne of Austria

**THE KINGS OF FRANCE
FROM CHARLES V TO LOUIS XIV**

This chart is selective and allows one to
trace the affiliation of reigning monarchs
with the dates of their reign, their consorts and
it includes other people mentioned in the guide

LOUIS XIV (1643-1715)
Maria Theresa of Austria

Prior to the Revolution, the Loire guild of mariners, dating from the 14C, was disbanded and gone was the animated commercial traffic on this great highway. Onetime exports included wine, wool from Berry, iron ores from the Massif Central, Forez coal, Beauce grain and fine materials from Tours while the upstream traffic consisted of cargoes of exotic goods from overseas. For a time the importance of the towns declined. Orléans closed its sugar refineries and its stocking and vinegar factories. Amboise ceased to weave cloth. The silk factories of Tours were abandoned and the cotton mills of Saumur stood idle.

Troubled times. – During the French Revolution, Anjou was one of the chief battlegrounds of the Blues (Republicans) and the Whites (Royalists). Angers was taken and retaken by both parties; Saumur was captured by the Whites. Then Santerre arrived from Paris with a troop of Revolutionaries, but the pleasures of the "Garden of France" so cooled their ardour that they laid down their muskets and cast off their accoutrements. In 1870 at the beginning of the Franco-Prussian War and following the surrender of the French army under the Emperor at Sedan, an improvised force, known as the *Armées de la Loire,* gathered to the north of the Loire. Despite two early victories at Orléans and Coulmiers, they were pushed back to Le Mans. The Provisional Government then left Tours to take refuge at Bordeaux.

During the First World War the Americans established their headquarters at Tours and the Loire was defended by American troops, the "Sammies".

On 10 June 1940, with the menace of the advancing German army, the Government left Paris for Tours. On the 13th the decision was taken to transfer the government once again to Bordeaux. This one week in June saw much destruction in the Loire country: bridges bombed and towns damaged. With September 1944 came the Liberation by the combined forces of the Americans and the French Resistance.

The region had suffered greatly but luckily it retained its essential charm.

17

THE COURT IN THE LOIRE VALLEY

(See chart of the Kings of France on page 17)

A Bourgeois Court. — The court resided regularly in the Loire Valley under Charles VII; these visits ended with the last of the Valois, Henri III. Charles VII's favourite residence was Chinon. Owing to the straitened circumstances to which the King of France was reduced his court was not brilliant; but the arrival of Joan of Arc in 1429 made the castle of Chinon for ever famous.

Louis XI disliked pomp and circumstance. He installed his wife, Charlotte de Savoie, at Amboise, but he himself rarely came there. He preferred his manor at Plessis-lès-Tours.

The Queen's court consisted of fifteen ladies in waiting, twelve women of the bedchamber and 100 officers (persons in charge of various functions, from the saddler to the librarian, including the doctor, the chaplain and the lute player). The budget amounted only to 37 000 *livres,* of which 800 *livres* were spent on minor pleasures: materials for needlework and embroidery, books, parchments and illuminating. Charlotte was a serious woman and a great reader; her library contained 100 volumes, a vast total for that time. They were works of piety and morality and books on history, botany and domestic science. A few lighter works, such as the *Tales of Boccaccio,* relieved this solemnity.

A Luxurious Court. — With the accession of Charles VIII, "the King of Amboise", at the end of the 15C, the taste for luxury appeared. Furnishings became rich: there were in the castle 220 Persian, Turkish and Syrian carpets, 45 beds, 60 chests, 60 tables, an incredible number of Flemish and Parisian tapestries and sumptuous silverware. A magnificent aviary contained rare birds. Lions and wild boars, which were made to fight with huge mastiffs, were kept in a menagerie. The armoury contained a fine collection of armour, the battle axes of Clovis, St Louis and Du Guesclin, the dagger of Charlemagne, the swords of Charles VII and Louis XI and the armour of Joan of Arc.

A Gallant Court. — Louis XII, who was miserly or at least frugal, was the bourgeois "King of Blois". But under François I (1515-47) the French court became a school of elegance, taste and culture.

The Cavalier King added men of science, poets and artists to the knights and bourgeois by whom his predecessors had been surrounded. Women, who until then had been relegated to the Queen's service and treated like pupils in a girls' school, played an effective part; the King made them the leaders of a new society. He expected them to dress perfectly and he gave them clothes which showed off their beauty: he would spend 200 000 *livres* at a time on fabrics and finery. He did not hesitate to pay 26 000 *livres* for the hangings and carpets of a single room.

The salamander
Crest of François I

At the same time the King took care that these ladies were treated with all courtesy and respect. A gentleman who had permitted himself to speak slightingly of them escaped the supreme penalty only by flight — "So great", says a contemporary historian, "was the King's anger, he swore that whoever reflected on the honour of these ladies would be hanged."

The festivals given by François I at Amboise, where he spent his childhood and the first years of his reign, were of unprecedented brilliance. Weddings, baptisms and the visits of princes were sumptuously celebrated.

The porcupine
Crest of Louis XII

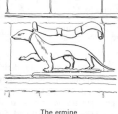

The ermine

Crest of Anne of Brittany
and Claude of France

The Franciscan girdle and ermine tufts
Crest of Anne of Brittany

The Last Valois. — Under Henri II and his sons, Blois remained the habitual seat of the court when it was not at the Louvre. It was Henri III who drew up the first code of etiquette and introduced the title "His Majesty", taken from the Roman Emperors.

The Queen Mother and the Queen had about 100 ladies in waiting. Catherine de' Medici also had her famous "Flying Squad" of pretty girls, who kept her informed and assisted her intrigues. About 100 pages, aged from fourteen to seventeen, acted as messengers.

The King's suite included 200 gentlemen in waiting and over 1 000 archers and Swiss guards. A multitude of servants were busy about the castle. Princes of the Blood and great lords also had their households. Thus, from the time of François I, about 15 000 people surrounded the king; when the court moved, 12 000 horses were needed.

Queens and Great Ladies. — The official position enjoyed by women at court around the king, often enabled them to play an important if not always a useful part in the political affairs of the country. It also enabled them to protect and develop the arts.

Agnès Sorel *(p 93)* adorned the court of Charles VII at Chinon and at Loches. She gave the King good advice and constantly reminded him of the urgent problems facing the country which had barely emerged from the Hundred Years War (1337-1453).

Louise de Savoie, the mother of François I, with her insatiable ambition lived only for the success and aggrandisement of her son, her "Caesar". Of his many mistresses, the duchesse d'Étampes, holds a place apart. Until the King's death she ruled the court.

Diane de Poitiers *(p 70)* the celebrated mistress of Henri II, made important decisions of policy, negotiated with the Protestants and distributed honours and magistracies.

The foreign beauty of Mary Stuart, the hapless wife of the little King François II, who died at seventeen after a few months' reign, threw a brief lustre over the court in the middle of the 16C.

A different type altogether was Marguerite de Valois, the famous Queen Margot, sister of François II, Charles IX — whose name is coupled with that of Marie Touchet — and Henri III. Her marriage to the future King Henri IV, did little to tame her.

THE ANGEVIN EMPIRE

This term applies to the territories extending from the north of England to the Pyrenees that were the suzerainty of Henry II and his successors who were known as the Angevin kings. Sometimes the surname Plantagenet is used for members of the family descended from Geoffrey of Anjou and usually includes all kings from Henry II to Edward III. The Angevin kings were more French than English in speech, habits and customs and their connections with the Loire country, at the heart of this Empire, were numerous and varied.

Geoffrey Plantagenet (1113-51), Count of Anjou, was born in Le Mans. It was his nickname, Plantagenet *(p 42)* which was adopted for the royal house. His marriage in 1128 to Matilda, the granddaughter of William the Conqueror and widow of the German Emperor, established an alliance between Normandy and Anjou and Maine. It was Matilda who fought with her cousin Stephen for the English throne on Henry I's death in 1135. Geoffrey died at the age of thirty-eight and was buried in Le Mans Cathedral. His enamelled tombal plaque can be seen in the Tessé Museum *(p 112)*.

The eldest son, Henry Plantagenet (1133-89) was quickly caught up in the dynastic struggles in both England and France. He was the creator of the great Angevin Empire. Henry acquired most of his continental lands before his accession to the English throne. Through his mother he inherited Normandy (1150), and Anjou, Maine and Touraine in 1151 and with his marriage the next year to Eleanor of Aquitaine he added Aquitaine, Gascony, Poitou and Auvergne. The King of France, Louis VII who had divorced Eleanor by the Second Council of Beaugency *(p 51)*, was confronted with a vassal whose empire equalled his own. Two years later Henry became King of England, ruler of an Anglo-French empire which rivalled that of his inveterate enemy the Capet. A great sovereign, Henry fought to consolidate his territorial gains but his reign was disturbed and empire imperilled by his quarrelling and discontented sons and his own dispute with his Chancellor Thomas Beckct.

Henry II outlived three of the Plantagenet princes. The youngest William died in infancy while his heir, Henry (1155-83), a true knight found his amusement on the jousting fields. He died at Martel having sacked St Amadour's shrine in Rocamadour. The third son Geoffrey (1156-86), a firm friend of Philippe-Auguste, was killed in a tournament in 1186. Henry had divided his empire among his remaining sons but this only led to quarrels and wars, often actively fostered by the French King. With Queen Eleanor imprisoned in England Henry II died a solitary death in Chinon, attended only by the faithful William Marshal.

Henry's heir, Richard Lionheart (1157-99) was a true Angevin, great warrior king, and Queen Eleanor's favourite. Soon after his accession he set out on the Third Crusade, accompanied by Philippe-Auguste. It was during this Crusade that Richard agreed to marry Berengaria of Navarre *(p 113)* despite his bethrothal twenty-one years previously to Alais, the French King's sister. Captured and imprisoned on his return journey he learned of his brother's treachery and on release he hastily returned to France, via England, to do combat with his arch enemy. The rest of his ten year reign was spent defending his French empire. He died in 1199 as a result of a wound incurred at the siege of Châlus. He was buried at Fontevraud *(p 82)* where his mother had retired in her old age.

The last of Henry II's sons, John Lackland (1166-1216) was no warrior and much of his time was spent intriguing. Philippe-Auguste was quick to wrest Normandy, Anjou, Maine and Touraine from him and, with his French possessions greatly diminished, he faced revolts by the Barons in England who were demanding a charter of liberties. The Magna Carta was signed in 1215.

The second half of the 13C saw the continuation of the Capet and Plantagenet struggles with each trying to consolidate their position and justify their territorial claims. Treaties were rife but the confiscation of Guyenne in 1337 and Edward III's renewed claim to the French throne led to the outbreak of hostilities known as the Hundred Years War (1337-1453). Early victories at Crécy and Calais were followed by a period of truces and then campaigns in the south led by the Black Prince and John of Gaunt against the great French warrior Du Guesclin. Both royal houses were troubled by dynastic problems. In France there was the bitter civil war between the Burgundian and Armagnac factions, with the English ultimately allied to the former. Agincourt in 1415 was their victory.

When Paris was occupied in 1418 by the Burgundians, the uncrowned Dauphin *(p 73)* fled to Bourges and was known by his enemies as the King of Bourges. The Loire became the theatre of the war. It was then that Charles invoked anew the Auld Alliance (1295) seeking Scots help in the face of Henry V's attacks. 6 000 Scottish soldiers arrived in 1419 under John the Earl of Buchan, later made High Constable of France, Archibald Douglas and Sir John Stuart of Darnley, rewarded with Aubigny *(p 47)*, and fought at Baugé and Cravant. The situation was critical, with half the kingdom in the hands of the English.

Joan of Arc's intervention in 1429 with the relief of Orléans was the beginning of the end of this once great empire. In spite of the efforts of military commanders such as the veteran general John Talbot, Earl of Shrewsbury and the Duke of Bedford, the brother of Henry V, the English rule in France was to end with the Battle of Castillon in 1453 and loss of Calais one hundred and five years later.

ART AND ARCHITECTURE

ECCLESIASTICAL ARCHITECTURE

To assist readers unfamiliar with the terminology employed in ecclesiastical architecture, we describe below the most commonly used terms.

The ground plan. – Basically a church consists of a chancel, where the clergy worship and where the high altar and reliquaries are to be found, and a nave, for the faithful. Early churches, which were rectangular in shape and were known as "basilical" in their plan, consisted of these elements only. It was the Romanesque architects who created the more usual Catholic plan based on the Cross. At the entrance a narthex was built to receive those who had not been baptised and, later, pilgrims who came for special services. Aisles were added to enlarge the nave. In pilgrimage churches, the aisles were prolonged to circle the chancel in an ambulatory, thus allowing the faithful to process freely. Chapels were sometimes built on to the apse (radiating chapels) and the arms of the transept (transept chapels).

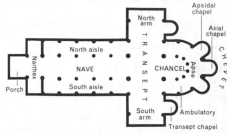

Romanesque (11-12C). – The year 1000 at the end of the troubled history of the early Middle Ages which had been marked by Norman invasions and conflicts between feudal lords, saw a renaissance in the art of building. Simultaneously the royal prerogative was asserted and there was an upsurge in religious faith expressed materially in monastic buildings. Churches became

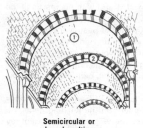

Semicircular or barrel vaulting
1 vault - 2 transverse arch

larger and loftier – heavy stone vaulting, replacing wood, tended to crush the supporting walls where openings were reduced to a minimum and side aisles were built tall to buttress the nave *(see cross section)*. Vaulting was semicircular or **barrel** with transverse ribs in the early periods, later to become **groined**. Columns were

Groined vaulting
1 main arch - 2 groin
3 transverse arch

generally cylindrical while arches were semicircular and decoration tended to represent floral or geometric motifs and fantastic figures. In England by contrast the equivalent Norman period produced long naves, flat east ends, towers and spires. The typical French sculptured doorway *(see illustration below)* was rare.

The Romanesque style had strong regional characteristics.

Orléanais. – The two most remarkable edifices are both Carolingian and monastic: the church at Germigny-des-Prés and the Benedictine basilica at St-Benoît-sur-Loire *(p 136)*.

The Cher Valley also has a rich heritage of Romanesque sanctuaries, namely at St-Aignan and Selles-sur-Cher.

Touraine. – Architecture in this region shows a strong Poitou influence with features such as column buttressed apsidal chapels; domes and doorways without tympana. The square or octagonal bell towers are crowned with spires and angle bell turrets *(see below)*.

Anjou. – Here the main examples of this style are to be found in the vicinity of Baugé and Saumur. The church at Cunault again shows a distinct Poitou influence with its five bays of broken barrel vaulted nave supported by groined vaulted side aisles, as does the abbey church at Fontevraud, the most northerly example of a domed church, more typical of the Aquitaine area.

Doorway
1 archivolt - 2 recessed orders or arches
3 tympanum - 4 splaying - 5 capitals

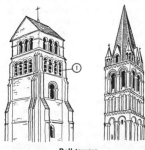

Bell towers
saddle-back roof   spire with
1 louvers   bell turrets

Romanesque to Gothic. – The **Plantagenet** or **Angevin** style got its name from Henry II Plantagenet *(p 42)*. This transitional style reached its zenith in the early 13C and was already superseded by the end of the same century. The most characteristic feature of the style was the Angevin vaulting. While in Gothic vaulting all the keys are at roughly the same level in the

St-Maurice Cathedral
Mid 12C

Angevin vaulting
Late 12C

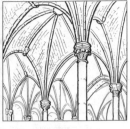

St-Serge : chancel
Early 13C

Plantagenet equivalent with its more rounded or domical form, the keys of the diagonal (ogive) arches are at least 3 m - 10 ft above the keys of the transverse and stringer arches (eg St-Maurice Cathedral, Angers).

Towards the end of the 12C Angevin vaulting became finer with more numerous and gracious ribs springing from slender columns. The early 13C saw the beginning of lierne vaulting with elegant sculptures.

From the Loire Valley this style spread to the Vendée, Poitou, Saintonge and Garonne.

Gothic (12-15C). –

The main features are the diagonal or ogive vaulting and systematic use of the pointed arch. A skeleton framework supported the main stress of the vaulting *(see cross section).* The stress passed from relieving arches to the pillars – later to become mere extensions of the arches – which were

Quadripartite vaulting
1 diagonal - 2 transverse
3 stringer - 4 flying buttress
5 keystone

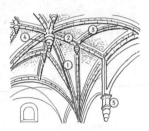

Lierne and tierceron vaulting
1 diagonal - 2 lierne
3 tierceron - 4 pendant
5 corbel

in turn directly supported by external flying buttresses. Walls became thin and openings were glazed with expanses of glass. The style was lofty and luminous.

Quadripartite vaulting, with its essential elements the diagonal and transverse ribs, was common and later followed by **sexpartite** vaulting, when covering rectangular instead of square bays. This involved the addition of a transverse arch, crossing the vault at its apex. From the 15C onwards the search for more decorative effects led to the adding of subsidiary ribs – called **lierne and tierceron** (St-Serge, Angers) – and the creation of a ridge rib with carved bosses and pendants.

The great French **chevets** date from this period. Strictly speaking the chevet includes the apse, surrounding ambulatory and radiating chapels. This form of east end with as many as thirteen chapels can be seen at Le Mans or Orléans *(illustration)*.

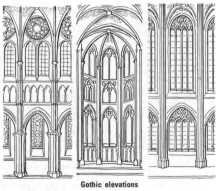

Gothic chevet
1 axial or lady chapel - 2 double course flying buttress - 3 north arm of transept
4 apse - 5 bell tower on the façade
6 spire over the transept crossing

Gothic elevations

Lancet
(13C)

Radiant
(late 13C-14C)

Flamboyant
(15C)

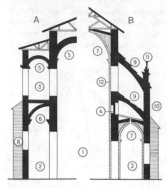

The three Gothic periods can be distinguished by decorative motifs: an initial or 13C phase was characterised by pointed arches and **lancet** windows with geometric tracery; a second or **Radiant** (Rayonnant) of 13-14C, with circular patterned tracery and the third or **Flamboyant** style (15C) showing flame like designs. These correspond with the English early, middle and late Gothic styles.

The abbey church of Vendôme is a good example of French Gothic while the evolution of the Gothic style is well represented by St-Gatien Cathedral in Tours (p 160).

Transverse section through nave

1 nave - 2 aisle - 3 gallery - 4 triforium
5 barrel vaulting - 6 half barrel vaulting
7 ogive vaulting - 8 buttress - 9 flying buttress
10 detached pier - 11 pinnacle - 12 clerestory

(A) Romanesque (B) Gothic

Renaissance and Classical (16-18C). – **Renaissance** ecclesiastical buildings in the Loire, like the châteaux show a strong Italian influence in their decoration (see p 23). The pointed arch, typical of the Gothic period, is replaced by basket handled or semicircular arches and statue filled niches become a common

feature. Although rare, the Renaissance edifices of the Loire region are well worthy of a visit, in particular, the church doorway at Montrésor (illustration adjoining) and the chapels at Ussé, Champigny-sur-Veude and La Bourgonnière.

Classical ecclesiastical buildings (17-18C) tend to be more majestic with superimposed Greek orders, pedimented doorways and domes.

Examples are the dome of Notre-Dame des Ardilliers, Saumur and the façade of St-Vincent's in Blois.

Renaissance doorway
Montrésor Church
1 basket-handle arch

Classical dome
Dome surmounted
by a lantern
1 flame ornament

Church Furnishings

Regrettably, much of the early church furniture – rood screens and beams, altarpieces, fonts, pulpits, pews, stalls and lecterns – especially the pieces in wood did not survive the various religious conflicts and the Revolution.

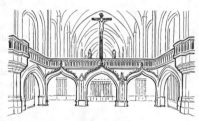

Rood beam of tref. – This supports the triumphal arch at the entrance to the chancel. The rood carries a Crucifix flanked by statues of the Virgin and St John and sometimes other personages from the Calvary.

Rood screen. – This replaces the rood beam in larger churches, and may be used for preaching and reading of the Epistles and Gospel. From the 17C onwards many disappeared as they tended to hide the altar.

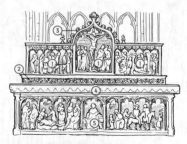

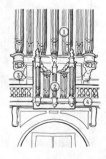

Stalls
1 high back
2 elbow rest
3 cheekpiece
4 misericord

Altar with retable or altarpiece
1 retable or altarpiece - 2 predella
3 crowning piece - 4 altar table - 5 altar front
Although they are becoming rare, certain
Baroque retables regroup several altars

Organ
1 great organ case
2 little organ case
3 caryatids
4 loft

SECULAR ARCHITECTURE

Rich in history this area has left us incomparable pieces of secular architecture among which the châteaux — mediaeval fortress or elegant residence — are the most famous.

During the Carolingian and early Capetian dynasties weak kings and a disunited kingdom encouraged the independence of turbulent and ambitious feudal lords. Touraine, the district of Blois, Anjou and Maine became so many separate States with local lords who raised armies, struck coinages and created small fortified cities — often encircled with ramparts, separated from the towns proper — as at Amboise, Loches and Angers. These feudal fortresses and strongholds were built to withstand numerous sieges.

Strategically sited, all strongholds were heavily fortified: sombre castles were encircled with ramparts and vested with massive towers with wooden hoardings, quadrangular keeps (Langeais, Montrichard, Beaugency and Montbazon) and curtain or revetment walls (Loches and Chinon). Against such defences the besiegers used a variety of assault weapons or tactics: including sapping, catapults (arbalests, tower crossbows, espringels, mangonels and trebuchets), battering rams and assault towers.

Corner towers became round or semicircular, following the First Crusade, and their bases were thickened. The wood hoardings gave way to stone machicolations. However the advent of the age of cannon (mid 15C) transformed military architecture, towers became low, squat bastions and curtain walls were reinforced by round or square flanking towers.

Towers and curtain walls
1 hoardings - 2 crenellations - 3 merlon
4 arrow slit or lancet
5 curtain wall
6 bridge or drawbridge

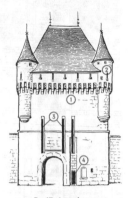

Fortified gatehouse
1 machicolations
2 watch turrets
3 slots for the arms of the drawbridge
4 postern

Gothic. — The 15C saw a new generation of buildings following on the mediaeval fortress. Not entirely free of the constraints of the Middle Ages these massive but elegant buildings showed a greater search for comfort, light and decoration, eg Le Plessis-Bourré and Plessis-Macé *(illustrations p 129)*. Many of the châteaux of the period were brick buildings with stone ornamentation (eg Le Moulin at Lassay). The manor Clos-Lucé at Amboise is another good example. Town houses were adorned with overhanging staircase turret and tall dormer windows, while houses of brick and timber work abounded.

Renaissance. — With the expulsion of the English (end of the Hundred Years War 1453) aided by Joan of Arc and the subsequent creation of a consolidated kingdom, military architecture as such was to become the exclusive domain of the king with a view to defending his frontiers. It was the Loire Valley that became the favourite abode of royalty and the court who abandoned the earlier royal residences of the Louvre, Bastille and Conciergerie in Paris. The king became

Renaissance ornament

Frieze on the grand staircase at Azay-le-Rideau

1 shell - 2 vase - 3 foliage
4 dragon - 5 nude child
6 cherub - 7 cornucopia
8 satyr

the promoter of all building: Louis XI built Langeais and Plessis-Lès-Tours; Charles VIII Amboise; Louis XIII a wing of Blois and François I another wing at Blois and Chambord.

This was the period of the itinerant court — and the attending French nobles, no longer feudal lords, and officers of State — also built elegant residences or town houses. Such was the case of the financiers Semblançay with a château of the same name, Robertet at the Hôtel d'Alluye in Blois and the Château du Bery, Bohier at Chenonceau and Berthelot at Azay-le-Rideau.

Prior to the Italian campaigns, Italian artists such as Francesco Laurana, Niccolo Spinelli and Jean Candida worked for both King René of Anjou and Louis XI doing sculpture and medallions. However it was with the return of Charles VIII from Naples in late 1495 accompa-

Renaissance coffered ceiling
Grand staircase at Azay-le-Rideau
1 pendant - 2 coffer - 3 medallion

Renaissance orders
François I Wing, Blois

1 chimney - 2 attic - 3 dormer window - 4 balustrade - 5 single mullioned window - 6 double mullioned window - 7 cornice - 8 pilaster - 9 moulding

nied by many craftsmen from Naples that the new Renaissance style began to flourish. The Italian influence favoured the imitation of Classical Antiquity. Semicircular arches replaced pointed ones while ceilings with compartments the ogival vaults.

Buildings such as Amboise, Chaumont, Chenonceau, Azay-le-Rideau, or Chambord retain a feudal aspect — curtain walls, rounded towers and moats — but the defensive devices were purely ornamental. Watchpaths tended to disappear although the machicolations were retained for their decorative effect. Façades were decorated with niches, medallions and large pilaster framed windows giving plenty of light. Steeply pitched and pointed roofs were adorned with highly decorated chimneystacks and tall pinnacled and pedimented dormer windows.

The château at Amboise, the Louis XII Wing at Blois and the north wing of Châteaudun all demonstrate early manifestations of the new Italian decorative style which triumphed on the inner façade of the François I Wing at Blois *(illustration adjoining)*.

Later as at Chambord and Le Lude, the decoration was adapted by local masters such as Pierre Trinqueau.

Architecturally the Italian influence is most noticeable in the outer façade of the François I Wing at Blois. With its rhythmic bay design, incorporating three tiers of open loggias, this front strongly resembles certain Italian Palaces.

The famous staircases of the Loire châteaux were also modelled on Italian examples whether they were superimposed spiral ones as at Chambord and Blois or straight flights with coffered ceilings as at Chenonceau, Azay-le-Rideau *(illustration p 23)* and Poncé-sur-le-Loir.

Civic architecture also showed Renaissance influences as in the town halls of Beaugency, with its characteristic semicircular arches and superimposed orders, Orléans and Loches. Private mansions typical of the Renaissance are to be found at Orléans (Hôtel Toutin), Blois (Hôtel d'Alluye), Tours (Hôtel Gouin) and Angers (Hôtel Pincé).

Classical (17-18C). — The late 16C was a period of unrest with the Wars of Religion (1562-98) and many of the châteaux remained uninhabited. The accession of Henri IV in 1589 restored peace and marked the end of the most brilliant period for the Loire. The court returned to Paris and the nobility sought to live in the shadow of the Sun King (1643-1715). Versailles was the greatest factor in the decline of the châteaux ; beautiful buildings were built by architects and sculptors and decorators were brought from Paris, eg J. Hardouin Mansart and Coysevox at Serrant and Pierre le Mercier at Richelieu.

In the 17C the style became more severe and there was a striving after majestic effects. The pompous manner of Louis XIV displaced the graceful fantasy of the Renaissance and feudal picturesqueness. Pediments, whether triangular or curvilinear, became the fashion, as did domes and the Greek orders, eg the Gaston d'Orléans Wing at Blois *(illustration adjoining)*. Towers were replaced by pavilions with great saloons and monumental chimneypieces adorned with caryatids. The exposed beams of the ceilings were elaborately painted. Steeply pitched or mansard roofs were common. Magnificent châteaux were built as at Ménars and Montgeoffroy, others were remodelled but the 18C was the great age of town planning. The projects at Orléans, Tours and Saumur included long vistas aligning with magnificent bridges, the work of Perronet, Soyer and Cessart.

Classical façade (17C)
Gaston d'Orléans Wing, Blois

Gardens and Parks

The earliest gardens were the orchards, vegetable and herb gardens of the monasteries. Flower beds were introduced in the 15C by Good King René and Louis XI (Plessis-lès-Tours) and were often accompanied by fountains, arbours, aviaries and menageries. An Italian designed for Charles VIII the first knot gardens at Amboise and Blois. Good examples exist today at Chenonceau and Villandry *(illustration p 167)* where arabesques of boxwood edge masses of flowers and clipped yew trees stand sentinel.

At Richelieu (1631) the garden was an extension of the building as at Versailles, while 18C Craon has a formal French garden extended by a park in the 18C English landscape style.

STATELY HOMES, CHÂTEAUX AND ROYAL PALACES

	THE LOIRE REGION	ILE-DE-FRANCE	ENGLAND
	Angers, Chinon, Loches, Luynes, Saumur	Bastille, Conciergerie, Louvre, Vincennes	Ightham Mote, Penshurst Place, The Tower, Palace of Westminster (1834*), Windsor.
15C	Montreuil-Bellay, Montsoreau, Plessis-Bourré, Plessis-Macé, Talcy, Ussé		Hever, Greenwich, Oxburgh Hall, Richmond
16C	Azay-le-Rideau, Beauregard, Blois, Chambord, Champigny-sur-Veude, Chaumont (décor), Chenonceau, Gué-Péan, Talcy, Valençay, Villandry, Villesavin	Chantilly (Petit Château), Ecouen, Fontainebleau, Louvre (Le Vieux Louvre), St-Germain-en-Laye (Château Vieux)	Bridewell Palace (1864*) Compton Wynyates, Hampton Court, Nonsuch Palace (1680*), St James
17C	Blois (Gaston d'Orléans Wing), Brissac (main building), Richelieu (19C*), Serrant (chapel), Valençay (south wing)	Luxembourg, Marly-le-Roi, Maisons-Laffitte, St-Germain-en-Laye (Château Vieux rebuilt), Vaux-le-Vicomte, Versailles	Audley End, Bolsover Castle, Chastleton House, Hatfield House, Knole
18C	Chanteloup (1823*), Menars, Montgeoffroy, Valençay (Tour Neuve)	Chantilly (stables), Compiègne (rebuilt), Petit Trianon	Blenheim Palace, Buckingham Palace, Castle Howard, Chatsworth, Chiswick House, Harewood, Kenwood House, Seaton Delaval, Syon House

Demolished or destroyed by fire

The vanished châteaux of the Loire

Bury: *Superb residence, built by Florimund Robertet, which fell into ruins.*
Champigny-sur-Veude: *Rebuilt 1508-43; destroyed on Richelieu's orders; chapel remains.*
Chanteloup: *Early 18C château enlarged by Choiseul, destroyed in 1823; pagoda remains.*
Richelieu: *Built early 17C for Richelieu, demolished after the Revolution.*
Le Verger: *Built in 1482 for Pierre de Rohan, demolished in 1776 on the Cardinal's orders.*

TRADITIONAL RURAL ARCHITECTURE

The varying character of rural architecture is determined in large part by the availability of local building materials.

On the plateaux and bocages. – The **Beauce**, a great grain growing plain, has large farms with steadings arranged around a courtyard. Access is through an imposing gateway. The plaster coated houses are roofed with flat tiles. **Dunois** and **Vendômois** houses feature a chequerwork pattern created by the alternation of stone and flint.

The long, low cottages of the **Sologne** and forested **Berry** are roofed with either flat tiles or thatch. The oldest have a timber framework with cob — a clay, gravel and straw mixture — for the intervening walls. More recent constructions resort to the use of brick.

On the plateaux between the Rivers Cher, Indre and Vienne, rural dwellings are often surrounded by clumps of walnut and chestnut trees. Flat tiles predominate in the countryside with slates more common in the towns and villages.

Between the Sologne and the Loire it is fairly common to find red brick houses with white tufa stone dressings.

In **Anjou** it is possible to distinguish three distinct areas: the white limestone of White Anjou to the east, the schists of Black Anjou, and the *bocage* countryside, namely Mauges, Craonnais and Segréen. The local blue black slates are found everywhere except in the Mauges. In the **Maine** limestone is used in the White Maine or Sarthe Department and granite or schist in the Black Maine or Mayenne Valley.

In the Valley. – In the Loire and its tributaries the charming flower decked houses resemble in many ways the typical vine grower's house. This one storeyed cottage has few and small windows, a beehive shaped oven for bread making adjoining an outside wall, an exterior staircase, with a door underneath giving access to the cellar. The building generally groups under one roof the communal living quarters or room, implement shed and the stable. A wistaria or rambling rose usually adorns the walls.

(After photo: Arthaud)

Cottage in the Val

Also characteristic of the valleys are the troglodyte dwellings *(p 11)* carved out of the tufa stone with their chimneys sprouting out from the plateau surface. Often enhanced by pot plants or a climbing vine, these dwellings usually have a southern aspect and are sheltered from the prevailing winds. Cosy in winter they are appreciated for their coolness in summer.

25

MURAL PAINTINGS AND FRESCOES

In the Middle Ages the interiors of ecclesiastical buildings were decorated with paintings, motifs or edifying scenes. There developed in the Loire Valley and its tributaries a school of mural painting akin to the famous Poitou school. The remaining works of this school are well preserved due to the mild climate and relative lack of humidity. The paintings of the Loire country are recognizable by the dull faint colours against light backgrounds. The style is livelier and less formalized than in Burgundy or the Massif Central while the composition is more sober than in Poitou. Two techniques were employed : **fresco work** (from the Italian word *fresco :* fresh) was done with watercolours on fresh plaster thus eliminating any retouching and **mural painting,** less durable where the colours were applied to a dry surface.

Romanesque Period. – The art of fresco work with its Byzantine origins was adopted by the Benedictines of Monte Cassino in Italy, who in turn transmitted the art to the monks of Cluny in Burgundy. The latter, responsible for the safe conduct and welfare of pilgrims on their way to Santiago de Compostela, used this art form in their abbeys and priories, from whence it spread throughout the whole country.

The technique. – The fresco technique was the one most commonly used, although beards and eyes were often added when the plaster was dry which accounts for the usual lack of these features. The figures, drawn with a red ochre, were sometimes highlighted with touches of black, green and the sky blue so characteristic of the region.

The subject matter. – Often inspired by miniatures the subjects were meant to instruct the people in the truths of religion and also to instil a fear of sinning and of Hell. The most common theme for the oven vaulting is Christ the King enthroned, majestic and severe, the reverse of the façade

often carries a Last Judgment, the walls show scenes from the New Testament, while the Saints and Apostles are often found on the pillars. Other frequently portrayed subjects are the Struggle of the Vices and Virtues and the Labours of the Months.

The most interesting examples. – Good examples of fresco painting are found throughout the Loir Valley, at Areines, Souday, St-Jacques-des-Guérets, Lavardin and especially St-Gilles in Montoire. The Cher Valley also retains a striking ensemble at St-Aignan. The crypt in the church of Tavant, in the Vienne Valley, still boasts lively works of a very high quality.

In Anjou a certain Foulques is said to have supervised the decoration of the cloisters of the Abbey of St-Aubin in Angers. His realistic style although slightly stilted in the drawing, would seem to spring from the Poitou school. More characteristic of the Loire Valley are the Virgin and Christ the King from Pontigné in the Baugé region.

There are also interesting Romanesque and Gothic frescoes at Pritz near Laval in the Maine.

(After photo: Éd. Plon)

Areines Church — Saint's head

Gothic Period. – The 13C frescoes still resembled those of the Romanesque period and it is not till the 15C and the end of the Hundred Years War that we see new compositions which remained till the mid 16C. These were more truly mural paintings than frescoes and new subjects were added to the traditional scenes : a gigantic St Christopher often appeared at the entrance to a church while the legend of the Three Living and the Three Dead, or three proud huntsmen meeting three skeletons, symbolized the brevity and vanity of human life.

The most interesting examples. – Mural paintings are found at Alluyes and Villiers in the Loir Valley. Two compositions with strange iconography are to be seen in the neighbouring churches of Asnières-sur-Vègre and Auvers-le-Hamon. On the borders of the Sologne the church of Lassay has a picturesque St Christopher.

Renaissance Period. – The 16C saw the decline of mural painting as a means of church decoration. Two examples however remain. The one at Jarzé portrays the Entombment while the second in the chapterhouse at Fontevraud represents the abbesses.

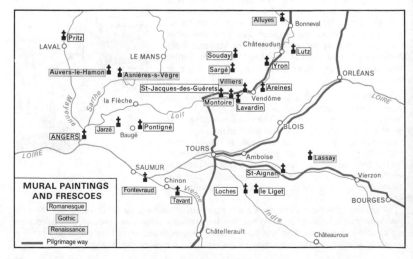

STAINED GLASS

A **stained glass window** is made up of a series of panels fixed with lead to an iron frame. The perpendicular divisions of a window are called lights. Metal oxides were added to the constituent materials of white glass to give a wide range of colours. Details were often drawn in

13C stained glass window
Angers — Cathedral

with dark paint and fixed by firing. Often quite surprising effects and variations were obtained by varying the length of firing, the impurities in the oxides and defects in the glass. The earliest stained glass windows date from the 10C but there are now no existing examples.

12-13C. – Colours were brilliant and intense with blues and reds predominating, the glass and leads were thick, the subject matter was naïve and restricted to superimposed medallions.

Grisaille windows were composed of clear through greenish glass with foliage designs on a cross hatched background giving a greyish or grisaille effect.

14-15C. – The master glaziers discovered yellow, tones were lighter, leads finer and windows themselves were bigger.

16C stained glass window
Champigny-sur-Veude

16C. – Windows became delicately coloured pictures, often copying Renaissance canvases. Examples remain at Champigny-sur-Veude, Laval, Montrésor and Sully.

17-19C. – The traditional stained glass was often replaced by coloured glass paints or enamels and painted glass. Orléans Cathedral has both 17 and 19C glass (the life of Joan of Arc).

20C. – With the need to restore and replace old glass there has been a revival in this art form. Present day painter glaziers include Max Ingrand, Alfred Manessier and Jean le Moal.

GEMMAIL

This modern art medium consists of assembling particles of coloured glass over an artificial light source. The inventors of this art form were the Frenchmen **Jean Crotti** (1878-1958) and the Malherbe-Navarre brothers. See the Gemmail Museum in Tours.

TAPESTRIES

It was the 14C before tapestries proper were to become popular, being employed to exclude draughts and divide up cavernous halls. The master weavers worked from cartoons or preparatory sketches using wool woven with silk, gold or silver threads on horizontal looms (low warp or *basse-lisse*) or vertical looms (high warp or *haute-lisse*).

Religious subjects. – Tapestries commissioned for châteaux or even specific rooms were later to find their way into churches. Perhaps the most famous 14C work is *The Angers Apocalypse* (Château d'Angers), a set of seven panels. *The Angels carrying the Instruments of the Passion* (Château d'Angers) is a late 16C work.

Mille-fleurs. – The *mille-fleurs* or thousand flowers tapestries evoke late mediaeval scenes – showing an idealized life of enticing gardens, tournaments and the hunt – against a green, blue or pink background strewn with flora and small animals. These are traditionally attributed to the Loire Valley workshops. Good examples exist at Saumur, Langeais and Angers.

Renaissance to 20C. – Paintings replace cartoons and finer weaving techniques and materials render greater detail possible. The number of colours multiply and panels are surrounded by borders.

In the 18C the art of portraiture is introduced into the tapestries.

(After photo: Archives photographiques)

Mille-fleurs Tapestry Angers : Lady at the Organ

The modern revival of this art is epitomized by the works of the famous French tapestry designer **Jean Lurçat** (1892-1966) whose great work, *Le Chant du Monde* is on exhibition in the Lurçat Museum at Angers. Three dimensional effects are part of the panoply of modern day weavers.

FAMOUS NAMES IN THE ARTS AND SCIENCES

Middle Ages. – Under St Martin's influence and even later in the 6C Tours was to become a centre of great learning. Bishop **Gregory of Tours**, the chronicler, wrote the history of the Gaulish people *(Historia Francorum)* and **Alcuin of York** was invited by the Emperor Charlemagne to found a school of calligraphy. Masterpieces produced included Charlemagne's Gospel Book and the Bible of Charles the Bald.

One of the most popular works of the later Middle Ages was *The Romance of the Rose,* a poem of courtly love by **Guillaume de Lorris** (*c* 1200/10-1240). Left unfinished, the conclusion was written by **Jean de Meung** and the whole became a highly influential work in European literature. The poem greatly influenced Geoffrey Chaucer who undertook the task of translating it into English.

Charles d'Orléans (1391-1465), a prince of royal blood and father of Louis XII, was one of the greatest of the courtly poets. Captured at Agincourt in 1415 he spent twenty-five years in exile in England where he also acquired a name for his verses in English. On his release, he returned to Blois, where he was patron of the lyric poet **François Villon** (1431-63) who was twice banished from Paris. Of his stays in the Loire one was as a prisoner in the Bishop of Orléans's cells at Meung-sur-Loire.

Renaissance and Humanism. – In the course of the Hundred Years War the centre of French culture moved with the court from Paris to Touraine and new universities were founded at Orléans (1305) and Angers (1364). These became centres of learning attracting scholars from far afield, including Erasmus and Calvin, William Elphinstone who was to found Aberdeen University and William Barclay the jurist who held the Chair of Law and died in Angers.

The humanist **Etienne Dolet** (1509-46) from Orléans was burnt at the stake for his atheistic doctrines and François I's valet **Clément Marot** (1496-1544), who attained the appointment of Court Poet, was suspected of heresy and exiled on several occasions.

Born near Chinon **Rabelais** (1494-1553) the archetype humanist writer and a physician is known for his satirical masterpiece, *Gargantua* and *Pantagruel* in which he portrays the preoccupations of the time. His native country is the setting for parts of the story *(p 76).*

(After engraving: photo Éd. Horizons de France)

Rabelais

La Pléiade. – In the 16C this group of seven writers aimed to develop and elevate the French language, in part by imitating Classical verse. Although the undoubted leader was **Pierre de Ronsard** from Vendôme it was **Joachim Du Bellay** who in 1549 wrote their manifesto, *The Defence and Illustration of the French Language.* The others were **Jean-Antoine de Baïf** from La Flèche, Jean Dorat, Etienne Jodelle and Pontus de Tyard. All held at some time the appointment of Court Poet and their odes and sonnets celebrated their native countryside.

Classicism and the Age of Enlightenment. – With the end of the Wars of Religion and the return of the court to the Ile-de-France the subject matter tended to become more philosophical. **Honorat de Bueil**, marquis de Racan manifested a great love of nature while **Théophraste Renaudot**, a native of Loudun is known as the "Father of French journalism".

It was the Protestant Academy at Saumur which approved the earliest works of the philosopher and mathematician, **René Descartes**. The founding in 1686 at Angers of the Academy of Fine Arts was to make this a truly active cultural centre. Chambord was the venue for the premières of two of Molière's plays.

In the following century **Nericault-Destouches**, a playwright from Tours was to follow in Molière's footsteps with his moralising comedies of character. Illustrious visitors to the region included Voltaire at Sully, Rousseau at Chenonceau and Beaumarchais, author of *The Barber of Seville,* sojourned at Vouvray from where he could readily visit the banished duc de Choiseul at Chanteloup.

The Romantics. – After the Empire it was no longer the great royal palaces but the smaller châteaux which were the centres of the literary world. The pamphleteer **Paul-Louis Courier** (1772-1825) and the popular song writer **Béranger** (1780-1857) during the second Bourbon restoration were both sceptical and anti monarchist, as well as politically liberal. **Alfred de Vigny** (1797-1863) a native of Loches and one of the foremost French Romantic writers told in his historical novel *Cinq-Mars* the tale of an idyllic Touraine.

However the great man of letters of the 19C was **Honoré de Balzac** (1799-1850), a native of Tours educated at Vendôme. He made his beloved countryside the setting for some of his novels in his great fresco of French society *The Human Comedy.* His retreat was the small Château de Saché.

The 20C. – The Orléans poet, **Charles Péguy** (1873-1914) wrote of Joan of Arc and the Beauce and Chartres in particular. Novelist and author **Marcel Proust** also made the Beauce the setting for his monumental work in several parts *A la recherche du temps perdu (Remembrance of Things Past).* **Max Jacob** (1876-1944), the poet and contemporary of Picasso retired to the calm and seclusion of the abbey at St-Benoît-sur-Loire.

Alain Fournier is famous for his novel *Le Grand Meaulnes (The Wanderer)* set in the Sologne. The Academician **Maurice Genevoix** (1890-1980) described his native country through the eyes of his famous poacher, Raboliot. **Georges Bernanos** (1888-1948), an original Catholic writer is interred at Pellevoisin.

The humorist **Georges Courteline** (1858-1929) came from the Touraine which was the retreat of many writers of international reputation. Maurice Maeterlinck, Nobel Prize winner in 1911, at Coudray-Montpensier, Anatole France, Nobel Prize winner in 1921, at La Béchellerie and Henri Bergson, Nobel Prize winner 1927, at La Gaudinière.

Although born in Paris, **René Benjamin** (1885-1948) adopted the Touraine where he wrote his prodigious *History of the Life of Balzac* and novels describing life in the area. Angers was the home of the Academician **René Bazin** (1853-1932), a novelist who was greatly attached to the simple virtues of provincial life and nature. His great nephew **Hervé Bazin** (b 1911), a rebel and Bohemian, was known for his virulent attacks against the traditional values of family, Church and motherhood, inspired it was said by his experiences in his native town of Angers.

Laval was the birthplace of **Alfred Jarry** (1873-1907), the author of *Ubu Roi,* considered to be the first work of the Theatre of the Absurd.

The Fine Arts. – The presence of many royal palaces and stately châteaµx attracted the very best of European craftsmen during two centuries. Only a few of the many who contributed to the fine arts can be mentioned here.

Jean Fouquet, Official Portraitist and Miniaturist to Charles VII and Louis XI, was the major French painter of the Renaissance. The altarpiece, *The Pietà of Nouans* is one of his better known works. Both the **Master of Moulins** and **Jean Bourdichon** left a small number of works. The musician Clement Janequin (1480-1565) adopted Anjou as his native countryside and was for a long time head of the Choir School at Angers Cathedral.

Jean Clouet of Flemish extraction and his son, **François,** were both Court Painters to the Valois dynasty. Their fine portrait drawings of notables of the period, including one of Mary Stuart, are of great historic interest.

Following the Renaissance there are two well known names with Loire connections – the engraver and sculptor **David d'Angers** (1788-1856), famous for his hundreds of portrait medallions of major figures of the time, and **Henri Rousseau,** called Le Douanier (1844-1910), another native of Angers and precursor of the Naive School.

The famous American sculptor **Alexander Calder** (1898-1976), inventor of mobiles and stabiles, lived near Saché.

Science. – The Loire Valley is one of the traditional homes of medical progress. It was here during the Renaissance that the notable surgeon **Ambroise Paré** (1517-90) laid the foundations of the science of modern surgery and among other achievements perfected the technique of ligaturing arteries. The Royal College of Surgeons was founded in Tours in 1756 and is now the Faculty of Medicine and Pharmacy.

It was also in Tours that **Bretonneau** (1778-1862) carried out his research on infectious diseases. His work was to be carried on by his pupils, **Trousseau** and **Velpeau.**

The inventor and physician **Denis Papin** (1647-1714) was born near Blois. Papin had already made his name with his work on the air vacuum and his invention of the steam digester or pressure cooker, before he was forced into exile by the Revocation of the Edict of Nantes in 1685. He spent many years in Marbourg and Cassel and then London where he died.

The physicist **Jacques-A. C. Charles** (1746-1823), inventor of Charles's Law, from Beaugency, built the first hydrogen balloon. The Mongolfier brothers, who were at the same time experimenting with hot air balloons assisted at the maiden flight of Charles's balloon in 1783 in Paris. In 1804 he married Julie who was the Elvire of the Romantic poet Lamartine's first collection *Méditations Poétiques.*

BOOKS TO READ

The Loire by Vivian Rowe *(Methuen – 1976)*
Loire Valley by J.J. and J. Walling *(Thomas Nelson Ltd – 1974)*
The Loire by S. Jennett *(Batsford – 1975)*
Valley of the Loire by G. Pillement translated by A. Rosin *(Johnson – 1965)*
Eleanor of Aquitaine and the Four Kings by Amy Kelly *(Harvard University Press – 1950)*
Francis I by R.J. Knecht *(Cambridge University Press - 1984)*
Joan of Arc by Marina Warner *(Penguin - 1983)*
Personal Recollections on Joan of Arc by Mark Twain *(Harper Row Publishers Inc.)*
Access in the Loire (Holiday guide for the disabled). Obtainable from Mr G. R. Couch, 68B
Castlebar Road, Ealing, London W5 200

Editions of works mentioned below can be obtained through public libraries.

Loire and its Châteaux by Pepin *(Thames & Hudson – 1971)*
The Châteaux of France by Ralph Dutton *(Batsford – 1957)*
The Châteaux of the Loire by Ian Dunlop *(Hamish Hamilton – 1969)*
The Cathedral's Crusade, The Rise of the Gothic style in France by Ian Dunlop *(Hamish Hamilton – 1982)*
Châteaux of the Loire by Jacques Levron *(Nicholas Kaye)*
The Loire Valley by Henry Myhill *(Faber & Faber – 1978)*

The following novels have settings in the area.

Honoré de Balzac: Eugénie Grandet, Le Curé de Tours, La Femme de Trente Ans, l'Illustre Gaudissart, Le Lys dans la Vallée.
René Benjamin: La Vie Tourangelle
Alain-Fournier (Henri-Alban Fournier) : Le Grand Meaulnes
Maurice Genevoix: Raboliot
Émile Zola: Earth
Marcel Proust: A la recherche du temps perdu, Jean Santeuil
Charles Péguy: Jeanne d'Arc
François Rabelais: Gargantua and Pantagruel comprising Pantagruel, Gargantua, Tiers Livre, Quart Livre

FOOD AND WINE

THE GOD OF WINE

"September soup". – The wines of France, and the Loire region in particular, have been held in great repute from time immemorial – Alcuin of York was to sing their praises, Rabelais declared that "the good September soup" was the greatest treasure of the Loire country and the *Dive Bouteille* or Sacred Bottle was the quest of his *Quart Livre.*

All wines marketed commercially come into three categories namely *Appellation Contrôlée* (AC), *Vins Délimités de Qualité Supérieure* (VDQS) and *vins de consommation.* The **Val de Loire** is one of the AC regions, a label which guarantees the geographical origin and method of manufacture. Within each region there are a variety of wines named after smaller areas, villages, parishes, châteaux, etc. *Coteaux* means vineyards.

The main varieties of vine *(cépage)* used are the *Cabernet Franc, Chasselas, Sauvignon, Chenin, Breton* and *Pineau (Pinot) de la Loire.* The term *pineau* is not to be confused with the French army slang word, *pinard,* meaning wine ration.

Local wines. – The best known white wines are Vouvray and Montlouis the *Pineau de la Loire* stock. Vines qualified as *breton* are a Cabernet Franc grape which originally came from the Bordelais and are now used in the region to produce red wines such as Bourgueil and Chinon. Other red Anjou wines are the Rouge de Cabernet and Saumur-Champigny with a raspberry flavour. The Cabernet de Saumur is a dry rosé. Another red comes from the Loudun slopes using the *breton* vines.

The Sancerre wines with their gunflint flavour from the *Sauvignon* grape are reputed. From a wealth of local wines others worthy of a mention are the *gris meuniers* from the Orléanais and the *gascon,* which are pale and have a low alcoholic content.

The Coteaux du Loir produce both a dry white wine and a bitter tasting red which improves with the keeping. From the Sologne, the Romorantin wine is light and pleasant. The wine of the Loire Valley has a delicate bouquet, tastes of the grape and is not very intoxicating.

For the vintage years see the current Michelin Guide France (Food and Wine).

The **cellars** are often former quarries, opening into the white chalk of the hillsides. The galleries may extend for several hundreds of metres, opening out at times to form halls which are used for the meetings and celebrations of local societies.

Wine growers' brotherhoods are similar in origin to the mediaeval guilds. Examples are the *Sacavins* (Angers), *Entonneurs rabelaisiens* (Chinon – *first Saturday in June, last Sunday in September and on the Feast of St Vincent, the patron saint's day)* la Chantepleure (Vouvray), *la Coterie des Closiers* (Montlouis). These local governing bodies preserve the tradition of fine drinking and joyously initiate new members, *chevaliers,* to the brotherhood.

Opportunities are numerous for visiting vineyards and inspecting cellars, tasting rooms and installations.

In the Temple of Bacchus. – Here you are, facing, as a guest, the barrels of the last vintage, firmly fixed on their stands ; it is *vin ordinaire* (common wine) that runs into the silver cup as the plug is withdrawn. You admire the ruby by daylight ; then the wine grower fills each glass. The glass has no foot ; you will not be tempted to set it down before it is empty. *Nunc est bibendum.* This wine must not be swallowed at a draught ; you must test the bouquet first, and then give a knowing glance to your host before drinking it in little sips. When you come to the end, no words of praise are necessary : just click your tongue.

From a large pocket in his grey apron the wine grower will take a huge key. A lock grates and the cellar, the sanctuary of the "Sacred Bottle", is open. The red, yellow, blue and white caps peep from pigeonholes sunk in the rock all around : Vouvray, heady Montlouis with its flintlock flavour, aromatic Sancerre, Chinon with its taste of violets, Bourgueil reminiscent of raspberries, and their brothers of Anjou, sparkling Saumur, wines from Serrant and the Layon. Finally, in a place to themselves, the vintages of 1943, 1945, 1947, 1949, 1953, 1955, 1959, 1969, 1970 and 1971 – the glory of the Loire, so much nectar to be tasted reverently.

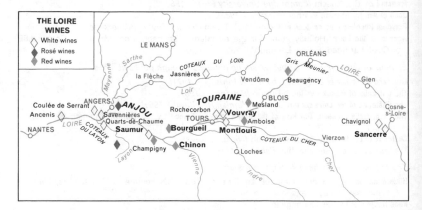

A few local proverbs

Thunder in April	*Shooting stars in September*
Augurs a good harvest	*Barrels overflowing in November*
Touraine and Anjou, the lands of	*After the soup a draught of wine*
Good fruit, great minds and good wines	*Keeps you healthy and fine*

REGIONAL SPECIALITIES

Here are some of the specialities with a selection of local wines *(see notes below).*

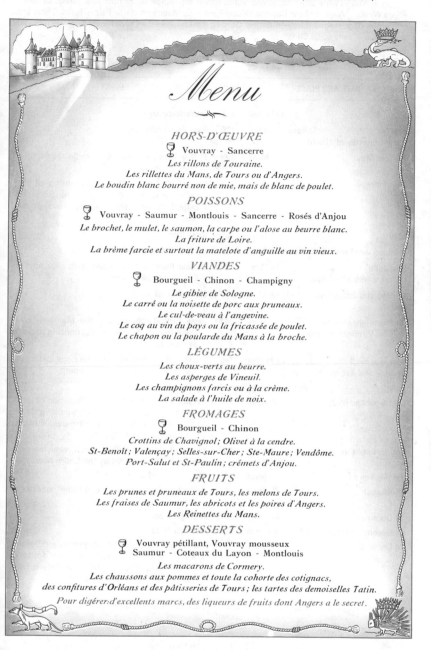

Menu

HORS-D'ŒUVRE
Vouvray - Sancerre

Les rillons de Touraine.
Les rillettes du Mans, de Tours ou d'Angers.
Le boudin blanc bourré non de mie, mais de blanc de poulet.

POISSONS
Vouvray - Saumur - Montlouis - Sancerre - Rosés d'Anjou

Le brochet, le mulet, le saumon, la carpe ou l'alose au beurre blanc.
La friture de Loire.
La brème farcie et surtout la matelote d'anguille au vin vieux.

VIANDES
Bourgueil - Chinon - Champigny

Le gibier de Sologne.
Le carré ou la noisette de porc aux pruneaux.
Le cul-de-veau à l'angevine.
Le coq au vin du pays ou la fricassée de poulet.
Le chapon ou la poularde du Mans à la broche.

LÉGUMES
Les choux-verts au beurre.
Les asperges de Vineuil.
Les champignons farcis ou à la crème.
La salade à l'huile de noix.

FROMAGES
Bourgueil - Chinon

Crottins de Chavignol ; Olivet à la cendre.
St-Benoît ; Valençay ; Selles-sur-Cher ; Ste-Maure ; Vendôme.
Port-Salut et St-Paulin ; crémets d'Anjou.

FRUITS
Les prunes et pruneaux de Tours, les melons de Tours.
Les fraises de Saumur, les abricots et les poires d'Angers.
Les Reinettes du Mans.

DESSERTS
Vouvray pétillant, Vouvray mousseux
Saumur - Coteaux du Layon - Montlouis

Les macarons de Cormery.
Les chaussons aux pommes et toute la cohorte des cotignacs,
des confitures d'Orléans et des pâtisseries de Tours ; les tartes des demoiselles Tatin.
Pour digérer:d'excellents marcs, des liqueurs de fruits dont Angers a le secret.

Hors-d'œuvre : various types of potted pork ; pork (blood) sausage stuffed with chicken meat.
Fish : pike, grey mullet, salmon, carp or shad with butter sauce (butter, shallots and vinegar) ; small fried fish from the Loire ; stuffed bream and eels simmered in matured wine with mushrooms, small onions and prunes (in Anjou).
Main course : game from Sologne ; pork with prunes ; veal in a cream sauce made with white wine and brandy ; casserole of chicken in a red wine sauce or in a white wine and cream sauce with onions and mushrooms ; spit roasted capon or large hen.
Vegetables : green cabbage with butter ; Vineuil asparagus ; mushrooms stuffed or with a cream sauce ; lettuce with walnut oil.
Cheese : St-Benoît, Vendôme, Port-Salut and St-Paulin are made from cow's milk ; Chavignol, Valençay, Selles-sur-Cher, Ste-Maure and crémets are made from goat's milk. The latter are small fresh goat's cream cheese ; Olivet is factory made with a coating of charcoal.
Fruit : plums and prunes from Tours ; melons from Tours ; Saumur strawberries ; apricots and pears from Angers ; Reinette apples from Le Mans.
Dessert : macaroons from Cormery ; apple pastries ; quince and apple jelly ; preserves from Orléans and Tours pastries ; caramelised apple turnovers.
Liqueurs : there are excellent marcs and fruit liqueurs, notably those from Angers.
Marcs : pure white spirit obtained from pressed grapes.

PRINCIPAL FESTIVALS

In addition to the principal events listed below the region plays host to a variety of fairs: Anjou Wines – Angers; Four Day and Onion Fairs – Le Mans and Garlic Fair – Tours. There are numerous pilgrimages (Cléry-St-André, Gardes, La Chapelle-du-Chêne) including the unusual pilgrimage – rally to St Christopher *(p 139)*.

CALENDAR OF EVENTS

DATE AND PLACE		PAGE	EVENT
Easter Sunday	Solesmes	149	Easter ceremony
Easter (Holy Saturday at 10pm)	St-Benoît-sur-Loire	136	Great Easter ceremony
April or May	Le Mans	109	24 Hour Race: annual motor cycle race on the Bugatti Circuit
7 and 8 May	Orléans	124	Festival of Joan of Arc: floodlighting of the cathedral on the 7th; religious service in the cathedral, procession, military parade on the 8th.
May	Tours	155	Corso fleuri
Whitsun weekend	Châteauneuf-sur-Loire	67	Rhododendron Carnival
Mid June or last weekend in June	Le Mans	109	24 Hour Race: annual automobile race on the Circuit des 24 heures.
Fridays and Saturdays in July	Sully-sur-Loire	152	Music Festival
2nd fortnight in June and 1st fortnight in July	Anjou	41	Anjou Festival: throughout the Maine-et-Loire Department: drama, music, dancing and art exhibitions.
Last weekend in June and 1st weekend in July	Grange de Meslay	162	Touraine Music Festival: with the participation of musicians of international repute
July	Doué-la-Fontaine	80	International Rose Show
Last weekend in July	La Ménitré		Headdress Parade: with the participation of local folklore groups. A hundred young girls in local costumes and headdresses. Further information Tel 41 45 63 63
2nd fortnight in July	Saumur	144	Military Tattoo: including motor vehicles and horses with displays by the *Cadre Noir*
1st weekend in August	Chinon	73	Mediaeval Market
15 August	Molineuf	58	Bric-à-brac Fair: antiques and other collector's items
24 December	Solesmes	149	Midnight Mass
24 December (11pm)	St-Benoît-sur-Loire	136	Midnight Mass
24 December	Anjou		The Naulets Mass: held each year in a different small country church. Angevin foklore groups sing carols in the local dialect. Further information Tel 41 88 69 93

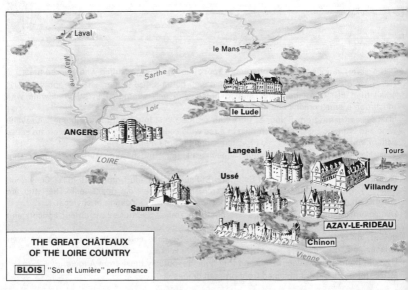

THE GREAT CHÂTEAUX
OF THE LOIRE COUNTRY

BLOIS "Son et Lumière" performance

SON ET LUMIÈRE PERFORMANCES

This type of performance was inaugurated at Chambord in 1952 by Mr. M. P. Robert-Houdin. The history of the châteaux and their owners is presented in an original manner with the shows lasting from 20 minutes to 2 hours.

Amboise : A la cour du roy François (At the Court of François I). – *Performances at 10.30pm on the last Saturday in June, Wednesdays, Saturdays and on some Fridays in July ; 10pm Wednesdays, Saturdays and on some Fridays and 15 August until mid-August. Time : 1 1/2 hours. Information : Tel 47 57 09 28. Price : 35F.*

Azay-le-Rideau : Puisque de vous n'avons autre visage★★ (A unique evocation of the Renaissance). – *Performances at 10.30pm late May to 31 July ; 10pm August and September. Time : 1 hour. Price : 22.50F. Information : Tel 47 61 61 23 Ext 2160.*

Blois : Les esprits aiment la nuit (Spirits prefer the night). – *Performances at 9.15pm in April and mid August to late September ; 10pm late April to mid-May and 1 to 15 August ; 10.30pm mid-May to late July. No performances on Thursdays excepting Ascension Day and in July and August and on certain days in June, July and August. Time : 3/4 hour. Price : 18F. Information : Tel 54 74 06 49.*

Chambord : Le combat du jour et de la nuit★★ (The conflict between day and night). – *Performances at 10pm during Easter weekend and Fridays, Saturdays, Sundays and holidays in April ; 10.15pm Fridays, Saturdays, Sundays and holidays in May ; 10.45pm 1 June to 20 July ; 10.30pm 21 July to 15 August ; 10pm 16 to 31 August ; 9.30pm 1 to 29 September. Time : 35 minutes. Price : 21F. Information : in Paris Tel (1) 42 74 22 22 ; Blois Tel 54 78 67 68 ; Chambord Tel 54 20 31 32.*

Chenonceau : Au temps des Dames de Chenonceau (The influence of the six châtelaines). – *Performances at 10 and 10.45 pm Friday, Saturday and Sunday at Whitsun and nightly mid-June to mid-September. Time : 3/4 hour. Price : 20F. Information : Tel 47 23 90 07.*

Cheverny : A la lueur des flambeaux (By the light of flaming torches). – *Performances at 10pm on two Saturdays in July, two Saturdays in August and 14 August. Time : 1 1/4 hours. Price : 32F. Information : Tel 54 79 96 29.*

Chinon : Charles VII, l'enfant maudit (Charles VII the accursed child). – *Performances at 10.30pm Fridays and Saturdays late June to mid July ; 10.15pm mid-July to mid-August ; 9.45pm mid-August to early September. Price : 35F. Information : Tel 47 93 17 85.*

Le Lude : Les glorieuses et fastueuses soirées au bord du Loir★★★ (Sumptuous nights on the banks of the Loir). – *Performances at 10.30pm from second weekend in June to first weekend in September, Fridays and Saturdays in June and July ; 10pm Fridays, Saturdays and some Thursdays in August ; 9.30pm Fridays and Saturdays in September. Time : 1 3/4 hours. Price : 25 to 45F.*
There are firework displays on Fridays and Saturdays : 15F supplement.

Valençay : La Reine Margot (Queen Margot). – *Performances at 10pm on some Fridays and Saturdays late June to mid-July ; 9.30pm on some Saturdays and Sundays in August and 14 August. Price : 40 or 45F. Information : Tel 54 00 04 42 (in season) or 54 00 14 33.*

It is advisable to confirm the above information by making further enquiries at the following Tourist Information Centres : Blois (Tel 54 74 06 49), Tours (Tel 47 05 58 08) and Le Lude (Tel 43 94 62 20). Places can also be reserved for evening bus tours to certain châteaux namely Amboise, Azay-le-Rideau and Le Lude. Apply to the Tourist Centre in Tours.

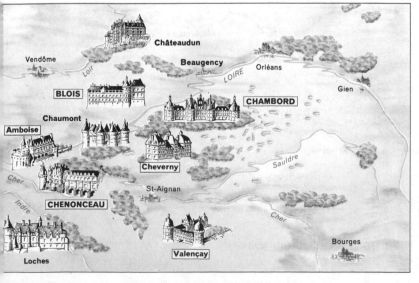

TOURING PROGRAMMES

ANJOU

Round tour from Angers via le Mans (450 km)
Round tour from Angers via Thouars (300 km)

0   10   20 km

LAVAL ★

D 130

Saulges

**LE MANS

D 112

Mayenne

D 79   Fillé ┼
la Suze-s-Sarthe
D 504

Asnières-s-Vègre ★

D 41

Château-Gontier

Sarthe Valley
p 142

Bercé
Forest ★

l' Escoublère ★

Malicorne-s-Sarthe

D 13   p 53   D 63

LA FLÈCHE ★

Luché-
Pringé

Château-du-Loir

D 162

D 78

Bazouges-s-le-Loir ★

D 13

Mayenne Valley ★
p 116

Durtal

N 23

Sarthe

Loir

Loir Valley ★★
p 96

le Lion-
d'Angers   ▲ l'Isle-Briand Stud ★

D 191   ┼ le Plessis-Bourré ★

Loir

D 18

le lude ┼

le Plessis-
Macé

D 141 Pontigné
Baugé   ★

Chandelais
Forest ★

N 162

ANGERS ★★★

Montgeoffroy ★

p 50

D 60   Cuon

★★ Serrant
p 104

D 111

D 952

D 74   Beaufort-en-Vallée

Loire Valley ★★★
p100

Béhuard ★

LOIRE

Angevin
Corniche

Rochefort-s-Loire ★

D 55

St-Maur
Abbey

D 152

les Rosiers

LOIRE

Chalonnes-
s-Loire

★★ Brissac

★★ Cunault   ■ Boumois ★

Beaulieu-s-Layon

D 125

p.103

SAUMUR ★★

D 83

★ Doué-la-
Fontaine

D 960

Layon Valley
p 91

D 178

▲ Asnières Abbey

Vienne

Layon

D 69

Montreuil-Bellay ★★

Passavant-s-Layon

D 159

Thouet

D 938

THOUARS ★

○	Overnight stop
✕	Castle or château
┼	Religious building
∴	Interesting ruins
▲	Miscellaneous sights
p.159	Route described on p 159

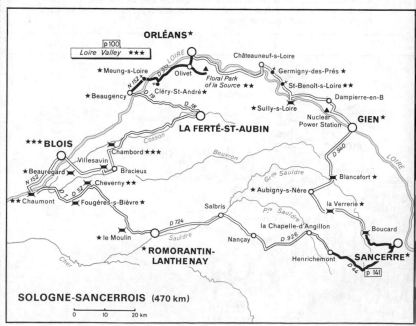

ORLÉANS ★

p 100
Loire Valley ★★★

LOIRE

Châteauneuf-s-Loire

★ Meung-s-Loire

D 951

Olivet

N 152

Cléry-St-André ★

Floral Park
of la Source ★★

★ Germigny-des-Prés ★

St-Benoît-s-Loire ★★

Dampierre-en-B

★ Beaugency

D 19

D 18

★ Sully-s-Loire

Nuclear
Power Station

GIEN ★

LA FERTÉ-ST-AUBIN

Cosson

B10

★★★ BLOIS

Chambord ★★★

Beuvron

D 940

LOIRE

Villesavin ✕

Bracieux

★ Beauregard

N 152

Cheverny ★★

D 52

Gde Sauldre

Blancafort ★

D 7

★ Aubigny-s-Nère

★★ Chaumont

Fougères-s-Bièvre ★

Salbris

la Verrerie ★

la Chapelle-d'Angillon

Boucard

D 724

Pte Sauldre

★ le Moulin

Sauldre

Nançay

D 926

Henrichemont

SANCERRE ★

Cher

★ ROMORANTIN-
LANTHENAY

D 44   p 141

SOLOGNE-SANCERROIS (470 km)

0   10   20 km

34

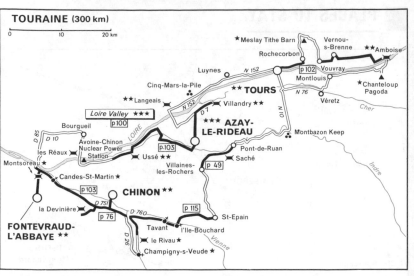

TOURAINE (300 km)

0 10 20 km

★ Meslay Tithe Barn   Vernou-s-Brenne   ★★ Amboise
Rochecorbon   ▲   Vouvray
Luynes   N 152   p 102   Montlouis
Cinq-Mars-la-Pile   ★★ TOURS   N 76   Véretz   ★ Chanteloup Pagoda
★★ Langeais   ★ Villandry ★★   N 10   Cher
Loire Valley ★★★   p 100   D 7   ★★★ AZAY-LE-RIDEAU
Bourgueil
D 85   D 10   Avoine-Chinon Nuclear Power Station   p 103   ▲ Montbazon Keep
les Réaux   LOIRE   Ussé ★★   Pont-de-Ruan
Montsoreau ★   Villaines-les-Rochers   p 49   Saché
★ Candes-St-Martin ★   Indre
p 103   CHINON ★★
la Devinière ★   D 751   D 760   p 115
p 76   Tavant   l'Ile-Bouchard   St-Epain
FONTEVRAUD-L'ABBAYE ★★   D 26   ★ le Rivau   Vienne
★ Champigny-s-Veude ★

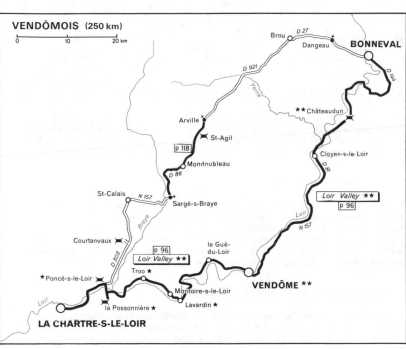

VENDÔMOIS (250 km)

0 10 20 km

Brou   D 27   Dangeau   BONNEVAL
D 921   Yerre   D 144
★★ Châteaudun
Arville
★ St-Agil   Cloyes-s-le-Loir
p 118   D 81
D 86   Mondoubleau
St-Calais   N 157   Loir Valley ★★   p 96
Sargé-s-Braye   Loir
Braye   N 157
Courtanvaux   le Gué-du-Loir
D 303   p 96
Loir Valley ★★
★ Poncé-s-le-Loir   Troo ★   Montoire-s-le-Loir   VENDÔME ★★
Loir   la Possonnière ★   Lavardin ★
LA CHARTRE-S-LE-LOIR

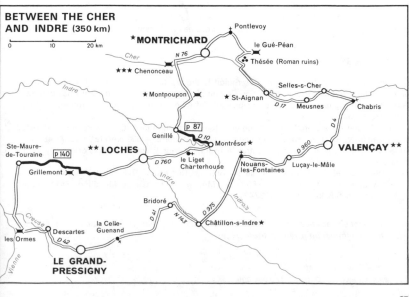

BETWEEN THE CHER AND INDRE (350 km)

0 10 20 km

Pontlevoy
★ MONTRICHARD   le Gué-Péan
Cher   N 76   Thésée (Roman ruins)
★★★ Chenonceau   Selles-s-Cher
Indre   ★ Montpoupon   ★ St-Aignan   Meusnes   Chabris
D 17   D 4
p 87
Genillé   D 10
Ste-Maure-de-Touraine   p 140   Montrésor ★   VALENÇAY ★★
★★ LOCHES   D 960   Luçay-le-Mâle
Grillemont   D 760   le Liget Charterhouse   Nouans-les-Fontaines
Indre
Bridoré   D 975   Châtillon-s-Indre ★
Creuse   la Celle-Guenand   D 41   N 143   Indrois
les Ormes   Descartes   D 42
Vienne   LE GRAND-PRESSIGNY

■ PLACES TO STAY

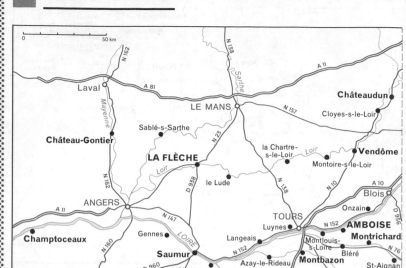

The map above indicates towns selected for the accommodation and leisure facilities, which they offer to the holidaymaker. To help you plan your route and choose your hotel, restaurant or camping site consult the Michelin publications, the traveller's friends.

Accommodation

The **Michelin Red Guide France** of hotels and restaurants and the **Michelin Guide Camping Caravaning France** are annual publications which present a selection of hotels, restaurants and camping sites. The final choice is based on regular on the spot enquiries and visits. Both the hotels and camping sites are classified according to the standard of comfort of their amenities. Establishments which are notable for their fortunate setting, their decor, their quiet and secluded location and their warm welcome are distinguished by special symbols.

Planning your route, sports and recreation

The **Michelin Sectional Map Series** at a scale of 1 : 200 000 covers the whole of France. For those concerning the region see the layout diagram on page 3. The maps are an essential complement to the tourist and annual guides, and all the publications are carefully cross referenced. The existence of a town plan and listing of hotel and restaurant ressources in the Red Guide are indicated on the map by a red frame and red underlining respectively. In addition to the wealth of road information, the touristic details include beaches, bathing spots, swimming pools, golf courses, racecourses, panoramas and scenic routes.

Paying guests

One of the greatest charms of this region is the wealth of châteaux and manor houses, often in calm and most attractive settings. Certain of these privately owned mansions open their doors to paying guests, who have the pleasure of enjoying the gracious surroundings for a moderate price.

For further details apply to the regional tourist organizations (Central Region : BP 2412, 45032 ORLÉANS CEDEX ; Pays de la Loire : 3 place St-Pierre, 44000 NANTES ; Tel 40 48 15 15, 40 48 24 20) the tourist information centres in Tours, Saumur, Chinon and Blois or directly to the organizations concerned such as :

Château Accueil : Mme la Vicomtesse de Bonneval, Château de Thaumiers, Thaumiers, 18210 CHARENTON-DU-CHER ; Tel 48 60 87 62 ; Mme Ide, Château de Mémillon, St-Maur-sur-le-Loir, 28800 BONNEVAL, Tel 37 47 28 57.

The mention facilities pp 36-37 under the individual headings in the body of the guide refers to the information given on these pages.

EUROPE on a single sheet
Michelin map No ▨▨▨ (scale 1/3 000 000)

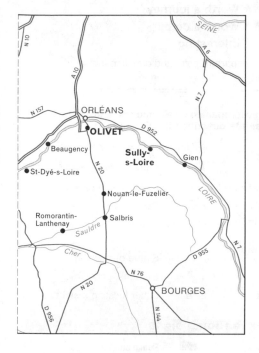

OUTDOOR ACTIVITIES

FORESTS

The numerous forests of the region make good walking country or simply a pleasant drive or stopping place. **Forest roads** are indicated on the Michelin Sectional Map Series (1 : 200 000). Respect the Country Code and protect wild life, wild plants and trees, leave no litter and guard against all risks of fire. The **Long Distance Footpaths** (GR : *sentiers de grande randonnée*), well signposted in the field and marked on Michelin maps, cross some of the area's forested tracts.

The **GR 3** follows the Loire and crosses the Orléans, Russy and Chinon Forests.

The **GR 3c** between Gien and Mont-près-Chambord is in Sologne country.

The **GR 31** links Mont-près-Chambord, on the edge of the Boulogne Forest and Sancerre passing through the Sologne Forest.

The **GR 32** crosses the Orléans Forest.

The **GR 33S** between the Loire and the Loir links Vouvray and Lavardin.

The **GR 35** follows the Loir Valley and crosses the countryside between Cloyes and Seiches-sur-le-Loir.

The **GR 36** or English Channel to Pyrenees route, runs between Le Mans and Thouars.

The **GR 46** follows the Indre Valley.

RIDING, PONY TREKKING

Noted for its studs and the National Riding School at St-Hilaire-St-Florent near Saumur, the region has numerous riding centres which are open to visitors. Some serve as an overnight halt for those on trekking holidays.

Trekking guides indicating the itineraries and overnight stops and further details, are available from the following organizations :

A.R.T.E. Val de Loire-Océan, 5 rue de Santeuil, 44000 NANTES ; Tel 40 73 57 19 (Wednesday and Thursday from 10am)

A.R.T.E. Val de Loire-Centre, M. Plchonnat, 13 rue du Tournebride, 36600 VALENÇAY ; Tel 54 00 00 10

A.N.T.E. 15 rue de Bruxelles, 75009 PARIS ; Tel (1) 42 81 42 82

Tourist Information Centres can also provide information on riding activities in the area.

CRUISING

In addition to the local sailing clubs centred on lakes, reservoirs and other stretches of water, the Loire basin offers opportunities for cruising enthusiasts to enjoy its waters. Pottering on the river is an original way to discover and appreciate to the full the beauty and calm of the riverside landscapes.

The **Maine** basin has good navigable stretches on the Oudon (downstream from Segré), on the Mayenne (downstream from Laval) and the Sarthe (downstream from Le Mans). Boats can be hired (no permit required) at Andouillé, Angers, Château-Gontier, Chenillé-Changé, Grez-Neuville, Laval-Salicome, Le Mans, Noyen-sur-Sarthe and Sablé. Reservations and further details from :

Syndicat interdépartemental du bassin Maine-Mayenne-Oudon-Sarthe, Place du Président-Kennedy, 49022 ANGERS CEDEX ; Tel 41 88 99 38

The **Loire** offers similar opportunities as do the various canals (Briare and Loire lateral canals) starting from Châtillon-sur-Loire (Loiret), Montargis (Loiret) and Rogny-les-7-Écluses (Yonne). Reservations and further details from :

Tourisme-Accueil-Loiret, Service de réservation, 3 rue de la Bretonnerie, 45000 ORLÉANS ; Tel 38 62 04 88.

For further information on cruising in the area apply to the Tourist Information Centres or to the Regional Tourist Organizations *(for addresses see under Paying Guests)*.

The companion guides in English in this series on France are
Brittany, Dordogne, French Riviera, Normandy, Paris, Provence

KEY

★★★ **Worth a journey**
★★ **Worth a detour**
★ **Interesting**

Sightseeing route with departure point and direction indicated

on the road   in town

The following symbols, when accompanied by a name or a letter in heavy type, locate the sights described in this guide

Mainly on local maps			*Mainly on town plans*	
✖	∴	Castle – Ruins	🏳 ⌂	Catholic, Protestant Church
♦	┼	Chapel – Cross or calvary		Building with main entrance
⁂	⩔	Panorama – View		Ramparts – Tower
⌕	✗	Lighthouse – Mill (wind or water)		Gateway
◡	✿	Dam – Factory or power station	◎	Fountain
☆	∪	Fort – Quarry	▪	Statue or building
▲		Miscellaneous sights		Gardens, park, woods
			B	Letter locating a sight

Conventional signs

▃▃▃	Motorway (unclassified)	🏢	Public building
▃▃▃	Dual carriageway	✚	Hospital
▃▃▃	Major through road	✉	Covered market
⋯⋯	Tree-lined street	⚔	Barracks
⋯⋯	Stepped street	⸭⸭⸭	Cemetery
╫	Pedestrian street	🏇 ⛳	Racecourse – Golf course
✗======	Impassable or under construction	⌕ ▢	Outdoor or indoor swimming pool
⋯⋯⋯	Footpath	⛸ ⊤	Skating rink – Viewing table
•–•–•	Trolleybus, tram	⸽	Telecommunications tower or mast
▅▆▃	Station	⌑ ⌇	Stadium – Water tower
⌐ A │ B	Reference grid letters for town plans	✈ ✈	Airport – Airfield
③	Reference number common to town plans and MICHELIN maps	🚌	Coach station
⌞ 12 ⌟	Distance in kilometres	🖃	Main post office (with poste restante)
→1429←	Pass – Altitude	🛈	Tourist information centre
		P	Car park

In all MICHELIN guides, plans and maps are always orientated with north at the top.
Main shopping streets are printed in a different colour at the beginning of the list of streets.

Abbreviations

A	Motorway (Autoroute)	*GR*	Long distance footpath (Sentier de Grande Randonnée)	*P*	Préfecture Sous-préfecture
A	Local agricultural office (Chambre d'Agriculture)			*POL.*	Police
C	Chamber of Commerce (Chambre de Commerce)	*H*	Town Hall (Hôtel de Ville)	*R.F.*	Forest Road (Route Forestière)
D	Secondary road (Route Départementale)	*J*	Law Courts (Palais de Justice)	*T*	Theatre
G	Police station (Gendarmerie)	*M*	Museum	*U*	University
		N	Trunk road (Route Nationale)		

With this guide

*use the **Michelin Maps** at a scale of 1:200 000.*
For coverage of this region see page three.

TOWNS, SIGHTS
AND TOURIST REGIONS

AMBOISE ★★

Michelin map 64 fold 16 – *Local map p 100* – Pop 11 415 – *Facilities pp 36-37*

Amboise appears at its most picturesque when seen from the north bank of the Loire or from the bridge. The château, high above the town, has been greatly reduced in the course of the centuries but still stands proudly, its history rich in dramatic events.

The Amboise Conspiracy (1560). – This abortive plot was led by a Protestant gentleman, **La Renaudie,** who formed a group of Reformers in Brittany who planned to go to Blois in twos and threes. Meeting there, they were to ask the young King, François II's permission to practise their religion, and also try, no doubt, to lay hands on the Guises, who were deadly enemies of the Huguenots.

But the plot was betrayed. The court immediately left Blois, which could not be defended, and took refuge at Amboise. The plotters were killed or arrested as they arrived. La Renaudie perished. The suppression of the revolt was pitiless.

■ THE CHÂTEAU★★ *time: 3/4 hour*

Historical notes. – The spur on which the château stands has been fortified since the Gallo-Roman era. A bridge was thrown across the river in the earliest times and the military importance of Amboise then increased *(1)*.

For part of the 11C there were two fortresses on the promontory and one in the town, all three keeping up perpetual warfare. The counts of Amboise gained the upper hand and the domain belonged to the family until it was confiscated by Charles VII.

The 15C is the golden age at Amboise; the château was constantly under construction: to be enlarged and embellished. Both Louis XI and Charles VIII were born here.

King Charles VIII's taste for luxury. – Charles VIII, on his return from Italy in 1495, had brought many treasures back to Amboise; furniture, pictures, fabrics and various utensils. He had also recruited a team of men of science, architects, sculptors, decorators, gardeners and tailors. As soon as he returned the King ordered the master gardener Pacello to lay out an ornamental garden on the terrace at Amboise. Among the architects who participated were Fra Giocondo and Il Boccadoro; they had both worked on Blois, Chambord and the town hall (Hôtel de Ville) of Paris.

The date – 1496 – marks the beginning of Italian influence on French art. At Amboise itself, where work had begun four years earlier, its effect was only barely perceptible, but it was accentuated under Louis XII and it was at its height in the reign of François I (1515-47).

Charles VIII died at Amboise in 1498 after a blow on the head sustained when passing through a low doorway on his way to see a game of fives being played in the moat of the castle.

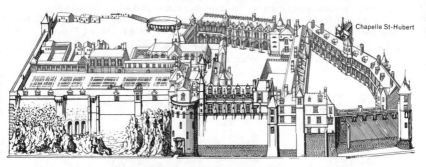

Chapelle St-Hubert

Amboise — Château in the 16C
Only those parts of the château drawn in black are now standing

The whirl of gaiety under François I (beginning of the 16C). – François d'Angoulême, the future François I, was only six when he arrived at Amboise with his mother, Louise de Savoie, and his sister Margaret, who was to be the famous and learned Margaret, Queen of Navarre. At the castle, where they now resided, the young François was given a complete intellectual, sporting and military education. He lived at Amboise for the first three years of his reign and this was the most brilliant period in the life of Amboise. Court life was organized and regulated. Magnificent festivals, comprising balls, tournaments, masquerades and wild beast fights, followed one another. François I finished the wing of the castle that had been begun by Louis XII. An enthusiast for the arts, he brought the great **Leonardo da Vinci** to Amboise, where the artist spent the last years of his life and was buried.

---

(1) In the Middle Ages there were only seven bridges between Gien and Angers. Troops then moved very slowly and the possession or loss of a bridge had a great influence on operations. Towns at bridgeheads drew great profit from the passage of merchandise.

Last phase. – Amboise passed with Blois into the hands of Gaston d'Orléans, the brother of Louis XIII. In 1631, during one of the many rebellions, the castle was taken by the royal troops and the outer fortifications were razed to the ground.

Returned to the Crown, Amboise served as a State prison.

Later Napoleon awarded it to Roger Ducos, a former member of the Directory. As there were no subsidies for its upkeep, the Senate had a large part of the castle demolished. The remains were damaged by bombing in 1940.

The château is now part of the Fondation St-Louis set up by the comte de Paris, Pretender to the French throne, which preserves the château as part of the French national heritage.

Tour. – *Guided tours 1 April to 30 June, 9am to noon and 2 to 6.30pm ; 1 July to 31 August, 9am to 6.30pm ; the rest of the year 9am to noon and 2 to 5pm ; time : 3/4 hour ; 15F.* Son et Lumière *performances are given in summer, see p 33.*

Terrace. – You enter the castle by a ramp which opens on to the terrace overlooking the river. From here there is a magnificent **view★★**, especially in the morning, of the Loire and its verdant valley, the town's pointed roofs and walls. The Tour de l'Horloge (**B F**) is set above one of the town gates ; to the west is silhouetted the Church of St-Denis with its squat bell tower ; and to the southeast the Clos Lucé (**B M¹**) can be seen.

In the time of Charles VIII the terrace was entirely surrounded by buildings. Festivals were held in this enclosed courtyard : tapestries adorned the walls, a sky blue awning gave protection from the weather.

Chapel of St-Hubert. – Curiously set astride the walls this jewel of Flamboyant Gothic architecture is all that remains of the buildings which once bordered the ramparts. With pleasing proportions, finely sculpted decoration and crowned by a delicate spire, it is the work of Flemish masters who were brought to Amboise by Louis XI ; they were also employed by Charles VIII before his admiration for Italian art began. Built in 1491 it was Anne of Brittany's oratory. Before entering admire the Gothic door panels and the finely carved lintel : on the left St Christopher carries the Infant Christ while on the right St Hubert, the patron saint of hunting, looks at a cross which has appeared between the antlers of a stag.

King's Apartments (Logis du Roi). – This is the only part of the château which escaped demolition *(see illustration p 39).* The Gothic Wing, built against the Minimes Tower – both built by Charles VIII – overlooks the Loire while the Renaissance wing, set at a right angle was constructed by Louis XII and raised by François I.

The tour includes a visit to the guardroom with its segmental ogive vaulting, the watchpath, with its beautiful view of the Loire and several rooms furnished in the Gothic or Renaissance style and hung with lovely tapestries. On the first floor the apartments arranged for Louis-Philippe contains Empire style furniture and portraits of the royal family by Winterhalter the official painter.

In the Gothic Wing, the **Hall of States** is a large room with ogive vaulting supported by a line of columns in the centre of the room. It was here that the Protestants headed by La Renaudie *(p 39)* were judged. It was also the home for nearly five years (1848-52) of the Algerian leader **Abd el-Kader.**

Minimes Tower (Tour des Minimes ou des Cavaliers). – This round tower is famous for its ramp which horsemen could ride up, assuring an easy access for the provisioning of supplies. It rises spirally round a core 9 m - 30 ft wide. From the top, one overlooks the northern face of the castle with its Plotters' Balcony and there is a fine extensive **view★★** of the Loire and its valley.

The Hurtault Tower resembles the Tour des Minimes but is broader (24 m - 79 ft), has thicker walls (4.30 m - 14 ft) and overlooks the southern side of the castle.

Gardens. – These pleasant gardens lie where parts of the château once stood. The bust of Leonardo da Vinci is on the site of the collegiate church, where he was buried.

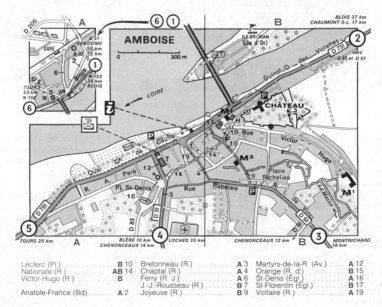

■ ADDITIONAL SIGHTS

Clos-Lucé★ (B M[1]). – *Guided tours 1 June to 31 September 9am to 7pm; the rest of the year 9am to noon and 2 to 7pm; closed in January and 25 December; 19F.*

A red brick manor house, Le Clos Lucé was acquired by Charles VIII in 1490. He had a small chapel built for his queen, Anne of Brittany. François I, Margaret of Navarre and their mother Louise of Savoie also resided here.

In 1516, François I invited **Leonardo da Vinci** to Amboise and had him stay at Le Clos Lucé where the great Renaissance man lived until his death on 2 May 1519.

The tour includes Anne of Brittany's chapel, the great hall, restored as it was in the 16C, and the saloons with 18C wainscoting and where Da Vinci most likely had his workshops installed.

On the first floor is the bedroom where the sixty-seven year old Da Vinci died. In the basement **museum** are exhibited models of machines made by Leonardo, showing the genius of this great man who was painter, sculptor, architect, engineer... The kitchens are also on this floor.

In the courtyard, north of the manor house is a Renaissance style garden – from here there is a view of the château and the chapel of St-Hubert.

Museum (Musée de l'hôtel de ville – B M[2]). – *Open weekdays only. Apply two days ahead of visit at the town hall,* ☎ 47570221; *3 F.*

This early 16C mansion was formerly the town hall. It contains a collection of royal signatures, a 14C Virgin and 19C paintings.

Tour de l'Horloge (B F). – The clock tower was built by Charles VIII.

Postal Museum (Musée de la Poste – B M[3]). – *Open 1 April to 30 September 9.30am to noon and 2 to 6.30; the rest of the year 10am to noon and 2 to 5pm; closed Tuesdays, 1 January, 1 May, Ascension Day, 1 November and 25 December; 7F.*

Installed in the Hôtel Joyeuse, an early 16C mansion, the museum has important collections on postmasters, messengers and their dispatches; uniforms, **badges**, a few coaches and motor vehicles. The two ground floor rooms depict the service in the early years when horses were used while the history of the letter post is traced on the first floor, and the maritime service on the second.

EXCURSION

Chanteloup Pagoda★ (Pagode de Chanteloup). – *3 km - 2 miles, leave Amboise by ④, the D 31, then take the avenue on the right, signposted, to the Pagoda. Open 1 April to 14 November 9am to noon and 2 to 6pm; the rest of the year, 10am to noon and 2 to 5pm; closed Mondays; 6F; walk around the pond 1.50F; picnic 3.50F.*

(After photo: Yvonne Sauvageot)

The Chanteloup Pagoda

This folly, a pagoda, is all that remains of a splendid 18C château built by the **duc de Choiseul**, Minister to Louis XV, in imitation of Versailles. The buildings fell into disuse and were demolished by property dealers in 1823.

When Choiseul was exiled to his estates, at the instigation of Mme du Barry, he made Chanteloup an intellectual and artistic centre. In gratitude for the loyalty of his friends he commissioned the architect, Le Camus, to build the pagoda (1775-78), following the Chinoiserie craze which was prevalent at the time.

The pagoda's **site★** *(best seen from the first floor),* surrounded by a fan-like basin, invaded by tall grasses, and its park, reveals the grandeur and sumptuousness Choiseul had sought while in exile.

ANGERS ★★★

Michelin map ██ fold 20 – *Local maps pp 104 and 117* – Pop 141 143 – *See plan of built up area in the current Michelin Guide France*

The former capital of Anjou stands on the banks of the Maine, formed by the confluence of the Mayenne and the Sarthe, 8 km - 5 miles before joining the Loire. For many centuries the population numbered 30 000. Today Angers is a lively town especially in the pedestrian precinct of the old town and along the Boulevard du Maréchal Foch.

A flourishing trade is based on Anjou wines, liqueurs, fruit and vegetables, cereals, flowers, medicinal plants and other horticultural products. The Sacavins wine brotherhood *(p 122)* which was founded in 1905 organizes an autumn wine festival *(late September).* There is an active electronics and car accessories industry.

The **Anjou Festival** *(p 32),* with its many varied events (drama, music, dance, poetry, art, etc), takes place throughout the Maine et Loire department and draws large crowds.

On the eastern outskirts of Angers, **Trélazé** is known for its slate, the production of which dates back to the 12C. When the Loire was used for navigation it was sent upstream by boat to provide the lovely blue-grey roofing for all the châteaux, manor houses and modest dwellings along the banks of the river.

HISTORICAL NOTES

In the 1C BC Angers was peopled by hunters and fishermen. Their chief was Domnacus, who took to the forests and heaths and never submitted to the Romans when they conquered the city.

The Normans at Angers (9C). – Repeatedly under attack from the Normans the town was taken in 867 and occupied for six years.

To drive them out, Charles the Bald and the King of Brittany revived the stratagem by which Cyrus took Babylon 1 500 years before. They dug a canal above Angers into which they meant to divert the waters of the Maine. Appalled at the prospect of seeing their boats grounded, the Normans hastened to abandon the town.

First House of Anjou (10-13C). – Under the first counts, Anjou lived through a particularly brilliant period. It was with **Foulques Nerra** (987-1040), who succeeded at seventeen, that the real Angevin power was created which at its height rivalled even the Capets, the ruling house of France. Ambitious and unscrupulous, criminally violent, greedy and grasping, he had fits of Christian humility and repentance when he would shower gifts and endowments on churches and monasteries or take the pilgrim's staff and set out for Jerusalem. A great builder, he erected twenty keeps and numerous ecclesiastical buildings in Anjou and Touraine (Chaumont, Langeais, Durtal...).

Second House and the Plantagenets. – It was Foulques V who married his son Geoffrey to Matilda *(1)* William the Conqueror's granddaughter. The young husband habitually wore a sprig of broom *(genêt)* in his cap, hence the name Plantagenet which was given to him and clung to his descendants.

The son of Geoffrey and Matilda, **Henri Plantagenet** married Eleanor of Aquitaine the divorced wife of the King of France, Louis VII, in 1152. To his domains which included Anjou, Maine, Touraine and Normandy, he then added Poitou, Perigord, Limousin, Angoumois, Saintonge, Gascony and suzerainty over Auvergne and the counties of Toulouse. Two years after his marriage he became King of England under the name of **Henry II** and his power was formidable.

The Capet monarchy cut a poor figure beside its former vassal. What saved it in the coming struggle was the separatist spirit in the provinces annexed by the Plantagenets. Henry's reign was troubled by personal quarrels, firstly with Thomas Becket, Archbishop of Canterbury, previously his trusted Chancellor *(see windows in cathedral)* and secondly with his sons, Richard Lionheart and John Lackland, for the division of his empire. Of his reign, Henry spent a nominal fourteen years in Britain and he was to die, lonely and abandoned, at Chinon. In the end, Henry II, Richard Lionheart and John Lackland were all faced in turn by Philippe-Auguste, one of the greatest kings of France. Anjou was added to the royal domains in 1204 but England and France continued to struggle for supremacy up to the end of the Hundred Years War (1337-1453).

Third House of Anjou. – Established as a county in 1246 by St Louis who gave it to his younger brother Charles it was raised to the status of a duchy in 1360 by Jean le Bon in favour of his son Louis. Thus from the 13C to the 15C the direct Capet princes and then the Valois held the coronet of Anjou.

At either end of this line of succession emerged two highly colourful figures, Charles I and King René. The former on an appeal from the Pope conquered Sicily and the Kingdom of Naples and dreamed of adding the Holy Land, Egypt and Constantinople to his conquests. However the Sicilian Vespers (1282) – with the massacre of 6000 Frenchmen – brought him rudely back to reality.

Good King René the last of the dukes – one of the most cultivated minds of his time – was also Count of Provence and titular King of Sicily. René was married twice, first when he was twelve to Isabelle de Lorraine and the second time to a young bride of twenty – one, Jeanne de Laval – the popular Queen Jeanne. At the end of his reign Anjou was annexed by his nephew Louis XI and he himself left Angers for his lands in the south, notably Aix-en-Provence, where he ended his days at the age of seventy-two in 1480.

It was during this period that the University of Angers was founded and it became a centre for students from many nations. The Scottish jurist William Barclay held the Chair of Law and died in Angers.

From Henri IV to our times. – It was at the Castle of Angers that Henri IV, in 1598, ended the League troubles by betrothing his son César *(p 164)* to Françoise de Lorraine, the daughter of the duc de Mercœur, leader of the opposing Catholic faction, the Leaguers. The bride and groom were six and four years old respectively. A week later the Edict of Nantes was signed ending the Wars of Religion.

From the beginning of the Revolution of 1789 Angers was strongly in favour of reform. The cathedral was sacked and turned into a Temple of Reason.

The uprising in Vendée *(p 115)* began in 1793 and the town of Angers was hotly disputed by both Republicans and Royalists.

------

(1) Matilda (1102-1164) was the daughter of Henry I by his first wife. She was married in childhood to the Emperor Henry V, and was herself still childless when her husband died in 1125. As both her brothers were now dead she returned to England and was recognized as her father's successor. The Great Council of England was reluctant to acknowledge a woman sovereign, and on Henry I's death both England and Normandy accepted his nephew Stephen as king. Matilda and her second husband attempted to win Normandy and, in 1141, after a revolt in the west of England and the capture of Stephen at Lincoln, Matilda was proclaimed Queen and crowned in London. After a defeat she was compelled to release Stephen, and in 1148 retired to Normandy, of which her husband had now gained possession.

■ THE CHÂTEAU★★★ (AZ) *time : 2 hours*

Open Palm Sunday to 30 June 9.30am to noon and 2 to 6pm; 1 July to 30 September 9.30am to 6.30pm; 1 October to Palm Sunday 9.30am to noon and 2 to 5.30pm; closed 1 January, 1 and 8 May, 1 and 11 November, 25 December; 20F; combined ticket 23F including admission to the Lurçat Museum, the cathedral treasury, the Fine Arts Museum, the David of Angers Gallery and the Pincé Museum.

The castle of Foulques was rebuilt by St Louis between 1228 and 1238 and is a fine specimen of feudal architecture *(p 23)* in red schist and white stone. The moats are now laid out as gardens. The seventeen round towers, strung out over 1 km - ½ mile, are 40 to 50 m - 131 to 164 ft high. Formerly one or two storeys taller they were crowned with pepperpot roofs and machicolations. The towers were lowered to the level of the curtain walls under Henri III during the Wars of Religion. The original order had been to dismantle the fortress, but the governor in charge of the operation delayed matters and by the King's death most of the building was still intact.

The château is renowned for its unique collection of tapestries which allows the visitor to follow the evolution of this art from the 14C to 17C.

Climbing to the top of the highest tower, the **Tour du Moulin,** on the north corner, there are interesting **views★** over the town, the cathedral towers and St-Aubin, the banks of the Maine and the gardens laid out at the foot of the château, and in the château precincts, the series of towers on the curtain wall, the careful design of the gardens punctuated with topiary arches, the chapel and the Logis Royal.

Continue by going round the **ramparts,** specially on the east side where a charming mediaeval garden is laid out with lavender, marguerites and hollyhocks growing in profusion, near vines like those which King René so loved to plant.

Apocalypse Tapestry★★★. – Sheltered in a specially designed building, this particularly famous piece is the oldest and largest which has come down to us. It was made in Paris between 1375 and 1380 commissioned by Nicolas Bataille for Duke Louis I of Anjou from Hennequin of Bruges' cartoons based on an illuminated manuscript of King Charles V. Bequeathed to the cathedral by King René, it was discarded, as a piece of no value. It was restored between 1849 to 1870.

Originally 130 m - 426 ft long and 5 m - 16 ½ ft high, it consisted of 7 sections of equal size, each with a major figure sitting under a canopy, their eyes turned towards two rows of 7 pictures, the alternating red and blue backgrounds of which form a chequered design.

The 75 pictures which have come down to us form a superb whole, despite the functional coldness of the large room (107 m - 350 ft) which holds them ; the biblical reference of each scene is placed in the window-recesses, opposite the tapestries.

One cannot remain unmoved by the scale of the work, the rigorous composition, as well as its great decorative value and purity of design. The tapestry closely follows the text of St John in the last book of the New Testament ; to rekindle the hope of Christians

(After photo : Arthaud, Grenoble)

Angers — Tapestry of the Instruments of the Passion

shattered by the violent persecutions, the artist shows the victory of Christ in the form of prophetic visions and, after many ordeals, the triumph of his Church.

Chapel and Logis Royal. – These 15C buildings stand inside the enclosure. In the vast and light chapel, note the finely sculptured Gothic leaves of the door, the small separate ducal chapel with a fireplace, and on a keystone, the representation of the Anjou cross *(see p 49 at Baugé).*

Take the adjacent staircase, the work of King René, to reach the upper floor of the logis where the **Passion Tapestry★** is on display. This is a series of four late 15C Flemish works which are wonderfully rich in colour. The hanging showing the Angels carrying the Instruments of the Passion, in spite of its religious theme, belongs to the group of *mille-fleurs* tapestries. Note the 16C Lady at the Organ and the fragment showing Penthesilea, the Queen of the Amazons, one of the Nine Heroines, women with chivalrous virtues.

Logis du Gouverneur. – This pleasant building modified in the 18C, half hidden between the east curtain wall against which it leans and the gardens, upstairs has a lovely collection of 15-18C **tapestries★** : Audenarde verdures (late 16C), Isaac and Jacob (early 16C), the Life of St Saturnin and the Legend of Samson (Brussels, 16C).

■ OLD TOWN★★ *time : about 2 1/2 hours*

Start from the château entrance and take the small Rue St-Aignan.

Hôtel du Croissant (AZ B). – This 15C mansion, with mullion windows and accolade arches, housed the registrar of the Ordre du Croissant, a military and religious chivalrous order founded by King René. The blazon on the façade bears the coat of arms of St-Maurice, patron of the order, a 4C Christian legionary put to death because he refused to kill his coreligionists. Opposite stand picturesque timber framed houses.

Continue to the St-Maurice Ascent, a long flight of stairs which leads to the cathedral square. Fine view of the cathedral.

St Maurice Cathedral★★ (Cathédrale St-Maurice – AZ). – This is a fine 12 and 13C building. The Calvary standing to the left of the façade is by David of Angers.

Façade. – It is surmounted by three towers, the central tower having been added in the 16C. The **doorway** was damaged by the Protestants and the Revolutionaries, and in the 18C by the canons, who removed the central pier and the lintel to make way for processions. Notice the fine statues on the splaying. The tympanum portrays Christ the King surrounded by the symbols of the Four Evangelists.

Above at the third storey level are eight niches containing roughly carved bearded figures in 16C military uniforms, St Maurice and his companions.

Interior. – The single nave is roofed with one of the earliest examples of Gothic vaulting which originated in Anjou in the mid 12C. This transitional style known as Angevin or Plantagenet vaulting *(see illustrations p 21)* has the characteristic feature that the keystones of the diagonal (ogive) arches are at least 3 m - 10 ft above the keys of the transverse and stringer arches giving a more rounded or domical form. In Gothic vaulting all the keys are at roughly the same level. The vaulting of St Maurice covers the widest nave built at that time measuring 16.38 m - 64 ft across, whereas the usual width was from 9 to 12 m - 30 to 40 ft; the capitals in the nave and the brackets supporting the gallery with its wrought iron balustrade are remarkably carved. The gallery is supported by a relieving arch at each bay.

The Angevin vaulting in the transept is of a later period than that in the nave. The ribs are more numerous, lighter and more graceful. The evolution of this style was to continue along these lines.

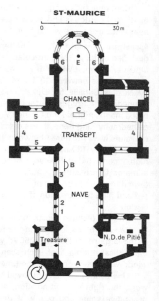

ST-MAURICE

The chancel, finished in the late 13C, has the same Angevin vaulting as the transept. The 13C stained glass has particularly vivid blues and reds.

The church is majestically furnished: high 18C organ (A) supported by colossal telamons, monumental 19C pulpit (B), high altar (C) surmounted with marble columns and a canopy of gilded wood (18C), 18C carved stalls (D) in front of which is a marble statue of St Cecilia by David of Angers (E). The walls are hung with tapestries, mostly by Aubusson.

St-Maurice's **stained glass windows★★** allow one to follow the evolution of the art of the master glaziers *(p 27)* from the 12C to the present day.

1 – St Catherine of Alexandria (12C).
2 – Dormition and Assumption of the Virgin (12C).
3 – The martyrdom of St Vincent of Spain (12C).
4 – Transept rose windows (15C): to the left Christ showing his wounds and to the right Christ in Majesty.
5 – North transept side windows (15C): St Rémi and Mary Magdalene.
6 – Chancel windows (13C) – from left to right: life of St Peter and St Eloi; St Christopher (16C); St Laurent; the tree of Jesse; St Julien; the life of Christ, and lives of the Saints Maurille, Martin, Thomas of Canterbury and John the Baptist.

Note to the right the window representing the life of Thomas Becket. The modern windows of the chapel Notre-Dame-de-Pitié and the south aisle bear witness to a revival of this art which had been in decline since the 16C. The organ dates from 18C.

Treasure★. – *Open 1 April to 30 September 9.30am to noon and 2 to 6.30pm; 1 November to 31 March 10am to noon and 2 to 5.30pm; closed in October and Sundays and Mondays except 1 July to 30 September; 10F.*

Among the most interesting items are a green marble Roman bath which served as a baptismal font for the dukes of Anjou; a red porphyry urn gifted by King René; the reliquary shrine of Bishop Ulger which was damaged during the Revolution; other reliquaries and gold and silver plate.

Walk past the Bishop's Palace to reach the Rue de l'Oisellerie. At nos 5 and 7, there are two lovely half timbered houses dating from the 16C.

Take the first road on the right.

Maison d'Adam★ (ABZ D). – Picturesque 16C half timbered house, with posts decorated with numerous carved figures. The house owes its name to the apple tree which appears to hold up the corner turret and was, until the Revolution, flanked by two statues of Adam and Eve. It so happened that in the 18C this house was inhabited by a consulting judge called Michel Adam.

Continue along the Rue Toussaint, to No 33 bis.

David of Angers Gallery★ (Galerie David d'Angers – AZ E). – *Open 10am to noon and 2 to 6pm; closed Mondays, 1 January, 1 May, 14 July, 1 and 11 November, 25 December; 5F including admission to the Fine Arts Museum. Combined ticket gallery and château: see p 43.*

The former 13C abbey church of Toussaint (restored) houses practically the complete collection of plaster casts donated by the sculptor David of Angers to his native town; its Plantagenet vaulting which caved in in 1815 has been replaced by a vast iron-framed glass roof.

The well-displayed collection comprises monumental statues *(King René, Gutenberg)*, funerary monuments, low-reliefs *(Epaminondas)*, the scale model of the Pantheon's pediment and busts of famous people of the time *(Chateaubriand, Victor Hugo, Goethe, Balzac)*, and medallions in bronze of the artist's contemporaries.

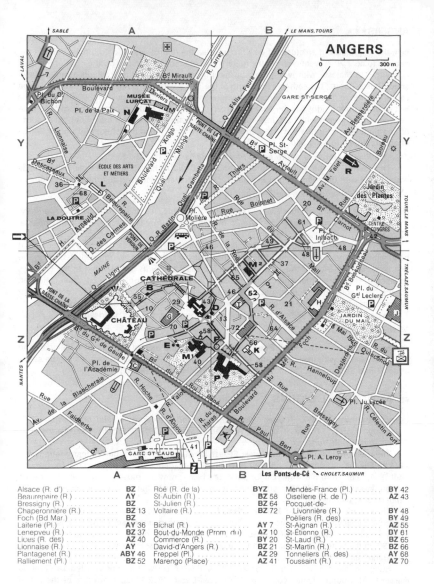

In the chancel with its square east end lit by a rose added in 18C are exhibited terracotta studies, drawings and sketch book as well as the graceful *"Young Greek Girl"* which adorned Markos Botzaris's tomb.

To the south of the church, next to the modern local library are the 18C cloisters with two remaining galleries.

Pass along the south side of the church to reach Logis Barrault.

Logis Barrault★ (Fine Arts Museum – AZM[1]). – *Open 10am to noon and 2 to 6pm; closed Mondays, 1 January, 1 May, 14 July, 1 and 11 November, 25 December; 1F. Combined ticket museum and château: see p 43.*

This beautiful late 15C residence was built by Olivier Barrault, the King's secretary, Treasurer to the Brittany States and Mayor of Angers. In the 17C it was taken over by the seminary, whose pupils included Talleyrand, the future Bishop of Autun *(p 163).*

On the first floor is a beautiful collection of the Middle Ages and the Renaissance: carved chests, statues (16C terracotta Virgin), excellently crafted enamels and ivories.

The second floor is devoted to paintings: lovely primitives, two remarkable small portraits of Charles IX as a young man and Catherine de' Medici after Clouet; 17C paintings (Philippe de Champaigne, Mignard) and above all the 18C French school (Chardin, Fragonard, Watteau, Boucher, Lancret, Greuze) together with sculptures by Lemoyne, Houdon and Falconet; and 19C works including sketches by David, Ingres, Gericault, Delacroix, landscapes by Corot and Jongkind and canvases by the local painters Lepneveu and Bodinier.

Tour St-Aubin (BZF). – 12C belfry of the former Abbey of St-Aubin, a wealthy Benedictine abbey founded in the 6C. It took its name from St-Aubin, Bishop of Angers (538-550), who was buried there.

The former monastery buildings have been taken over by the Préfecture.

Continue to the Préfecture.

Préfecture★ (BZP). – *To visit apply to the keeper's lodge.*

In these 17C buildings of the former St-Aubin abbey a **Romanesque arcade★★** has been uncovered on the left of the courtyard, which has sculptures of remarkably delicate craftsmanship. It was a cloistered arcade; through the door with sculptured arching was the chapter hall, the neighbouring arcatures of which permitted the monks who had no official voice in the debates to hear what went on from the gallery ; decorating the twin bay on the right of the door is a Virgin in Majesty with two angels burning incense while on the archivolt a multitude of angels bustle about ; beneath this the scene of the Three Wise Men is painted : on the left Herod sends his men to massacre the innocents, while on the right the star guides the Wise Men. The last arcature on the right has the best preserved scene of all : in the centre the unequal combat between David armed with his sling and the giant Goliath in his coat of mail, is about to start ; on the right the victorious David is cutting off the head of the vanquished, and on the left he offers his trophy to King Saul.

*Take the Rue St-Martin to return to the Place du Ralliement (**BZ52**).*

The centre of the town, animated and lined with shops, the **Place du Ralliement** is embellished with the monumental façade of the theatre, adorned with columns and statues.

Take the Rue Lenepveu then the first road on the left.

Hôtel Pincé★ (BZM²). – *Open 10am to noon and 2 to 6pm ; closed on Mondays and 1 January, 1 May, 14 July, 1 and 11 November and 25 December ; 1F, free Wednesdays 15 September to 30 June.*

The Hôtel Pincé is a graceful Renaissance mansion built for a Mayor of Angers and bequeathed to the town in 1861. It houses the **Turpin de Crissé Museum**, originally based on the fine personal collection of this local painter (1772-1859) who was chamberlain to the Empress Josephine. There are Greek and Etruscan vases on the ground floor and an Egyptian collection on the 1st floor. But the principal attraction is on the 2nd floor, a beautiful collection of ceramics, masks and Japanese engravings, the bequest of the Count of St Genys, nephew of Turpin de Crissé, as well as the Chinese collection (ceramics, bronzes, fabrics).

Make for the Rue St-Laud.

St-Laud Quarter. – The small Rue St-Laud (**BZ65**) is the axis of a pleasant pedestrian and shopping quarter with lively bars and restaurants, where several ancient façades can be seen : at no 21 Rue St-Laud (15C), and at no 9 Rue des Poëliers (16C) (**BY49**).

■ ADDITIONAL SIGHTS

Lurçat Museum★★ (AY). – *Open 10am to noon and 2 to 6pm ; closed on Mondays and 1 January, 1 May, 14 July, 1 and 11 November and 25 December ; 3F, free Wednesdays 15 September to 30 June.*

The museum is housed in the **former St-Jean Hospital★** (Ancien Hôpital St-Jean), founded in 1174 by Étienne de Marcay, Seneschal of Henry II Plantagenet. The hospital cared for the sick until 1854. Apart from the large hall for patients which is now the museum, one can still see the Roman **cloister** at the back, covered with greenery, and more to the west, the **former granary** (12C) (**N**) decorated with twin bays.

The old and very beautiful **hall for patients** (12C) has 3 naves of equal height with gracefully shaped Angevin vaulting ; on the right on entering is the former **dispensary★** of the hospital with lovely wooden panelling executed in 1612 and filled with pots, trivets, vessels and jars of the 17 and 19C. In the central niche there is a large compounding vessel in pewter (1720) containing a preparation used for snake bites.

Hung around the room is a remarkable series of Lurçat tapestries called **Le Chant du Monde★★** (The Song of the World). In 1938, **Jean Lurçat** (1892-1966), renovator of the art of tapestry, discovered with admiration the Apocalypse tapestry and had been profoundly influenced by it ; 19 years later he started the work shown here, his masterpiece, a set of 10 compositions which cover 80 m - 260 ft in length. The notes placed before each tapestry help to express, by form, rhythm and colour, his philosophical concept of the world and life.

La Doutre★ (AY). – This quarter "beyond" the Maine has kept its old timber framed houses in good repair : in the pretty Place de la Laiterie (**AY36**), in the Rue Beaurepaire which links this square to the bridge (particularly no 67, the former residence (1582) of Simon Poisson, the apothecary, decorated with statues) and all along the Rue des Tonneliers (**AY68**).

The **Church of La Trinité (AYL)** is a 12C building with a 16C bell tower.

St-Serge★ (BYR). – *Open weekdays.*

Until 1802 it was the church of the Benedictine abbey of the same name, founded in the 7C. The 13C **chancel★★** is remarkably wide, elegant and luminous, a perfect example of the Angevin style at its best, with its lierne vaulting descending in feathered clusters on to slender columns. It forms a contrast to the 15C nave, which seems narrower because of its massive pillars ; at the end graceful 15C stained glass in tones of grey is set in the high windows.

Gardens (Jardin des Plantes – **BY)**. – Attractive landscape gardens, undulating and in English style, with beautiful trees and a lake in the lower part. A section reserved for succulent plants forms an exotic garden. *Children's games.*

EXCURSION

Les Ponts-de-Cé. – Pop 11 072. *7 km - 4 miles to the south by the N 160.* A straggling town, the main street crosses a canal and several arms of the Loire, affording some fine views from the bridges. The history of this small town includes many bloody episodes. Firstly under Charles IX 800 camp-followers were thrown into the Loire and again in 1562 when the château was taken from the Huguenots, any surviving defenders were treated to a similar fate. In 1793 numerous Vendéens were shot on the island that surrounds the château. •

On the edge of the road, overlooking the Loire, stand the remains of a château (today the town hall), an ancient 15C fortress crowned with machicolations.

Michelin map **64** northwest of fold 2 – *Local map p 143* – Pop 356

Asnières lies in an attractive setting, on the floor of the Vègre Valley. Coming from Poillé by the D 190 there is an attractive view over the old houses with their high pitched roofs, the church and the residence called the Cour d'Asnières.

Bridge. – This mediaeval hump backed structure provides a charming **view**★ of the river with long grasses swaying smoothly in the current, of the old mill still in working order, in its setting of fine trees and of the elegant manor with its turret and dormer windows on the right bank. Close to the mill stands a château known as the Moulin Vieux dating from the 17 and 18C.

Church. – This church with a Romanesque bell tower has Gothic **wall paintings**★ – 13C in the nave and 15C in the chancel. The most famous, on the inside wall of the main façade, shows Hell. On the left Christ is preparing to release the souls trapped in Limbo, attacking with a lance the three headed dog, Cerberus ; in the centre Leviathan is swallowing up the Damned.

The walls of the nave and chancel evoke the New Testament cycle. The scenes on the north wall of the nave represent the Adoration of the Magi, Jesus' Presentation in the Temple and the Flight into Egypt. Note in the chancel a Baptism of Christ, a Flagellation and a Crucifixion.

Cour d'Asnières. – Standing a little to the south of the church is a large but elongated Gothic building, with attractively paired windows. It was here that the canons of Le Mans, the one time lords of Asnières, exercised their seigneurial rights, hence the name *cour* meaning court.

Château de Verdelles. – *2.5 km - 1 1/2 miles by the D 190 in the direction of Poillé. Restoration work in progress.*

This late 15C château has remained unaltered since its construction by Colas Le Clerc, Lord of Juigné. The building marking the transition between the feudal castle and stately home, incorporates four towers grouped closely together round the central part of the château with its moulded windows. Admire the attractive suspended turret decorated with Gothic arcades.

Michelin map **65** fold 11 – Pop 5 693 – *See town plan in the current Michelin Guide France*

Aubigny, small yet animated, is a picturesque village, crossed by the Nère. As in the past it is an active town with its fairs, electric motor and lingerie factories and sports ground.

The Stuart City. – In 1423 Charles VII gave Aubigny to a Scotsman, John Stuart, his ally against the English, who was succeeded by Berand Stuart. The latter was responsible for a reconciliation between Louis XI and his cousin, the future Louis XII. Next came Robert Stuart, known as the Marshal of Aubigny, who fought in Italy under François I.

Gentlemen and craftsmen from Scotland settled here. They established glassmaking and weaving using the white wool from the Sologne. Before the 19C the importance of cloth manufacture was so great that the town was known as Aubigny-les-Cardeux or the Carders' Aubigny. Rue des Foulons recalls the days when these craftsmen dressed the cloth by fulling it in the waters of the Nère.

■ SIGHTS

Old houses★. – A number of early 16C half timbered houses have survived. The oaks used in their construction were gifted by Robert Stuart from the nearby Forest of Ivoy. There are several along Rue Cambournac and especially the charming and busy Rue du Prieuré which becomes the Rue des Dames. At the corner of Rue de l'Église and Rue du Bourg-Coutant stands the attractive **François I's house**. In the Rue du Bourg-Coutant, across from the Maison St-Jean is the **Maison du Bailli**★ with its carved beams. The tiny Rue du Charbon is also lined with half timbered houses and the only 15C house to have survived the fire of 1512 stands in Rue du Pont-aux-Foulons.

St-Martin. – *Closed Sunday and holiday afternoons.* At the entrance to the chancel two 17C statues represent a charming Virgin and Child and a dramatic Christ Reviled, while in the chancel a 16C stained glass window depicts the life of St Martin. In the third chapel to the right there is an admirable 17C wood *Pietà*.

Town Hall. – It is located in the former Stuart castle. The entrance gatehouse, dating from the time of Robert Stuart, is flanked by attractive brick bartizans ; the keystone of the vault is emblazoned with the Stuart coat of arms. Pass into the interior courtyard with its mullioned windows and turreted staircases.

Duchess of Portsmouth's Park. – These gardens, still called the Grands Jardins, were laid out in the 17C and adorned with clipped hedges, arbours and fine trees.

Ramparts. – Of the old wall built originally by Philippe-Auguste remain the layout of the streets marking off the town centre and the three round towers overlooking the Mall which parallels the Nère with its various footbridges. There are views of the half timbered houses and the small gardens.

EXCURSION

Château de la Verrerie★. – *11 km - 7 miles to the southeast by the D 89. Guided tours 15 February to 15 November 10am to noon and 2 to 7pm ; time : 1/2 hour ; 15F.*

This large isolated château near the Forest of Ivoy benefits from its lovely **setting**★ beside a lake. It is believed that the château inspired Alain-Fournier for one of the episodes of his novel *Le Grand Meaulnes (p 28)*.

AUBIGNY-SUR-NÈRE★

The château was originally built on a square plan around a central courtyard; the oldest part was built by Charles VII. John Stuart received it from the French king at the same time as he received Aubigny *(p 47)*. Returned to the French in 1670, the château was again given to the English, three years later, when Louis XIV gave it to the Duchess of Portsmouth, Charles II's favourite.

To enter the courtyard pass through the gatehouse flanked by elegant bartizans. A graceful **Renaissance gallery★** in pink brick and white stone and built in 1525 by Robert Stuart, faces the entrance. Under the gallery are reproductions of frescoes from the first floor depicting the Stuarts. The 15C chapel, with its pointed spire was decorated with frescoes in 1525; note the carved wood tabernacle of the Renaissance period.

The visit includes the wing, behind the Renaissance gallery, added in the 19C. Its rooms are decorated with furnishings of the Renaissance to the Louis XVI period, silver, paintings and portraits. In the dining room hang two large 18C tapestries from Beauvais; in the saloon a Renaissance cupboard contains four 15C alabaster weepers from Jean de Berry's tomb. In the boudoir is a collection of 19C dolls and their furnishings. The library contains memorabilia belonging to Melchior de Voguë (1829-1916). Archaeologist and diplomat he headed the excavations in Palestine and Syria.

AZAY-LE-RIDEAU ★★★

Michelin map 🔢 fold 4 − *Local map 100* − Pop 2 915 − *Facilities pp 36-37*

A tree clad setting on the banks of the Indre provides the backdrop for the Château d'Azay, one of the gems of the Renaissance. Akin to Chenonceau, but less grandiose, its lines and dimensions suit the site so perfectly that it gives an unforgettable impression of elegance and harmony.

HISTORICAL NOTES

Azay-le-Brûlé (15C). − Strategically sited at a bridging point on the Indre on the main road from Tours to Chinon, Azay was fortified early.

The most tragic incident in its history was the massacre of 1418. When Charles VII was Dauphin he was insulted by the Burgundian guard as he passed through Azay. Instant reprisals followed. The town was seized and burnt and the Captain and his 350 soldiers were executed. Azay was called Azay-le-Brûlé (Azay the Burnt) until the 16C.

A financier's creation (16C). − When it rose from its ruins Azay became the property of **Gilles Berthelot**, one of the great financiers of the time. He had the present delightful mansion built between 1518 and 1529. His wife, Philippe Lesbahy, directed the work, as Catherine Briçonnet had directed that of Chenonceau.

But under the monarchy, fortune's wheel turned quickly for financiers. The rich Semblançay ended his career on the gibbet at Montfaucon. Berthelot saw the fatal noose draw near, took fright, fled and later died in exile. François I confiscated Azay and gave it to the Captain of his Guard, who was succeeded by several other proprietors. In 1905 the State bought the château.

■ THE CHÂTEAU★★★ *time: 3/4 hour*

Enter from Rue de Pineau.

Guided tours of château and park Palm Sunday to 30 September 9.15am to noon and 2 to 6.30pm (5pm 1 October to 15 November); 16 November to Palm Sunday 9.30am to noon and 2 to 4.45pm; closed 1 January, 1 May, 1 and 11 November and 25 December; 15F (9F 1 October to 31 March).

Son et Lumière★★ *performance see p 33.*

Though Gothic in outline, Azay is modern in its bright appearance and its living accommodation. The mediaeval defences are purely symbolic and testify only to the high rank of the owners. The massive towers of other days have given way to harmless turrets with graceful forms. Dormer windows spring from the corbelled watchpath, the machicolations lend themselves to ornament and the moats are mere placid reflecting pools. Partly built over the Indre, the château consists

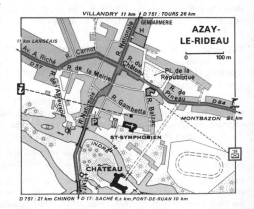

of two main wings at right angles. The decoration shows the influence of the buildings erected by François I at Blois: pilasters flank the windows, mouldings separate the storeys but here there is a strict symmetry throughout the design of the building.

The most remarkable part of the mansion is the great gable with double openings containing the grand staircase. At Blois the staircase is still spiral and projects from the façade; at Azay as at Chenonceau which was built a few years earlier, it is internal with a straight ramp.

The interior is decorated with fine furniture and Renaissance and 17C tapestries.

■ ADDITIONAL SIGHT

St-Symphorien. – This curious 11C church, altered in the 12 and 16C, has a double gabled **façade★**. Embedded to the right are remains of the original 5 and 6C building : two rows of statuettes and diapered brickwork.

EXCURSION

The Indre Valley from Azay to Pont-de-Ruan. – *Round tour of 26 km – 16 miles to the east via the D 17 and D 84 – about 2 hours.* Leave Azay from the south by the bridge over the Indre (lovely view of the château). *Bear left immediately on to the D 17 and right onto the D 57.*

Villaines-les-Rochers. – Pop 939. Wickerwork has always been the mainstay of the village of Villaines-les-Rochers. The green rushes and black and yellow osiers are cut in winter and steeped in water until May when they are taken out, stripped and woven.

The products are on sale at the *Coopérative (signposted ; open 9am – 10am Sundays and holidays – to noon and 2 to 7pm ; closed Sunday and holiday mornings from 1 October to Palm Sunday).*

Return to the D 17 via the D 217.

Saché – Pop. 738. The village has had two famous residents : Honoré de Balzac and Alexander Calder (1898-1976), originator of mobiles and stabiles. Several outdoor works can be seen at Le Carroi to the north of the village.

(After photo: Sylvain Knecht)

Château de Saché

The **Château de Saché** houses a Balzac museum. *Open 9am to noon and 2 to 6pm (5pm 1 October to 14 March) ; closed Wednesdays out of season and December and January ; 10F.* This château of the 16 and 18C belonged to a friend of **Balzac ;** it was here that he wrote some of his works : *Le Père Goriot, The Quest of the Absolute, The Lily of the Valley.* His bedroom remains as it was in his lifetime and other rooms have been arranged as a museum : portraits, manuscripts, first editions and other souvenirs of 1850.

Pont-de-Ruan. – Pop 510. On crossing the Indre, a lovely picture is presented of two windmills each on an island in a lovely verdant setting.

After the bridge take the D 8 for 500 m - 1/3 mile then bear left on the D 84 which follows the north bank to Azay.

BAUGÉ

Michelin map 🆖 folds 2 and 12 – Pop 3 906

Baugé, a peaceful town with noble dwellings, is the capital and market town of the surrounding region, a countryside of heaths, forests and vast clearings. There is a good view of the town with its ruined walls from the Rue Foulques Nerra to the west.

The True Cross of Anjou. – Brought from the Holy Land by Jean d'Alluye, the one time overlord of Baugé, this relic of the True Cross was given to the Abbey of La Boissière *(p 108).* It was transferred for safe keeping in 1790 to a hospice in Baugé where it now remains *(see opposite).* Initially known as the Cross of Anjou this double armed cross was adopted by the House of Lorraine, and finally became the emblem of the Free French Forces in 1940.

■ SIGHTS

Château. – *Museum open 15 June to 15 September 11am to noon and 3 to 6pm ; 3.50F.* This much restored 15C building now serves as town hall, tourist information centre and **museum** (arms, faience and numismatic collections).

In the 15C Baugé was one of the favourite residences of Yolande d'Aragon and of her son the Good King René. It was the King himself who supervised in 1455 the building of the turrets, dormer windows, the oratory and the intriguing bartizan on the rear façade, where the master masons are portrayed. An ogee arched doorway gives access to the **spiral staircase** which terminates with a magnificent palm tree vault, decorated with the Anjou-Sicily coat of arms.

Clemenceau (R. G.)		Girouardière (R. de la)	9
		Le-Gouz-de-la-B. (Av.)	10
Berthelot (R. M.)	2	Lofficial (R.)	12
Cygne (R. du)	3	Melun (R. Anne-de)	14
Église (R. de l')	5	Renan (R. Ernest)	15
Gaulle (Av. Gén. de)	7	Victor-Hugo (R.)	16

Les Filles du Cœur de Marie Chapel (B). – *Guided tours Mondays to Saturdays 10am to noon and 2.30 to 4.30pm and 6 to 7pm; Sundays and holidays 3 to 4pm and 6 to 7pm; closed first Sunday in July and 24, 25, 26 July; time: 1/4 hour; ring the doorbell at 8 Rue de la Girouardière.*

Formerly part of an 18C hospice the chapel is now the sanctuary for the famous **Cross of Anjou**★★ *(see p 49).* Supposedly part of the True Cross, brought from the Holy Land in 1241, it was ornamented in the 14C with gold crucifixes on both sides and precious stones.

Hôpital St-Joseph. – *Guided tours 10am (10.30am Sundays and holidays) to noon and 3 to 5.30pm (4.30pm 1 October to 31 May); time: 1/2 hour.*

The hospice which was founded in 1643, is now run by the nuns of the St-Joseph Order of Hospitallers.

The **dispensary**★ with its fine parquet flooring and wall panelling has a colourful collection of faience pots (16-17C) from Lyon and Narbonne with Italian or Hispano-Moresque decoration.

The chapel, separated from the ward by a corridor, has a large altarpiece with a gilded wooden tabernacle, dating from the 17C.

Hôtels. – Noble mansions with tall doorways line the peaceful streets of old Baugé: Rues de l'Église, de la Girouardière and du Cygne and especially the Place de la Croix-Orée.

EXCURSIONS

The Baugeois. – *Round tour of 38 km - 24 miles – about 1 hour – Local map below.*

Leave Baugé towards the east by the D 141 which follows the Couasnon Valley before entering forested countryside.

Dolmen de la Pierre Couverte. – About 3 km - 2 miles from Baugé branch off to the left taking the sign-posted path leading to the dolmen standing in a forest clearing *(1/2 hour on foot Rtn).*

By car again, take the D 141 in the direction of Pontigné, which affords fine views to the right of the Couasnon Valley and the forested massif of Chandelais.

Pontigné. – Pop 299. The church, dedicated to St Denis, whose effigy is above the Romanesque portal, is crowned by an unusual twisting spiral bell tower. Inside Angevin vaulting covers the nave while the capitals of the transept sport monstrous heads and water leaf motifs. In the apsidals 13-14C **mural paintings**★ depict Christ the King and the Resurrection of Lazarus on one side and the Virgin Enthroned, the Nativity and the Adoration of the Shepherds on the other.

Follow the road behind the church, and turn right on to the D 766. The road affords a fine view of the valley. *Then bear left and turn right in the direction of Bocé.*

Chandelais Forest★ (Forêt de Chandelais). – This is a magnificent State owned property, covering 800 hectares - 2000 acres. The splendid full grown oaks and beech trees are replanted every 210 years.

Follow the forest road to the central crossroads before turning right in the direction of Bocé. Then take the D 938 to the left towards Cuon.

Cuon. – Pop 413. Behind the church with the curious conical spire is a charming 15C manor house.

From Cuon take the road to Chartrené. The wooded park on the left marks the site of the Château de la Grafinière.

Beyond Chartrené turn left to the D 60. After 4.5 km - 3 miles follow the D 211 to your right, crossing heaths and woodlands, to reach Fontaine-Guérin.

Fontaine-Guérin. – Pop 579. The belfry of the much altered Romanesque church is crowned by a twisting spire.

Inside the 15C roof is decorated with 126 colourful painted panels (15-16C) with secular themes.

Follow the Couasnon Valley, taking the D 144 in the direction of Le Vieil-Baugé and passing within sight of the ruins of the Château de la Tour du Pin.

Le Vieil-Baugé. – Pop 1104. Le Vieil-Baugé is the site of a battle in 1421 when the English were defeated by an Angevin army supported by Scottish mercenaries led by John, the Earl of Buchan, who was later rewarded with the baton of High Constable of France.

Dominating the valley from its hilltop position the town is renowned for the curiously twisting and leaning spire of its church. The **choir**★ is 13C with Angevin vaulting while the façade adorned with pilasters and the south transept arm with its coffered ceiling are both Renaissance and are by Jean de Lespine. *Closed Sundays and holidays.*

La Boissière. – *22 km - 14 miles to the east via the D 766 and the D 767. Description p 108.* The chapel was originally built to house the True Cross of Anjou *(see p 49).*

Jarzé ; Montplacé. – *Round tour of 20 km - 12 miles – about 1/2 hour. Leave Baugé to the northwest by the D 788.*

Jarzé. – Pop 1 368. In the one time domain of Jean Bourré *(p 129)*, Jarzé's former collegiate church built on 11C remains, is in the Flamboyant style. The stalls (16C) in the chancel have amusingly historiated cheekpieces, while the seigneurial chapel to the right is covered with lierne and tierceron vaulting. The 15C statuette in a recess on the last pillar before the chancel probably represents the son of Jean Bourré holding a pear, recalling that his father introduced the good Christian pear into Anjou *(p 12)*. At the end of the apse the remains of an early 16C **mural painting** *(partly rubbed out)* represents the Entombment.

4 km - 2 1/2 miles from Jarzé on the road to La Flèche, the D 82, turn right.

Notre-Dame de Montplacé Chapel. – *Apply for the key at the old people's home near the church in Jarzé.* Standing in a beautiful setting this chapel has a remarkable west doorway (17C) dedicated to the Virgin. The plain, illuminated interior is adorned with three 17C altars. The altar on the left contains in its niche the venerated *Pietà.*

BEAUGENCY ★

Michelin map **64** fold 8 – *Local map p 101* – Pop 7 339 – *Facilities pp 36-37*

Once a walled and fortified town, Beaugency remains a picture of the Middle Ages in its green and pleasant riverside setting.

It is best to arrive from the south bank crossing the 14C **bridge** which affords a fine view of the town dominated by the Tour St-Firmin and the keep.

The Two Councils of Beaugency (12C). – It is curious that both should have had to deal with difficulties in the royal families. The First Council (1104) excommunicated **Philippe I** who had repudiated the Queen and abducted and married Bertrade, the wife of the Count of Anjou. After his reconciliation with the Church, Philippe was buried at the Abbey of St-Benoît-sur-Loire *(p 136).*

The Second Council (1 152) annulled the marriage of **Louis VII** with **Eleanor of Aquitaine**. The King accused the Queen of misconduct ; the Queen alleged her own consanguinity with her husband to a degree forbidden by the Church. This was one of the great events of the Middle Ages ; later, the Queen was to marry again with Henry Plantagenet, the future King Henry II of England. Eleanor's dowry, almost all of southwestern France, then passed under English rule.

A disputed town. – Beaugency commanded the only bridge that crossed the Loire between Blois and Orléans before modern times. For this reason the town was often attacked *(see note 1 p 39).* During the Hundred Years War (1337-1453) it fell into English hands four times : in 1356, 1412, 1421 and 1428. It was delivered by Joan of Arc in 1429.

The town was then caught up in the turmoil of the Wars of Religion (1562-98). Leaguers and Protestants held it by turns. At the time of the fire started by the Huguenots in 1567, the abbey was burnt down, the roof of Notre-Dame collapsed and so did that of the keep.

■ SIGHTS

Notre-Dame★. – This was built in the 12C as the church to the former abbey and it was here that the Councils deliberated. To replace the Romanesque vaulting destroyed by fire, false Gothic vaulting of wood was painted to look like stone. However, placed too low, it has spoilt the building's proportions.

Near the church are the 18C buildings of the Abbey of Notre-Dame. At the bottom of the small Rue de l'Abbaye, the **Tour du Diable** (D) was part of the fortifications protecting the bridgehead. In the Middle Ages the Loire washed around the foot of the tower.

The **Place Dunois**, opposite the church and the keep, forms with the **Place St-Firmin** a picturesque area. At night this quarter is lit by old street lamps that give it a particular charm.

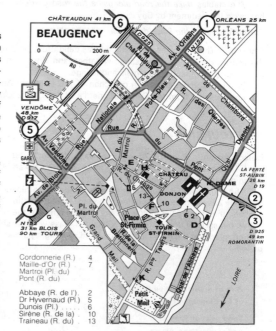

Cordonnerie (R.) 4
Maille-d'Or (R.) 7
Martroi (Pl. du)
Pont (R. du)

Abbaye (R. de l') 2
Dr Hyvernaud (Pl.) 5
Dunois (Pl.) 6
Sirène (R. de la) 10
Traineau (R. du) 13

Keep★ (Donjon). – This is a fine example of 11C military architecture. At the time, keeps were rectangular and supported by buttresses, becoming circular later. This one is impressively massive. The five storeys of the interior are in ruins.

BEAUGENCY★

Château Dunois. — This former mediaeval fortress was converted into a 15C residence by Dunois, Joan of Arc's companion.

Museum of the Orléans district. — *Guided tours 9am to noon and 2 to 6pm (4pm 1 October to Palm Sunday); closed Tuesdays out of season; time: 3/4 hour; 7F.* The rooms of the château contain collections of costumes, headdresses, waistcoats and furniture of the Orléans district. Other sections deal with souvenirs of local celebrities. The visit ends in the loft to admire the 15C timberwork of the roof.

Tour St-Firmin. — This tower is all that remains of a 16C church destroyed during the Revolution. A street used to pass under the tower.

To the right is the former hospice, Villa Notre-Dame. Open the door a little way to get a glimpse of the charming courtyard.

Maison des Templiers (F). — Interesting Romanesque windows.

Hôtel de Ville (H). — *Apply to the caretaker 9am to noon and 2 to 5pm; closed Wednesdays and holidays; 2F.*

This pretty restored Renaissance building looks out over the Place de la Poste. In the council chamber are eight embroidered **hangings★** dating from the 17C and originally from the Abbey of Notre-Dame.

Tour de l'Horloge (E). — The tower was a gateway in the 12C city wall.

Petit Mail. — Dominating the Loire the Little Mall planted with large trees affords a beautiful view over the valley.

Porte Tavers (K). — Formerly part of the old city wall.

BELLEGARDE

Michelin map fold 11 — Pop 1 582

Lying in the midst of a fertile countryside of grain fields, market gardens and rose nurseries, Bellegarde groups its houses round a vast square.

Formerly known as Choisy-aux-Loges it was renamed in 1645 when it was bought by the Duke of Bellegarde.

■ SIGHTS

Château★. — The 14C château, with its square **keep** quartered with bartizans and surrounded by a moat, forms a charming picture. Around the courtyard the brick **pavilions** with stone dressings were intended to lodge staff and guests. From left to right are: the Steward's pavilion surmounted by a pinnacle turret, the Captain's tower a massive round brick tower, the kitchens, the pavilion to the right of the gate (now the town hall) and on the other side of the gate, a pavilion with a mansard roof.

Around the moat a rose **garden** has been planted.

The stables *(take the road alongside the rose garden)* are decorated with three horses' heads on the pediment by Coysevox.

Turn left to reach the Place du Marché and the church.

Church. — This Romanesque building has a delightfully harmonious façade. The decoration of the central doorway is interesting: wreathed and ringed engaged piers support sculptured capitals depicting fantastic animals and foliage.

In the wide nave there is a collection of 17C **paintings**: Annibale Carracci's *St Sebastian;* Lebrun's *Descent from the Cross;* Mignard's *St John the Baptist* with the infant Louis XIV as St John.

EXCURSION

Boiscommun. — *Pop 810. 7.5 km - 5 miles to the northwest by the D 44.*

Of the castle only two towers and other ruins remain and these can be seen from the path which now follows the line of the former moat.

The church with its Romanesque doorway has a Gothic nave with a majestic elevation. It is relatively easy to discern the different periods of construction by looking at the changes in the capitals, the form of the high windows and openings of the triforium. At the end of the aisle, above the sacristy door, is a late 12C stained glass window showing the Virgin and Child. On leaving, glance at the organ loft, ornamented with eight painted figures (16C) in costumes of the period.

Join us in our never ending task of keeping up to date.

Send us your comments and suggestions, please.

Michelin Tyre PLC,
Tourism Department
Lyon Road, HARROW, Middlesex HA1 2 DQ.

Michelin map **64** fold 4

The Bercé Forest is all that remains of the once immense natural Forest of Le Mans which formerly extended from the Sarthe to the Loir. The 5 414 hectares - 21 sq miles cover a plateau incised by small valleys. This state owned forest includes a mixture of oak, chestnut and beech trees. It is exploited for quality oak which yields a pale yellow wood with a fine grain much in demand for veneering and for export.

TOUR

16 km - 10 miles from St Hubert to La Futaie des Clos – about 3/4 hour

Fontaine de la Coudre. – This is the source of the Dinan, a tributary of the Loir. It is to be found amidst the tall oaks of the grove known as the Futaie des Forges.

Sources de l'Hermitière★. – Resurgent springs in a wooded valley.

Futaie des Clos★. – *Guided tours (4 km - 3 miles) by the Forestry Service in July and August at 9.30am and 3pm; closed Tues-days; meet at car park at*

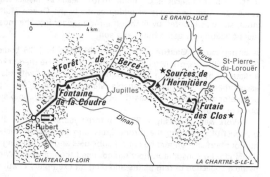

chêne Boppe. This, the finest grove in the forest, contains great soaring oaks, many of which are between 300 and 340 years old. Go on foot to see these patriarchs of the forest; both oaks: chêne Boppe, now only a stump protected by a roof, was felled by lightning in 1934 at the venerable age of 262; nearby is chêne Rouleau, 43 m - 141 ft tall and a mere 340 years old.

Michelin map **64** fold 7 – *Local map p 101* – Pop 49 422

Border town between the Beauce to the north of the Loire and the Sologne to the south, county town of the Loir-et-Cher department, Blois is the commercial centre of an agricultural region producing mainly wheat (in the Beauce) and down in the river valley, wine, strawberries, bulbs and vegetables. The foremost vegetable crop is asparagus which was first cultivated in the immediate vicinity of Blois, at Vineuil and St-Claude; it has since spread towards Contres, between the Loire and Cher rivers, and to the Sologne, wherever the soil is light and fertile.

Blois is built on the right bank of the Loire, on the hillside which overlooks the river; it is a sharply contoured town which has kept a number of steep and tortuous mediaeval alleys, linked here and there by flights of steps. The characteristic tricoloured harmony of Blois comes from the roof terracing: white façades, blue slate roofs and red brick chimneys.

HISTORICAL NOTES

From the Counts of Blois to the Dukes of Orléans. – In the Middle Ages, the Counts of Blois were powerful lords, despite repeated assaults by their neighbours and rivals, the Counts of Anjou, and in particular by the formidable Foulques Nerra *(p 42)*, who annexed large sections of the Blois estates bit by bit. In 1391, the last of the Counts, with no descendants and weighed down with debts, sold the county to Charles VI's brother, Louis, Duke of Orléans. Thereafter the Court of Orléans was held in Blois. Louis was involved in the power struggle with the dukes of Burgundy and in 1407 he was assassinated in Paris by order of the Duke of Burgundy, John the Fearless. Louis's widow, Valentina Visconti, retired to Blois and carved on its walls the disillusioned motto: *Plus ne m'est rien, rien ne m'est plus* (Nothing means anything to me any more). She died, inconsolable, the following year.

A poet: Charles d'Orléans (1391-1465). – Charles, the eldest son of Louis d'Orléans, inherited the castle. He was the poet of the family. At fifteen he married the daughter of Charles VI, but she died in childbirth. At twenty he married again. He went to fight the English and proved a poor general at the Battle of Agincourt where he was taken prisoner, but his poetic gift helped him to survive twenty-five years of captivity in England. He returned to France in 1440, and being once more a widower he married, at the age of fifty, Marie de Clèves, who was then fourteen. The château of Blois was his favourite residence. He demolished part of the grim old fortress and built a more comfortable mansion. Charles formed a little court of artists and men of letters. Great joy came to him in old age: at seventy-one he had at long last a son and heir, the future Louis XII.

The Versailles of the Renaissance (16C). – Having become a royal residence, Blois was to play a part comparable with that of Versailles in later centuries. **Louis XII** and his wife, **Anne of Brittany,** liked the castle. The King added a wing and had great terraces and gardens, which have since disappeared, designed by Pacello, the Italian master gardener of Amboise. These covered the Place Victor-Hugo and what is now the station quarter.

In 1515 **François I** succeeded Louis XII, and it is to him that we owe the finest part of the château. His wife, **Claude de France,** was the late King's daughter. She was brought up at Blois and was very fond of it. She died in 1524, when barely twenty-five, after having given the King seven children in eight years.

Assassination of the duc de Guise (1588). – The historical interest of the château reached its peak under **Henri III.** The States-General twice met at Blois. The first time was in 1576, when there was a demand for the suppression of the Protestant Church. In 1588 **Henri de Guise,** the Lieutenant-General of the kingdom and all powerful head of the League in Paris, supported by the King of Spain, forced Henri III to call a second meeting of the States-General, which was then the equivalent of Parliament. Five hundred deputies, nearly all supporters of Guise, attended. Guise expected them to depose the King. The latter, feeling himself to be on the brink of the abyss, could think of no other means than murder to get rid of his rival. The killing took place in the château itself, on the second floor. Eight months later Henri III himself succumbed to the dagger of Jacques Clément. In 1617 **Marie de' Medici** was banished to Blois by her son, Louis XIII. After two years of gilded captivity the Queen Mother escaped. Although she was stout, she was lowered by night on a rope ladder into the moat. After this exploit there was a reconciliation between mother and son.

A conspirator: Gaston d'Orléans (1608-60). – In 1626 Louis XIII, to get rid of his brother, Gaston d'Orléans, granted him the county of Blois. He tried to keep that perpetual conspirator at a distance by persuading him to rebuild the château with his financial aid. Gaston d'Orléans asked the great architect François Mansart (1598-1666 – generally considered to be the originator of the great "mansard" or curb roof) to draw up plans for a huge building to take the place of its predecessor.

Work went on busily at Blois for three years. Then the future Louis XIV was born and the prospect of ascending the throne grew dim for Gaston. Richelieu thought it unnecessary to humour him any longer: he cut off subsidies and the building slowed down. For the last years of his life the conspirator, now tamed, used the François I Wing. He embellished the gardens, made a collection of rare plants and died an exemplary death surrounded by his little court.

■ THE CHÂTEAU★★★

Guided tours 1 April to 31 August 9am to 6.30pm; 15 to 31 March and in September 9am to noon and 2 to 6.30pm; the rest of the year 9am to noon and 2 to 5pm; closed morning on 1 January and 25 December; 13.50F including admission to the St-Saturnin Cloisters.

Son et Lumière★ *performance see p 33.*
Park your car in the Place du Château.

Place du Château. – This vast esplanade is the former "farmyard" of the château. Slightly below, the terraced gardens offer a wide view over the roofs behind which can be seen the bridge over the Loire, and at the foot of the retaining wall, the St-Nicolas church. Immediately on the left the cathedral with its Renaissance tower stands out.

The **façade** of the château on the esplanade has two main parts: on the right the pointed gable of the Chamber of the States-General (1), relic of the former feudal castle (13C), and then the pretty building of brick and stone erected by Louis XII (5). The latter building shows no symmetry and open-

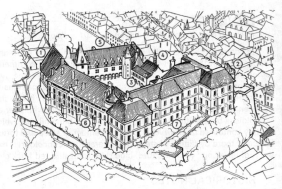

(After photo: Cie Aérienne Française)

Château de Blois

Feudal period:
1 Salle des États Généraux (13C); 2 Tour de Foix (13C)

Gothic-Renaissance transitional period:
3 Charles d'Orléans Gallery (late 15-early 16C);
4 St-Calais Chapel (1498-1503); 5 Louis XII Wing (1498-1503)

Renaissance period:
6 François I Wing: Façade des Loges (1515-1524)

Classical period:
7 Gaston d'Orléans Wing (1635-1638)

ings were still placed according to the amiable whims of the Middle Ages.

Two windows on the first floor have balconies. The one on the left opened from Louis XII's bedroom. His Minister, Cardinal d'Amboise, lived in the nearby house, which was destroyed in June 1940 and has since been rebuilt with only moderate success. When the King and the Cardinal took the air on their balconies they could chat together. The great Flamboyant gateway is surmounted by an alcove containing a modern copy of an equestrian statue of Louis XII. The windows' consoles are adorned with spirited carvings. The coarse humour of the period is sometimes displayed with great candour (first and fourth windows to the left of the gateway).

The inner courtyard. – Cross the courtyard to reach the delightful terrace (good view of St-Nicolas Church and the Loire) on which stands the **Tour du Foix** (2) which formed part of the mediaeval wall.

Return to the courtyard which is lined with buildings from every period which, together, make up the château, one of the great sights of the Loire valley.

St-Calais Chapel (4). – Of the King's private chapel which was rebuilt by Louis XII, only the chancel remains. Mansart demolished the nave when he built the Gaston d'Orléans Wing. The modern stained glass windows are by Max Ingrand.

Charles d'Orléans Gallery (3). – Although called Charles d'Orléans it is probable that this gallery dates from the Louis XII period. Till the alterations in the 19C this gallery was twice its present length and connected the two wings at either end of the courtyard. Note the unusual basket-handle arches.

Louis XII Wing (5). – The corridor or gallery serving the various rooms in the wing marks a step forward in the search for more comfort and convenience. Originally rooms opened on to one another. At each end of the wing a spiral staircase gave access to the different floors. The decoration is richer and Italianate panels of arabesques adorn the pillars.

François I Wing (6). – The building extends between the 17C Gaston d'Orléans Wing and the 13C feudal hall, Salle des États Généraux (1). Only twelve years passed between the completion of the Louis XII Wing and the commencement of the François I Wing, but the progress made was important. It meant the triumph of the Italian decorative style.

Château de Blois — François I staircase

French originality, however, persisted in the general plan. The windows were made to correspond with the internal arrangement of the rooms, without regard for symmetry ; they were sometimes close together, sometimes far apart ; their mullions were sometimes double, sometimes single ; and pilasters sometimes flanked the window openings, sometimes occupied the middle of the bay.

A magnificent **staircase** was added to the façade and it was to be the first of a series. Since Mansart demolished part of the wing to make room for the Gaston d'Orléans building, this staircase is no longer in the centre of the façade. It climbs spirally in an octagonal well, three faces of which are embedded in the wall. This masterpiece of architecture and sculpture was evidently designed for great receptions. The well is open between the buttresses and forms a series of balconies from which members of the court could watch the arrival of important people. The guards who saluted the guests stood on these balconies.

The decoration is varied and elaborate. The royal insignia are used together with all the customary themes of the Renaissance *(p 23)*.

Gaston d'Orléans Wing (7). – This range by François Mansart in the Classical style, is in sharp contrast to the rest of the building. Seen from the inner courtyard the comparison with the other façades is unfavourable. To judge Mansart's work fairly it must be seen from outside the château and imagined in the context of the original design. The proposed building would have occupied not only the site of the château but also the square and it would have been linked with the forest by a series of terraces occupying the present station quarter.

Royal Apartments in the François I Wing. – You climb the François I staircase to reach the first floor where the guide shows various rooms in detail, some containing splendid fireplaces, tapestries, busts and portraits, furniture. The interior decoration was restored by Duban (19C) and the effect is now almost too gorgeous. In bygone times smoke from the great fireplaces, candles and torches quickly toned down the décor.

First floor. – The most interesting room is that of Catherine de' Medici. It still has its 237 carved wood panels concealing secret cupboards which may have been used to hide poisons, jewels or State papers or may have been made in accordance with the practice of having wall cupboards in Italian style rooms. They were opened by pressing a pedal concealed in the skirting board.

Second floor. – This is the scene of the murder of the duc de Guise. The rooms have been altered and the King's study is now included in the Gaston d'Orléans Wing. It is therefore, rather difficult to follow the phases of the assassination on the spot.

After the murder Henri III went down to his mother, Catherine de' Medici, and told her joyfully : "I no longer have a colleague, the King of Paris is dead !" "God grant", replied Catherine, "that you have not become the King of Nothing at All !" Untroubled by his conscience, the King went to hear Mass in the St-Calais Chapel.

The next day the Duke's brother, Cardinal de Lorraine, who had been thrown into gaol directly after the murder, was assassinated. His body was left with that of Guise in the Cabinet neuf, before being burnt and the ashes thrown into the Loire.

Salle des États Généraux (1). – This is the oldest part of the château and served as the council hall or great hall – the equivalent of Westminster Hall – to the counts of Blois. The States-General of 1576 and 1588 were held here.

On the ground floor of the François I Wing, in the former outbuildings, there is an **audio-visual presentation** on the château *(in the tourist season only ; time : 1/4 hour ; entrance at the foot of the staircase)*, as well as a small **archaeological museum** where Gallo-Roman remains, discovered in Blois during recent excavations, are displayed.

Fine Arts Museum★. – *1st floor of the Louis XII wing.* This museum is of interest mainly for its 16 and 17C portraits and paintings, particularly the portraits of Marie de' Medici symbolizing France by Rubens, of Gaston d'Orléans, Anne of Austria and Louis XIV by Mignard.

Façade des Loges and Gaston d'Orléans Façade. – *Description in Old Blois p 56*

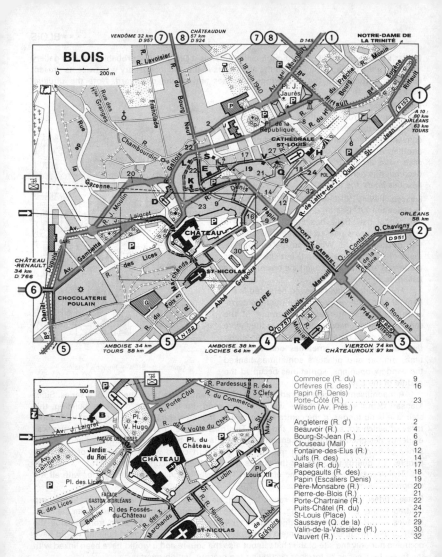

■ OLD BLOIS★ *time : 2 hours on foot*

Pavillon Anne de Bretagne★ (B). – This graceful little building of stone and brick is now the Tourist Centre. Note the cable mouldings which emphasize the corners, and the openwork sculptured stone balustrade with the initials of Louis XII and Anne of Brittany, his wife. Originally the Pavilion was in the middle of the château gardens (the Avenue Jean-Laigret was later opened up) and the royal couple often went to say novenas in the small oratory, in order to have a son.

On the right along the Avenue Jean-Laigret, the Pavilion extends into a long half timbered wing, also built under Louis XII and which was later used as an **orangery**.

Walk along the Place Victor-Hugo, which is lined on the north by the façade of the **Church of St-Vincent (D)** (17C) built in the style known as Jesuit, and on the south by the beautiful Façade des Loges of the château.

Jardin du Roi. – This small terraced garden, overlooking the Place Victor-Hugo, is all that remains of the vast château gardens, formerly directly accessible from the François I wing by a footbridge over the moat, and extending as far as the railway station. From near the balustrade there is an excellent **view★** to the left over the high slate roof topping the Anne of Brittany Pavilion which was built in these gardens, as was the neighbouring orangery, and to the right over the Church of St-Vincent and the Place Victor-Hugo ; in the background is the massive square silhouette of the Beauvoir tower, and to its right is the cathedral steeple ; on the right runs the beautiful Façade des Loges or the François I Wing of the château, which the return angle of the Gaston d'Orléans wing is backed on to.

Façade des Loges. – The interior part of François I's first construction backed on to the feudal wall and had no outside view. This troubled the King and so he decided to add on against the outside of the ramparts a second building which would have a great many apertures. Since from here it is a sheer drop into the gully, the building had to be supported on a stone foundation.

The two storeys of *loges* and the upper gallery of this façade make it very different from other parts of the building. It somewhat resembles certain Italian palaces. But here again, the asymmetry of the windows, watchtowers, balconies, pilasters and the foundations, is very typically French.

There is an impressive row of gargoyles above the top floor of the *loges*.

Returning to the Place des Lices, one can take in at a glance the majestic **Gaston d'Orléans Façade** which overlooks the moat, its Classical style no longer comparing unfavourably with the gay and lively Renaissance façades.

St-Nicolas★. − A beautiful building of the 12 and 13C, extremely homogeneous, the church was formerly part of the Benedictine Abbey of St-Laumer whose sober monastic buildings, in Classical style, extend to the Loire. Note the Benedictine plan (large chancel surrounded by an ambulatory and radiating chapels) and also the lovely historiated capitals in the chancel. To the left is a 15C altarpiece.

In the square, the **Louis XII fountain** (N) is a copy of the original badly damaged, which was erected in Flamboyant Gothic style by the king it is named after.

At the corner of the Rue des 3 Clefs, note a 16C half timbered house.

Hôtel de la Chancellerie (K). − This late 16C mansion is one of the biggest in Blois. Behind the 17C carriage entrance note at the back of the courtyard the superb staircase with straight banisters.

Hôtel de Guise (L). − *At no 18 Rue Chemonton.* Renaissance building with windows surrounded by pilasters and a façade decorated with a wide frieze of medallions.

Hôtel d'Alluye★ (E). − A fine private mansion built in 1508 for Florimond Robertet, Treasurer successively of Charles VIII, Louis XII and François I. When accompanying Charles VIII on an expedition to Naples, the financier took a liking to Italian art. Behind the façade of the mansion with its delicate Gothic Renaissance sculptures, a large courtyard opens up with pure Renaissance Italianate galleries *(can be seen during office hours)*.

Beauvoir Tower (S). − This ancient square keep (12C) of a fief was originally separated from that of the château, then redeemed in the 13C. Later the tower was integrated into the town's fortifications.

Old half timbered façades line the Rue Beauvoir (nos 5, 13, 15 and 21), surrounding a 15C stone house (no 19).

Denis-Papin Stairs (19). − At the top of the stairs a long view suddenly opens up towards the south. Dominating the view is the statue of **Denis Papin**, recognized as the father of the steam machine. Born in Chitenay (12 km south of Blois) in 1647, he was forced into exile by the Revocation of the Edict of Nantes and published his memorandum on "How to soften bones and cook meat quickly and cheaply" in England; his "digester" known as Papin's cooking pot, thus became the forerunner of today's pressure cooker. In Germany for the Landgrave of Hesse, Papin discovered "a new way of raising water by the use of fire"; in Kassel in 1706 he carried out public tests demonstrating the motive power of steam. After the death of his patron, he died in poverty in 1714.

Maison des Acrobates. (V). − *At no 3 Place St-Louis.* This is a typical mediaeval house, with its half timbered façade, its two corbelled storeys, and posts carved with acrobats, jugglers, etc.

St-Louis Cathedral. − *To visit the crypt apply to the sacristan.*

Built in the 16C and flanked by a high Renaissance tower with a lantern, the cathedral was almost entirely destroyed in 1678 by a hurricane. Thanks to the intervention of Colbert, whose wife was a native of Blois, it was rapidly reconstructed in the Gothic style. In the nave, above the large arches, one can still see the projecting stones which were to be sculptured like those in the bays of the chancel.

Town Hall and gardens of the Bishop's palace (H). − *Access by the gate to the left of the cathedral.* Situated behind the cathedral, the town hall is in the former bishop's palace, built at the beginning of the 18C by Jacques-Jules Gabriel, father of the architect of the Place de la Concorde in Paris.

Further towards the east, the gardens of the bishop's palace form a terrace overlooking the Loire, with a lovely **view★** (stand near the statue of Joan of Arc) over the river, its wooded slopes and the roofs of the town; to the south is the pinnacle of the Church of St-Saturnin, and to the right on the north bank, the pure spires of the Church of St-Nicolas. Lovely view also of the cathedral chevet.

At the foot of the cathedral there is a picturesque view extending over an old quarter with its narrow alleys intersected by stairways.

■ ADDITIONAL SIGHTS

Denis-Papin House (Q). − Also called Hôtel de Villebresme, this lovely Gothic house at the top of the Rue Pierre-de-Blois spans the road with a timber framed footbridge.

At the bottom of the Rue Pierre-de-Blois on the left a lovely Renaissance door stands out bearing the Latin inscription "Usu vetera nova" which can be translated either "through use, the new becomes old" or on the contrary "the old becomes new again".

Go down the Rue des Juifs: at no 3 is the 16-17C Hôtel de Condé, with its Classical courtyard. Lower down on the left, bordering a half timbered house, is the crossroads of the Rue des Papegaults (16C houses at nos 4, 10 and 14) and the Rue du Puits-Châtel.

Rue du Puits-Châtel (24). − Many interior courtyards are worth a glance through half open entrance doors.

At no 3 there is an outside staircase with a half timbered balcony (16C); at no 5 the staircase turret is in stone and there are vaulted galleries and sculptured balconies at the landings (early 16C); next door at no 7 the Hôtel Sardini has a courtyard with Renaissance arcades and above the door of the staircase turret is Louis XII's porcupine.

BLOIS★★★

St-Saturnin Cloisters (R). – *Entrance indicated on the Quai Villebois-Mareuil. Open 15 March to 31 October except Mondays and Tuesdays, 10am to 12.30pm and 2.30 to 5.30pm ; the rest of the year on Wednesdays, Saturdays and Sundays 10am to noon and 2 to 5pm ; closed 1 January and 25 December. Combined ticket with château.*

This former cemetery with timber-roofed galleries, was built under François I. It serves as a lapidary museum, containing fragments of sculptures from the houses of Blois destroyed in 1940.

Basilica Notre-Dame-de-la-Trinité. – *Northeast on the plan.*

This building designed by the architect Paul Rouvière, built between 1937 and 1944, has some fine stained glass and a Stations of the Cross sculptured out of cement by Lambert-Rucki. The 60 m - 200 ft high campanile affords an extensive view of the surrounding countryside *(240 steps ; admission free).* The carillon consists of 48 bells, the largest weighing over 5.3 tonnes — 5 tons. It is one of the best in Europe.

Carillon concerts during the tourist season.

Poulain Chocolate Factory (Chocolaterie Poulain). – *Guided tours Monday to Thursday and Friday morning at fixed hours ; time : 1 1/2 hours. Apply by telephone : (54) 78 39 21. 2F ; children 1F.*

Auguste Poulain was born in 1825, the son of a modest farmer in the vicinity of Blois. While still very young he went to Paris and became an apprentice in a high-class grocery.

A few years later, he had saved enough to buy a shop in Blois and became a chocolate artisan, then opened his own factory in 1848.

Today Poulain Chocolate Factory produces 33 000 tons of chocolate a year and employs 900 people.

EXCURSIONS

Château de Beauregard★. – *9 km - 6 miles by ③ and the D 956 to Cellettes or from the D 765. Guided tours 1 April to 30 September 9.30am to noon and 2 to 6.30pm (5pm out of season), 9.30am to 6.30pm in July and August ; closed on Wednesdays out of season, 25 December and from early January to early February ; 14F.*

Set in large grounds with geometrical paths, the Château de Beauregard mostly dates from the beginning of the 17C, but the main body decorated with an arcaded gallery, has all the characteristics of the 16C.

The château is renowned for its remarkable **Portrait Gallery★★** of notable people which is above the ground floor arcades. Decorated for Paul Ardier, the Lord of Beauregard at the beginning of the 17C, and Treasurer of the Exchequer under Louis XIII, this long room has preserved its strange old Delft tiling depicting an army on the march, cavalry, artillery, infantry, musketeers, etc. in period costume ; the wainscoting and beamed ceiling still have the paintings of Jean Mosnier who also decorated the château at Cheverny ; but this room is most interesting for the 363 historical portraits which cover the walls. Arranged in rows, each devoted to the reign of a King of France – you can see the complete succession of kings from the first Valois, Philippe VI, up to Louis XIII –, portraits of the queen, the main figures of the Court and famous contemporary foreigners are collected around the portrait of the king. So it is that next to Louis XII one finds Isabella of Castila, her daughter Joan the Mad, and Amerigo Vespucci, the Florentine navigator who gave his name to America. The dates of each reign and each king's emblem are also displayed. A good history lesson !

On the same floor is the **Cabinet des Grelots★**, a charming little room fitted out towards the middle of the 16C for Jean du Thiers, Secretary of State for Henri II, then Lord of Beauregard. His coat of arms, azure with three gold spherical bells, decorates the coffered ceiling, while the spherical bells are repeated as a decorative motif on the carved oak woodwork which covers the walls, concealing the closets which contain the château's archives.

One can also see the large 16C kitchen with two fireplaces.

Château de Ménars★. – *8 km - 5 miles to the northeast by ①, the N 152. Closed for restoration.*

This 17C château overlooking the Loire was bought in 1760 by Madame de Pompadour, by then the Marquise, who had the residence greatly modified by the architect Gabriel. The Marquis de Marigny, brother of the former favourite of Louis XV and inheritor of the Marquisate of Ménars, employed the architect Soufflot, who laid out the gardens, in particular.

Mulsans. – *Pop 367. 14 km - 9 miles to the north by ⑧, the D 924, before turning right to Villerbon and then taking the D 50.*

A small farming village on the edge of the Beauce, as can be seen from the flatness of the surrounding countryside and the existence of walled-in farmyards, Mulsans has a delightful **church** *(to visit apply at the presbytery)* with Flamboyant bays surmounted by a fine 12C Romanesque bell tower decorated with arcatures and vaulted twin bays. A Renaissance gallery with carved wooden columns surrounds the whole lower nave and amply houses the porch. This typical bit of regional architecture has been dubbed a *caquetoire* (place to chatter) as people tend to linger after Sunday services.

Molineuf ; Cisse Valley. – *Round tour of 24 km - 15 miles – about 1/2 hour. Leave Blois by ⑥, the D 766, which crosses the beautiful Blois Forest.*

Molineuf. – Pop 776. This village lies in the Cisse Valley on the outskirts of the Blois Forest.

Follow the D 766 to Orchaise where you turn right on to the D 135A.

Return to Molineuf by the D 135 following the Cisse (fine glimpses of the river) amidst vineyards and crops.

BONNEVAL

Michelin map **60** fold 17 – *Local map p 96* – Pop 4864

Bonneval was built around the Benedictine abbey of St-Florentin (9C) in the Middle Ages. This charming former walled town, surrounded by canals used for defence purposes, has kept vestiges of its past.

Former abbey. – Now a psychiatric hospital the abbey buildings include an elegant **fortified gate★**, with its 13C pointed arch, remodelled in the 15C. The whole, flanked by two machicolated towers, is enhanced by the chequerboard pattern of the stonework. Dormer windows with carved gables top the construction. On the right is the abbot's residence and a massive round tower.

In front of the abbey is the **Grève**, a large shaded square beside the canal. West of town, at the beginning of the Rue des Fossés-St-Jacques, there is a charming view of the village : its church spire and ruined towers reflecting in the placid waters.

Notre-Dame. – *Closed Sunday and holiday afternoons.* This church, an early 13C edifice, was built in the Gothic style. Note the lovely rose window above the flat east end.

From the nearby bridge, Rue de la Résistance, the picture of the canal bordered by washing houses and the towers is quite enchanting.

Porte St-Roch and **Tour du Roi.** – From the Rue St-Roch lined by several old houses one arrives at the Porte St-Roch. This gate is flanked by two round towers. Beside it is the Tour du Roi, the old keep, pierced by loopholes and crowned by a pepperpot roof. This part of the curtain wall and the Mail canal were built in the 15C, cutting the fortified town in half for defence purposes.

Porte Boisville and **Pont du Moulin.** – West of town, the 13C Boisville gate is all that remains of the perimeter wall in the 15C.

Not far from there, take the Rue du Pont de Boisville, then take the old Pont du Moulin (13C) over the river into a tranquil verdant setting.

EXCURSION

Alluyes. – Pop 626. *7 km - 4 miles to the northwest.* In the late 15C the overlord was Florimond Robertet, Royal Treasurer to successive kings and owner of the Hôtel d'Alluye in Blois *(p 57)* and the Château de Bury to the southwest of Blois. Of the old **castle** *(medical centre)* there remain a round tower part of the keep, and a fortified gate.

On the left bank of the river, the 15 and 16C **church** presents, on its south side, a succession of pointed gables corresponding with each bay of the aisle – a feature commonly found in churches of the area.

On the wall on the left of the nave two Gothic mural paintings depict St Christopher and the Legend of the Three Living and the Three Dead *(p 26).* A 16C Virgin, north of the nave, carries a Trinity, and at its base Florimond Robertet's coat of arms.

La BOURGONNIÈRE Chapel ★

Michelin map **63** fold 18 – 9 km - 6 miles southeast of Ancenis – *Local map p 104*

On the south side of the D 751 between Marillais and Bouzillé stands the gate onto the Bourgonnière property.
Enter the park ; apply at the steps left of the château 10am to noon and 2 to 6pm (4pm out of season) ; time : 1/2 hour ; 5F.

St-Sauveur Chapel★. – Towered, turreted and buttressed, the chapel, built between 1508 and 1523 is decorated with shells, the initials LC and the Greek letter tau (τ) – all attributes of the Antonines, mediaeval Order of Hospitallers who nursed those with St Anthony's Fire, or ergotism.

The doorway is surmounted by an ornately decorated lintel while the door panels are carved with taus *(see above).*

The nave's beautiful star vaulting has coats of arms and pendants. The oratory to the right has a rare seigneurial pew embellished with 16C Italianate grotesques. The centre retable is surmounted by a remarkable statue of Our Lady, attributed to Michel Colombe between St Sebastian and St Anthony the Hermit. The **altarpiece★** on the left, highly ornamented with foliated scrolls and cherubs is probably the work of a Tuscan or Northern Italian artist.

BOURGUEIL

Michelin map **64** fold 13 – *Local map p 105* – Pop 4185

Bourgueil is well situated in a fertile region where the hillsides are carpeted with vines. Ronsard often stayed there and it was there that he met the ''Marie'' of his love songs. Nowadays the little town's renown derives from the full bodied red wines produced by the Breton vines found only in that area. Rabelais mentions it in his works. A Wine Fair is held on the 1st Saturday in February.

Parish Church. – *Closed Sunday and holiday afternoons, Monday and Tuesday after Easter.*
Illuminated by lancet windows, the large Gothic chancel is divided into three and covered with Angevin vaulting of equal height. Its width contrasts with the narrow and simple 11C Romanesque nave.

Halles. – Across from the church note the elegant marketplace with stone arcades *(annual wine exhibition at Easter).*

BOURGUEIL

Abbey. – *East of town on the road to Restigné. Guided tours Easter to 30 September only Sundays and holidays 2 to 6pm (also Fridays to Mondays 1 July to 31 August); closed Tuesdays to Thursdays; time: 3/4 hour; 9F.*

This Benedictine abbey was founded in the late 10C and was at one time one of the wealthiest in the Anjou. In the 13 and 14C it was fortified and surrounded by a moat. Also built during this period was the building (on the road side), with its gable flanked by turrets capped with stone octagonal spires, which contained the **cellar and granaries**. The **tour** takes the visitor to a building built in 1739 which has a dining room decorated with 18C woodwork.

EXCURSIONS

Restigné. – Pop 1 210. *5 km - 3 miles to the east by the D 35.*

The church in this wine growers' village, which lies a little way off the main road, has an interesting diapered façade and a south doorway whose lintel is carved with fantastic beasts and a representation of Daniel in the Lions' Den. Inside, the Angevin chancel has a square east end and resembles that of Bourgueil with lofty vaulting and sculptured keystones. The late 15C vaulting above the 11C nave is of wood. *Open Saturdays 9.30am to 5pm.*

Les Réaux. – *4 km - 2 ½ miles south on the D 749, first right after the railway line.*

Built in the 15C the château *(not open to the public)* belonged, in the 17C, to a certain Tallemant des Réaux whose *Historiettes* described early 17C society. There now remains a fine brick and stone gatehouse, flanked by round towers and where defence has been put aside and decoration encouraged: dormer windows, a salamander above the entrance and soldiers for weather vanes etc. *Paying Guests see p 36.*

Chouzé-sur-Loire. – Pop 2 075. *7 km - 4 miles south on the D 749 and N 152.*

This village was once an active port. It was in the charming 15C **manor house** *(on Rue de l'Église,* near the main square), with its turrets and sculpted dormer windows, that Marie d'Harcourt, the wife of Dunois, the Bastard of Orléans *(p 64),* died on 1 September 1464.

▐ BRISSAC, Château de ▐ ★★

Michelin map ▐64▌ fold 11 – *Local map p 105*

Guided tours 15 July to 31 August (half-hourly) 9.30 to 11.30am and 2.15 to 5.45pm; 1 April to 14 July and 1 September to 15 October (hourly) 9.30 to 11.30am and 2.15 to 5.15pm; 16 October to 3 November (hourly) 9.30 to 11.30am and 2.15 to 4.15pm; closed 4 November to 31 March and Tuesdays except 1 July to 15 September; time: 1 hour; 18F.

"A new château not completed in an old castle only half destroyed", the words of the present twelfth Duke of Brissac. In an elegant park beside the Aubance stands this imposing château; the mixture of styles does not detract from the grandeur of the historic mansion still lived in by the De Cossé family.

The first château was built around 1455 by Pierre de Brézé, who was minister under Charles VII and Louis XI. Bought in 1502 by René de Cossé, the château was damaged during the Wars of Religion. René's grandson, **Charles de Cossé**, Count of Brissac was the Governor of Paris. It was he, who, in the name of the Holy League, opened the city gates in 1494 to Henri IV, after his conversion; the king made him duke. The Duke started the construction of the present day château on the ruins of the 15C castle, however, work ceased on his death in 1621 leaving the château incomplete and as we see it today.

The central pavilion ornamented with pilasters, broken pediments and niches containing statues is flanked on one side by a mediaeval tower, the remains of the castle built by De Brézé, and on the other by a Gothic tower – both have finely carved machicolations and conical roofs. Inside, the tour leads through twelve of the château's two hundred rooms. The richly furnished rooms have intricately painted and gilded **ceilings** and are hung with 17C paintings and **tapestries**. The Grand Saloon with its Gobelins tapestries (18C) and crystal chandeliers contains 18C furniture as does the Petit Saloon. In the dining room lovely silverware is displayed. Hanging in the Portrait Gallery, on the first floor, are portraits of the Dukes of Brissac. The chapel has elegant, finely carved Italian Renaissance choir stalls.

On the second floor a door surmounted by a lyre opens into a delightful 17C style theatre (restored) built in 18C. The stalls can seat 200 spectators.

To the north of Brissac, on the road to Angers, a windmill *(illustration p 11)* adds a picturesque note.

▐ CANDES-ST-MARTIN ▐ ★

Michelin map ▐64▌ southwest of fold 13 – *Local map p 105* – Pop 268

The old village of Candes *(illustration p 9),* which used to be fortified, stands at the confluence of the Loire and the Vienne. It has a fine church, built on the spot where the legendary St Martin died in 397 *(p 155).*

Church★. – The building was erected in the 12 and 13C and provided with defences in the 15C. The roadside façade is remarkable for its combination of military architecture and rich decoration. The vault of the porch is supported by a central pillar on to which the ribs fall in a cluster. The doorway, inside the porch, is flanked by interesting statues.

Inside, the nave is buttressed by aisles of the same height which are in their turn supported outside by simple buttresses. The Angevin vaulting rests on soaring piers, and the whole gives an impression of lightness. The older chancel is out of line with the nave.

By taking a byroad to the right of the church you can reach in a ¼ hour a nearby hillside, which affords a good **view** of the confluence of the two rivers.

CHAMBORD, Château de ★★★

Michelin map 🔲 south of folds 7 and 8 – *Local map p 101*

Chambord with its 440 rooms is the largest of the Loire country châteaux. Its scale foreshadows Versailles. Its sudden apparition at the end of an avenue and the sight of its white mass gradually widening and becoming clearer in detail, make a deep impression, even more striking at sunset. To this must be added the fine structural unity of the building, the rich decoration it owes to the Renaissance, which was then at its height, and finally two wonderful features: the great staircase and the terrace.

HISTORICAL NOTES

A grandiose creation of François I (16C). – The counts of Blois, who were great hunters, built a fortified castle in this lonely corner of the game filled Forest of Boulogne, four leagues from their capital. This building was demolished by François I in 1519 when he came to build the present château. This construction he pursued with passionate enthusiasm.

Even when the Treasury was empty and the King had no money to pay the ransoms of his two sons held by Spain, when he was forced to raid the treasuries of his churches or to melt down his subjects' silver, work at Chambord went on steadily. François I in his zeal wished to divert the Loire and bring it to the foot of the château, but the architects demurred before such a task, and a smaller river, the Cosson, was diverted instead.

Royal visits. – In 1539 the king was able to receive **Charles V** at Chambord. A group of young women dressed as Greek divinities went to meet the Emperor and strewed flowers at his feet. The visitor, charmed by this reception and amazed by the mansion, said to his host: "Chambord is a summary of human industry".

Henri II continued the building. It was at Chambord, in 1552, that the treaty with three German princes was ratified, bringing the three bishoprics of Metz, Toul and Verdun to the Crown. François II and Charles IX often came to hunt in the forest. Henri III and Henri IV hardly appeared at Chambord, but Louis XIII renewed the link.

The sport of kings. – Set in a forested area renowned for its good hunting, the first building on the site was no more than a hunting lodge. The domain was rich in game and lent itself to hawking. At one time there were more than three hundred falcons. The royal packs received every attention and for breeding purposes, the best dogs were brought from the four corners of Europe to improve the strain. Hunting was the favourite mediaeval sport and princes were brought up to it from their very earliest days. Many women were also accomplished at the sport such as Diane de Poitiers. Louis XII took 5 m - 16 ft ditches in his stride. Despite his delicate constitution Charles IX used to hunt for as long as ten hours at a stretch, tiring in the process five horses and often spitting blood such were his exertions. He was invariably ill after each hunt and realized the exploit of stalking a stag without tiring the hounds.

La Grande Mademoiselle (17C). – Chambord was part of the county of Blois which Louis XIII granted to his brother, Gaston d'Orléans *(p 54)*. One can be both a conspirator and a good father: Gaston's daughter, "La Grande Mademoiselle", relates that her favourite game was to make her father go up and down one of the double spiral staircases while she passed him in the opposite direction, without ever meeting him. Later, it was at Chambord that she declared her love to Lauzun. She led him to a looking glass, breathed on it and traced the name of the irresistible charmer with her finger.

Louis XIV and Molière. – The King stayed in Chambord nine times. It was there that Molière created *Monsieur de Pourceaugnac* and *Le Bourgeois Gentilhomme.*

At the first performance of *Pourceaugnac* the King never smiled. Lully, the author of the music, who played the part of an apothecary, had an inspiration: he jumped from the stage on to the harpsichord and fell through it. The King laughed and the play was saved.

Le Bourgeois Gentilhomme caused Molière renewed anguish. The King was icy at the first performance. The courtiers who were made fun of in the play were ready to be sarcastic. But after the second performance the King expressed his pleasure and the whole court changed their criticisms into compliments.

Maréchal de Saxe (18C). – Louis XV put the château at the disposal of his father in law, Stanislas Leczinski, the deposed King of Poland. Then he presented the domain, with 40 000 *livres* revenue, to the Maréchal de Saxe as a reward for his victory at Fontenoy. Was this a coincidence or a piece of mischief by the son in law? Maurice de Saxe was the natural son of Augustus of Poland, the lucky rival of Stanislas and the man who drove him from the throne.

The luxury loving, proud and violent Marshal filled the château with life and excitement. To satisfy his taste for arms he found quarters there for two regiments of cavalry composed of Tartars, Wallachians and even Negroes, whom he brought from Martinique. These strange troops rode fiery horses from the Ukraine which were allowed to run wild in the park and trained to assemble at the sound of a trumpet. The Marshal imposed iron discipline. For the least fault he hanged the culprits from the branches of an old elm. More by terror than by courtship Maurice de Saxe won the favours of a well known actress, Mme Favart, and compelled her to remain at Chambord. He re-erected Molière's stage for her amusement. Monsieur Favart played the triple role of director, author and consenting husband.

The Marshal died at fifty-four, killed, some said, in a duel by the prince de Conti whose wife he had seduced. Others ascribed his death to a neglected chill. Vainglorious even in death, Maurice de Saxe had given orders that the six cannon he had placed in the main courtyard of the château should be fired every quarter of an hour for sixteen days as a sign of mourning.

From the Revolution to the Restoration. – After the Marshal's death the château was neglected and gradually fell into disrepair. The Revolution destroyed what furniture was left.

In 1809 Napoleon gave Chambord as an entailed estate to Marshal Berthier. Berthier sold the timber and left the estate unoccupied. After his death the Princess was authorized to sell it. It was bought by public subscription in 1821 for the duc de Bordeaux.

■ THE CHÂTEAU★★★ *time : 1 1/2 hours*

Open 1 April to 30 September 9.30am to noon and 2 to 6pm ; the rest of the year 9.30am to noon and 2 to 5pm ; 20F, (9F 1 October to 31 March). Visitors no longer admitted half hour before closing time.

Son et Lumière★★ performance see p 33.

The park. – The Chambord estate, the home since 1948 of the National Hunting Reserve, is immense. It covers 5 500 hectares - 13 600 acres of which 4 500 hectares - 11 120 acres are forested. The longest wall in France – 32 km - 20 miles – surrounds the park and has six gateways leading respectively into the same number of fine avenues.

Visitors are allowed into an area to the west of the estate, the rest being a protected zone. For those who wish to observe the game (deer, roe, wild boar...) feeding at dawn and dusk there are four observation points.

The Cosson, which was diverted for the purpose of feeding the moats and had then been filled up by Leczinski, flows once again through the park.

The buildings. – The plan of Chambord is feudal : a central **keep** with four towers and a wall. But the Renaissance architecture evokes no warlike memories. This was a royal palace of pleasure. The northwest front is particularly imposing.

Visitors enter by the Porte-Royale. A plan of the château is on sale, 3F.

The main courtyard. – From here there is a view of the keep which is joined to the corner towers by means of arcades surmounted by two storey galleries. In the original design these galleries did not exist. There was only a terrace, a device which emphasised the massiveness of the keep.

The staircase. – The famous staircase is in the middle of the guardroom. At first it stood alone and rose straight to the roof ; its effect was tremendous. But serious drawbacks – violent draughts and difficulty of access – compelled François I to have floors built connecting the staircase with the various storeys.

This unusual staircase consists of two spirals which are superimposed but do not meet. The central nucleus is pierced in such a way that one can see from one spiral to the other. The decoration in the Italian style, though not as good as that of Blois, is fine.

The apartments. – For a long time the château was almost bare of furniture and interest was focused on the rich decorative sculpture as in the coffered ceilings of the halls at each level. Note throughout the crest of François I, the Salamander and the King's crowned initial, the Franciscan Girdle and ermine tufts.

Rooms on the ground and first floors have been refurbished to bring alive the memory of many of the personalities who came to Chambord.

On the **ground floor** the Salle des Soleils or Sun Room is so named after the sunbursts decorating the shutters. The painting by Baron François Gérard shows the Recognition of the Duke of Anjou as King of Spain while the Brussels tapestry portrays the Call of Abraham. The François I Hunting Room is hung with a series of 16C tapestries after cartoons by Laurent Guyot.

On the **first floor** the apartments originally arranged during Louis XIV's reign are hung with tapestries and paintings, notably a portrait of Henri III by Clouet and another of Anne of Austria by Mignard. In François I's Bedchamber note the 16C gold embroidered velvet bedspread. One of these window panes supposedly carried a melancholy couplet summing up the knightly King's long experience of love : *Souvent femme varie, bien fol est qui s'y fie* (Woman often changes, he who trusts her is a fool).

François I's Cabinet was used as an oratory by Catherine Opalinska the wife of Stanislas Leczinski.

The Queen's Suite is hung with tapestries relating the History of Constantine, after cartoons by Rubens.

After the Queen's Suite there is in the François I Tower, the Royal Bedchamber, which was occupied successively by Louis XIV, Stanislas Leczinski and Maurice de Saxe, retains the Regency panelling installed in 1748 for the latter. In the King's Guards' Room is the huge porcelain stove, a souvenir of Maurice de Saxe.

The Dauphin's Suite contains many mementoes of the comte de Chambord : paintings, the state bed presented by his followers, statues of Henri IV and the duc de Bordeaux, the first and last comte de Chambord, as children ; and the collection of miniature artillery used by the young Prince. The cannon fired shot which could pierce a wall. Also on view is his manifesto of 5 July 1871 when he declared "Henri V will not abandon the white flag of Henri IV".

The **second floor** is devoted to the hunt : arms, trophies and other related items. One room has a series of animal paintings by 17C Flemish painters such as Snyders, Fyt and Boël. The adjoining rooms, in the Henri V Tower, are hung with tapestries relating the History of Meleager, who in Greek mythology was the leader of the Calydonian Boar Hunt, and the History of Diana after cartoons by Toussaint Dubreuil.

The terrace. – Directly inspired by Italy, this presents a unique spectacle. The lantern, the gables, the dormer windows, 800 capitals, 365 chimneys, spires and bell turrets stand together. All are carved intricately.

It was here that the court spent most of its time watching the start and return of the hunts, military reviews and manœuvres, tournaments and festivals. The thousand nooks and crannies of the terraces invited confidences, intrigues and assignations which played a great part in the life of that brilliant society.

Above the terrace the staircase has only one spiral. It winds within a magnificent lantern 32 m - 105 ft high.

CHAMPIGNY-SUR-VEUDE ★

Michelin map ⬛ fold 10 – 6 km - 4 miles north of Richelieu – Pop 950

Champigny lies in the green Valley of the Veude and still has some 16C houses (Rue des Cloîtres and Route d'Assay.) The most interesting sight, however, is the chapel, with its fine Renaissance windows, of the now vanished château.

Sainte-Chapelle★. – *Guided tours 1 April to 15 October 9am to noon and 2 to 6pm; time: 1/2 hour; 11F.*

The chapel, which is a remarkable example of Renaissance art at its height, was part of a castle built from 1508 to 1543 by Louis I and Louis II de Bourbon-Montpensier. The castle itself was later demolished on the orders of Cardinal Richelieu who felt that its magnificence outshone his nearby Château de Richelieu. Only outhouses remain but even these give some idea of the size and splendour of the château that was pulled down. The Sainte-Chapelle was saved by the intervention of Pope Urban VIII.

Louis I of Bourbon, who had accompanied Charles VIII to Naples, wanted the chapel to be in the transitional Gothic-Renaissance style.

The peristyle, which was built later, is decidedly Italian in character: the detailed sculptured ornament is based on the insignia of Louis II of Bourbon and includes crowned and plain Ls, lances, pilgrims' staffs, flowers, fruit, etc. The porch has a coffered ceiling.

A fine wooden door dating from the 16C, carved with panels depicting the Cardinal Virtues, leads to the nave which has ogive vaulting with liernes and tiercerons. There also the visitor will see at prayer the figure of Henri de Bourbon, last Duke of Montpensier, carved by Simon Guillain at the beginning of the 17C.

Stained glass windows★★. – Installed in the middle of the 16C, these windows are the chapel's most precious jewel. The windows all together form a remarkable example of Renaissance glasswork *(see illustration p 27).*

The subjects portrayed are: at the bottom – thirty-four portraits of the Bourbon-Montpensier House from the time of St Louis; above, the principal events in the life of St Louis; at the top – scenes from the Passion. The window in the centre of the chevet shows a moving representation of the Crucifixion. The vividness and delicate combination of colours throughout should be noticed, particularly the purplish blues with their bronze highlights which are beyond compare.

La CHAPELLE-D'ANGILLON

Michelin map ⬛ fold 11 – Pop 756

Lying in a hollow, La Chapelle-d'Angillon stands on the banks of the Petite Sauldre. It was here, on 5 October 1886, that the author of *Le Grand Meaulnes*, Alain-Fournier (Henri Alban Fournier) was born. This is the Ferté-d'Angillon of the novel and Fournier's house is on the left hand side of the road on the D 940 leading to Gien, 100 m from the crossroads. 6 km - 3 1/2 miles to the south lies the **Forest of St-Palais**.

Château de Béthune. – *Open Palm Sunday April to 31 October 9am to noon and 2 to 7pm; closed Sunday mornings; 15F.*

This feudal castle, square in plan, with its towers and keep is surrounded by a moat. In the 17C the castle belonged to the Duke of Sully, Maximilien de Béthune. His descendants gave the castle to Louis XV.

Via the postern gate one enters the interior courtyard dominated by the 11C square keep and bordered by the living quarters, altered in the 16C, as can be seen by the opening up of the dormer windows, addition of mullioned windows and by the turreted staircases of brick with stone courses. Near the well are two lovely Renaissance arcades, perhaps once part of a tennis court.

During the visit note in particular: a tapestry by the Felletin tapestry factory in the great saloon; two lovely Italian Renaissance cabinets incrusted with ivory and ebony in the dining room; and the groined vaulting in the guardroom. There is an **audio-visual presentation** *(time: 10 min)* on Alain-Fournier.

St-Jacques. – The façade has a great Flamboyant window. Behind the altar a 16C stained glass window portrays the Crucifixion with angels collecting the blood of Christ. On the wall on the right, a console holds the 17C reliquary bust of St-Jacques of Saxeau, a 9C hermit from Constantinople. Note Fournier's name on the First World War memorial: his parents are buried in the adjoining churchyard.

*The **Michelin Guide France***
lists hotels and restaurants serving good meals at moderate prices.
Use the current annual guide.

Michelin map **60** fold 17 – *Local map p 96* – Pop 16094 – *Facilities pp 36-37*

Picturesquely perched on a promontory, rising up out of the Beauce Plain, Châteaudun and its castle command the meandering Loir. The market town for the Beauce and Le Perche, both rich agricultural regions, Châteaudun, in the 18 and 19C was an important centre for the grain trade. It still witnesses a thriving market on the vast Place du 18-Octobre every Thursday. In the past the poppies of the Beauce furnished a poppy seed oil and the wool from the surrounding flocks was the staple of a textile industry evoked by certain street names such as Rue des Filoirs and des Fouleries.

The town suffered a series of conflagrations : burnt down in 1723, it was rebuilt in part to the plan of Jules Hardouin, only to be severely damaged in 1870 during a Prussian attack and again in 1940.

HISTORICAL NOTES

The town was the domain of the counts of Blois from the 10C onwards and it was the last of this line who in 1391 sold it to Louis d'Orléans *(p 53)*, father of the poet Charles d'Orléans. The latter gave the countship to his halfbrother, Dunois, the Bastard of Orléans and it was his successors, the Orléans-Longueville family who owned Châteaudun till the end of the 17C.

Dunois, the Bastard of Orléans. – The handsome Dunois (c 1403-68), faithful companion to the Maid, Joan of Arc, was the natural son of Louis d'Orléans. He fought the English from the age of fifteen and was to play a decisive role in the final French victory in the Hundred Years War. He is buried in the basilica at Cléry St-André *(p 77)*.

■ THE CHÂTEAU★★

time : 3/4 hour

CHÂTEAU DE CHÂTEAUDUN

0   40m

LONGUEVILLE WING

Terrace

Gothic staircase

Renaissance staircase

Terrace

DUNOIS WING

Main courtyard

STE-CHAPELLE

KEEP

LOIR →

Rue St-Jean

Rue   des   Fouleries

Guided tours from Palm Sunday to 31 October 7.30 to 11.45am (9.30am to 1.15pm Sundays and holidays) and 2 to 6pm; 1 October to Palm Sunday 10 to 11.45am and 2 to 6pm; closed 1 January, 1 May, 1 and 11 November, 25 December; 18F.

The château rising vertically above the river, is impressive for its massive strength. There is a good view of the château from near the bridge on the right bank. Dating in part from the 12 and 16C the château has been restored with great taste and care. The rooms are graced with fine furniture and rich tapestries (17 and 18C).

From outside it has the austerity of a fortress, while the buildings round the main courtyard resemble a stately mansion. The 12C keep, 31 m - 102 ft high (not including the roof), is one of the first round keeps and one of the most imposing and best preserved.

The **lower levels** extend below the Dunois Wing *(access at the foot of the Gothic staircase)*. Two large adjoining rooms, the kitchens, are decorated with palm tree vaulting ; each possesses a double fireplace. The very small rooms to the north, where the guards kept watch over the prisoners, gave onto the prison cells, some of which have ogive vaulting.

Sainte-Chapelle. – Built in the 15C for Dunois, this elegant construction is flanked by a square belfry and two oratories. The upper chapel with its fine wooden ceiling was intended for the servants. The well lit lower chapel has attractive ogive vaulting while the south oratory is adorned by a colourful late 15C mural painting depicting the Last Judgement. The series of fifteen charming **statues**★★ on imposts round the walls are excellent examples of the variety and scope of the local Loire workshops towards the end of the 15C. Twelve of them, placed there during Dunois's lifetime, are lifesize, polychrome statues representing different saints: St Elizabeth, St Mary of Egypt with her long tresses, St Radegund the Queen with her sceptre, St Apollinia with her instrument of torture, St Barbara and her tower where she was held captive, St Geneviève with her book, St Catherine of Alexandria with her martyr's crown and the wheel, the instrument of her martyrdom, Mary Magdalene, the two

(After photo : Revue géographique et industrielle de France)

Châteaudun from the river Loir

St Johns, the Baptist and Evangelist, the patron saints of Dunois, St Martha with the dragon, a majestic Virgin and Child, patroness of Marie d'Harcourt, Dunois's wife. Three smaller statues — St Francis, St Agnes and Dunois himself — were added later by Dunois's son François d'Orléans-Longueville and his daughter in law Agnès de Savoie.

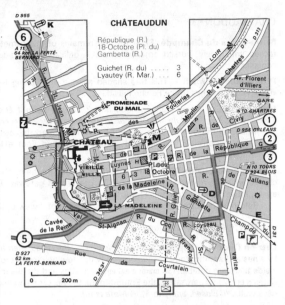

Dunois Wing. — Started in 1460, it is in the true Gothic tradition, but it shows a greater concern for comfort and convenience typical of buildings of the period following the upheavals of the Hundred Years War. The living quarters have attractive wooden ceilings with several massive main beams supporting other smaller rafters and they are hung with fine tapestries. You also visit the Hall of Justice. The room was arranged in such a way as to separate, by wainscoting (17C) and benches, the public from the court of law, while the lord overlooked the assembly from his throne, placed on the platform. Painted with the arms of Louis XIV, on the occasion of one of his visits to Châteaudun, the room became, in 1793, the Revolutionary Tribunal. The watchpath leads to the guardroom.

Longueville Wing. — Completing the work of his father, François had a staircase built in the Gothic style — a transition between the usual mediaeval turreted staircase of the Dunois Wing and the Renaissance staircase, as can be seen on the eastern side of the building. Three storeys high, the staircase's courtyard façade is pierced by twin openings with Flamboyant tracery and decoration. Built by the next generation of the Orléans-Longueville branch of the family from 1511 to 1532 on foundations dating from the previous century, the right wing, the Longueville Wing, was however, left unfinished. On the courtyard façade the Italianate cornice supports a Flamboyant balustrade. The central column of the Renaissance staircase to the right, is decorated with panels of Renaissance motifs which are framed by Gothic mouldings.

The ground floor rooms including the Guard Room are hung with tapestries. Note in the large room on the first floor 16C carved chests. The monumental chimneypieces are either Gothic or Renaissance.

■ ADDITIONAL SIGHTS

Old town★ (Vieille ville). — *Itinerary (time: 1/2 hour) shown on the accompanying plan.* Starting from the Promenade St-Lubin, continue along Rue du Château, lined by overhanging houses, to a charming small square. One of the two old houses here is early 16C with sculpted pilasters, beams and medallions, while the second, restored house, has historiated corner beams (deteriorated).

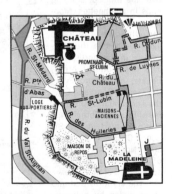

The Rue de la Cuirasserie, with an admirable hôtel with 16C corner turret, opens on to the Square de la Madeleine where the building to the right, a rest home (maison de repos), has a fine projecting frontispiece; and the building to the left, the former Augustinian abbey in Classical style, houses the Law Courts.

La Madeleine★. — The church presents a series of pointed gables on its north façade, an arrangement common in the region. Built in the 12C, La Madeleine was never completed — a plan too ambitious and a lack of funds were the cause. Yet the large interior strikes you by its airy, luminous quality and, although the pillars in the nave are missing the ogive vaulting above them, this does not detract from the soaring effect they present. Giving onto the ravine, the south side has a Romanesque doorway with a recessed arch carved with human figures and fantastic-looking animals.

Continue down Rue des Huileries to Rue de la Porte-d'Abas where on the left, near the ruins of a Roman gateway, stands the 16C Porters' Lodge (La Loge aux Portiers).

Return to the Rue St-Lubin, picturesque with its central stream. Once back in front of the castle, walk underneath the doorway at the beginning of the Rue de Luynes, into the Impasse du Cloître St-Roch and bear right into the narrow, windy Ruelle des Ribaudes, which gives onto a small square. From here there is a pleasant **view** of the Loir and its valley.

On the right of the square, note the 15C house with its Flamboyant style door and mullioned windows. *Return to the castle by the Rue Dodun.*

St-Valérien (D). — Distinguished by its tall belfry crowned by a crocketed spire, the church, on its south side, has a fine Romanesque multi-foil doorway.

CHÂTEAUDUN★★

Notre-Dame-du-Champdé (E). – All that remains of this cemetery chapel is a Flamboyant façade with finely worked ornamentation. A delicate balustrade is supported by sculpted consoles.

Promenade du Mail. – This tree shaded avenue dominating the Loir affords an extensive **view★** which reaches to the Perche hillsides.

Museum (M). – *Open 10am to noon and 2 to 6pm (5pm 1 October to 31 March); closed Tuesdays, 1 May, 14 July, 15 October to 15 November, 25 December and 1 January; 5.60F.*
This local museum houses, on its first floor, a remarkable **collection of birds★** (stuffed) and fine Oriental porcelain, jewelry and arms. The ground floor exhibits Egyptian objects and mementoes from the Prussian attack in 1870.

St-Jean-de-la-Chaîne (K). – In the suburb of St-Jean on the north bank of the Loir, stands this church which is reached by an early 16C ogee arched gateway. Built mainly in the 15C, the apses, however, date from the 11 and 12C.
Returning back towards Châteaudun, there is a good view of the castle's north façade.

EXCURSION

Lutz-en-Dunois. – Pop 383. *7 km - 4 miles by ②, the D 955, then turn left after the aerodrome.* Lutz has a charming Romanesque church with a low bell tower crowned by a saddleback roof. Inside there are notable 13C **mural paintings** : Apostles and the Bishop Saints on the oven vault ; Christ's entry into Jerusalem, the Entombment, the Resurrection and Descent into Limbo on the nave walls. *(If closed, apply to M. & Mme Ison).*

CHÂTEAU-GONTIER

Michelin map 🔢 fold 10 – *Local map p 117* – *Pop 8 352* – *Facilities pp 36-37*

This attractive old town in the very heart of Chouan country *(p 88)* was founded in the 11C by Foulques Nerra. The old town with its narrow, winding streets is grouped round the town hall (**H**) and Church of St-Jean. The hospital, convents and religious communities are all on the east bank. The Royalist leader Mercier, son of an innkeeper was born in Rue Trouvée. The confidant of Cadoudal, he was killed in 1801 at the Battle of Loudéac, aged twenty-six.

The spacious quays recall the former glory of Château-Gontier as a busy port on the canalised Mayenne. Today the calf sales are among the most important in France and Europe and on Thursday, market day, nearly 5 000 head of cattle are sold.

St-Jean. – This 11C Romanesque building in flint and red sandstone was built on land given by Foulques Nerra to Benedictines from Angers.

The **interior★** is remarkable for its forceful yet pure Romanesque style. The dome on pendentives over the transept crossing ends in colonnettes. Modern stained glass adorns the windows. There are 12C frescoes in the transept – in the north arm : The Creation (of birds, beasts, Adam and Eve) ; the Tree of Good and Evil ; the Temptation and Downfall of Eve. The Three Kings are portrayed in the St-Benoît Chapel. In the south arm : Noah's Ark, the End of the Flood with the appearance of the Dove.

The crypt divided into three aisles by columns has groined vaulting.

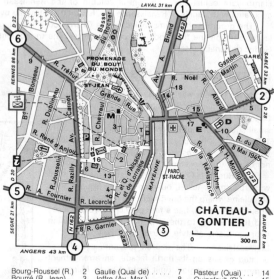

Bourg-Roussel (R.)	2	Gaulle (Quai de)	7	Pasteur (Quai)	14
Bourré (R. Jean)	3	Joffre (Av. Mar.)	8	Quinefault (Pl.)	15
Cahour (R. Abel)	4	Leclerc (R. de la Div.)	9	République (Pl.)	16
Foch (Av. Mar.)	5	Lemonnier (R. Gén.)	10	Thiers (R.)	17
Gambetta (R.)	6	Olivet (R. d')	13	Trouvée (R.)	18

Viewpoint. – Behind St-Jean's chevet, terraces laid out on the former ramparts afford fine views of the Mayenne.

Promenade du Bout-du-Monde. – These gardens, affording glimpses of the river, were laid out on the site of the former priory grounds.

Museum (M). – *Open 10am to noon and 2 to 7pm ; closed Mondays and in February ; time : 3/4 hour.*
Housed in a lovely recently restored 17C hôtel, this museum contains in addition to Graeco-Roman antiquities, some good paintings and sculptures. Note the drawing by Le Brun, *The Battle between Constantine and Maxentius* ; canvases by the 17C Dutch school ; an important 16C Italian work, *Cleopatra* ; an admirable wooden **statue of St Martha** by late 15C French school and a 14C marble Virgin.

La Trinité (D). – This 17C church was formerly the Ursulines' chapel. The pilastered façade is adorned by a statue of St Ursula. It was in this chapel that Lucrèce Mercier came to pray after the execution of her fiancé the Royalist leader, Cadoudal. She was later to take her vows with the Ursulines.

Notre-Dame-du-Genneteil (E). – This former church built of schist in the Romanesque style was once the college chapel.

CHÂTEAU-LA-VALLIÈRE

Michelin map 🔢 northwest of fold 14 – Pop 1 628

This calm, small town ideal for tourists seeking a quiet haven is situated in a wooded region interspersed with many stretches of water.

Louise de la Baume le Blanc, or better known as Duchess of La Vallière, spent her childhood at La Vallière Manor, near the village of Reugny to the northeast of Tours.

Lady in waiting to Charles I of England's widow, Henrietta Maria, the gentle, gracious Louise captured the heart of the Sun King, Louis XIV, at Fontainebleau in 1662. She remained the royal mistress for five years before giving way to the haughty Mme de Montespan. Following her fall from favour, she retired to the Carmelite Convent in Rue St Jacques in Paris where she eventually took her vows. For the thirty-six years of her stay her piety, modesty and tolerance never failed her.

Étang du Val Joyeux. – This vast stretch of water *(bathing and sailing facilities)*, formed by the River Fare, lies in an attractive wooded setting. The nearby hill is crowned by a church.

Château-la-Vallière Forest. – This vast forest of pines and oaks, interspersed with stretches of heath is ideal for hunting.

EXCURSION

Château de Vaujours. – *3.5 km - 2 miles by the D 959 the Tours road, and afterwards the D 34 to the right.*

The romantic ruins of this château are preceded by a fortified barbican and a rampart wall marked out at intervals by round towers. Only one of the once battlemented towers stands in its entirety. The courtyard is bordered by the remains of the chapel and main building dating from the 15C. Louise de La Vallière also retained the title of duchesse de Vaujours, but only visited the château once in 1669.

CHÂTEAUNEUF-SUR-LOIRE

Michelin map 🔢 fold 10 – Pop 6 029

Although Châteauneuf-sur-Loire suffered in 1940 from the bombardments like many other bridgeheads on the Loire, it has recovered and become a small pleasant town.

Castle park. – On the site of the former fortified castle where Charles IV the Fair died in 1328, La Vrillière, Louis XIV's Secretary of State, had a small "Versailles" built. Only the domed rotunda, which is used as the town hall, the outbuildings and the pavilions in the forecourt remain. The park is bordered by a moat, the west section of which is filled with water and crossed by a stone footbridge. It is at its best at the end of May or the beginning of June when the giant **rhododendrons** are in flower.

Loire Maritime Museum (Musée de la Marine de Loire). – *Open July and August 10am to noon and 2 to 5.30pm; June and September weekdays afternoons only, Saturdays, Sundays and holidays 10am to noon and 2 to 5.30pm; April and May Saturdays, Sundays and holidays only 10am to noon and 2 to 5.30pm; closed 1 October to 31 March and Tuesdays; 5F.*

Bear right, round the town hall and go down a few steps to enter the basement where the museum has been installed. Engravings showing the former river traffic, navigational instruments, models and photographs of the different craft, recall former days.

St-Martial. – The Gothic style end of 16C church lost its nave in the bombings in 1940; all that remains is a double arcade. Inside, La Vrillière's (d 1681) marble **mausoleum★**, carved in Italy by a student of Bernini, is an imposing Baroque monument – two skeletons enframe it.

St Peter's covered market (Halle St-Pierre). – Adjoining the church, this picturesque building, with wooden columns, was built in 1854.

EXCURSIONS

Fay-aux-Loges. – Pop 2 135. *9 km - 5 1/2 miles northwest via the D 11.*
This small village on the Orléans Canal *(p 106)* possesses a squat 11-13C **church** made in the local stone. Behind the church, the presbytery is located in a fortified house.

Combreux. – Pop 183. *13 km - 8 miles northeast by the D 10 and D 9.*
Combreux also lies along the banks of the Orléans Canal. Its 16-17C **château** (north of village on the D 9) of bricks marked at the angles with stone quoins, is surrounded by a moat.

Étang de la Vallée★. – *2 km - 1 mile west.* This reservoir of the Orléans Canal is situated in a wild setting amidst dense woodland and tall grasses where water hens and ducks take refuge. Facilities are provided for the fisherman and tourist: bathing place, yachting and boardsailing is permitted. *Boats and pedal boats for hire.*

Michelin map 🔟 southwest of fold 6 – Pop 6170

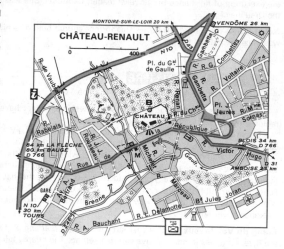

Founded in 1066 by Renault, son of Geoffroi de Château-Gontier, the town stands on a promontory at the confluence of the Gault and the Brenne. The main street curves as it descends to the level of the two rivers.

The chemical and electronics industries have been added to the traditional activity of leather working. There are plans to open a museum devoted to leatherwork *(work in progress)*.

Château. – Pass through the 14C gateway to reach the lime planted terraces which afford a fine **view★** over the town. The 12C **keep (B)** has been dismantled; the 17C château now houses the town hall. The château belonged to the owners of the château in Châteaudun, followed by two illustrious sailors: the Marquis de Château-Renault, who served under Louis XIV and the Comte d'Estaing, who was beheaded in 1793.

CHÂTILLON-SUR-INDRE ★

Michelin map 🔟 fold 6 – Pop 3560

Châtillon, a small town curiously clustered on to a mound dominating the Indre, is a jumble of tortuous streets, alleys and stairways bordered by ancient houses with old roofs. The town's activity is mainly based on agriculture, and market days with transactions relating mainly to cattle and agricultural machinery are lively occasions.

Notre-Dame. – Although the transept and chancel without their original vaulting date from the 11C, the church is essentially a Romanesque building dating from 1112. The façade finished in 1180 is pierced by a **doorway** with remarkable historiated capitals: fantastic animals (Harpies and Sphinx); the symbolic dove feeding on the fruit of the vine; men struggling with monsters (vices); Adam and Eve expelled from the Garden of Eden; the miser's torment and a buffoon leading donkeys in a dance. The south gable is ornamented with a bas-relief depicting Christ the King surrounded by seraphim.

Inside admire the height of the nave and the formidable surge of the Romanesque columns supporting the cradle vaulting. The capitals of the nave are ornamented with plant motifs and masks while those in the transept are historiated: Daniel in the Lions' Den; the monkey trainer; and scenes from the Life of St Austrégisile, the church's patron saint.

Château. – *Open 9am to noon and 2 to 7pm (5pm in winter); apply to the caretaker; 4F.* Still surrounded in parts by its revetment wall *(p 23)*, the round **keep** dates from the early 13C. From the summit there is a pleasant panorama of the town and Indre Valley.

EXCURSIONS

Bridoré. – Pop 426. *9 km - 5 1/2 miles northwest by the N 143 and D 241.*

The late 15C **church,** dedicated to St Roch, contains a monumental 15C statue of the Saint, to the right in the nave. The legend of St Hubert is evoked on a 16C bas-relief.

The 14-15C **castle** *(not open)* forms an imposing ensemble bordered on three sides by deep, dry moats. The most interesting parts are the gatehouse and the rectangular keep with a Louis XII style dormer window and lateral bartizans with pepper pot roofs. The main apartments adjoin the keep.

Verneuil-sur-Indre. – Pop 542. *16 km - 10 miles northwest by the N 143 and D 12.*

The château, now used by a horticultural centre *(gardens open to the public June to October only)*, comprises a keep, remodelled in 1820 in the style of the 15C and an 18C building, surmounted by a dome with gores. Good view of the château from the bridge.

The former fortress of Chaumont was demolished twice; it was rebuilt between 1465 and 1510 by Pierre d'Amboise, by the eldest of his seventeen children, Charles I d'Amboise, and by his grandson, Charles II. The latter, thanks to his uncle, Cardinal Georges d'Amboise, who was in great favour with King Louis XII, became Grand Master of the King's Household, Marshal, Admiral of France and Lieutenant-General in Italy.

In 1560 Catherine de' Medici, the widow of Henri II, acquired the castle only as a means of revenge against Diane de Poitiers, the mistress of the late King *(p 70)*. The Queen compelled her rival to give up her favourite residence of Chenonceau in exchange for Chaumont. Diane de Poitiers, however, did not remain at Chaumont but retired to Anet where she died in 1566.

The stay of Catherine de' Medici at Chaumont and the existence there of a room connected by a staircase with the top of a tower have given rise to conjecture. The room was said to be the study for **Ruggieri**, the Queen's Astrologer, and the tower, the observatory from which Catherine and her master plotter consulted the stars. It is said to be at Chaumont that Catherine read in the future the grim fate awaiting her three sons, François II, Charles IX, and Henri III (all of whom died violent deaths) and the accession of the Bourbons with Henri IV of Navarre.

Mass produced medallions. – In the 18C one of the proprietors of the castle, Le Ray, Governor of the Invalides, hired for 1 200 *livres* a year, plus lodging and heating, the services of the famous Italian artist **Nini**, a glass engraver and potter. Nini fitted out a workshop in the stables and an oven in a dovecote. With a hollow mould he reproduced many copies of medallions of more than a hundred famous people of the time. Le Ray made a large profit from this new industrial method of portraiture.

19C. – Exiled from Paris by Napoleon, Madame de Staël spent some time in 1810 at Chaumont. When her guests praised the landscape of the Loire, she replied sadly: "Yes' it's an admirable scene, but how much I prefer my gutter in the Rue du Bac."

In 1875 the castle was bought by the Princess de Broglie. This was for Chaumont an era of luxury and magnificent festivities. Chaumont has belonged to the State since 1938.

■ THE CHÂTEAU★★ *time: 1 1/2 hours*

Open 1 April to 30 September 9 to 11.20am and 1.30 to 5.20pm; the rest of the year 9.30 to 11.45am and 1.45 to 5.45pm; closed 1 January, 1 May, 1 and 11 November and 25 December; the stables remain open 3/4 hour after the château's closing time; château and stables: 20F, park: 10F.

Chaumont has a site overlooking the Loire. There is an admirable **view★** of the valley from its terrace. Surrounded by a beautiful park the building's feudal grimness is softened by Renaissance influences. The luxurious stables are a reminder of coaching days.

The park. – An uphill walk along a shady avenue giving glimpses of the Loire leads to the castle. This is a pleasant walk and will give an idea of the fine park with its centuries old cedars.

The building. – The outer west façade, which is the oldest, is severely military. Most of the windows that can be seen now did not exist originally. The two other façades, though they still have a feudal look, show the influence of the Renaissance.

At ground floor level there is a frieze bearing the interlaced Cs of Charles d'Amboise and his wife, Catherine, alternating with the emblem of the castle: a volcano or *chaud mont* (Chaumont). The emblem of Diane de Poitiers is carved in front of each machicolation: it consists either of two intertwined Ds or of the hunting horn, bow and quiver of Diana the Huntress.

Beyond the drawbridge, the entrance gate is adorned with the arms of France, together with the initials of Louis XII and Anne of

(After photo: Yvon)

Château de Chaumont

Brittany. The hat of Cardinal d'Amboise is carved on the tower on the left, and the arms of Charles d'Amboise, Admiral and Marshal of France, on the right hand tower. These emblems are protected by small structures in a mixed Gothic and Italian Renaissance style. On entering the courtyard go first to the terrace. It was built in the 18C on the site of the north wing, which had been demolished by an owner who liked the view. A magnificent Loire landscape can be seen from it.

The apartments. – Note the room of the two rivals Catherine de' Medici and Diane de Poitiers, Ruggieri's study and the Council Room, paved with Renaissance majolica tiles from Sicily. They contain fine tapestries, good furniture and a collection of Nini's medallions.

The stables. – They are about 50 m from the château. Their size and appointments give an idea of the part played by horses in the lives of princely families.

Built in 1877 by the Prince de Broglie the stables were used until 1917, when the Prince went bankrupt and was forced to sell his horses.

In a corner of the stables note the double-roofed tower, the former dovecote, transformed into an oven for Nini *(see above)*, which later became the castle children's riding school.

Michelin map 🔟 fold 16 — 7 km - 4 miles to the east of Bléré — *Local map p 100*

A tour of the principal Châteaux of the Loire is not complete without a visit to Chenonceau *(1)*. Generous planning and a well proportioned distribution of water and greenery have increased the beauty of a naturally fine setting. The buildings are elegantly decorated. Inside, magnificent furnishings gladden the eye of art lovers.

HISTORICAL NOTES

"The Château of Six Women". — The present château was built between 1513 and 1521 by **Thomas Bohier**, Collector of Taxes under Charles VIII, Louis XII and François I. The acquisition of Chenonceau by Bohier reads like a novel by Balzac.

The estate was the property of the Marques family, whose extravagance caused their ruin. The land was sold bit by bit. Bohier, who had his eye on Chenonceau, bought each of these lots. The owners, feeling the spider's web being spun round the château, tried desperately to avoid the inevitable. After twenty years of struggle, in 1512, they had to admit defeat. Bohier bought the château for 12 500 *livres* and had it all pulled down except the keep. The very next year the delightful mansion the tourist can see today began to rise on the Cher.

From that time onward there was an original feature in the history to Chenonceau. It could be called "The Château of Six Women" because of the leading part its hostesses played there for 400 years.

Katherine Briçonnet, the Builder (beginning of 16C). — Bohier married Katherine Briçonnet, a woman from Touraine who belonged to a family of great financiers. As Bohier was kept busy by his duties and often had to be with the armies in the area of Milan he could not supervise the works at Chenonceau, thus Katherine was the moving spirit.

(After photo: Yvon)

Château de Chenonceau

One feels the feminine influence in the site chosen for the castle and its arrangement with an eye to comfort and convenience. For instance, for the first time, the rooms are placed on either side of a central vestibule, which makes service easier. Another novelty at Chenonceau was the straight flighted staircase, more practical and better suited for receptions than a spiral staircase.

Bohier died in 1524 and Katherine two years later. François I then had his Treasurer's accounts examined. He was found to owe large sums to the Treasury. To pay his debt his son gave up Chenonceau to the King.

Diane de Poitiers "the Ever-Beautiful". — In 1547, Henri II gave Chenonceau to his mistress, Diane de Poitiers. She was twenty years older than he, but her beauty and charm were famous and in no way lessened by the years. "I saw her", wrote a contemporary, "at the age of seventy (in fact, she died at sixty-seven) "as beautiful to look upon and as attractive as at thirty. Above all, she had a wonderfully white skin and did not paint it. But they say she took some sort of broth and various drugs every morning. I don't know what they were".

Diane was the widow of Louis de Brézé. She had a splendid tomb built for him in Rouen Cathedral and she always wore mourning : black and white. Her influence over Henri II was such that he also wore mourning. Diane ordered a fine garden and had a bridge built between the château and the bank of the Cher. She drew ample funds from the tax of twenty *livres* on every church bell levied by her lover, about which Rabelais said : "The King has hung all the bells in the kingdom round the neck of his mare."

The death of Henri II, killed by Montgomery's lance thrust in a tournament in 1559, brought his favourite face to face with Catherine de' Medici, who had become Regent. The Queen, who was patient and retiring, had accepted the situation in her husband's lifetime ; now she meant to enjoy her revenge. Diane was greatly attached to Chenonceau and Catherine knew she would touch a tender spot by forcing her to yield it to her in exchange for Chaumont. With bitter despair the favourite left the banks of the Cher, made a short visit to Chaumont and retired to the Château d'Anet, where she died seven years later.

Catherine de' Medici, the Magnificent. — With her love of the arts Catherine de' Medici also had a love of magnificence, and she satisfied both at Chenonceau. She had a park laid out, built a two storey gallery on the bridge and added large outbuildings. Grand festivals were frequent and the people marvelled at them. One was given for the arrival of François II and Mary Stuart ; another for Charles IX was even more brilliant. Young women disguised as mermaids welcomed the visitors from the moats along the avenue leading to the château. Their singing was matched by that of the nymphs emerging from the thickets. But the appearance of satyrs scattered the graceful chorus. Nothing was lacking from these festivities. There were banquets, dances, masquerades, fireworks and a naval battle on the Cher.

Henri III presided over a sylvan festival that cost 100 000 *livres* and made a sensation. "The most beautiful and virtuous ladies of the court", we are told, "appeared half naked, with their hair loose, like brides, and with the Queen's daughters, waited on the guests."

---

(1) The town of Chenonceaux has an x, not the château.

Louise of Lorraine, the Inconsolable (end of 16C). – Catherine bequeathed Chenonceau to her daughter in law, Louise of Lorraine, wife of Henri III. After the King's assassination by Jacques Clément, Louise retired to the château, put on white mourning according to royal custom and wore it to the end of her life. Her bedroom, her bed, her carpets and chairs were covered with black velvet, and the curtains were of black damask; crowns of thorns and Franciscan girdles were painted in white on black ceilings. For eleven years, faithful to the memory of her husband, Louise divided her time between prayer, needlework and reading.

Madame Dupin, Lover of Letters (18C). – After Louise of Lorraine, Chenonceau fell into disuse until Dupin, the Farmer-General, became its owner. Mme Dupin kept a salon which all the celebrities of the period attended. **Jean-Jacques Rousseau** was tutor to her son. It was for the benefit of this boy that he composed his treatise on education, *Émile*. In his *Confessions* he speaks warmly of that happy time. Mme Dupin grew old at Chenonceau, much beloved by the villagers, so that the château came through the Revolution undamaged.

Madame Pelouze, Lover of Antiquity (19C). – In 1864 Mme Pelouze bought Chenonceau and made it her life's work to restore the château. She refurbished it, recreating the interiors of Bohier's time. Catherine de' Medici had altered the main façade by doubling the windows and placing caryatids between them. The new openings were now walled up and the caryatids were moved into the park. A building which had been added between the chapel and the library was removed. The château is now the property of the Menier family.

■ THE CHÂTEAU★★★

Open 16 March to 15 September 9am to 7pm; 16 to 30 September 9am to 6.30pm; October 9am to 6pm; 1 to 15 November 9am to 5pm; 16 November to 15 February 9am to noon and 2 to 4.30pm; 16 to 28 February 9am to 5.30pm; 1 to 15 March 9am to 6pm. Tea room, snack bar; children's crèche in summer; 17F, combined ticket château and museum : 11.35F.

In July and August an electric train (1F) links the entrance gate to the main courtyard of the château. In summer, when the water level permits, there are boat trips on the Cher.

Son et Lumière★ performances are given in summer see p 33 and below.

Arrival. – You will reach the château along a magnificent avenue of plane trees. The tourist who likes to indulge his fancy can try to imagine the entry of Charles IX, among mermaids, nymphs and satyrs. Standing back on the left, at the end of a path, you will see the caryatids moved from the façade by Mme Pelouze; the outbuildings erected to the plans of Philibert Delorme are on the right.

After crossing a drawbridge you reach a terrace surrounded by moats. To the left is Diane de Poitiers's Italian garden; to the right, that of Catherine de' Medici, bounded by the great trees in the park. On the terrace stands the keep of the original château remodelled by Bohier. Here you will read the initials "TBK" (Thomas Bohier and Katherine). You will find them again in the château, with the motto: *S'il vient à point, me souviendra.* The meaning of this motto is rather obscure. it may be : "If the building is finished it will preserve the memory of the man who built it."

The château. – The château consists of a rectangular mansion with turrets at the corners. It stands on two piers of the former mill, resting on the bed of the Cher. The library and the chapel project on the left.

Catherine de' Medici's two storeyed gallery stands on the bridge over the river. This building by Philibert Delorme has a classical simplicity contrasting with the rich, gay appearance given to the older portion by the sculptures on the balustrades, roof and dormer windows.

Ground floor. – The former guardroom is paved with majolica tiles and adorned with 16C Flemish tapestries; in the chapel is a 16C marble bas-relief of a Virgin and Child; the fireplace in Diane de Poitiers's bedroom was designed by Jean Goujon; pictures hang in Catherine de' Medici's Green Cabinet as well as an Oudenaarde tapestry. The great gallery overlooking the Cher is 60 m - 197 ft long and has black and white chequered paving; incorporated in its ceiling is the ceiling of Louise of Lorraine's bedroom. In François I's bedroom hang paintings by Van Loo *(Three Graces)*, Il Primaticcio *(Diane de Poitiers as the Huntress Diana)*, and, a handsome 15C Italian piece of furniture inlaid in ivory and mother of pearl is worth noting ; in a salon with a magnificent French style ceiling are works by Rubens *(Jesus and St John)*, Mignard, Nattier *(Mme Dupin)* and a portrait of Louis XIV by Rigaud.

First floor. – One reaches it by a straight staircase, which at the time it was built was an innovation in France. From the vestibule, with its Oudenaarde tapestries depicting hunting scenes and Carrara marble statues of Roman emperors brought by Catherine de' Medici from Florence, walk through to Gabrielle d'Estrée's bedroom, the Royal, or Five Queens' Bedroom, the bedroom of Catherine de' Medici and finally to that of César de Vendôme. All the rooms are furnished and adorned with fine Gobelins tapestries.

A small convent for Capuchin nuns was installed in the attics, complete with a drawbridge which was raised at night to separate the nuns from the castle's other occupants.

The kitchens. – There is an attractive dresser and a series of brass containers.

CHENONCEAU, Château de★★★

Waxworks Museum. – *Same visiting times as the château ; 4F.*

In the Dômes building, so named because of the configuration of the roof, are fifteen scenes evoking life in the château and the personalities connected with it.

The park. – Views of the château from the banks of the Cher and the gardens.

EXCURSION

Montlouis-sur-Loire via the Cher Valley. – *Round tour of 48 km - 30 miles – about 1 3/4 hours.*

Leave Chenonceaux via Montrichard, after crossing the Loire bear right on to the N 76 towards Tours.

Bléré. – Pop 4 060. *Facilities pp 36-37.* On entering Bléré, on the Place de la République, the site of the former cemetery, stands the **funerary chapel** of Guillaume de Saigne, Treasurer of the Royal Artillery under François I. Erected in 1526, this elegant monument has carved decoration in the Italian style.

Château de Leugny. – *Guided tours late July to early September, a to 6pm. ; time : 1/2 hour ; admission : 10F.*

Overlooking the Cher, the château was the work of the architect Portier, a student of Gabriel, for his own use. It is furnished with Louis XVI period furniture.

Véretz. – Pop 2 379. A pleasant small village snugly fitted between the Cher and the hillside, Véretz presents a charming picture from the north bank of the river : its houses and church are prolonged on the right by the château's tree-lined paths and terraces.

Take the D 85 to Montlouis-sur-Loire.

Montlouis-sur-Loire. – *Description p 162.*

Leave Montlouis in the direction of Amboise then bear right into the D 40.

St-Martin-le-Beau. – Pop 2 051. The church has a finely sculpted Romanesque doorway.

Return to Chenonceaux via the D 40.

Respect the life of the countryside
Go carefully on country roads
Protect wildlife, plants and trees.

CHEVERNY, Château de ★★

Michelin map 🔠 fold 17

Not far from the châteaux of Blois and Chambord, Cheverny with its Classical white façade and slate roof, stands on the edge of the Sologne Forest.

Built without interruption between 1604 and 1634 by Count Henri Hurault de Cheverny, the château presents a rare unity of style in both its architecture and decoration. The symmetry and majesty of its façade are characteristic features of the Classical period. The interior is sumptuously decorated with furniture, sculpture, gilt, marble, multicoloured panelling...

Son et Lumière *performances are given in summer – see p 33.*

(After photo: F. de Bertier)
Château de Cheverny

■ THE APARTMENTS★★★

Open 9am (9.30am in winter) to noon and 2.15 to 5pm or 5.30, 6, 6.15, 6.30pm according to the season ; 16F.

In the **Grand Salon**, on the ground floor, the ceiling is entirely covered, as is the wall panelling, with painted decoration enhanced with gilt. Among the paintings note the portrait of Cosimo de' Medici by Titian, that of Jeanne d'Aragon from the School of Raphaël and, on the chimneypiece, a portrait by Mignard of Marie-Johanne de Saumery, Countess of Cheverny. In the **Petit Salon**, which follows, hang five 17C tapestries from Flanders after cartoons by Téniers. Both rooms contain Louis XIV and Louis XV period furnishings. Note, in particular, the Louis XV Chinese lacquered commode and the Louis XV clock, decorated with bronzes by Caffiéri. In a suite of three richly furnished salons are some fine paintings, in particular Clouet's Countess of Cheverny and Rigaud's Self-portrait.

On the other side of the hall is the **dining room**. Although refitted in the 19C, it has preserved its painted ceiling and small painted wall panels – recounting the story of Don Quixote – both by Jean Mosnier (1600-56) a painter from Blois, as well as its walls of Cordova leather, embossed with the Hurault coat of arms.

The majestic great staircase with a straight ramp, leads to the **armoury**. Mosnier was the painter of the ceiling, wainscoting, inside shutters and the canvas, flanked by statues of Mercury and Venus, on the gilded wooden chimneypiece. On the walls hang 15 and 16C arms and armour. The Paris tapestry (1610) which precedes the Gobelins factory, depicts *The Abduction of Helen.*

In the **King's Bedroom**, the coffered ceiling, painted by Mosnier is enhanced with gilt as is the Renaissance chimneypiece. The tapestries (1640) covering the walls are after cartoons by Simon Vouet (1590-1649); they are also from the Paris factory. The canopied bed is entirely covered in 16C Persian embroidery.

The outbuildings. — The **kennel** houses a pack sixty strong. The **Trophy Room** contains a collection of 2 000 deer antlers.

Cour-Cheverny. — On leaving, note the graceful village church with its rustic porch dating from the 16C.

EXCURSION

Château de Troussay. — *4.5 km - 3 miles to the west by Cour-Cheverny, the D 52 and a road to the right. Guided tours Easter holidays to 11 November Sundays and holidays only (daily during school holidays) 10am to 12.30pm and 2 to 6pm (7pm in summer, 5pm mid-September to 11 November); time : 1/2 hour; 14F.*

This small Renaissance château was refurbished in the late 19C by the historian Louis de la Saussaye with furnishings and items from other now vanished historic buildings of the region, in particular the wood carvings and stone sculpture including the Louis XII porcupine adorning the rear façade and the fine chapel **door★** with linenfold panels from Florimond Robertet's former Château de Bury. Note the Louis XII floor tiles on the ground floor.

The outbuildings contain a collection of agricultural implements and tools and domestic objects, all typical of the Sologne region.

CHINON ★★

Michelin map **67** fold 9 – *Local maps pp 101 and 105* – Pop 8 873 – *Facilities pp 36-37*
Son et Lumière *performances are given in summer, see p 33.*

Chinon lies in the fertile **Véron**, the countryside between the Loire and the Vienne composed of light alluvial soils or alluvial sediments deposited by the two rivers. It is located in the heart of the well-known wine country and the splendid **Chinon Forest.** Chinon, dominated by the ruined walls of its castle, retains its mediaeval aspect especially during its annual **mediaeval market** *(p 32).*

Arrive from the south for a good **view★★** of the town and the castle's unique positioning perched over the Vienne. *(We suggest you park your car on the Quai Danton).* From here the different parts of the castle are clearly visible : the Fort du Coudray, all the way to the left ; in the middle the massive Château du Milieu (Middle Castle) which extends to the narrow Tour de l'Horloge (Clock Tower) — it still has its roof and machicolations ; and to the right the Fort St-Georges, now dismantled.

Literary associations as well as beautiful views and setting add to the town's artistic and historical interest. The great man of Chinon, **François Rabelais** (1494-1553) was born at La Devinière *(p 76)* and spent his childhood at Chinon, which he left only to complete his studies first at Angers and then at Montpellier.

To stroll along the banks of the Vienne is especially agreeable and particularly in the landscaped **English garden** (B) where the Loire's mild climate permits palm and plane trees to flourish.

HISTORICAL NOTES

For a long time a fortress belonging to the Counts of Blois, Chinon fell into the hands of the Counts of Anjou in the 11C. Henry Plantagenet, the creator of the Angevin Empire *(p 19)* and King of England (1154) had the greater part of the castle built. He died in Chinon in 1189.

John Lackland. — The youngest son of Henry II and Eleanor of Aquitaine, John, on Richard Lionheart's death (1199) became King of England and Count of Anjou. He lost his French possessions to Philippe Auguste, when in 1202 he failed to answer a summons to the vassalic court of his lord. Philippe Auguste confiscated his fiefs and conquered Maine, Anjou and Touraine between 1204-06 — Chinon passed into French hands in 1205.

The Court of the "King of Bourges" (beginning of the 15C). — At the accession of **Charles VII**, France was in an almost desperate situation.

Henry VI, King of England, was also "King of Paris". Charles VII was only "King of Bourges" when, in 1427, he brought his little court to Chinon. The following year he called a meeting of the States-General of the central and southern provinces which had remained faithful to him. They voted him 400 000 *livres* to organize the defence of Orléans, then besieged by the English *(p 124).*

Joan of Arc at Chinon (1429). — Escorted by six men at arms, Joan travelled from Lorraine to Chinon without encountering any of the armed bands which were ravaging the country. The people took this for a clear sign of divine protection. Waiting to be received by Charles VII, Joan spent two days at an inn in the lower town, fasting and praying.

When the peasant girl of eighteen was admitted to the palace, an attempt was made to put her out of countenance. The great hall was lit by 50 torches ; 300 gentlemen in rich apparel were assembled there. The King hid among the crowd. A courtier wore his robes.

Joan advanced shyly, immediately recognized the King and went straight to him. "Gentle Dauphin", she said — for Charles, not having been crowned, was only the Dauphin to her — "my name is Jehanne la Pucelle [Joan the Maid]. The King of Heaven sends word by me that you will be anointed and crowned in the city of Reims, and you will be the Lieutenant of the King of Heaven, who is the King of France".

Charles was obsessed with doubts; he wondered whether Charles VI was really his father. His mother was Isabella of Bavaria, whose conduct was scandalous. When the Maid said to him: "I tell you in the name of Our Lord Christ that you are the heir of France and the true son of the King", he was reassured and almost believed in the heroine's mission.

His advisers were more stubborn. The poor girl was made to appear before the court at Poitiers. A bench of doctors and matrons was to decide whether she was bewitched or inspired. For three weeks she was cross examined. Her naïve replies, her swift repartee, her piety and confidence in her heavenly mission convinced the most sceptical. She was recognized as the "Messenger of God". The Maid returned to Chinon, where she was equipped and given armed men. She left on 20 April 1429 to accomplish her miraculous and tragic destiny *(see map p 16. "An Outline of the Campaign of Joan of Arc in the Loire Country ")*.

■ OLD CHINON★★ (Vieux Chinon) *time : 3/4 hour*

Once surrounded by walls, thus its name "fortified town" – Ville Fort – old Chinon is nestled between the Vienne and the castle's escarpment. Recently restored, the old town, with its narrow streets, pointed roofs, half timbered houses with carved beams, corner turrets, mullioned windows and carved portals evokes the atmosphere of a mediaeval town.

Park the car at the Place du Général de Gaulle. Start in the **Rue Voltaire★**, the main street of the old town and then take a right into Rue du Dr-Gendron where in the cellars a small **wine museum (A M[1]**) has been installed *(guided tours in April 2 to 6pm; 1 May to 30 September 10am to noon and 2 to 6pm; closed Thursdays; time: 1/2 hour; 10F; wine tasting)*. Also branching off the Rue Voltaire is the Rue des Caves Peintes which looks out on the vinecovered slopes; at the end of the street are the **Painted Cellars** (Caves Peintes), former quarries where Rabelais's character Pantagruel used to come to refresh himself with a glass or two of chilled wine. The wall paintings have since disappeared, yet the worship of the Sacred Bottle has been kept alive and it is here that the annual ceremony of the *Entonneurs Rabelaisiens,* the wine growers' brotherhood *(p 30)* are held. At no 19 Rue Voltaire stands a 14C half timbered house; further on take the Rue Jeanne d'Arc which climbs to the castle; a sign indicates the site of the **well**, which, tradition has it, Joan of Arc used to dismount; continue climbing to the 18C **Hôtel Torterue de Langardière,** its Classical façade adorned with elegant wrought iron balconies.

Once at the **Grand Carroi★★** *(carroi = crossroads)* (**A B**), the centre of activity during the Middle Ages, you will see some charming old houses. At no 38 note the half timbered brick **Maison Rouge,** with its overhanging storey; no 45 is also half timbered; at no 44 is the **Hôtel of the States-General** (Hôtel des États-Généraux) an elegant 15 and 16C stone building which contains the Museum of Old Chinon *(see below)*; at no 48 the 17C **Hôtel du Gouvernement's** large stone portal opens on to an arched courtyard. Continue along the **Rue Haute-St-Maurice,** at no 71 is the **Hostellerie Gargantua.** The façade on the Rue Jacques-Coeur is lovely with its corbelled turret and crocketed gable, a decorative motif characteristic of the Flamboyant period.

The nave and chancel of **St-Maurice** (12-16C) (**A E**) are in a very pure Angevin style.

Further on at no 81 is the 15 and 16C **Hôtel Bodard de la Jacopierre**; and at no 82 the 16C **Hôtel des Eaux et Forêts** with its turret and lovely dormer windows.

Museum of Old Chinon (Musée du Vieux Chinon – **A M[2]**). – *Open 1 June to 31 August 10am to noon and 3 to 7pm (5pm the rest of the year); closed Tuesdays and January; 10F.*

This museum is housed in the Hôtel of the States-General, which is not only associated with the death of Richard Lionheart in 1199 but also the meetings of the States-General called by Charles VII in 1428.

The ground floor exhibits are mainly concerned with folk art. There are beautiful rooms: the main hall on the first floor has a full portrait of Rabelais by Delacroix; and the second floor, where the roof is in the form of a ship's hull, contains the collections of a local historical society. There are also Joan of Arc's relics (1431) and St Mexme's cope brought back from the Holy Land during one of the Crusades, as well as Gothic chests and wooden statues of the Virgin.

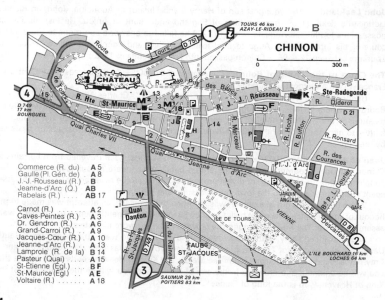

Commerce (R. du)	A 5
Gaulle (Pl. Gén. de)	A 8
J.-J.-Rousseau (R.)	B
Jeanne-d'Arc (Q.)	AB
Rabelais (R.)	AB 17
Carnot (R.)	A 2
Caves-Peintes (R.)	A 3
Dr. Gendron (R.)	A 6
Grand-Carroi (R.)	A 9
Jacques-Cœur (R.)	A 10
Jeanne-d'Arc (R.)	A 13
Lamproie (R. de la)	B 14
Pasteur (Quai)	A 15
St-Étienne (Égl.)	B F
St-Maurice (Égl.)	A E
Voltaire (R.)	A 18

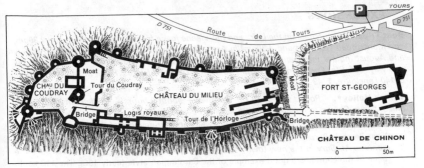

Moat
CHĀU DU COUDRAY   Tour du Coudray
CHÂTEAU DU MILIEU   FORT ST-GEORGES
Bridge   Logis royaux   Moat
Tour de l'Horloge   Bridge
CHÂTEAU DE CHINON
0   50m

■ THE CASTLE★★ *time: 1 hour*

Open 15 March to 30 September 9am to noon and 2 to 6pm (5pm the rest of the year); in July and August the castle is open between noon and 2pm; closed Wednesdays out of season and December and January; 10F.

It is best to arrive at the castle from the Route de Tours, which skirts the massive walls on the north side. Built on a spur overlooking the Vienne, this vast fortress (400 m by 70 m - 1 312 ft by 230 ft) dates mostly from the reign of Henry II (12C) with some later additions. Abandoned in the 15C by the court and bought in the 17C by Richelieu (it stayed in his family until the Revolution), it was badly kept and the fortifications and buildings began to crumble — nothing but the skeleton of a great fortress remains.

The lay-out consisted of three distinct parts separated by deep dry moats: to the east the **Fort St-Georges**, now dismantled, protected the castle open to attacks from the plateau.

Cross the moat and enter the **Château du Milieu** or Middle Castle by the 14C Clock Tower or Tour de l'Horloge, a curiously narrow structure 5 m - 16 ft wide. A bell (1399), known as the Marie Javelle, hung in a lantern turret abutting the platform, still rings the hour. The gardens can be visited; the south curtain wall affords picturesque **views★★** of old Chinon, the Vienne and its valley. To the west of the gardens a second bridge crosses over to the **Fort du Coudray** at the tip of the spur. To the right of the bridge the Coudray keep was built by Philippe Auguste in the early 13C. The Templars were imprisoned here *(p 119)* by Philip the Fair in 1308 and are

(After photo: Arthaud, Grenoble)

The Clock Tower

responsible for the wall graffiti to be seen on the ground floor's north wall (of the present edifice). Joan of Arc occupied the first floor in 1429.

The **guided tour** *(time: 1/2 hour)* is the only mode of access to the **Logis Royaux** or royal apartments, the remains of which rest against the south wall of the Château du Milieu. On the first floor was the great hall where Joan of Arc was received — now in ruins, all that is left is the fireplace. The ground floor rooms have been restored and house a museum: in the guardroom is a model of the castle as it looked in the 15C; in the kitchens a lovely 17C Aubusson tapestry represents the Maid recognizing the Dauphin; also on exhibit are genealogies of the Capetians, Valois and Plantagenets and a map of France in 1420, at the time of the Treaty of Troyes *(p 14)*. After a small lapidary exhibition, the tour ends in the 13C Boissy Tower; this vaulted chamber was used as a chapel.

■ ADDITIONAL SIGHTS

St-Étienne (B F). – Rebuilt in ten months by Philippe de Commines (*c* 1480), the church has a Flamboyant door carved with his coat of arms.

Rue Jean-Jacques Rousseau (B). – Several picturesque mediaeval houses can be seen, especially at the crossroads with the Rue du Puy des Bancs.

St-Mexme (B K). – *Restoration work in progress.* Now a school, this 10 and 11C church has preserved only its nave and narthex. Its two imposing towers overlook the Place St-Mexme.

Ste-Radegonde Chapel. – *Access: on foot by the steep rise to the north of St-Mexme; by car take the Rue Diderot and the Rue Paul Huet, after crossing under the railway line turn left immediately; then take the narrow path to the left. To visit apply to the tourist information centre – guided tours in season only 10am to 6pm; 5F.*

The steep rise is bordered by troglodyte houses. In the 6C a pious hermit had his cell built in the cave. Radegund the wife of King Chlotar I came to consult the hermit about her intentions to leave the court and found the Ste-Croix convent at Poitiers — the cell was later enlarged into a chapel where the hermit was buried. A Romanesque portal leads into the chapel. On the left is a Romanesque fresco depicting a Royal Hunt; on the right 17C paintings recount St Radegund's life.

EXCURSIONS

Boat Trips. – *Excursions on the Loire and the Vienne leave from Chinon (8.15am and 2.30pm) and Montsoreau (10.15am and 4.30pm) in April, May, June, September and October. For July and August inquire in advance. Time: about 2 hours. 75F one way; 120F Rtn; children 35F one way, 60F Rtn. For information apply to Val de Loire Croisières, Place de la Liberté-Thuré 86140 Lencloitre, ☎ 49 93 89 46.*

Vienne Valley★. – *Round tour of 60 km - 38 miles – about 3 hours – Michelin map* 64 *folds 8 and 9. Leave Chinon to the east by the Rue Diderot and the D21.*
The road follows the chalky slope through the well-known vineyards of Cravant-les-Côteaux.

Vieux-Bourg de Cravant. – *1 km - 1/2 mile north of Cravant-les-Côteaux. To visit the church apply to M. Bury in the new town; ☎ 4793 12 40 ; 2.30 to 6pm except Tuesdays; 5F.* The nave of the church is a good example of the Carolingian style (early 10C). The 11C south portal is adorned with a twisted fringe; just at the entrance to the chancel two rectangular pillars have been adorned with Merovingian interlacing. These pillars used to support the roof of the south portal. In the south chapel, added in the 15C, there are remains of a fresco (on the west wall) representing the church's donors. There is also a lapidary museum.

Follow the D 21 to Panzoult and then take the D 221 to Crouzilles.

Crouzilles. – Pop 453. Built in the 12C and covered with Angevin vaulting in the 13C, the church *(to visit apply at the town hall)* is fascinating due to the unique way in which the statues have been incorporated into the church's structure. The buttresses on either side of the Romanesque door have been carved with a niche to hold a statue; in the apse statues have been placed at the springing line of the vault: St Peter, the Virgin, St John, St Paul and in the southeast corner of the south transept the "beau Dieu de Crouzilles".

Take the D 760 to L'Ile-Bouchard.

L'Ile-Bouchard. – *Description p 86.*

The road passes in front of the church of St-Gilles, then crosses the Vienne. *Take the D 18 to Parçay-sur-Vienne.*

Parçay-sur-Vienne. – Pop 1 538. This 12C church has a fine Romanesque doorway flanked by blind arcades. It is decorated with carved archivolts representing bearded faces, foliated scrolls and palmettes and the ensemble is adorned with a motif resembling fish scales.

Return to L'Ile-Bouchard and follow the D 760.

Tavant. – Pop 218. This Romanesque church *(to visit apply to Mme Ferrand, who lives in the house on the right, in the street leading to the church; 6F)* is of special interest due to its 12C **frescoes★** which adorn the vaulting and crypt. More marked in the crypt than in the church, the figures show a power of expression and a degree of realism extremely rare during the Romanesque period.

Continue along the D 760 past the **Château de Brétignolles,** *a Louis XII style building. Take the D 749 to the left.*

Château du Rivau★. – *Guided tours 15 March to 31 October 10am to noon and 2 to 7pm; time: 3/4 hour; 15F. Apply in advance to Mme Rival ☎ 47 9571 15.* Built in the 13C, Le Rivau was fortified in the 15C by Pierre de Beauvau, Chamberlain to Charles VII. Le Rivau also figures in Rabelais's work: after the Picrocholean War, Gargantua gave the château to one of his knights.
The drawbridge, overlooked by the keep, leads to the court of honour.
Inside there are elegant rooms paved in white tufa and Gothic and Renaissance furniture. In the armoury are a monumental fireplace and a 15C Gothic sidetable with the royal coat of arms. In the room communicating with the oratory there is a handsome Renaissance bed. Throughout the château are contemporary paintings.

Return to Chinon via the D 749 and ③ of the town plan.

Rabelais's Country. – *25 km - 15 miles by ③.* The road runs beneath a continuous arch of enormous plane trees as far as St-Lazare where you turn right into the D 751, once a Roman road. 3 km - 2 miles further on, turn left into the D 759 and right on to the D 24, which is continued by the D 117.

La Devinière. – *Open 15 March to 30 September 9am to noon and 2 to 6pm (5pm the rest of the year); closed Wednesdays out of season and December and January; 8F.*
This manor was where **François Rabelais** (1494-1553), the author of the great satirical work *Gargantua* and *Pantagruel,* spent his childhood. Son of a Chinon lawyer, Rabelais, the writer and scholar was also a Franciscan priest and eminent physician. Published in parts,

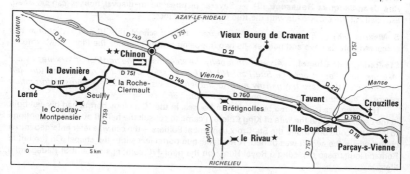

his great work presents the preoccupations of the day through the lively exploits of the two main characters. His native region is the scene of the Picrocholean War and therefore associations with Rabelais or his works abound in the area.

The visit includes Rabelais's room and a museum illustrating the writer's life and works.

Return to the D 117.

Across the way is the **Château du Coudray-Montpensier** (1481) ; drive through **Seuilly-Côteaux,** with its main street lined with troglodyte houses. The young Rabelais was educated at the Benedictine abbey which once stood in Seuilly. He was later to satirize the Benedictines in *Gargantua* through the character of Frère Jean.

Lerné. – Pop 338. This picturesque village of yellow tufa is where, according to Rabelais, the bakers of a special bread – *fouace* – used to set out to sell their wares in Chinon. It was an incident between these bakers and some shepherds from nearby Seuilly, that sparked off the Picrocholean War described in *Gargantua.*

To return to Chinon take the D 224 which crosses Seuilly-Bourg ; on your right is the **Château de la Roche-Clermault.** In Rabelais's tale, this château was owned by Grandgousier, Gargantua's father and was actively disputed on both sides during the Picrocholean War.

Avoine-Chinon Nuclear Power Station. – *11 km - 7 miles northwest of Chinon. Leave Chinon by ④ and take the D 749 to the station. A belvedere is equipped with plans and models which enable one to understand the working of the reactors.*

Put into service in 1963 Chinon A was the first nuclear power reactor in France to generate electricity. This dual purpose plan combines plutonium and power production, with the emphasis on the latter. E.D.F. 1, the prototype, was shut down in 1973 but not destroyed and its great dome, with a diameter of 55 m - 180 ft, is the most striking feature. The present production units, known as E.D.F. 2 and 3 put into service respectively in 1965 and 1966, have an installed capacity of 540 000 kW and an average annual production of 3 500 million kWh (compare Wylfa, Gwynedd with an installed capacity of 1 001 000 kW and an average annual production of 5 910 million kWh).

Presently under construction the new nuclear power station Chinon B will include four production units (B 1 to B 4) each with an installed capacity of 900 000 kW. They will produce 24 000 million kWh. Chinon B 1 began functioning in 1982 ; Chinon B 2 in 1983 ; B 3 and B 4 will start operating in 1986 and 1987.

CLÉRY-ST-ANDRÉ ★

Michelin map **64** fold 8 – *Local map p 101* – Pop 2 242

The only interesting feature of Cléry, is its basilica in which Louis XI is buried.

The present church had its origin in a humble chapel to which, in 1280, some ploughmen carried a statue of the Virgin found in a thicket. The cult of this statue spread throughout the district, and the chapel, being too small to accommodate the pilgrims *(1),* was transformed into a church served by a college of canons. This was destroyed in 1428 by the English commander Salisbury, on his march to Orléans.

Charles VII and Dunois supplied the first funds for rebuilding, but the great benefactor of Cléry was **Louis XI.** When still Dauphin, during the siege of Dieppe, he made a vow : if he were victorious, he would give his weight in silver to Notre-Dame de Cléry. His prayer was answered and he kept his vow. When he became King, Louis XI dedicated himself to the Virgin and his attachment to Cléry was strengthened thereby. He was buried there by his wish and the building was completed by his son, Charles VIII.

■ THE BASILICA★ *time : 1/2 hour*

To visit the vault of Louis XI, St James's Chapel and the oratory of Louis XI, apply at the presbytery 1 Rue du Cloître, behind the chevet of the church or at the sacristy.

The house (now a school) in which Louis XI stayed during his visits to Cléry is on the right of the church, opposite the entrance.

Notre-Dame de Cléry is a 15C building with the exception of its square tower abutting the north side of the church which is 14C and alone escaped destruction by the English. *Enter through the door into the transept.*

The interior of the church is both plain and graceful : there are no capitals on the pillars and no triforium. Austere yet elegant, the church should be imagined in the warm light of its former stained glass windows and hung with tapestries.

The Tomb of Louis XI. – The tomb stands on the north side of the nave and is aligned with the Virgin's altar, so that it lies at an oblique angle to the axis of the church.

The King's marble statue is the work of an Orléans sculptor, Bourdin (1622). It took the place of the original bronze statue melted down by the Huguenots.

Louis XI's Vault. – Louis XI's bones and those of his wife, Charlotte de Savoie, are still in the vault which opens on to the nave near the tomb. The two skulls, sawn open for embalming, are in a glass case. Note the *litre (2)* which runs round the vaulting.

Tanguy de Châtel, who was killed during a siege while saving the life of Louis XI, is buried under a flagstone alongside the royal vault. Further to the right another stone covers the urn containing the heart of Charles VIII. The inscription on this urn is repeated on the nearest pillar.

(1) The pilgrimage is still popular. It takes place on 8 September and the following Sunday.
(2) A litre is a black painted band, bearing the arms of a lord, which runs round a church or a chapel. The higher the rank of the nobleman, the higher it is placed.

St James's Chapel★. – *South aisle.* This was built by Gilles de Pontbriand, Dean of the church, and his brother to serve as their tomb. The Gothic decoration is very rich. The vaulting is decorated with girdles, pilgrims' purses, for Cléry is on the pilgrimage route to St James's shrine in Santiago de Compostela, Spain. The walls are studded with ermines' tails and bridges (the arms of the Pontbriands). There are three fine statues of which two are of wood: St James in a pilgrim's cloak is 16C, St Sebastian is 17C, and the Virgin with the very delicate features is 16C and of stone. The wooden grille was offered by Louis XIII in 1622.

Dunois Chapel. – *From the St James's Chapel the second door to the left.* Dunois and his family lie here *(p 64).* The church at Cléry was finished when this chapel was added (1464) so that the construction of the vaulting was complicated by the presence of a buttress.

Stalls. – These were presented by Henri II. Their seats are carved with masks and the initials of the donor and his mistress, Diane de Poitiers (see cheekpieces of second row on the right).

Chancel. – On the modern high altar is a statue in wood of Notre-Dame de Cléry. In the central window a fine piece of 16C stained glass represents Henri III founding the Order of the Holy Spirit.

Sacristy and oratory of Louis XI. – In the second ambulatory bay on the right is the beautiful door to the sacristy, in pure Flamboyant style. Above it a small opening leads to an oratory *(access by a spiral staircase in the sacristy)* from which Louis XI could follow the services.

COURTANVAUX, Château de

Michelin map 🔢 fold 5 – 2 km - 1 mile to the northwest of Bessé-sur-Braye

Guided tours 1 May to 30 September 10, 11am, 2, 3, 4, 5 and 6pm; the rest of the year Sundays and public holidays only at the aforementioned times; closed Tuesdays; time: 1 hour; 6F. In summer theatrical and musical evenings and art exhibitions.

Set in a shaded vale this Gothic building was the seat of a marquisate held successively by the Louvois and Montesquiou families; in particular by Louis XIV's Secretary of State for War, Michel Le Tellier, Marquis de Louvois.

On the downfall of the Empire in 1815, the château was to emerge from 150 years of abandonment when the King of Rome's (Napoleon Bonaparte's son by Marie-Louise) governess came to live here.

An avenue shaded by plane trees leads to the Renaissance gatehouse. The buildings have typical 15 and 16C features: tall roofs, mullioned windows and pointed pediments. The inner courtyard forms a terrace which is itself dominated by two terraces, all of which give a good idea of the château's **site**. The main building called the "grand château", has on the first floor a suite of four rooms (47 m - 154 ft long) which were redecorated in 1882.

CRAON

Michelin map 🔢 fold 9 – Pop 5 021

Astride the Oudon, this calm Angevin town lies in the heart of the *bocage* country. Arable farming and stock raising are the main activities of the region.

Craon is well known for its horse race *(in September).* From the esplanade behind the church there is a pleasant view of Craon. This was the birthplace of the philosopher writer, Volney, who enjoyed great fame in his lifetime (1757-1820).

Château. – *Park open 9am to noon and 2 to 6.30pm (closed 1 November to 31 March); guided tours of the interior 1 July to 31 August 2 to 6.30pm; closed Tuesdays; 9F château and park, 4.50F park only. Enter from the Laval road.*

The façade of this elegant château built in the local white tufa (c 1720) presents a curvilinear pediment and windows adorned by festoons characteristic of the Louis XVI period. The courtyard front is in a severe neo-Classical style. Inside several 18C rooms with Louis XVI furnishings are shown.

In the pleasant English type park, crossed by the winding Oudon, is the underground ice house built in the 19C. Snow and ice collected during the winter were used to keep the temperature of the "house" ice cold in the summer.

EXCURSIONS

Château de Mortiercrolles. – *11 km - 7 miles to the southeast by the D 25 and then a road to the left. Guided tours 14 July to 31 August 3, 4 and 5pm; closed Tuesdays; time: 3/4 hour; 7F.*

This elegant château was built in the late 15C by Pierre de Rohan. A wide moat encircles the long wall with corner towers which is guarded by a remarkable **gatehouse★** with alternating courses of brick and stonework, and fine machicolations in white tufa.

In the courtyard to the right, the façade of the main apartments is ornamented by superb dormer windows with frontons. At the rear of the courtyard the chapel of brick with stone courses was reroofed in 1969: note the lovely Renaissance side door and piscina.

La Frénouse. – *14 km - 9 miles to the northeast of Craon by the N 171 and D 126.* An avenue bordered by giant statues leads to La Frénouse, a former farm now restored and the unusual museum of sculpture.

Robert Tatin Museum. – *Open 10am to noon and 2 to 7pm (6pm 1 November to 31 March); 6.80F.*

This somewhat surprising open-air museum consists of a sculptured ensemble surrounding a basin. The work of a single man, Robert Tatin, the totem pole like structures show a decidedly Latin American influence.

CUNAULT ★★

Michelin map 64 fold 12 — 12 km - 8 miles to the northwest of Saumur — *Local map p 105*

Cunault, a fine Romanesque church erected from the 11 to the 13C, was founded in 847 by the monks from Noirmoutier who were fleeing the Norman invaders and who, in 862, had to leave Cunault and flee even further — as far as Tournus in Burgundy. Cunault, thus, became part of the rich Benedictine priory dependent on the Abbey of Tournus.

Church★★. — It is the majesty of the edifice which impresses the visitor. Note the massive 11C bell tower crowned by a 15C stone spire. The façade, adorned in great simplicity with arcades below and three bays above, is ornamented with an Adoration of the Virgin on the tympanum.

As you enter, the pure lines of the nave's elevation and the whiteness of the stone are striking. The vastness of its interior is accounted for by the needs of this monastic community which had seven liturgical ceremonies a day and an important pilgrimage dedicated to Our Lady on 8 September. The ambulatory and the radiating chapels were built to hold large processions; the wide side aisles and the raised chancel permitted the worshippers to see the priest officiating.

Although the church is now empty, the richness of the 223 carved **capitals** (11-12C) is remarkable (on entering the chancel note to the right nine monks standing and to the left St-Philibert welcoming a sinner). Binoculars are advisable especially for the sculpture on the keystones, friezes and arcades.

(After photo: Arthaud)

Cunault Church
Saint Catherine

The furnishings in the radiating chapels are worth examining (starting from the left): a 16C *Pietà*, a 16C ash vestment wardrobe and a rare 13C carved, painted wooden **shrine of St-Maxenceul**.

An attractive 16C house formerly the prior's residence is across from the church.

DAMPIERRE-EN-BURLY

Michelin map 65 fold 1 — 13 km - 8 miles west of Gien — Pop 909

Coming from Ouzouer-sur-Loire, the picture of Dampierre is one of a charming village. As you cross over the pools of water, the château walls, the remains of the curtain walls come into view.

The church spire rises up from behind; on its square stands one of the château's 17C entrance pavilions, topped by a pointed roof and adorned with bossed pilasters.

Dampierre Nuclear Power Station. — *3 km - 2 miles to the south on the signposted road. The information centre is open 9am to noon and 2 to 6pm.*

Sticking out of the flat Loire Valley these four gigantic cooling towers (165m - 541ft high and 135m - 443ft diameter at the base) use, like Chinon *(p 77)* and St-Laurent-des-Eaux *(p 102)*, the river for its cooling system.

Put into service 1980-81 Dampierre includes four production units with an output of 900 MW with enriched uranium reactors and pressurized water.

From the neighbouring observation point you will see at the base of the cooling towers water fall from 20m - 65 1/2 ft which creates a powerful cooling draught.

A **guided tour** *(time: 3 hours with 1 1/2 hours of film, talks)* of the power station *(by appointment only ☎ 38 29 70 04 except Sundays and holidays)* takes you to the machine room, and to the base of the reactors and cooling towers.

DESCARTES

Michelin map 68 fold 5 — Pop 4 357

It was in Descartes, formerly known as La Haye, that **René Descartes** (1590-1650), the famous French philosopher, physicist and mathematician was baptised, although the family home was in the neighbouring town of Châtellerault. At the age of eight he was sent to the Jesuit College of Henri IV in La Flèche where he received a semi military education, before joining the army under the Prince of Nassau. While pursuing his military career, he travelled widely in Europe, devoting most of his time to study, and the pursuit of his life's mission as it was revealed to him on 10 November 1619. In 1629 he went again to Holland where he stayed for twenty years, studying at various universities and writing and publishing some of his most famous works. In 1649 he accepted an invitation to the Swedish royal court, where he died on 11 February 1650.

Cartesian thought. — In 1637 Descartes had *Discourse on Method* published. It was exceptionally written in French and not in Latin, the common language of all learned works. The *Discourse* has radically influenced modern philosophical thought — it introduced a new mentality and thus new problems.

Descartes explained how he was deceived by the knowledge he had received from education and books. He suggested the rejection of all accepted ideas and opinions — to doubt until convinced of the contrary by self-evident facts. He concluded his thought with : " ... I who doubt, I who am deceived, at least while I doubt, I must exist and as doubting is thinking, it is indubitable that while I think I am."

Descartes Museum. — *29 Rue Descartes. Guided tours 2 to 6.30pm; closed Tuesdays; time: 1 hour; 2F.*

This house is where Descartes was born. Documents recounting his life and works are displayed.

EXCURSIONS

Balesmes. – *2 km - 1 mile to the northwest by the D 750.* Standing amidst this charming village with its houses roofed in rose-coloured tiles, the church presents an attractive belfry over the transept crossing.

Les Ormes. – *7 km - 4 miles to the west on the N 10.* The **château** gates border the road (as you leave the village by the north). A magnificent alley of chestnut and plane trees leads to the vast grass-covered courtyard. The central building, an early 20C reconstruction, is linked to two 18C pavilions by means of single storey arcades with roof top terraces. Two wings (18C) at right angles to the main front, face one another across the courtyard.

The former stables, known as **La Bergerie**, present a severe but striking Classical pediment on the other side of the N 10.

Ferrière-Larçon. – *16 km - 10 miles to the east by the D 100.*

Château du Châtellier. – Standing on a rocky outcrop, commanding the Brignon Valley, this castle (rebuilt 15 and 17C) has preserved some of its mediaeval fortifications : moats, drawbridges and to the east of its rampart, an imposing round keep with a spur.

Ferrière-Larçon. – Pop 348. The picturesque tile roofs of this village climb haphazardly up the valley slopes.

The **church** is an interesting mixture of styles with a narrow Romanesque nave (12C) and a vast, luminous Gothic chancel (13C). The elegant Romanesque bell tower is capped by an octagonal stone spire with a pinnacle at each corner.

DOUÉ-LA-FONTAINE ★

Michelin map 🔢 fold 8 – *Local map p 92* – Pop 6 855

Doué has preserved a certain number of houses with turrets and external staircases as well as several troglodyte dwellings. The town, one of the oldest in the Anjou Region, is built over a network of underground quarries and galleries excavated out of the limestone rock.

The town's main activities are nursery gardening and rose growing, examples of which can be seen in the **Rose Garden** (Jardin des Roses – *a park open to the public on the road to Soulanger)* and during the well-known annual floral display **Journées de la Rose** *(in the Arena in mid-July).*

Leave Doué via Saumur. A solitary windmill is the only one left of the many that once used to cover these slopes.

Zoo★★ (Parc Zoologique des Minières). – *Open Easter to 15 September 8am to 7pm ; the rest of the year 9am to noon and 2 to 6pm ; 28F, children : 14F.*

On the outskirts of town, on the road to Cholet, this 8 hectares - 20 acre zoo is located amidst beautiful **surroundings★**. The site is unique ; it occupies former quarries and is pleasantly embellished with foliage. The quarries' ovens, grottoes, and tunnels are incorporated into the zoo's setting. The careful attention paid to the natural habitat of each species ; the contact the public has with the various animals (in summer monkeys cavort in liberty while the macaws find peace in the trees) ; and the explanatory notices describing the animal's mode of life and its character are some of the elements which make this zoo outstanding.

As well as the primates you will see pumas, zebras, wolves, lions, hyenas, camels, etc. Housed in one of the quarries is the Vulture-Safari, a huge free-flight aviary which permits the visitor to observe the different birds of prey in liberty. In the Emeu-Safari the tourist is invited to watch these friendly Australian ostriches in their natural habitat. Eight troops of rare apes roam freely on eight islands.

Arena. – *Open 1 April to 30 September 8am to noon and 2 to 7pm ; the rest of the year 9am to noon and 2 to 5pm ; closed Tuesdays ; time : 20 minutes ; 3.50F.*

Situated in the **Douces** quarter of the town, the so called arena was in reality a quarry which was transformed in the 15C when rows of seats were cut out of the solid rock. The quarry is now used for theatrical and musical performances as well as flower shows *(see above).* The vast caves under the seating, were for a long time inhabited and kitchens and other rooms are still visible. Vendéen prisoners were confined there.

Carolingian House (Maison Carolingienne). – *South of Doué on Boulevard du Docteur Lionet near the road (D 69) to Argenton-Château.*

Excavations in 1967 uncovered this 9C fortified construction, later turned into a keep.

■ TROGLODYTE HOUSES★

Doué and its environs lie on a chalky plateau which through the centuries have been carved out for different uses : for the chalk itself, to live in – known as **cave dwellings** – as store rooms, wine cellars, cattle sheds etc... Contrary to those carved out of the hillsides, as in the Loire Valley, these dwellings, not visible from the road, are carved from under the ground, around a pit, which forms the courtyard. Some of these dwellings are now open to the public.

Troglodyte Village (Village Troglodytique de Rochemenier). – *6 km - 3 1/2 miles north on the D 69 and D 177. Open 1 April to 30 September 9.30am to noon and 2 to 7pm, closed Mondays except July and August; 1 to 15 October 2 to 6pm only; 16 October to 30 November and 1 February to 31 March Saturdays, Sundays and holidays 2 to 6pm; January and December inquire in advance.* ☏ *41 59 18 15; 10F.* Rochemenier, once a rather large "underground" village, has succumbed to modernization and the new "above ground" village hides the older "underground" one. Two troglodyte farms (abandoned since 1930's) are open to the public.

La Fosse. – *5.5 km - 3 miles north of Doué via the D 214. Open 15 March to 1 April and 1 September to 15 October 10am to noon and 2 to 6.30pm, closed Monday; July and August 9am to 7.30pm; the rest of the year Saturday, Sunday and holiday afternoons only; closed January and December; time: 3/4 hour; 10F.* The cave's interest lies in the fact that you can observe the way of life of "cave dwellers". Astute small farmers took full advantage of the natural resources the cave and its surroundings offered them: the chalk, carved out to make the ovens, chimneys, silo, vegetable shed etc... was sold, a hole, dug directly into the ground, was all that was needed to store the crops!

Carved Cave (Caverne Sculptée). – *Denezé-sous-Doué. 5.5 km - 3 miles north by the D 69. Open 1 April to 30 June and 1 September to 31 October 2 to 8pm; 1 July to 31 August 10am to 8pm; the rest of the year 2 to 6pm; closed December and January; 10F.* This cave, the sides of which are carved with grotesque figures, was discovered in 1956. After having carefully studied the costumes, the attitudes of the personages and the musical instruments they play, the archaeologists have dated these carved figures to the 16C. It is believed that these caves were where a secret community of stone carvers held their meetings. The carved figures recount the initiation ceremonies.

La FLÈCHE ★

Michelin map **64** fold 2 – *Local map p 98* – Pop 16421

This charming Angevin town, pleasantly situated on the banks of the Loir, is renowned for its *Prytanée,* a military college which has trained generations of officers.

Market town for the varied fruit produce from the Maine, La Flèche has recently experienced an industrial expansion with the building of several large factories, including the printing works of the paperback publishers *Livre de Poche.*

Students tend to group around the Henri IV Fountain (on the square of the same name); and yet a stroll along the Boulevard Latouche and Carmes Gardens is also pleasant.

Henri IV, the Gay Old Spark. – La Flèche was given as part of a dowry to Charles de Bourbon-Vendôme, the grandfather of Henri IV of Navarre, of "Paris is well worth a Mass" fame.

It was here that the young Prince Henri happily spent his childhood and where in 1604 he founded a Jesuit college, which was to become the *Prytanée.*

Cradle for officers. – The Jesuit college developed rapidly and at its height in 1625 the college had 1 500 pupils and counted among the more famous, Descartes. Following the Jesuits expulsion from France in 1762, the college became a military school before being made in 1808 a *Prytanée militaire (see below).*

Missionaries in Canada. – A native of La Flèche, **Jérôme le Royer de la Dauversière,** founded with a group of forty, Montréal in 1642. In 1646 several Jesuit priests from La Flèche : Fathers **Jogues, Lalemant** and **Brébeuf,** were massacred by the Iroquois (Lalemant and Brébeuf were canonized in 1930). **Monsignor de Laval,** also a graduate of the college, became in 1674 the first bishop of Québec. *For more details consult the Michelin Green Guide to Canada.*

■ SIGHTS

Prytanée militaire★. – *Guided tours during school holidays apply in advance to Mr. le Colonel commandant le Prytanée National 72808 La Flèche Cedex; time: 1/2 hour.*

The *Prytanée* is essentially a school for the sons of officers and in certain cases of civil servants, leading to the school leaving certificate, the *baccalauréat.* In addition preparatory classes are provided for the entrance examinations to the prestigious *grandes écoles,* especially the service academies.

A monumental Baroque doorway, surmounted by a bust of Henri IV, marks the entrance to this former Jesuit college. It opens onto the main courtyard, also known as the Austerlitz courtyard, at the end of which is the Louis XVI style hôtel (1784), which is used as the commanding officer's lodging. To the left of this courtyard is the more austere Sébastopol courtyard, overlooked by the **St-Louis chapel★** (1607-37).

The chapel is typical of the lay-out adopted by the

Carnot (R.) 3
Grande Rue
Grollier (R.) 9
Marché-au-Blé (Pl. du) . . 12

Boierie (R. de la) 2
Collège (R. du) 4
Dauversière (R. de la) . . 5
Foch (Promenade Mar.) . 6
Gallieni (R. du Mar.) . . . 8
Henri-IV (Pl.) 10
Montréal (Bd de) 13
Moulin (Bd J.) 15
Rhin-et-Danube (Av.) . . . 16
Thury-Harcourt (Av.) . . . 17

Society of Jesus : a single nave, with Doric pilasters, lined by chapels, large galleries and the whole well lit. Its Baroque decoration is noteworthy — the reredos of the high altar and organ case (1640), supported by a graceful loft. It is the unity of the style and the majesty of the ensemble which are remarkable. In the north arm of the transept is a lead gilt urn, in the shape of a heart, containing the ashes of the hearts of Henri IV and Marie de' Medici, his wife.

Notre-Dame-des-Vertus. — This is a charming Romanesque chapel with a semicircular arched doorway and oven vaulted apses.

The nave vaulting in wood is completely decorated with 17C paintings (scrolls and medallions). The Renaissance **woodwork★** originally from the chapel of the Château du Verger *(p 99)* will fascinate, particularly the "Muslim warrior" on the back of the main door with its Renaissance panels. The nave carvings include medallions and religious attributes : the Last Supper near the pulpit.

Château des Carmes (H). — The town hall is located in this château made up of 17C buildings and built on the ruins of a 15C fortress. From the Loir side, the château presents a pointed gable flanked by two machicolated turrets. Hemmed in by more recent buildings, the **Carmes Gardens** is an agreeable public garden beside the Loir. From the bridge there is a lovely view of the river and the château and gardens reflected in it.

EXCURSION

Le Tertre Rouge★ (Parc zoologique du Tertre Rouge). — *5 km - 3 miles. Leave La Flèche by ② and take the D 104 to the right. Follow the road for 1 km - 1/2 mile after the third level crossing. Open 9.30am to 7pm (dusk, 1 October to 31 March) ; 30F ; children : 17F.*

In a forest setting, the zoo includes mammals, birds, reptiles, etc. The **museum of natural science**, situated in the zoo, exhibits more than 600 examples of the local fauna (stuffed) in their natural environment.

FONTEVRAUD-L'ABBAYE ★★

Michelin map 64 southwest of fold 13 — *Local maps p 105* — Pop 1 850

Built within the limits of the Anjou, Touraine and Poitou regions, Fontevraud-L'Abbaye, in spite of its deterioration, remains the largest ensemble of monastic buildings in France. There is a general view of the abbey and village from the Loudon road.

Located in the abbey, the **Centre Culturel de l'Ouest** organizes concerts, exhibitions, conferences etc. *(Information ☎ 41 51 73 52)* and is responsible for the monument's conservation.

HISTORICAL NOTES

Foundation (1099). — The Order at Fontevraud was founded by **Robert d'Arbrissel**, a preacher famous throughout Brittany and Anjou, who had previously spent some time as a hermit in the Mayenne Forest. The abbey was unique as a religious establishment in that it grouped five different monasteries : Ste-Marie housed the nuns, St-Lazare the lepers, St-Benoît the sick, La Madeleine the fallen women, and St-Jean de l'Habit the monks. Each unit had its own church, cloister, refectory, dormitory and kitchen.

At the head of this community Robert d'Arbrissel placed a woman who took the rank of Abbess and was later designated as the "Head and General of the Order". The Order had dependent houses in England and Spain. The one at Amesbury was founded by Henry II in repentance for the murder of Becket.

An aristocratic Order. — The success of the new Order was immediate and it quickly took on an aristocratic character ; the abbesses, who were members of noble families, procured rich gifts and powerful protection for the abbey. It became the refuge for repudiated queens and daughters of royal or exalted families who took leave of the world voluntarily or under compulsion. There were thirty-six abbesses, many of royal blood including five from the House of Bourbon, between 1115 and 1789.

The Westminster of the Plantagenets. — As a family the **Plantagenets** or counts of Anjou poured wealth and blessings on the abbey and it was in the crypt that Henry II, his Queen, Eleanor of Aquitaine and their son Richard Lionheart found their resting place.

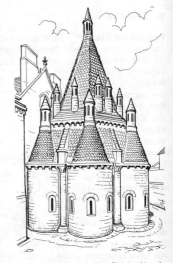

(After photo: Archives Photographiques)

Fontevraud Abbey — Kitchen

Later transfers to the crypt included the hearts of John Lackland and of his son Henry III, the rebuilder of Westminster Abbey which in the 13C became the traditional sanctuary of English sovereigns.

The Violation of the Abbey. — The Huguenots desecrated the abbey in 1562 and the Revolutionaries pillaged and completely destroyed the monks' monastery in 1793. In 1804 Napoleon converted the remaining buildings into a national prison which was only closed in 1963.

■ THE ABBEY★★ *time: 1 hour*

Guided tours 1 April to 30 September 9am to noon and 2 to 6.30pm (4pm the rest of the year); closed Tuesdays, 1 January, 1 and 8 May, 1 and 11 November and 25 December; time: 1 hour; 20F.

The lecture tours organized by the Centre Culturel de l'Ouest (separate from the guided tours) are particularly interesting. For information ☎ 41 51 73 52.

Among the buildings around the entrance court, most of which date from the 19C are, on the left, the vast 18C stables *(la fannerie)* and on the right, the 17 and 18C abbess's house adorned with garlands and bas-reliefs.

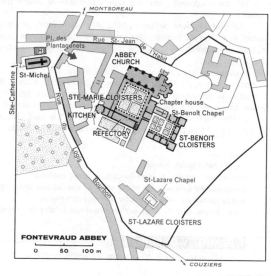

Abbey church★★. – This vast 12C church divided into storeys at the time it served as a prison has again found its original purity.

The wide nave with its delicately carved capitals is roofed by a series of domes, a characteristic of churches found in the southwest of France (Cahors, Périgueux, Angoulême, etc.). Fontevraud is the northernmost example of these curious domed churches and this can be explained by the important links between the Anjou and Aquitaine during the Plantagenet reign.

Built several decades earlier than the nave, the transept and chancel resemble more the Benedictine plan: with an ambulatory and radiating chapels and where the luminosity and repetition of vertical lines – slender columns, arcades, pillars – signify the closer contact with the Heavenly Father.

In the south arm of the transept are the **Plantagenet tombs★**, polychrome recumbent figures representing Henry II, his wife Eleanor of Aquitaine, who died at Fontevraud in 1204, their son Richard Lionheart and lastly Isabelle of Angoulême, second wife of their son, England's King John Lackland. In the 16C these recumbent figures laid in the kings' cemetery *(cimetière des rois)* of which only the base still stands in the nave to the left of the chancel's entrance.

All the church's furnishings have disappeared, destroyed or dispersed during the Revolution; and yet the purity of the construction remains.

Ste-Marie Cloisters. – The cloisters in the nuns' convent, or the Great Cloisters, have Renaissance vaulting except on the south side, which is still Gothic inspired. Go through a richly sculptured doorway in the east gallery, paved with the coat of arms of the Bourbons, to enter the **chapter house★** which is decorated with 16C mural paintings representing the abbesses.

St-Benoît Cloisters. – Restored in parts (17-18C) the cloisters used to lead to the infirmary. The north wing includes the 12C St-Benoît Chapel.

Refectory. – This large hall (45m-148ft long) with its Romanesque walls is roofed with Gothic vaulting which replaced a timber ceiling in 1515.

Kitchen★★. – This is the only Romanesque kitchen which has been conserved over the centuries – inspite of its alterations. In many respects it resembles the kitchen at Glastonbury.

The technical skill of the architect backed by his artistic feeling combines to form a most intriguing building. The kitchen is roofed with overlapping stones and topped by a number of chimneys; built on an octagonal plan and capped by an octagonal hood, the building was originally flanked by eight apsidal chapels, three of which were destroyed in the 16C, when the kitchen was attached to the Refectory. The kitchen's large size can be explained by the great number of people it had to feed and the large amount of smoked meat and fish (it was also used as a smoke room) consumed as part of the daily diet (especially in winter) at that time.

■ ADDITIONAL SIGHTS

St-Michel★. – *Recorded music and lighting; 1F (for 3 minutes).* A low lean-to gallery was built against the walls of this parish church in the 18C, giving it an unexpected character. Although the church was enlarged and remodelled in the 13 and 15C, an inner arcade with small columns and typical Plantagenet style vaulting remain of the original Romanesque building.

The church contains numerous **works of art★**. The high altar was made at the behest of the Abbess, Louise de Bourbon, in 1621. In a north side chapel is a 15C wooden Crucifix simultaneously tormented and at peace, and an impressive 16C Crowning with Thorns by the pupils of Caravaggio. In a Crucifixion painted on wood in an archaic style by Étienne Dumonstier, the artist sought to portray the pitiful waste of the struggles between Catholics and Protestants by depicting the protagonists at the foot of the Cross. One can make out Catherine de' Medici as Mary Magdalene, Henri II as the soldier piercing the heart of Christ, and their three sons, François II, Charles IX and Henri III. Mary Stuart is the Holy Woman with a crown.

Ste-Catherine. – This 13C chapel stands in what was originally the churchyard.

FOUGÈRES-SUR-BIÈVRE, Château de ★

Michelin map 🔢 fold 17 — 8 km - 5 miles northwest of Contres

Guided tours 1 April to 30 September 9 to 11.15am and 2 to 6pm; the rest of the year 10 to 11.15am and 2 to 3.30pm; closed Tuesdays and Wednesdays, 1 January, 1 May, 1 and 11 November and 25 December; time: 1/2 hour; 10F.

In the charming village of Fougères, surrounded by nursery gardens and fields of asparagus, stands the austere yet noble north façade of the feudal looking château of Pierre de Refuge, Louis XI's Chancellor.

Without much difficulty you can pick out the moats, drawbridge, arrow slits — replaced in the 16C by windows — and the keep's battlements which disappeared when the roof was added.

The building was begun in 1470. Already, twenty years before, Charles d'Orléans had pulled down the old fortified castle at Blois and built a more cheerful residence in its place. The builder of Fougères did not follow the new fashion. He built a true stronghold round the square 11C keep.

However, when completed by his son-in-law, the château acquired a certain grace: a court of honour, the east wing of which has a gallery of arcades with lovely dormer windows; the attractive turreted staircase in the northwest corner with its windows flanked by pilasters with Renaissance motifs; and the south wing with large bays added in the 18C.

Inside, the vastness of the rooms is striking. The lord's house is covered with a framework in the form of a ship's hull while that of the towers is in the form of a cone.

Each year
*the **Michelin Guide France***
revises its selection of stars for cuisine (good cooking)
accompanied by a mention of the culinary specialities and local wines;
and proposes a choice of simpler restaurants offering
a well prepared meal, often with regional specialities for a moderate price.

GERMIGNY-DES-PRÉS ★

Michelin map 🔢 fold 10 — 4 km - 3 miles to the southeast of Châteauneuf-sur-Loire — Pop 398

A rare jewel and an important example of Carolingian art, the small **church**★ of Germigny is one of the oldest existing churches in France.

About AD 800 Theodulf, Bishop of Orléans and Abbot of nearby St-Benoît-sur-Loire and friend and counsellor of Charlemagne, founded Germigny. The small church served as the chapel for his "villa" or country house. The "villa" was burnt down and destroyed by the Normans in the 9C.

The careful restoration of the church — the architectural and decorative elements were scrupulously maintained — enables tourists and scholars alike to admire not a church in ruins but a rare example of Carolingian art.

The east apse — the only original portion — has a **mosaic**★★ fixed to its roof. The subject is the Arc of the Covenant, which housed the two tablets of the Law given to Moses by God, and it is surmounted by the two traditional cherubim. Two archangels, whose figures follow the shape of the vaulting, are showing the Ark. Between them the hand of God reaches down from the sky.

The mosaic was discovered in 1840, when archaeologists noticed small boys playing with little cubes of glass found in the church. Once the mosaic was stripped of the thick plaster, an array of colours — gold, silver, blue, green and red — was discovered, revealing the influence of the School of Ravenna.

Underneath the mosaic runs an arcade embellished with a carved decoration which is repeated around the three windows and two niches in the apse — this decoration, as well as that of the horseshoe arches, confirms the influence of Oriental or Byzantine art.

The early church, built in the form of a Greek plan, was made up of four similar apses; the interior was sumptuously decorated with coloured mosaics, stucco ornamentation and the floor paved with inlaid marble and porphyry.

In the centre a square lantern tower, the small openings of which are fitted with panes of alabaster (at that time the artisan had not yet discovered the art of stained glass) illuminates the "new" altar. The nave, now standing, replaced the fourth apse and dates from the 15C.

GIEN ★

Michelin map 🔢 fold 2 — Pop 16784 — *Facilities pp 36-37*

Built on a hill overlooking the north bank of the Loire, Gien, a small town with many flowers, is well known for its faience. It was bombed several times between 1940 and 1944, and it suffered cruelly, as did other bridgeheads on the Loire, but its recovery was rapid. Respect for the traditional forms of regional architecture and a careful use of local materials have given the reconstructed quarters an original and attractive appearance.

From the bridge there is a lovely **view**★ of the château, the houses along the quays and the Loire.

The first château on the Loire. — Built on an old hunting site of Charlemagne's, the château was the first château in the middle course of the Loire.

Historically it is a significant location: in 1410 during the Hundred Years War, the civil strife between the Armagnac and Burgundian faction came to a head *(p 19)* here. Later on **Anne de Beaujeu** (1460-1522), Countess of Gien, had the château rebuilt. She was Louis XI's eldest daughter and on her father's death, she became, at twenty-three, Regent while waiting her brother, Charles VIII's (1483-91) majority. She revealed qualities of great statesmanship and her authority was respected by those around her. Gien is again a place of historical importance during the Fronde (the name given to a civil war in France which lasted from 1648-52 and to its sequel, the war with Spain in 1653-59).

Anne of Austria, Mazarin and the young Louis XIV, being forced to flee from Paris, took refuge at Gien. Turenne enabled them to return by defeating Condé and the Frondeurs at the Battle of Bléneau (1652).

GIEN

■ SIGHTS

International Hunting Museum★★ (Musée International de la Chasse – M). – *Open 9.15 to 11.45am and 2.15 to 6.30pm (5.30pm 1 November to Palm Sunday); time: 2 hours; 11.05F.*

Just skirting the Forest of Orléans and the Sologne, a region abounding in game, Gien is an ideal place for a hunting museum.

The museum is located in the **château★** built by Anne de Beaujeu in 1484. The sober lines of this brick construction, topped with a slate roof, are adorned by turreted staircases and the geometric design of black bricks on the red brick walls – this handsome ensemble is touched up with white stone.

The **museum**'s large and varied presentation of the hunt and its large rooms embellished with handsome fireplaces and woodbeam ceilings combine to make this a remarkable museum on the subject. It is a combination art museum – with its beautiful cynegetic works of art (tapestries, faience, paintings, pipes, etc.) and armoury museum – with its displays of hunting weapons from prehistory to the present (powder flasks, crossbows, harquebuses and sporting guns – ornamented with such detail as to be considered works of art in themselves, etc.).

Hunting scenes depict either mythological (Diana the Huntress) or Christian legends (St Hubert, patron saint of hunters). Displays include the fashioning of gun flints; or the sophisticated workmanship of sporting rifles with damascening. The falcon gallery explains the significance of the different coloured falcon hoods.

The large hall with its fine timberwork ceiling contains a remarkable collection of paintings by the animal painter François Desportes (1661-1743); in another room are works by Florentin Brigaud (1886-1958), sculptor and engraver, whose subjects were mainly animals. In another room is a large collection of buttons (about 5000), these small *objets d'art* closed hunter's jackets. The visit ends in the trophy room which contains 500 antlers, a gift to the museum from the great hunter, Claude Hettier de Boislambert.

From the château's terrace there is a **view★** of the Loire and the town's roof tops.

One side of the courtyard is closed by the **Church of Ste-Jeanne-d'Arc**, rebuilt in 1954 against the 15C stone bell tower, all that was left of the collegiate church founded by Anne de Beaujeu. The interior, with its slender round pillars ringed by carved capitals exudes that peaceful, welcoming atmosphere so often found in the Romanesque church.

(After photo: Syndicat d'Initiative)

Gien

Faience Factory (Faïencerie). – *Leave Gien by* ④ *of the town plan, west of town. Access either by the quay or the Rue Paul Bert. Guided tours 9.30 to 11am and 2 to 3.30pm by appointment :* ☎ *38 67 00 05 Ext 208 ; closed Saturdays, Sundays and holidays ; time : 1 hour.*

When in 1821, the faience factory was founded, Gien was the obvious spot to choose : it was near the deposits of clay and sand used to make the porcelain ; the wood, abounding in the forests nearby was used to heat the ovens ; and the Loire River transported the finished product to its final destination.

The Gien faience factory known mainly for its dinner services and its *objets d'art*, discovered and developed, during the end of the 19C, a unique decoration called *bleu de Gien* – Gien blue. It is a deep blue enhanced by a golden yellow decoration.

The factory continues its costly handmade produced pieces, however, the more modern yet lovely services are also displayed. Wares currently on sale in shops are on show in the exhibition hall.

Museum. – *Open 9 to 11am and 2 to 3.30pm ; 10F.*

Some 400 pieces of 19C faience illustrate the production techniques and rich decoration developed by the Gien factory.

Le GRAND-PRESSIGNY

Michelin map 🔢 fold 5 – Pop 1 185 – *Facilities pp 36-37*

Situated in a picturesque setting at the confluence of the Claise and the Aigronne, Le Grand-Pressigny was protected in earlier times by its castle perched on the hillside.

Museum of Prehistory★. – *In the castle. Open 9am to noon and 2 to 6pm (5pm out of season); closed December, January and Wednesdays in season ; 10F.*

The **castle** has preserved its fortress-like aspect : 14C perimeter wall, round towers, fortified gate and 12C square keep. In the well-kept gardens stands the overlord's house, a 16C building with an elegant façade of Renaissance arcades.

The **museum★** was created in 1910 by Dr. Édouard Chaumié, who did much research on rock shelters and prehistoric sites which were centres of flint-working industries in Neolithic times. The collections of flint artifacts, hand-axes, arrow-heads and polishing tools are among the most complete, making this an important centre for scientific research into the Stone Age.

EXCURSION

La Celle-Guenand. – Pop 365. *8.5 km - 5 miles to the northeast by the D 13.*

Situated in a small tributary valley of the Aigronne, la Celle-Guenand has a harmonious church. The sober Romanesque façade has a central doorway with finely sculpted covings portraying masks and fantastic figures. The transept crossing is covered by a dome on squinches. Note the carved fretwork on the abacus of the massive capitals.

To the right of the entrance an enormous monolithic column decorated with masks, serves as a baptismal stoup (12C).

L'ILE-BOUCHARD

Michelin map 🔢 fold 4 – *Local map p 76* – Pop 1 796

Formerly one of the Vienne ports, the ancient settlement of L'Ile-Bouchard spreads out on both banks amidst gardens and orchards.

Its name is derived from the midstream island where a certain Bouchard is said to have built a fortress in the 9C, which was destroyed in the 17C. The estate was bought by Cardinal Richelieu and belonged to his descendants until 1789.

St-Léonard Priory. – *South of town, signposted. To visit apply to Mme Berton, Rue St-Léonard.*

All that remains standing of the priory church, nestled on the lower slopes of the valley side, are the 11C Romanesque apse in white tufa, an ambulatory and radiating chapels. The arcades are unusual having been added a century later to strengthen the construction.

The fascinating series of historiated **capitals★** represent from left to right :

First pillar : Annunciation and Visitation, Nativity, Adoration of the Shepherds and the Magi. Second pillar : Circumcision, Massacre of the Innocents, Flight into Egypt, Jesus amidst the Pharisees. Third pillar : Judas's kiss, Crucifixion, Last Supper. Fourth pillar : Jesus's entry into Jerusalem, Descent into Limbo, Beheading of St John the Baptist.

St-Maurice. – *To visit apply to Mme Page, 3 Rue de la Vallée-aux-Nains.*

The church's octagonal tower, dating from 1480, is crowned by a stone spire with openwork. The main vessel in the transitional Flamboyant-Renaissance style is supported by pilasters decorated with Renaissance medallions. The early 16C **bishop's throne★** in the chancel has sculptured Renaissance panels portraying the Annunciation, Nativity and Flight into Egypt. The craftsmen are represented on the cheekpieces.

Standing near the church is a charming early 17C manor with pedimented dormer windows.

St-Gilles. – On the north bank of the Vienne, on the D 760, this 11C church (nave) was enlarged in the 12C and altered again in the 15C (chancel).

Two attractive Romanesque doorways, without tympana, have remarkable geometrical and foliage decoration. The dome on squinches over the transept crossing is surmounted by a squat Romanesque tower.

The old mill behind the church ceased to operate in 1970.

INDROIS Valley ★

Michelin map **64** folds 16 and 17

This tributary of the Indre cuts through the clays and chalks of the Montrésor *gâtine*. The river course is lined by willows, alders and poplars with lush meadowlands beyond. Fruit trees and vineyards cling to the well exposed slopes.

From Nouans-les-Fontaines to Azay-sur-Indre – *33 km - 20 1/2 miles – about 2 hours*

Nouans-les-Fontaines. – Pop 883. The 13C church harbours a masterpiece of primitive art: the **Deposition★★** or *Pietà of Nouans* (behind the high altar). By Jean Fouquet and his school, this painting on wood, of monumental dimensions (2.36m by 1.47m - 6 3/4ft by 3 1/2ft), is one of the finest late 15C French works. The deliberately neutral colours employed, the resigned expressions of the figures, and their majestic attitudes make this a moving composition.

Coulangé. – At the entrance of this pleasant hamlet stands (on the right) the bell tower of the former parish church (12C). Positioned on the opposite bank of the river is a round tower and part of a wall, all that remains of the fortifications which once protected the former Benedictine abbey of Villeloin.

Montrésor★. – *Description p 121.*

After Montrésor the D 10 offers scenic views of the lake of Chemillé-sur-Indrois and east of Genillé.

Genillé. – Pop 1 420. The houses climb up from the river to the late 15C château with its angle towers and dovecote. Dominated outside by its belfry the interior of the church possesses a 16C Gothic chancel.

St-Quentin-sur-Indrois. – Pop 425. A pleasantly situated village.

Leave the village on the D 10; the Loches Forest offers a pleasant picture on the left. *At Azay-sur-Indre the road follows the Indre Valley (p 95).*

If you wish to explore the neighbouring areas
*buy the following **Michelin Green Guides***
Normandy, Brittany and Dordogne

LANGEAIS ★★

Michelin map **64** fold 14 – Pop 4 142 – *Facilities pp 36-37*

The town's white houses nestle below the château's walls. Facing the château there is a lovely Renaissance house decorated with pilasters; the church's tower is also Renaissance.

Louis XI's château. – It is Foulques Nerra *(p 42)* who, at the end of the 10C, built the keep, the ruins of which still stand in the gardens – it is the oldest existing keep in France.

The château, now extant, was built by Louis XI from 1465-69 as a strongpoint on the road from Nantes, the route most likely to be taken by an invading Breton army. This threat vanished after the marriage of Charles VIII and Anne of Brittany was celebrated at Langeais itself in 1491.

■ THE CHÂTEAU★★ *time: 1 hour*

Guided tours July and August 9am to 6.30pm; 15 March to 30 June and in September 9am to noon and 2 to 6.30pm (6pm 1 October to 2 November, 5pm the rest of the year); closed 25 December, Monday mornings 15 March to 30 September, all day Monday the rest of the year; 12F; recorded commentary in each room.

The château is one of the most interesting in the Loire Valley. It was built all in one piece, in four years, which is rare; it has undergone no alterations or additions, which is rarer still. Moreover, it has been admirably furnished, in the 15C style, by the patient efforts of the last owner, M. Siegfried, who presented it to the Institut de France in 1904.

Seen from the outside it has the appearance of a powerful mediaeval fortress: high walls, massive round towers, crenellated watchpaths, machicolations, drawbridge and moat. Seen from the inner courtyard, it is less severe, more the residence of a great lord of the 15C: mullioned and dormer windows; the two wings are set at right angles; and the courtyard is bordered on the west side by gardens, which extend to the keep, at the foot of which is the tomb of the Siegfrieds.

The apartments★★★. – Well presented with contemporary period furnishings the atmosphere is more alive than in most other old castles and gives an accurate picture of aristocratic life in the 15C and early Renaissance. There are many fine tapestries mostly Flemish but with some *mille-fleurs.* Note the repetition of the monogram K and A for Charles VIII and Anne of Brittany.

The guardroom, now transformed into a dining room, has a monumental chimneypiece the hood of which represents a castle with battlements manned by small figures.

One of the first floor bedchambers has an early four poster bed, a credence table and Gothic chest. The room where Charles VIII and Anne of Brittany celebrated their marriage is hung with a series of tapestries portraying the Nine Heroes. Charles VIII's chamber has a fine Gothic chest and a curious 17C clock. The upper great hall, rising through two storeys, has a chestnut timber roof in the form of a ship's keel. The Creation is the theme of the Renaissance tapestries hanging here.

The visit ends on the watchpath, a covered gallery the length of the façade, offering views of the Loire and the town's pointed roof tops.

EXCURSIONS

Cinq-Mars-la-Pile. – Pop 2438. *5 km - 3 miles northeast by the N 152.*

The village gets its name from a curious monument in the form of a slim tower, dating from the Gallo-Roman period, which dominates the ridge. The structure with sides of 5 m - 16 1/2 ft and 30 m - 98 ft high, ends in four small pyramidal structures at each corner. Its origin and purpose are wrapped in mystery.

Château. – *Guided tours 1 March to 30 September, 9am to noon and 2 to 7pm (6pm 1 October to 1 November; closed non holiday Mondays; 7F.*

Two towers dating from the 11 and 12C point out the remains of this feudal castle where the celebrated favourite of Louis XIII, Henri d'Effiat, Marquis of Cinq-Mars was born. With his friend De Thou he was convicted of having conspired against Richelieu, and was beheaded at Lyon at the age of twenty-two.

Each tower contains three rooms with lovely ogive vaulting. From the top there is an extensive view of the Loire Valley.

The **park★** is a delightful combination of the romantic garden, thick forest and maze of foliage.

St-Étienne-de-Chigny. – Pop 846. *7.5 km - 4 1/2 miles northeast on the N 152; bear left on the D 76 and left again on the D 126.*

Standing back from the river this old village is sited in the Bresme Valley.

The **church★** *(to visit apply at the grocer's shop; closed Mondays)* built in 1542 by a former Mayor of Tours, **Jean Binet**, has a mourning band *(litre)* both inside and out, figuring his coat of arms. This lordly privilege was common in the Middle Ages and the height of the black band corresponded to the degree of nobility.

The nave has a quite remarkable **hammerbeam roof** with tie beams sculptured in the form of large grotesque masks and in the choir Jonah inside the Whale. In the chevet a 16C **stained glass window**, depicting the Crucifixion, figures the donors, Jean Binet and his wife, Jeanne de la Lande. In the north transept is a Virgin and Child by the 16C French school.

Admire the 16C baptismal font.

Luynes. – Pop 3925. *12 km - 7 1/2 miles northeast on the N 152 then left on the D 49.*

The N 152, running along the river's embankment, offers a good view of this picturesque village, with its cellars carved out of the rock face, clinging to the slope.

In the village worth noting are the marketplace *(halles)* in wood – its high roof covered with flat tiles – and several half timbered houses. Opposite the church, in Rue Paul-Louis-Courier is a house with carved beams depicting St Christopher, a *Pietà* and a Virgin.

Via the D 49, which climbs through the vineyard clad slopes, there is a lovely view, looking back, of the feudal **castle** (13C) watching over its village.

The times indicated in this guide
when given with the distance allow one to enjoy the scenery
when given for sightseeing are intended to give an idea of
the possible brevity or length of a visit.

LAVAL ★

Michelin map **63** fold 10 – *Local map p 117* – Pop 53766 – *Cruising p 37*

This attractive town in the Bas-Maine is pleasantly situated on the banks of the Mayenne. The old town, clustered round the 11C castle, stands on the west bank with modern urban development confined to the north of the walls and on the opposite bank of the river. From the vast Square du Maréchal Foch the main shopping streets begin : Rue du Général de Gaulle, Rue des Déportés, and Rue de la Paix (on the other side of the river).

Although Laval was formerly a linen manufacturing centre *(toiles de Laval)*, today linen has been replaced with cotton and synthetics and yet industry also plays an important role in the town's economy. The presence of the Préfecture of the Mayenne has given an added importance to the city's service industries. The livestock market is one of the most important in the region.

HISTORICAL NOTES

The "Chouannerie". – During the Vendéen War *(p 115)*, the name **Chouan** was applied to the Royalist supporters (Whites) from the Laval area led by the Cottereau brothers, who had adopted the hooting of the tawny owl as their rallying cry *(chat-huant)*. As part of the campaign north of the Loire, Laval, occupied by the Royalists, saw the defeat of the Republican (Blues) Army under its very walls. During a general retreat towards the Loire, the Royalist commander La Rochejaquelein withdrew his forces from Laval. During this operation, a certain La Trémoille, prince de Talmont and leader of the Vendéen cavalry was captured and guillotined at the gateway to his own castle.

Famous citizens of Laval. – Many of the sons of Laval have gained fame. The notable Renaissance surgeon **Ambroise Paré** (1517-90) served several French monarchs and is regarded as the father of modern surgery. His innovations included the treatment of wounds, the ligature of arteries during amputations and the invention of new surgical instruments. **Henri Rousseau** (1844-1910), nicknamed "Le Douanier", was the forerunner of the naïve school of painters. His works were vividly colourful and full of meticulous detail. Rousseau was friendly with another Laval notable, the writer **Alfred Jarry** (1873-1907), who was known as the creator of the drama *Ubu roi*; the production caused riots; it is generally acknowledged as the first work of the Theatre of the Absurd. The navigator, **Alain Gerbault** (1893-1941) was also known as the tennis partner of the French champion Jean Borotra.

■ SIGHTS

Quays★. – The quays along the left bank offer the best **views★** of Laval, a lovely site beside the tranquil Mayenne River canalized since the 19C. From the Pont Aristide-Briand, you can see the Pont Vieux and the tiered arrangement of the old town dominated by the dark mass of the Old Castle and the lighter tones of the New Castle.

As you stand on the once fortified **Pont Vieux**, a 13C hump-backed bridge, the old town reveals itself: half timbered houses with slate roofs bordering narrow streets and the Old Castle, which is crowned with hoardings and pierced by large Renaissance windows.

Along the Quai Paul Boudet the last remaining **washing houses** are docked. They appeared along the river during the 1880's (the last one ceased activity in 1960). *One of these washing houses the* St-Julien *is open to the public during temporary expositions.*

Château★. – *Guided tours 15 June to 15 September every 1/2 hour, 9am to 5pm ; the rest of the year 2, 3, 4 and 5pm ; closed Mondays and holidays ; 3.30F.*

On the far side of the Place de la Trémoille is the Renaissance façade of the New Castle or **Nouveau Château** ; in the 16C it became the residence of the Counts of Laval. Enlarged in the 19C it houses the Law Courts (Palais de Justice).

Vieux Château★ (Old Castle). – To the right of the Law Courts stands the 17C gatehouse, with its pilasters and groovings, which adjoins an early 16C half timbered house. Pass through the gatehouse to the courtyard of the Old Castle, which is surrounded by ramparts, from the top of which are attractive **views★** of the old town. Overlooking the Mayenne, on the terrace to the left of the castle is a statue of Beatrix de Gavre, Baroness of Laval during the 14C, who helped develop the manufacturing of linen at that time.

The 12C crypt and keep are the oldest parts of the castle, as the castle dates essentially from the 13 and 15C with modifications in the 16C : addition of white tufa bays and dormer windows, the latter ornamented with sculptured Italian motifs.

The Romanesque **crypt** has groined vaulting which springs from finely carved capitals *(temporarily closed ; access via staircase near the castle's entrance).*

The **keep**, once separated from the courtyard by a ditch, became part of the castle, when the two castle wings were connected. It has kept its original roofs and hoarding (best seen from the river) which is an overhanging gallery protected by boarding in front, projecting from the surface of the wall, and which enabled the defenders to protect the foot of the wall as well as the bridge.

Its **timber roof★★** built in around 1100 is unique in France. It looks like the spokes of a wheel. The central pivot (90 cm-35 ins in diameter) is supported by great oak beams solidly maintained, they extend outside to form the hoardings. *(For more details on timberwork see p 153.)*

Museum of Naïve Paintings★. – *Open 10am to noon and 2 to 6pm ; closed Mondays and holidays ; combined ticket château and museum : 3.30F.* The castle houses an interesting collection of naïve paintings grouped around a canvas and other mementoes by Le Douanier Rousseau. The collection includes 400 works of art (French, Yugoslav, Brazilian, German, etc.) exhibited on a rotating basis.

On the first floor, the Great Hall, 32 m - 105 ft long, with its wooden roof, contains several frescoes and sculpture including the 15C tombs of Guy XII of Laval, his wife and his mother *(the hall is only open during temporary exhibitions).*

Old Town★ (Vieille Ville). – Start from the Place de la Trémoille, the name of the last lords of Laval ; in front of the castle take Rue des Orfèvres lined by fine 16C houses with overhanging upper storeys and 18C *hôtels.* At the junction with the Grande-Rue stands the Renaissance mansion of the Master of the Royal Hunt *(Grand Veneur).*

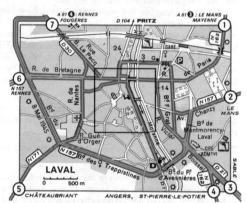

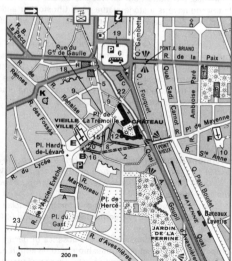

Déportés (R. des)	5	Orfèvres (R. des)	12
Gaulle (R. Gén. de)		Paradis (R. de)	14
Paix (R. de la)		Pin-Doré (R. du)	15
		Serruriers (R. des)	16
Chapelle (R. de)	2	Souchu-Servinière (R.)	18
Crossardière (R.)	3	Strasbourg (R. de)	19
Foch (Square Mar.)	6	Trinité (R.)	20
Grande-Rue	8	Val-de-Mayenne (R.)	22
Jeu-de-Paume (R.)	9	Vaufleury (R.)	23
Le Doyen (Pl. G.)	10	Vieux-St-Louis (R.)	24

The main street of the mediaeval town, Grande-Rue, goes down to the Mayenne lined alternately by half timbered dwellings with overhangs or stone built houses with Renaissance decoration. Bear right on the Rue de Chapelle, which climbs between mediaeval and Renaissance houses : at the top, note in a niche to the right, the statue of St René. You reach the 14C **Porte Beucheresse (B)** which is flanked by two round machicolated towers and was formerly part of Laval's perimeter wall. Henri Rousseau was born in the right hand tower, where his father exercised the trade of tinsmith.

Cross the Place Hardy-de-Lévaré and enter the **cathedral (E** – *closed noon to 2pm – 6pm Sundays)*. The structure has been greatly altered over the centuries. Its nave and transept are covered with Angevin vaulting *(p 21)*. Early 17C Aubusson tapestries portray the story of Judith and Holofernes in six hangings.

In front of the chancel, against the left pillar note the remarkable triptych by the 16C Antwerp Mannerist school which depicts the martyrdom of John the Evangelist when closed, and three scenes of John the Baptist's life when open.

On leaving the cathedral go around the east end to the northeast doorway adorned with 17C terracotta statues.

Take the Rue de la Trinité ; one of the houses along this street is decorated with statues of the Virgin and Saints (note St Christopher) ; by the Rue du Pin-Doré return to the Place de la Trémoille.

Gardens★ (Jardin de la Perrine). – These terraced gardens offer very good views of the Mayenne, the lower town and the keep.

Lakes, a rose garden and waterfalls alternate with lawns, flowerbeds and many fine trees : palms, limes, chestnuts, Lebanese cedars and larches.

Basilica of Notre-Dame-d'Avénières (D). – It is from the Pont d'Avénières that the Romanesque **chevet★** of this 12C basilica is best appreciated : note the volume of the chancel and ambulatory and the ring of five apsidal chapels.

The sanctuary is crowned by a lovely spire in the Gothic-Renaissance style, designed in 1538 and rebuilt in 1871. Although this basilica, dedicated to Our Lady, was reconstructed in the 19C, the unity of style has not been altered.

Inside, the sombre but welcoming atmosphere, often found in Romanesque churches, envelops the visitor.

On either side of the entrance are two enormous polychrome wooden statues representing Christ (15C) and St Christopher carrying the Infant Jesus (16C).

In the fine Romanesque chancel with a three storey elevation note the carved capitals, a 15C polychrome wooden statue of Christ and at the triforium level the miraculous statue of Our Lady. The modern stained glass is by Max Ingrand. In the axial chapel there is a terracotta *Pietà* of Breton origin.

St-Vénérand (F). – This church with one principal and four collateral naves is entered through a Flamboyant doorway with a 17C terracotta Virgin and pedimented canopy with Renaissance motifs. *The nave is closed due to restoration.*

Tower (Tour Renaise – K). – This 15C round tower with machicolations was formerly part of the city wall.

Pritz Church. – *2 km - 1 mile to the north. Leave Laval by the Rue du Vieux-St-Louis and the D 104.* This church stands in a garden on the right of the road. Dating from approximately the year 1000, the modest edifice was altered and enlarged during the Romanesque period. To the left of the nave is a stone statue of St Christopher and a 17C terracotta of Christ bearing the Cross. The Renaissance wooden chancel railing was restored in 1776. The retable dates from 1677.

The church's main feature is the series of **mural paintings**. Above the chancel fine 11C frescoes represent scenes from the life of the Virgin : Visitation, Nursing Virgin (the only known example of the Romanesque period), Nativity ; at the triumphal arch a 13C Calendar of the Months ; in the chancel the Old Men of the Apocalypse ; at the double arch three Signs of the Zodiac ; in the nave a Virgin and Child, the Bringing of the Good News to the Shepherds (14C), and a 15C St Christopher partly effaced by a 16C one.

EXCURSION

Clermont Abbey (or Clairmont). – *15 km - 9 miles to the northwest. Leave Laval by ⑥ the N 157, and at La Chapelle-du-Chêne turn right into the D 115. Michelin map 🆖🆖 north of fold 9.*

Open 1 May to 30 September, 8am to 8pm ; 1 March to 30 April, 9am to 7pm ; the rest of the year 9am to 5pm ; 10F.

Set in pastoral surroundings this former Cistercian abbey, belonging to the Cluniac order, was founded in 1152 by St Bernard with the support of Guy V, Count of Laval. Restoration work is under way.

Built on the Cistercian plan the absence of decoration and the emphasis on harmonious proportions and exact craftsmanship are to be admired.

At the entrance a 17C edifice with dormer windows is where the Fathers resided ; skirt this wing to the right, around the flat east end to the soberly decorated façade with its Romanesque porch. The side aisles were destroyed and yet the severe elegance of the edifice remains. It is the purity of execution and luminosity which prevail. Note the three storey chancel with the unusual placement of the bays ; as well as the three transept chapels on either side of the chancel.

In the west wing, reserved to the laymen, is the cellar covered with groined vaulting springing from four central pillars and the refectory with its three pillars.

Michelin map 64 fold 5 − *Local map p 99* − Pop 256

The romantic ruins of this feudal fortress present a jagged silhouette towering high above the village on a rocky promontory. Stronghold of the counts of Vendôme in the Middle Ages, its strategic importance greatly increased as early as the 12C when the area became borderland country between the kingdoms of the Capetians and Angevins. The fortress was dismantled on the orders of Henri IV during the Wars of Religion.

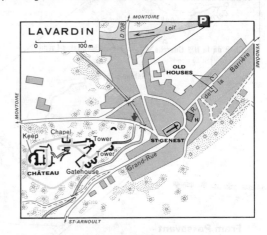

■ SIGHTS

Château★. − *Ruins open during spring and summer school holidays, 9am to noon and 2 to 7pm; time: 3/4 hour; 8F. Restoration work in progress.*

The track running along the south side of the fortress offers good views of the gatehouse and keep.

Of the three sets of ramparts originally surrounding this fortress, the outer one was defended by a small 14C gatehouse. An underground passage led below the second wall, passing the storerooms dug out of the living rock. Incorporated into the second rampart was a 15C building with a fine staircase and prismatic vaulting. Below the stairs is an interesting vaulted room. The third rampart or revetment wall defended the 11C rectangular **keep** 26 m - 85 ft high, to which towers were added in the 12C. A doorway adorned with the Bourbon-Vendôme blazon gives access to the staircase turret now in a ruinous state.

St-Genest. − *If closed apply to Mr. Perrault at the town hall.* The church, preceded by a square belfry porch, was built in an archaic Romanesque style. The bas-reliefs of the apse represent the Signs of the Zodiac.

Interior. − The vessel is divided into three by square piers with delicately carved early 12C imposts. A triumphal arch gives access to the chancel, terminated by an oven vaulted apse, where curious Romanesque pillars support roughly hewn capitals. Framing the windows of the north aisle are delightful twisted Romanesque colonnettes *(see illustration)*.

The numerous **mural paintings** date from the 12 to 16C. The oldest, most stylized and majestic ones are on the pillar at the entrance to the left apsidal chapel: Baptism of Christ and a Tree of Jesse.

The well conserved group in the chancel and apse shows scenes from the Passion: to the right the Feet Washing, to the left Christ in Majesty surrounded by the symbols of the Evangelists.

In the right apsidal chapel note a St Christopher and Last Judgement (15C) where Paradise and Hell are colourfully portrayed. On the pillars in the nave and side aisles are 16C figures of saints venerated locally. Note the Martyrdom of St Margaret on the wall of the south aisle and the Crucifixion of St Peter on a pillar on the north side of the nave.

Old houses. − One is 15C and half timbered while the other is Renaissance with an overhanging oratory, pilastered, mullioned dormer windows and a loggia overlooking the courtyard.

*(After photo:
Éd. du Zodiaque)*

St-Genest Church
Romanesque colonnette

The Green Guides (picturesque scenery, buildings and scenic routes)
Austria - Canada - England: The West Country - Germany - Italy - London - New England -
New York City - Portugal - Spain - Switzerland and 7 guides on France

LAYON Valley

Michelin map 67 folds 6 and 7

The Layon, canalized under Louis XVI, follows the junction between the Mauges schists *(p 115)* and the Saumur limestone escarpments, except between Beaulieu and St-Aubin where the river has traversed the ancient massif. In the clear air, the deeply incised meanders sometimes create an impression of a hilly terrain. The region has a certain attraction with its vineyards, its crops sometimes interspersed with fruit trees (walnut, peach, plum, etc.), its hillsides crowned with windmills, its wine growers' villages with their cemeteries planted with cypresses.

The "Coteaux du Layon". − The delicious fruity, liqueur like white wines of the Layon vineyards are produced by the *chenin* often known as *pineau* variety of vine. They are harvested in late September when the grapes begin to be covered with a mould known as *pourriture noble.*

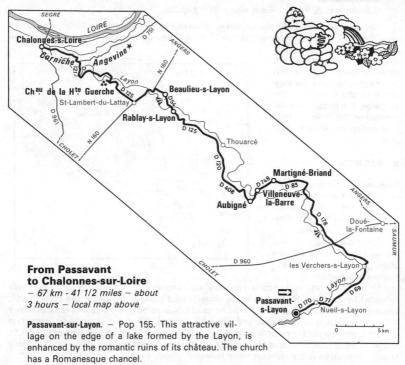

From Passavant
to Chalonnes-sur-Loire
*— 67 km - 41 1/2 miles — about
3 hours — local map above*

Passavant-sur-Layon. — Pop 155. This attractive village on the edge of a lake formed by the Layon, is enhanced by the romantic ruins of its château. The church has a Romanesque chancel.

Take the D 170 to Neuil-sur-Layon, turn right after the church into the D 77 ; after the bridge over the Layon bear left onto the D 69 towards Doué-la-Fontaine.

The landscape at this point is still typical of the Poitou with its hedgerows, sunken paths and farmsteads with Roman tiles. The vineyards are grouped on the well exposed slopes and at Neuil slate roofing appears.

On the other side of Les Verchers bear left onto the D 178 towards Concourson.
Crossing fertile countryside, the road, overlooking the Layon, offers an extensive view of the valley after Concourson.

Continue on the D 178, on the road to Brigne, go through St-Georges, further on bear left onto the D 83 to Martigné-Briand.

Martigné-Briand. — Pop 1 835. This wine growers' village clusters round its ruined château, burnt during the struggles between the Blues and the Whites *(p 115)*.

Leave Martigné on the road to Aubigné (D 748) ; bear right on the road to Villeneuve-la-Barre.

Villeneuve-la-Barre. — Cross this picturesque village, gaily decorated with flowers to the **Benedictine monastery**, a handsome edifice with a courtyard. The rather austere chapel, in a former barn, has white stained glass windows with abstract motifs.

Aubigné. — Pop 258. This picturesque village has preserved several elegant town houses. Near the church stands an old fortified gateway, the remains of the portcullis and drawbridge can be seen.

Leave Aubigné on the road to Faveraye-Mâchelles (D 408) and turn right on the D 120 which crosses the village. Cross the D 24 ; continue on the D 125 to Rablay-sur-Layon.

Rablay-sur-Layon. — Pop 592. This well sheltered attractive wine growers' village has, in its Grande Rue, a brick and half timbered house with an overhanging upper storey.

Take the D 54 to Beaulieu. This road crosses the Layon, then skirts a vine covered cirque ; from the plateau there is an extensive view of the valley.

Beaulieu-sur-Layon. — Pop 995. This wine grower's village *(panoramic table)* in the midst of the Layon vineyards has attractive mansard roofed houses including the town hall. As you leave Beaulieu to the west by the D 55, to the right in a low building is a **Caveau du Vin** with a collection of old Angevin wine bottles and glasses. *Open 9am to 7pm.*

Take the N 160 towards Chemillé. The route descends into the valley with its steep sides riddled with caves and quarries. The bridge over the Layon offers an attractive view of the river and a ruined mediaeval bridge. *At St-Lambert-du-Lattay bear right on the D 125 to St-Aubin-de-Laigné.* This scenic road, winding and hilly, runs amidst the vineyards which produce the *Quart de Chaume* wine.

Before St-Aubin turn left into the D 106 and soon after turn right.

Château de la Haute-Guerche. — *Open 1 July to 31 August 9am to noon and 2 to 7pm.* This romantic ruin was built during the reign of Charles VII and burnt down at the time of the Vendéen War *(p 115)*. There is a wide view of the environs.

Take the D 125 in the direction of Chaudefonds. Turn right into D 121 which leads to Ardenay on the Angevin corniche road.

Angevin Corniche Road★. — *Description p 104.*

Chalonnes-sur-Loire. — *Description p 105.*

Michelin map 🔲 fold 16 – Pop 7019 – *Facilities pp 36-37*

This charming town lies in a pleasant setting on the banks of the Indre. Dominated by its mediaeval city, heavily fortified on a rocky spur, it is a gem of great historical and architectural interest.

HISTORICAL NOTES

A fortress and prison. – The naturally strong position of Loches was used from the earliest times. A great feudal family, the counts of Anjou *(p 42)* established a large entrenched camp on it. After the death of Henry II, while Richard Lionheart was in captivity in Durnstein following his return from the Third Crusade, Philippe-Auguste intrigued with John Lackland (England's Bad King John), Richard's brother, and obtained possession of Loches. The impetuous Richard, soon after he was ransomed hastened to the spot and recaptured the castle by a surprise attack in three hours. Ten years later, in 1205, Philippe-Auguste had his revenge, but less brilliantly : his siege lasted a year. Loches then became the great French State prison and the kings of France tried to make it impregnable.

Agnès Sorel. – In the 15C a woman's smile brightens the dark history of the castle. Agnès Sorel, the "Lady of Beauty" *(1)* and favourite of Charles VII came to live at Loches. She deserted the court of Chinon, where the Dauphin – the future Louis XI – had made things difficult for her.

The King picked her out from among the Queen's maids of honour. They were an ill assorted couple : Agnès enchanting and the King ill favoured. The favourite had a great influence on Charles VII. Her advice was often good, but her taste for luxury, accompanied by her great generosity, was a heavy burden on the finances of the kingdom. In order to be buried in the collegiate church, Agnès loaded the chapter with gifts. After her death the canons were of the opinion that the presence of a notorious sinner in the sacred precincts was unedifying. They asked Louis XI to remove her remains to the castle. The old fox agreed, but on condition that the gifts took the same road. At this the scruples of the chapter promptly evaporated.

Louis XI's cages (end of 15C). – When inspecting the castle the visitor will see dungeons and barred cells, but he will not find the cages in which Louis XI liked to confine his prisoners as these "monuments to tyranny" were destroyed by the inhabitants of Loches in 1790.

The cages were made of wooden trelliswork, covered with iron. The most comfortable measured 2 m - 6 1/2 ft on all sides. But there was a smaller model, in which the prisoner could only lie or sit. It is said that the prisoner never came out alive ; and yet the said inventor of the cage, the **Cardinal La Balue** (1421-91) withstood eleven years imprisonment (1469-80) before being freed. The son of a Poitiers tailor he became counsellor to Louis XI. He betrayed his master to Charles the Bold, the Duke of Burgundy but was unmasked and imprisoned. These cages are believed to have been used only at night or to transport the prisoner.

■ THE MEDIAEVAL CITY★★ (La cité médiévale) *time : 2 hours*

There is a tour of the mediaeval city starting at 9pm every evening from the Tourist Centre from 1 July to 15 September ; 12F.

Leave the car on the Mail de la Poterie.

Porte Royale★ and the museums (M). – The 13C gateway, Porte Royale, massive and powerfully fortified, now stands flanked by two 15C towers. The slots through which the drawbridge chains ran and the machicolations can still be seen.

Go past the Porte Royale to the Rue Lansyer on the left. A few yards further on are the entrances to the Lansyer and Folklore Museums. Open 9 to 11.45am and 2 to 6pm (5pm March and October, 4pm 1 November to 28 February) ; closed Fridays ; 5.50F.

The **Lansyer Museum** contains works by the local landscape painter Lansyer (1835-93). There are also curios from the Far East.

A visit to the **Folklore Museum** (Musée du Terroir) enables you to see inside the Porte Royale. There is a fine view of Loches.

St-Ours★. – This former collegiate church is distinguished by two octagonal pyramids which rise between its towers ; these are formed by the vaulting over the nave.

The porch with vaulting in the Angevin style *(p 21)* shelters a richly decorated Romanesque doorway. A Gallo-Roman altar is used as a stoup.

In the nave you will see the famous pyramid vaulting, known as *dubes,* which was erected in the 12C by the Prior, Thomas Pactius.

(After photo : Éd. du Zodiaque)

St-Ours — From the château courtyard

(1) "Beauty" here had a double meaning. Agnès was very pretty and also owned a château at Beauté (now Nogent-sur-Marne, near Paris).

Château★★. – *Guided tours 9am to noon and 2 to 6pm (5pm 1 October to 14 March); open all day July and August; closed Wednesday out of season and December and January; combined ticket for château and keep : 10F.*

Tour Agnès Sorel. – This 13C tower has been known since the 16C as the ''Beautiful Agnès Tower''.

Logis Royaux (Royal Residence). – From the castle terrace, overlooking a fine view of Loches and the Indre Valley, one sees that the building is in two parts which were erected at different periods. The Vieux Logis (14C) the older, taller building is heavily fortified with four turrets linked by a watchpath at the base of the roof. It was enlarged under Charles VIII and Louis XII by the addition of the more recent Nouveau Logis, in the manner and style of the Renaissance.

Enter the **Vieux Logis** by the room known as Charles VII's ante-chamber where a copy of the manuscript of the proceedings of Joan of Arc's trial (1431) is on display. On the wall hang a 16C tapestry narrating an allegorical depiction of music as well as a portrait of Charles VII, a copy of the painting by Jean Fouquet. Then enter the great hall with the large fireplace where on 3 and 5 June 1429 Joan of Arc came to urge Charles VII to go to Reims. She was accompanied at the time by Robert Le Masson, Dunois *(p 64)* and Gilles de Rais *(p 169)*. Lovely tapestries *(Verdures and Oudenaarde)* adorn the walls.

The **recumbent figure of Agnès Sorel★**, placed in the Charles VIII Room, attracts the attention of the visitor. During the Revolution, soldiers of the Indre battalions, whose historical knowledge was not equal to their Revolutionary zeal, took the favourite of Charles VII for a saint, chopped up her statue, desecrated her grave and scattered her remains. The alabaster monument was restored in Paris under the Empire and again on the occasion of its transfer to the Nouveau Logis. Agnès is shown recumbent, with two angels supporting her lovely head and two lambs lying at her feet. In the same room you will see the portrait by Fouquet of the Virgin, whose face is that of the beautiful Agnès, amidst red and blue angels (the original is in Antwerp).

Another room contains an interesting **triptych★** from the school of Jean Fouquet (15C), which originally came from St-Antoine church, with panels evoking the Crucifixion, Carrying of the Cross and Deposition. The tour ends in Anne of Brittany's oratory, a tiny room finely worked and decorated with the ermine of Brittany and the girdle of St Francis *(p 18)*. The canopy opposite the altar originally surmounted the royal pew and the only door was the one to the right of the altar.

Return to the Church of St-Ours and by way of the Rue Thomas-Pactius, make for the Mail du Donjon. Turn round, after a bend to the right, to get a view of the church.

Keep★★ (Donjon). – *Open 9.30am to 12.30pm and 2.30 to 6.30pm (5.30pm 1 October to 14 March); all day July and August; closed January, December and Wednesdays out of season ; combined ticket keep and château : 10F.*

The keep was built in the 11C by Foulques Nerra to defend the fortified town from the south, its only vulnerable side. It is a powerful square construction which, together with the towers Ronde and Martelet, forms an imposing fortified group.

On the outside can still be seen the putlog holes in which the timbers supporting the hoardings rested. To the left of the entrance in Philippe de Commines's dungeon, is an iron collar weighing 16 kg - 35 lb.

The floors of the three storeys have vanished but three sets of fireplaces and windows can still be seen on the walls. A staircase of 157 steps enables you to climb to the top of the keep from which there is a fine view.

Tour Ronde (F). – This round tower, which like the Martelet was built in the 15C to complete the fortifications where they formed part of the main wall of the castle, the keep and of the town, was, in fact, another keep.

Known as the Louis XI Tower, the round tower contains four rooms, one above the other. Over the torture chamber is a vaulted cell in which Cardinal La Balue is said to have been imprisoned.

Martelet (L). – The most impressive dungeons, occupying several floors below ground, are to be found in this building. The first was that of **Ludovico Sforza** the Moor, Duke of Milan, who was taken prisoner by Louis XII. For eight years (1500-08) at Loches, he paid for his trickeries and treacheries. On the day of his release the

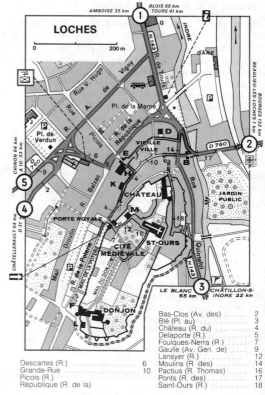

LOCHES

0   200 m

Bas-Clos (Av. des)	2
Blé (Pl. au)	3
Château (R. du)	4
Delaporte (R.)	5
Foulques-Nerra (R.)	7
Gaulle (Av. Gén. de)	9
Lansyer (R.)	12
Moulins (R. des)	14
Pactius (R. Thomas)	16
Ponts (R. des)	17
Saint-Ours (R.)	18

Descartes (R.)	6
Grande-Rue	10
Picois (R.)	
République (R. de la)	

sunlight was so bright and the excitement of freedom so great that he fell dead. Ludovico, who was Leonardo da Vinci's patron, covered the walls of his prison with paintings and inscriptions. Next to the stars, cannons and helmets, may be seen a phrase, hardly surprising in the circumstances : *celui qui n'est pas contan* (he who is not content).

Below, lit by a solitary ray of light, is the dungeon where the Bishops of Autun and Le Puy, both implicated in the Constable of France or Charles, Duke of Bourbon's change of allegiance to the Emperor Charles V, found leisure to hollow out of the wall a small altar and a symbolic Stations of the Cross. In another cell was interned the Count of St-Vallier, father of Diane de Poitiers *(p 70)*. He was sentenced to death and informed of his reprieve − on the intervention of his daughter − only when on the scaffold.

On the same underground level as the dungeons, galleries open off to quarries, which in the 13C, provided stone for the small fortified covered passageways flanking the ramparts.

Tourists who are pressed for time should turn right on leaving the Martelet to reach the Mail de la Poterie and their cars. For those with another 1/2 hour to spare, we would highly recommend a walk round the outside of the ramparts.

Walk round the outside of the ramparts and the old town★. − *Turn left on coming out of the Martelet.*

This walk *(3/4 hour on foot)* shows one that this mediaeval town was in fact an entrenched camp, complete with all its own defences. The perimeter wall is more than 1 km - 3/4 mile long and is pierced by only two gateways. Note first the three spur towers built in the 13C in front of the keep, then walk inside the moat to the Rue Quintefol before coming up onto the ramparts : good view of St-Ours's east end. Here you are in the second perimeter wall where the Rue St-Ours twists around picturesque old houses. Once out of the perimeter wall take one of the narrow pedestrian streets, across the way, which leads to the late 15C **Porte des Cordeliers** (**B**), which, with the Porte Picois *(see below)* are the only two remaining gates of the town's original four. It was the main gate of the city and the road to Spain passed by it. Go through the gate to see its riverside façade with machicolations and flanked by bartizans. On to the 16C **Tour St-Antoine** (**D**) one of the rare belfries in central France ; then to the 15C **Porte Picois** (**E**) also with machicolations ; it is adjacent to the **town hall★** (**H**) a dignified Renaissance building adorned with flowered balconies. Continue to the **Maison de la Chancellerie** (**K**) of the Henri II period (mid 16C), embellished with fluted columns, pilasters and wrought-iron balconies.

Continue on the Rue du Château to the Porte Royale and the Mail de la Poterie.

■ ADDITIONAL SIGHT

Beaulieu-lès-Loches. − Pop 1 769. *1 km - 3/4 mile by ② on the plan.*

This old village contains the ruins of a famous abbey founded in 1004 by Foulques Nerra *(p 42)*, who was buried there by his wish. The **abbey church** *(to visit apply to Mme Allibrand, 2 Rue Foulques Nerra ; in summer apply at the town hall)* is dominated by a majestic, square Romanesque tower which is surmounted by an octagonal spire. The arms of the transept also date from the Romanesque period but the nave and the chancel were rebuilt in the 15C following their destruction by the English in 1412. At the back of the choir traces of the original Romanesque apse can still be seen. Among the church's works of art note the 15C *Pietà*, the 18C terracotta statues in the chancel and, in the sacristy, the 17C portraits and a bas-relief of the Last Supper.

A curious outdoor pulpit stands in the adjoining abbot's lodging on the site of the old cloisters, to the right of the church.

The former **Church of St-Laurent** still has three fine aisles with domical Angevin vaulting and a beautiful Romanesque tower.

EXCURSION

Indre Valley★. − Michelin maps 64 folds 15 and 16 and 68 fold 6 − *27 km - 16 miles northwest by ①, the N 143 and D 17 − about 1 hour.*

From Chambourg-sur-Indre to Esvres the D 17 follows a scenic stretch along the Indre's valley floor.

Azay-sur-Indre. − Pop 282. Azay stands in a pleasant site at the confluence of the Indre and the Indrois *(p 87)*. Adjoining is the park of the château that once belonged to La Fayette.

Reignac. − Pop 855. Visible from the bridge over the Indre (on the road to Cigogné), in a pastoral setting, is the Reignac windmill.

Continue along the D 17.

Cormery. − Pop 1 169. This picturesque town is renowned for its macaroons. Near its bridge, hidden amidst weeping willows is a windmill ; downstream is an old washing house.

The former Benedictine abbey was founded in 791 and destroyed in 1791. The massive 11C belfry porch, Tour St-Paul, in ruins, marked the entrance to the church. Note the decorative motifs and Romanesque bas-reliefs on its façade. At the foot of the tower the prior's lodging has an elegant staircase turret ; on the north side the arches of the former refectory (13C) can be seen. The graceful Gothic Abbot's chapel (15C) is all that remains of the church ; the turreted Abbot's lodging (15C) communicated with the chapel.

The church of **Notre-Dame-du-Fougeray** has elements which are typical of the Poitou region ; a large apse with three apsidal chapels, storiated brackets, a frieze and a dome on pendentives over the transept crossing. In the cemetery there is an altar and 12C lantern of the dead (or Hosanna cross).

Cross the Indre and follow the N 143 towards Tours for 1 km - 1/2 mile then bear left on the D 17.

The trip ends at Esvres, located in lovely surroundings.

Michelin maps **60** and 17 and **64** folds 2 to 7

Placid and slow the Loir from L'Ile-de-France to Anjou flows through a countryside more deeply rural than its mother river the Loire. Green meadow landscapes, attractive towns and charming villages all go to epitomize the saying *La Douce France* (Gentle France).

Over 350 km - 218 miles from its source to its confluence with the Sarthe, the meanders of this slow flowing river have steep banks on the outside of its bends. Riddled with caves or troglodyte dwellings, many have been inhabited since Neolithic times.

Lines of trembling poplars, alders and silver willows follow the river's course through chalky terrain; lush green meadows, orchards and gardens alternate along the banks, while vineyards cling to the hill slopes.

Originally navigable up to Château-du-Loir, few boats pass except for the flat bottomed ones of the fishermen in search of a good catch of trout, gudgeon, perch, pike and eel.

During the Middle Ages the pilgrims on the land route to Santiago de Compostela *(see Michelin Green Guide to Spain)* followed the valley before joining Tours. Traces of their religious ardour remain along the way : priories, commanderies, churches and chapels often decorated with frescoes on characteristic light backgrounds.

1 From Bonneval to Vendôme – *77 km - 47 miles – allow one day – local map below*

For the most part this itinerary follows the signposted tourist route (Route touristique de la Vallée du Loir).

Leave Bonneval *(p 59)* by the D 144 which affords some far reaching views. On arriving at **Conie**, cross the river of the same name in a lovely location. The route continues through **Moléans**, dominated by its 17C château. There are picturesque views of the tranquil Loir as the road continues to **St-Christophe** from where you pick up the D 361 to Marboué.

Marboué. – Pop 1017. Site of a Gallo-Roman settlement this village has a good spot for river bathing, and a crocketed spire towering above its 15C belfry porch.

Leave Marboué on the N 10 and take the direction of Châteaudun.

Châteaudun. – *Description p 64.*

Leave Châteaudun by ⑤ (D 927) then bear left on the D 111⁴ towards Cloyes.

Montigny-le-Gannelon. – Pop 334. Between the cliff face with its troglodyte dwellings and the Loir, this once fortified stronghold retains a 12C gateway on the plateau side. The 15C brick and stone château, restored in the 19C, overlooks the Loir.

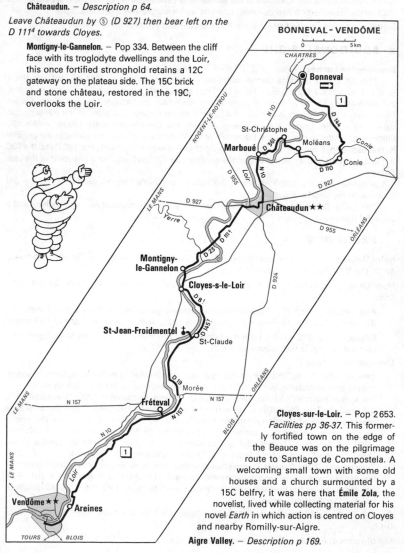

BONNEVAL - VENDÔME

Cloyes-sur-le-Loir. – Pop 2 653. *Facilities pp 36-37.* This formerly fortified town on the edge of the Beauce was on the pilgrimage route to Santiago de Compostela. A welcoming small town with some old houses and a church surmounted by a 15C belfry, it was here that **Émile Zola**, the novelist, lived while collecting material for his novel *Earth* in which action is centred on Cloyes and nearby Romilly-sur-Aigre.

Aigre Valley. – *Description p 169.*

From Cloyes follow the D 8 (eastwards) then follow the D 8¹ to Bouches-d'Aigre. This picturesque stretch of road the D 145⁷ follows the Loir and goes through **St-Claude** before arriving at the bridge of St-Jean-Froidmentel.

St-Jean-Froidmentel. – Pop 418. The village on the far bank has a church with an attractive Gothic-Renaissance doorway.

Return to the left bank. The road at this point runs very close to the river, passing on the way various quarries and mills. Note in particular the mill, Moulin St-Jean, which is still operated with water power. Between Morée and Fréteval, there is a succession of fishermen's huts and charming little houses.

Fréteval. – Pop 909. Known for its fishing, Fréteval on the far bank is dominated by a ruined feudal **fortress** *(access : 1/4 hour on foot Rtn)* perched on a rocky spur on the near bank. The forest on the west bank is known as the Forêt de Fréteval.

Beyond Fréteval the houses cling to the slopes to avoid the river in spate. Soon the signposted itinerary (Route touristique) strays from the river only to unveil the charm of this valley with its elegant houses and lovely little churches.

Areines – *Description p 166.*

Arrive in Vendôme (p 164) by ②.

② **From Vendôme to La Chartre** – *78 km - 49 miles – allow one day – local map p 99*

Leave Vendôme (p 164) by ⑥, D 957, bear left on the D 5 towards Villiers and Savigny-sur-Braye.
The road drives through vineyards which produce the rosé de Vendôme : wine cooperatives.

Villiers-sur-Loir. – Pop 1001. Clinging to the hillside above the vineyards this village looks across to the Château de Rochambeau. There are 16C mural paintings in the church *(open 9.30am to 5pm)* : portrayed on the north wall are St Christopher *(p 26)* carrying the Infant Jesus and the Legend of the Three Living and the Three Dead *(p 26).* 15C choir stalls.

Take the road to Thoré and bear left immediately after the bridge over the Loir.

Rochambeau. – The route, crossing this picturesque village with its troglodyte houses, leads to the Château de Rochambeau, the birthplace of General Rochambeau (1725-1807) the commander of the French forces in the American War of Independence. He is buried at nearby Thoré.

Return to the north bank and bear left on the D 5.

Le Gué-du-Loir. – Standing at the confluence of the Boulon with the Loir, this hamlet is surrounded by lush prairies. At the beginning of the D 5 via Savigny skirt the curtain wall, with its round turrets, of the **Bonaventure Manor.** It belonged to Antoine de Bourbon-Vendôme, father of the future Henri IV and later to the poet **Alfred de Musset's** family.

Continue along the D 5 towards Savigny, take the second road to the right (C 13) at a wayside cross. Through a wooded valley the road leads to **Mazangé**, its houses grouped round its charming church with its Gothic doorway.

Return to Gué-du-Loir ; bear right on the D 24 to Montoire. The road cuts a large bend in the Loir, where the river has cleared the cliff face enabling the inhabitants of Asnières to build troglodyte dwellings.

Bear right on the D 82 to Lunay.

Lunay. – Pop 1 207. The main square is bordered by several old houses. The Church of St-Martin, Flamboyant in style, has an attractive doorway with finely sculptured splayings.

Return to the D 24.

Les Roches-l'Évêque. – Pop 256. This once fortified village is well known for its troglodyte dwellings which are often decorated with lilac and wistaria.

Follow the signposted tourist road crossing the Loir ; on arriving at St-Rimay turn right to Lavardin.

Lavardin★ – *Description p 91.*

At the church's east end take the small picturesque road along the river's south bank.

Montoire-sur-le-Loir – *Description p 120.*

Leave Montoire by the D 917 towards Château-du-Loir ; the silhouette of Troo's church stands out clearly.

Troo★ – *Description p 162.*

Continue along the D 917 towards Songé, then follow the signposted tourist road towards Artins.

Vieux-Bourg d'Artins. – Situated on the banks of the Loir, the village church has retained its Romanesque walls pierced with Flamboyant windows and a pointed arched doorway. *To visit apply to Mr Mercier at Antins.*

9 km - 2 miles beyond Artins turn right into the road signposted L'Isle Verte and after 100 m turn left to pass in front of the Château du Pin. From the bridge opposite the castle there is a view upstream of the **L'Isle Verte** at the confluence of the Braye and the Loir. It was Ronsard's wish to be buried here.

Couture-sur-Loir. – Pop 467. The church *(open 9am to 6pm, 1 May to 31 October)* has a Gothic chancel with Angevin vaulting. The chapel to the right of the chancel has 17C woodwork. The recumbent figures in the nave are those of Ronsard's parents.

The D 57 takes you to La Possonnière Manor.

La Possonnière Manor★. – *Description p 130.*

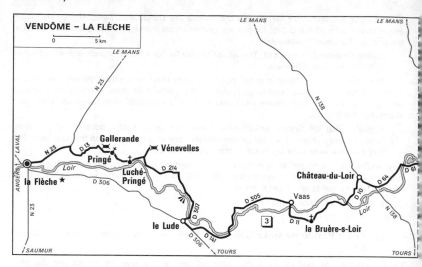

Return to Couture and leave the signposted tourist road for the D 57 crossing the Loir. Up ahead high on a wooded slope is the Château de la Flotte.

Along the north bank, bear left on to the D 305.

Poncé-sur-le-Loir. – *Description p 130.*

Continue along the D 305; at Ruillé bear left on to the D 80 which crosses the Loir. The road, quite pretty, especially from Tréhet, hugs the slope riddled with caves.

Villedieu-le-Château. – Pop 553. This attractive village in a pleasant **setting** is surrounded by slopes covered with vineyards and fruit trees and interspersed by troglodyte houses. The houses standing in colourful gardens, the ruined ramparts and belfry of the former priory of St-Jean compose a charming picture.

Return to Tréhet and pick up the signposted tourist road, on the left, on the D 10.

La Chartre-sur-le Loir. – Pop 1791. *Facilities pp 36-37.* Near the Jasnières estate which produces a sweet white wine which ages well but is little known, and the Bercé Forest.

③ **From La Chartre to La Flèche** – *74 km - 46 miles – about 1/2 day – local map above*

The countryside is peaceful from La Chartre to Marçon (well known wines). At Marçon bear right on the D 61 crossing the Loir plain, high on the slope is the Ste-Cécile Chapel. Bear left on the D 64 which follows the cliff face pierced here and there with troglodyte dwellings.

Château-du-Loir. – Pop 5891. This small town spreads itself out in the small valley of the Yre, a tributary of the Loir. The old part of the town clusters round the **Church of St-Guingalois.** The monumental terracotta *Pietà* standing at the far end of the chancel, is by Barthélemy de Mello (17C) who also did the St-Martin on Horseback in the chapel to the right. Note in the north transept two wooden panels representing a Nativity (15C) and a Resurrection (late 15C) by the Flemish Mannerist school. In the Romanesque crypt is a fine 16C wooden Christ Reviled.

In the gardens near the town hall stands the **keep**, all that remains of the former château; from the top there is a view of the town and neighbouring countryside. Underneath the keep are prisons.

Leave Château-du-Loir on the D 10 towards Château-la-Vallière. After the Nogent bridge turn right immediately into the C 2.

La Bruère. – Pop 279. The church has graceful Renaissance vaulting over the chancel and 16C stained glass windows. Note the statues of saints in the nave.

Leave La Bruère on the D 11 towards Vaas; bear right on to the D 30. On recrossing the river admire **Vaas** with its dam, church, houses, gardens and riverside washing houses, attractively situated on the north bank.

Take the D 305 on the left towards Le Lude. Meadows, nursery gardens and conifer forests succeed one another. Follow the tourist road, bearing left on the D 188 to La Chapelle-aux-Choux. Then drive along the river's verdant south bank to Le Lude, skirting its park.

Le Lude. – *Description p 108.*

Leave Le Lude to the northeast on the D 305, turn left immediately on the D 307 and left again towards Mansigné. A viewpoint opens up, before passing the Château de la Grifferie, on to the valley where fruit trees, asparagus, potatoes and maize grow. *Bear left onto the D 214 towards Luché-Pringé. After the bridge over the Aune, leave the signposted tourist road, bearing right on the D 13 to Vénevelles Manor.*

Vénevelles Manor. – This 15-17C building in a pleasant setting is surrounded by moats.

Return to the D 214.

Luché-Pringé. – Pop 1433. The church (13-16C) has a curious exterior: its gables and small figures representing musicians seated at the roof corners on either side of the façade. Above the entrance doorway is a bas-relief depicting St Martin on horseback. As

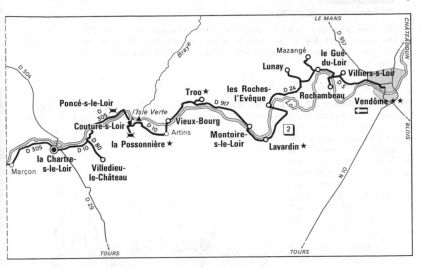

you enter on the right there is a remarkable *Pietà* (early 16C) carved in walnut wood. The large 13C chancel with its flat east end and Angevin vaulting springing from tall, slender columns is the pure Plantegenet style.

The house (13-15C) with the octagonal turret, in front of the church, is the priory.

Pringé. – The small Romanesque church is pierced by a doorway with splaying. Inside *(for the key apply to M. Herteloup, as you leave the village to the north)* are 16C mural paintings.

The D 13 skirts the moats which surround the park of the **Château du Gallerande**, where peacocks strut on lawns bordered by cedars, limes and oaks. From the railing of the courtyard one sees the northeast front, flanked by round machicolated towers. It includes a curious octagonal keep.

Make for La Flèche (p 80) by the N 23 and ①.

From La Flèche to Angers – *50 km - 31 miles – about 2 hours*

Leave La Flèche by ④, the N 23, and after 7 km - 4 miles reach Bazouges.

Bazouges-sur-le-Loir. – Pop 1 313. From the bridge there is a charming **view★** of Bazouges in its riverside setting.

The 15-16C **château** *(open Saturday before Easter to 30 June Saturdays 2 to 5pm also on Easter Monday, Ascension Day and Monday after Whitsun; 1 July to 15 September Tuesdays 10am to noon, Thursdays and Saturdays 2 to 5pm; 8F; on coming east out of Bazouges take the tree planted avenue)* still has a watermill intact. Two massive machicolated towers with pepperpot roofs flank the entrance. One of the towers contains the 15C chapel with elegant Angevin vaulting and several old statues. Above a guards' chamber is connected to the watchpath. Also included in the visit are the Guards' Room with its imposing stone fireplace, the 18C saloons and the French style park.

The **church** dates from the 12C.

Continue along the N 23 to St-Leonard where you cross the river to reach Durtal.

Durtal. – Pop 3 240. Attractively situated Durtal offers a choice of recreations: bathing, fishing, walking in the nearby **Forest of Chambiers** and a racecourse. The **château** *(courtyard open; views from the watchpath)*, now an old people's home, has 15 and 16C machicolated towers with pepperpot roofs and a six storey keep while the main wing and other buildings are typical of the Louis XIII style. The 15C **Porte Verron** is a vestige of the château's curtain wall. From the old **bridge** there is a good view of the village, its château and windmills.

Continue to follow the N 23 on the south bank of the Loir and 2 km - 1 mile beyond Bourgneuf take the local road to the right to reach the Château du Verger.

(After photo: René Jacques)

Durtal

Château du Verger. – An imposing gatehouse, outbuildings, wide moat and flint towers with white tufa ornamentations and machicolations recall the once stately dwelling which belonged to the Rohan family. Started in 1482 by **Pierre de Rohan**, Marshal of France, the château was to suffer an ignominious fate when in 1776 Cardinal Rohan, of the Diamond Necklace Affair ordered its destruction. Priceless works of art were dispersed.

Return to the N 23 which leaves the Loir to reach Angers (p 41).

The Loire, so often sung by the poets since Ronsard and Du Bellay, for long brought life to the countryside, but today no river traffic plies the great waterway. None the less, the river still gives its character to the region and the finest landscapes are those it adorns with its long vistas and graceful curves.

GEOGRAPHICAL NOTES

The Loire, a former tributary of the Seine. – The longest river in France – 1 020 km – 634 miles – rises at the foot of the peak, Gerbier-de-Jonc on the southern edge of the Massif Central, but only its middle course is treated in this guide.

Originally a tributary of the Seine, the Upper Loire was captured when an earth movement tilted the southwestern part of the Paris Basin causing the swing westward to a newly created arm of the Atlantic extending up to Blois.

(After engraving: photo Éd. Larousse, Paris)

The Loire at Saumur. — Gabarres and N.-D.-des-Ardilliers

A fickle river. – The Loire with its irregular and capricious régime is sometimes furious and sometimes indolent. In summer, only a few rivulets *(luisettes)* trickle between the sand or gravel banks *(grèves)*. In these conditions it has the appearance of a "sandy river", but in autumn, during the rains, or at the end of winter, when the snow melts, it is in spate and its swirling waters then run high. It sometimes bursts the dikes, known as *levées* or *turcies,* built to protect the countryside from floods. Many village walls bear the tragic dates of great floods : 1846, 1856, 1866 and 1910.

Shipping on the Loire. – Up to the mid 19C the Loire in spite of its whims – sandbanks, whirlpools, floods and tolls – was a much used means of communication. As early as the 14C navigation was organised by a guild of mariners centred on Orléans. In addition to merchandise – wood and coal from the Forez, pottery from Nevers, grain from the Beauce, wines from Touraine and Anjou – there was a great flow of passengers who preferred the river to the road. The journey from Orléans to Nantes by river took six days, and from ten to twenty for the return journey with a good wind. Coaches were transported on rafts. The river traffic comprised flat bottomed barges (scows or lighters) with large square sails. **Toues,** barges without rigging, still used today, transported hay and livestock ; **sapines** with a greater capacity and rudely made of fir planks, were destroyed at the end of the voyage ; **gabarres** were much larger vessels with sails up to 20 m - 66 ft high. The boats travelled in groups with a mother ship pulling two decreasingly smaller boats, one of which carried the bargee's cabin. The convoy was preceded by a wherry or punt to sound the river bed. The bargees had to be skilled on the upstream voyage to negotiate the bridges, especially the Ponts-de-Cé and at Beaugency where ropes from the bridge were used to guide the boats.

The "Unexplodables". – In 1832 the first steamboat service was started between Orléans and Nantes. It caused a sensation. Two days were enough for the journey, but there were accidents, for boilers exploded. Enthusiasm died down. The appearance of new steamboats nicknamed "unexplodables" restored confidence so much so that in 1843 more than 100 000 passengers were carried on the Loire and the Allier by the various steamboat companies which ran the services between Moulins and Nantes.

With the development of the railway, navigation on the Loire declined. In 1862 the last shipping company closed down.

■ VIEWS OF THE LOIRE

The itineraries described below link the sights of prime importance with the most picturesque stretches of road.

Certain sections of the route are beautiful on both banks of the river *(see the road sections outlined in green on the Michelin maps 🈳 and 🈳.*

On the **north bank,** the N 152 only offers rare glimpses, as far as Blois, of the Loire; and yet after Blois the road follows the embankment closely and lovely vistas succeed one another as far as the outskirts of Tours; between Tours and Angers the road continues along the river offering picturesque stretches of road.

On the **south bank,** the D 751 wanders slightly from the Loire. Nevertheless, scenic views may be enjoyed a couple of miles downstream from Blois as well as between Amboise and Tours; and further along downstream from Saumur and along the Angevin Corniche Road.

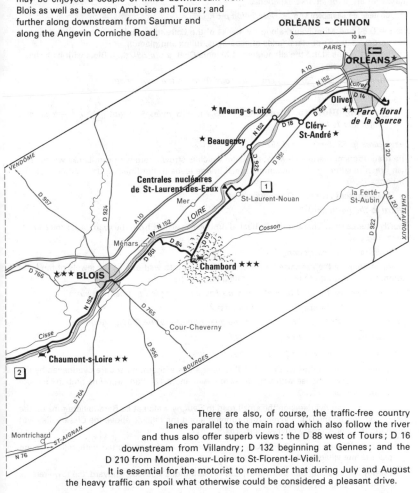

There are also, of course, the traffic-free country lanes parallel to the main road which also follow the river and thus also offer superb views: the D 88 west of Tours; D 16 downstream from Villandry; D 132 beginning at Gennes; and the D 210 from Montjean-sur-Loire to St-Florent-le-Vieil.

It is essential for the motorist to remember that during July and August the heavy traffic can spoil what otherwise could be considered a pleasant drive.

⬚ **From Orléans to Blois**★★★ – *84 km - 52 miles – about 6 hours – local map above*

Take Avenue Dauphine (south of the plan) to leave Orléans (p 124). Nursery gardens line both sides of the road until the bridge over the Loiret, flowing between wooded banks.

Olivet. – *Description p 128.*

In Olivet take the D 14 to the left which leads to the Floral Park of La Source.

Floral Park of La Source★★. – *Description p 128.*

Return on the D 14 to Cléry. Lining this road are neat little houses with pretty gardens.

Cléry-St-André★. – *Description p 77.*

Meung-sur-Loire★. – *Description p 118.*

Take the N 152 to Beaugency; soon the large towers of the St-Laurent Nuclear Power Station are visible on the horizon.

Beaugency★★. – *Description p 51.*

Leave by ③ or D 925 and after 6 km - 4 miles take the D 951 to the right. Turn right again just before St-Laurent-Nouan.

St-Laurent-des Eaux Nuclear Power Station. – Built on an artificial island in the Loire the nuclear power station is made up of two district power reactors: SLA, functioning since 1969, the two production units (output 500 MW) of which employ natural uranium, graphite and carbonic gas; SLB, the two production units (output 900 MW) of which employ enriched uranium and pressurized water. SLB's production units have been functioning since 1981. The information centre *(open 9am to 6pm; time: 1/2 hour)* explains the problems of nuclear energy, its importance and the workings of the plant. A belvedere gives an overall view of the various installations.

Note to the east, along the road to St-Laurent-Nouan, the vast experimental fish farm and the green houses – both use the heated water from the reactors.

Guided tours (2 1/2 hours) of the power station on weekdays by prior appointment only ☎ 54 87 75 66. Minimum age: 14.

After Nouan-sur-Loire the road enters the walled Chambord Estate where motorists are advised to drive slowly.

The sudden apparition of the stately façade of the Château de Chambord on the Cosson River, makes for an unforgettable experience.

Château de Chambord★★★. – *Description p 61.*

Via the D 84 and Montlivault, along the banks of the Loire, the road offers beautiful **views★** of this verdant setting: poplars, fields of asparagus, tulips and gladioli.

On the north bank stand the silhouettes of Ménars Château *(p 58),* then Blois with its basilica, cathedral and castle.

On arriving in Blois (p 53) by ② cross the Loire to reach the town centre.

② **From Blois to Tours★★★** – *89 km - 55 miles – about 4 hours – local map pp 100-101*

Leave Blois (p 53) by ⑤, the N 152.

The road offers numerous views of the Loire which is strewn here with sandbanks which are a lush green in summer. The Chaumont metal bridge leads to the Château de Chaumont on the far bank.

Chaumont-sur-Loire★★. – *Description p 69.*

Return to the north bank.

Shortly after Le Haut-Chantier the Château d'Amboise is visible from the road. *Cross the Loire to reach Amboise.*

Amboise★★. – *Description p 39.*

A short detour via the Amboise Forest allows the tourist to visit one of the jewels of the Loire region, the Château de Chenonceau, standing on the Cher.

Leave Amboise on the D 81 then at Civray de Touraine bear left to Chenonceaux.

Château de Chenonceau★★★. – *Description p 70.*

Return by the D 40; at La Croix de Touraine bear right on to the D 31 to Amboise.

Chanteloup Pagoda★. – *Description p 41.*

At Amboise, cross back over the river towards Tours.

Négron. – Standing below the N 152 this village has a charming square overlooked by the church, a Gothic house with a Renaissance front and a 12C barn with fine timberwork roof *(in summer art shows).*

Continue along the riverbank on the small road to Reugny which at La Bardouillère runs up the slope; bear left on the D 1, a lovely road running along the hillside above the Cisse Valley and bordering the well-known Vouvray vineyards.

Vernou-sur-Brenne. – Pop 2050. Leaning against the cliff face, dotted with cellars, is the picturesque village with its old houses, set in the Vouvray vineyards.

Vouvray. – Pop 2598. Situated at the heart of the famous Vouvray vineyard, the town retains numerous troglodyte houses.

Vouvray is known for its sparkling white wine. *Local wine growers and merchants welcome visitors to their cellars.* **Cave de la Bonne Dame,** holds in early January and on 15 August a wine exhibition.

Take the N 152 to Tours. As you approach the small village of **Rochecorbon** (pop 2711), the cliffs of which are dotted with troglodyte dwellings, note on the crest of the hill a watch tower known as the **lanterne.** A bit further on, after a wall, appears, on the right, an imposing 13C doorway belonging to the former **Marmoutier Abbey,** founded by St Martin in 372 and fortified in the 13 and 14C.

Enter Tours (p 155) by ④ of the town plan.

③ **From Tours to Chinon**★★★ — *61 km - 38 miles — about 5 hours — local map p 101*

Leave Tours *(p 155)* to the west by the D 88 passing on the way the Priory of St-Cosme *(p 161)*, continue along the embankment between gardens and vegetable patches. Fine views of the opposite side of the river.

At L'Aireau-des-Bergeons turn left on to the D 288 to Savonnières.

Savonnières — Pop 1813. The church has a pleasing Romanesque doorway, decorated with affronting animals and doves. Leaving in the direction of Villandry there are two limestone **caves** with calcite formations *(inquire at the café ; guided tours 1 April to 30 September 9am to 7pm ; 8 February to 30 March and 1 October to 20 December 9am to noon and 2 to 6pm ; closed 21 December to 7 February ; time : 1 hour ; 14F ; cave temperature : 14° C - 57° F)*. This particular cave system, a former (12C) quarry, is partially covered by a lake. The infiltration of water saturated with limestone has given stalactites and flowstone in the process of formation.
Petrified objects can be seen. Wine tasting.

Villandry★★. — *Description p 167.*

Once beyond Villandry you are out of the region of troglodyte dwellings ; continue by the D 39 to reach the Indre Valley and Azay-le-Rideau.

Azay-le-Rideau★★★. — *Description p 48.*

The D 17 runs between the river and the Forest of Chinon. *At Quincay, take the D 7 to the right then the D 119 towards Bréhémont.* Branch left on to the D 16, a narrow but pleasant road winding between hedges and spinneys and offering at various intervals glimpses of the river. From the bridge over the Indre one gets one of the best views of the Château d'Ussé.

Ussé★★. — *Description p 163.*

After Ussé cross the highly fertile **Véron** *(p 73)*. The crops grown here include cereals, vines and fruit trees (plums for the famous prunes of Tours). Via the village of Huismes you reach Chinon dominated by the ruins of its massive fortress.

④ **From Chinon to Saumur**★★★ — *38 km - 23 1/2 miles — about 3 hours — local map p 105*

Leave Chinon *(p 73)* by ③ ; *at the end of the archway of plane trees bear right on to the D 751 to Saumur. Just before entering Candes go right on to the bridge across the Vienne.* The village is in a lovely **site**★ at the confluence of the Loire and the Vienne. *Return to the south bank.*

Candes-St-Martin★. — *Description p 60.*

Montsoreau★. — *Description p 123.*

In Montsoreau bear left on the D 947 to Fontevraud.

Fontevraud Abbey★★. — *Description p 83.*

Return to Montsoreau.

From the bridge at Montsoreau there is a fine view upstream of Candes and Montsoreau and downstream in the direction of Saumur, where the castle is just distinguishable. Continue along the D 947 lined with troglodyte dwellings and white Renaissance houses.

Small wine growers' villages are nestled between the road and the limestone cliffs, which are riddled with caves and former quarries — some of which have now been converted into caves for mushroom growing. The slopes are carpeted with vines which produce a dry or medium dry white wine ; a *rosé* — **Cabernet de Saumur** and a red wine — **Champigny**.

Skirt the imposing church Notre-Dame-des-Ardilliers before arriving in Saumur by ③.

⑤ **From Saumur to Angers**★ — *48 km - 30 miles — about 3 1/2 hours — local map pp 104-105*

Leave Saumur *(p 144)* by ⑤ of the town plan.

St-Hilaire-St-Florent. — *Description p 146.*

To the right vast meadows, protected by dikes, are bordered with trees.

Chênehutte-les-Tuffeaux. — Pop 668. Standing beside the road (north of the village) is the lovely Romanesque church with its elegant Romanesque door.

Trèves-Cunault. — Pop 467. At the foot of the 15C crenellated tower, all that remains of the castle is the small village **church**★. Inside admire the beauty of the vast Romanesque nave bordered by arcades. At the entrance to the chancel the triumphal arch still has its rood beam carrying a Crucifix. Also worth noting are : the porphyry stoup with its primitive statues ; a recumbent figure in the south transept and an elegant reliquary in the north transept.

(After photo: Éd. du Lys, Clermont-Ferrand)

Trèves — Church and tower

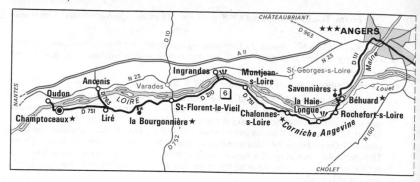

Cunault★★★. – *Description p 79.*

At Gennes cross the Loire to Les Rosiers (p 135).
Cross back over the bridge and bear right immediately on to the D 132 which skirts the river.

Le Thoureil. – Pop 359. This quiet, spruce little village was formerly a very active river port for the handling of apples. Inside the **church**, on either side of the choir there are two beautiful wooden reliquary shrines dating from the late 16C, which originally belonged to the nearby St-Maur-de-Glanfeuil Abbey. They are adorned with statuettes of saints.

St-Maur-de-Glanfeuil Abbey. – Facing the Loire this ruined Benedictine abbey *(now an international ecumenical centre)* is named after St Maurus, a hermit who came from Angers and founded a monastery in the 6C on the site of the Roman villa of Glanfeuil. In the courtyard excavations have uncovered a 4C Gallo-Roman temple dedicated to the nymphs, the base of this temple's columns were used by St Maurus to build a chapel.

On the first floor is the austere chapel, built in 1955 and decorated with stained glass windows. On the second floor there is a superb **Carolingian cross** carved on the gable of the former 9C church destroyed by the Normans, and set into the wall rebuilt in 11C.

Cross the Loire between St-Rémy-la-Varenne and St-Mathurin : this scenic route runs alongside the Loire. The road leaves the Loire just before reaching Angers (p 41) via ③.

⑥ From Angers to Champtoceaux★ – *83 km - 50 miles – about 4 hours – local map p 104*

Leave Angers (p 41) by the Boulevard du Bon-Pasteur and take the D 111 to the left to Bouchemaine. Beyond La Pointe, the road leaves the river to cross vineyard country. The road after Epiré overlooks a small valley.

Savennières – Pop 1813. The lovely village church has a Romanesque east end decorated with modillions and carved friezes ; the south door is also Romanesque. Note the nave's schist wall with its unusual brick decoration.

Leave the north bank for the island of Béhuard.

Béhuard★ – Pop 93. Attractively situated on an island of the same name this very old village with its 15 and 16C houses, in some cases raised to save them from river flooding, makes a picturesque **setting★**. Across from the souvenir shop in the former king's residence (15C) built for Louis XI, is the 15C **church** erected by Louis XI, following a vow he made when he was once in danger of drowning. Part of the nave is formed by living rock. Votive chains hang from the gallery while the 16C stalls have delightfully malicious carved misericords. The highly venerated statue of Our Lady of Béhuard stands in a niche in the choir. A late 15C window of the Crucifixion in the side aisle shows the donor, Louis XI on the left. *Closed noon to 2pm.*

A short path near the wayside cross takes you to the Loire and its sandy beach. A particularly pleasant **walk** is one to the end of the island *(3/4 hour on foot)* ; take the path to the left of the poplars in front of the wayside cross – a lovely site where the river separates to go round Béhuard.

Rochefort-sur-Loire. – Pop 1819. Rochefort lies in a rural setting beside the Louet, a side-stream of the Loire. The nearby vineyards produce the famous **Quart de Chaume**, a distinctive and heady wine. Several old houses, with turrets or watch towers line the square below the D 751.

Bear right on the D 751.

The Angevin Corniche Road★ (La Corniche Angevine). – As far as Chalonnes the road is a series of tight bends. The road cut into the cliff face, affords as from La Haie-Longue bird's eye views across the full width of the valley and also of the small towns bordering the Loire.

(After photo: Knecht)

Salmon fishing

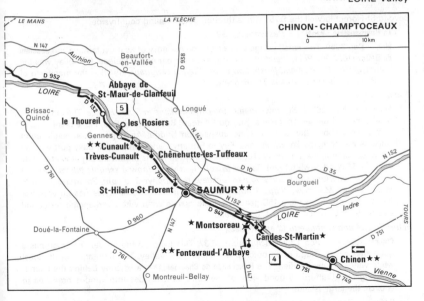

CHINON - CHAMPTOCEAUX

0   10 km

La Haie-Longue. — As you approach La Haie-Longue you will see from a bend a chapel dedicated to Our Lady of Loreto, the patron saint of aviators. Opposite is a viewing table from which there is a remarkable **view★** of the Loire with its sidestreams, glinting silver in the light, and of meadows, turreted manor houses and hillside vineyards. The wine from these vineyards is known as *Coteaux du Layon (p 91)*.

Chalonnes-sur-Loire. — Pop 5 358. Chalonnes has a pleasant setting and was the birthplace of St Maurille, a 5C Bishop of Angers. There are attractive views of the river to be had from the quayside which is lined with plane trees. The old port now harbours more pleasure craft than fishing boats.

After Chalonnes the D 751 follows the edge of the plateau, cut at intervals by small tributary streams, till reaching Montjean.

Montjean-sur-Loire. — Pop 2 492. Montjean, with its tightly packed streets, stands on a rocky spur overlooking the Loire. The terrace beside the church affords a wide view of the valley, the suspension bridge and the numerous villages with their grey slate roofs.

From Montjean to St-Florent-le-Vieil use the D 210. The **road★** following the embankment affords views to the north of the river and to the south of the vineyard clad slopes rising above the Thau, a former sidestream of the Loire. Nice view on arriving at Ingrandes.

Ingrandes. — Pop 1 450. The deserted quays and berths and imposing 17 and 18C houses are evidence of the former prosperity of this once bustling port, best observed from the south bank. In the past, the town served as a link between Brittany and Anjou. Since salt was stored here and Anjou was not exempt from the salt tax *(la Gabelle)*, contraband dealing by

smugglers flourished in the region. The **church** *(closed Sunday afternoons)* rebuilt in 1956 in the local style has an unusual bell tower and remarkable modern stained glass in brilliant colours by master glaziers from Chartres (Les Ateliers Loire) following cartoons by the artist Bertrand.

Return on to the D 210.

St-Florent-le-Vieil. — Pop 2 560. A good view of the **site** of this village perched on a rocky spur, dominated by its church, can be had from the bridge over the Loire. St-Florent was one of the first centres of Royalist insurrection in what

(After lithograph: photo Éd. Horizons de France)

St-Florent in the 19C

was to be known as the Vendéen War *(see Les Mauges)* following the execution of Louis XVI in March 1793. On 18 October, after a defeat at Cholet the Royalists with their mortally wounded leader, **Bonchamps**, a man of noble birth, withdrew to St-Florent. In revenge it was proposed to massacre the Republican prisoners gathered in the church. Only by the clemency of Bonchamps were the lives of the Republican captives spared — including among their number the father of the sculptor, David d'Angers who in thanks made the moving memorial in front of the church.

The **church** contains in a chapel to the left Bonchamps's **tomb★** of white marble (1825), a moving work executed by David d'Angers himself. From the tree planted esplanade extending round the church there is an extensive **view★** of the Loire Valley.

Beyond St-Florent-le-Vieil the D 751 winds through gently rolling countryside.

La Bourgonnière Chapel★. – *Description p 59.*

Liré. – Pop 2 250. This small village keeps alive the memory of its most famous son **Joachim du Bellay** (1522-60). Poet, friend of Ronsard, and member of the Pléiade, Du Bellay was the author of *The Defence and Illustration of the French Language* (1549) – the manifesto of the Pléiade. His finest work is *The Regrets*.

The D 763 leads to Ancenis.

Ancenis. – Pop 7 263. – *See town plan in the current Michelin Guide France.* The old houses of Ancenis – Rue des Tonneliers, Rue du Château, Basse Grand-Rue, Place des Halles – rise in tiers above the Loire and the suspension bridge. An important strategic point Ancenis was formerly known as the "Key to Brittany" and was once a busy port with an active sailcloth making industry. Today it is renowned for its important pig market and its wines – Muscadet (white) and Gamay *(rosé).* The **château** *(now a school: guided tours of part of the interior in July and August, Tuesdays to Sundays 3 to 6pm, Saturdays 11am to noon; closed Mondays; time: 1 hour; 10F)* with its mixture of styles has an entrance flanked by round towers, a 15C gallery, a Renaissance wing with overhanging turret and elegant dormer windows and 17C pavilions.

Return to Liré and continue to Champtoceaux.

Champtoceaux★. – Pop 1 396. *Facilities pp 36-37.* This town on the borders of Anjou has a good **site★** on the ridge of an outcrop dominating the valley. The reputation of the local white wines is fully justified. The **Promenade de Champalud★★**, a balcony behind the church *(viewing table),* affords a good view of the Loire as it divides into various branches to encircle the large islands.

Oudon. – Pop 2 001. *2 km - 1 mile from Champtoceaux by the D 751.* The village is dominated by a mediaeval keep. The use of limestone – in layers to mark each storey and alternating stones to emphasize the corners and crown the crenellations – overcomes the severity of the main building stone, schist. From the top *(open 1 July to 31 August 10am to noon and 3 to 5pm; 2.50F)* there is a fine view of the Loire Valley.

LORRIS ★

Michelin map 🗺 fold 1 – Pop 2 592

Lorris is famous for its customary law or *coutumes,* which is said to be the oldest in the kingdom. These varied from one region to the next and were in force prior to the Revolution throughout France. Hunting seat of the Capetian kings the town was often the place of residence of Blanche of Castille and her son St Louis, Louis IX of France. This town was the birthplace (c 1215) of Guillaume de Lorris, the author of the first part of the *Roman de la Rose* or *Romance of the Rose,* a poem of courtly love which so influenced Chaucer in his writings.

Notre-Dame★. – The church is noteworthy not only for the purity of its architecture (12-13C) but also for its furnishings. By the elegant Romanesque doorway enter the luminous Gothic nave. High up in the nave the early 16C **organ loft★** is carved with pilasters and medallions. The late 15C **choir stalls★** are historiated portraying Prophets and Sibyls on the cheekpieces and scenes from *The Golden Legend,* New Testament and everyday life on the misericords. Above the altar hang two 18C angels; nearby is a handsome lectern of the same period. Also worth noting are polychrome statues in the ambulatory and an alabaster Virgin (late 15C) near the baptismal fonts.

Place du Martroi. – This spacious square is the centre of the village. The 16C **town hall**, of brick with stone courses and heavily ornamented dormer windows, stands on the main street. Opposite is the **market** *(les halles)* covered with an oak timber roof (1542).

EXCURSION

Orléans Canal. – *Round tour of 14 km - 9 miles.* The itinerary follows the canal, which crosses peaceful, scenic countryside.

Completed in 1692 the canal links the Loire and the Loing, downstream from Montargis. It is now out of service and yet fishermen continue lining its banks.

Leave Lorris by the V 5 to the west and then turn right.

Grignon. – The hamlet occupies a calm setting overlooking the canal with its three locks.

Bear left on the D 444. The road passes through **Vieilles-Maisons,** where the church porch is timber framed.

Étang des Bois. – This lake, very busy in summer, is set amidst woodland.

Return to Lorris via the D 88.

---

*The **Michelin Map series** at a scale of 1 : 200 000*
(1cm:2km) covers the whole of France. For the
maps to use with this guide see page three.
You may pick out at a glance
   the motorways and major roads for a quick journey
      the secondary or alternative roads for a traffic free run
         the country lanes for a leisurely drive
These maps are a must for your holidays.

Michelin map **67** fold 9 – Pop 8 448

Situated on a mound encircled by shady boulevards taking the place of its former ramparts, Loudun's activities are based on a few new industries and its fairs.

Prosperous in the Middle Ages, the town had some 20 000 inhabitants in the 17C. The heritage of this former prosperity is a great diversity of dwellings lining the old winding streets.

The Golden Age (17C). – In the early 17C Loudun was known as a meeting place for great minds and where the ideas of the Reformation found ready acceptance. Among the more notable local intellectuals were the doctor **Théophraste Renaudot** (1586-1653) who was to found the first printed newspaper *La Gazette de France* in 1631 and **Urbain Grandier**, a cultured and brilliant priest whose scathing comments about the religious Orders and lax moral standards earned him many enemies. In 1634 the young priest was accused of bewitching the Ursulines of a Loudun convent. Found guilty, he was condemned and burned at the stake on the Place Ste-Croix.

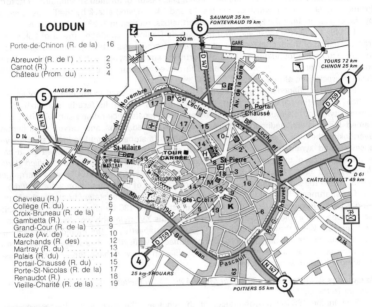

LOUDUN

Porte-de-Chinon (R. de la)	16
Abreuvoir (R. de l')	2
Carnot (R.)	3
Château (Prom. du)	4
Chevreau (R.)	5
Collège (R. du)	6
Croix-Bruneau (R. de la)	7
Gambetta (R.)	8
Grand-Cour (R. de la)	9
Leuze (Av. de)	10
Marchands (R. des)	12
Martray (R. du)	13
Palais (R. du)	14
Portail-Chaussé (R. du)	15
Porte-St-Nicolas (R. de la)	17
Renaudot (R.)	18
Vieille-Charité (R. de la)	19

■ SIGHTS

Tour Carrée. – *Open 15 June to 15 September 2 to 7pm (6pm the rest of the year); 6F.*

Rising above the rooftops of Loudun this buttressed tower was built in 1040 by Foulques Nerra *(p 42)*. The crown was dismantled in 1631 on Richelieu's orders at the same time as the razing of the adjoining castle. From the top *(143 steps)* there is a remarkable **panorama★** of the surrounding countryside.

Promenade du Château (4). – This forms an esplanade overlooking the countryside with the typical features of lime lined mall, sandy alleys and bandstand.

St-Hilaire-du-Martray. – Begun in the 14C the entrance on the south side has a fine 16C doorway with covings adorned by canopied niches containing incense burning angels. Inside the primitive doorway is ornamented with vine branches. Above the 17C altar in the south aisle is a 15C **painting on wood** attributed to Gerard David of the school of Bruges representing the Virgin and Child. The great Flamboyant window behind the high altar has 19C stained glass. Downhill from the church is one of the town's former gateways, the **Porte du Martray.**

St-Pierre-du-Marché. – Founded in 1218 by Philippe-Auguste and continued by Saint Louis, the church, identified from afar by its 15C stone spire has an imposing Renaissance doorway. Angels and medallions adorn the recessed arches.

Ste-Croix (K). – This former church was greatly altered when it was transformed into a covered market. The Romanesque chancel with its historiated capitals, is still visible.

EXCURSION

The scenic route "La Côte Loudunaise". – *Round tour of 26 km - 16 miles. Leave Loudun by ④, the D 759 and after 6.5 km - 4 miles turn right into the D 19.* The scenic route from Glénouze via Ranton, Curçay and Ternay follows the crest of the hills which dominate the Dive Valley and crosses a countryside of vineyards and orchards.

Glénouze. – Pop 128. Small Romanesque church with a bell gable.

Ranton. – Pop 174. Huddled around the small picturesque square are the castle's 15C fortified gateway with traces of a drawbridge and flanked by a tower with machicolations; and the church with its Romanesque doorway.

Curçay-sur-Dive. – Pop 245. This small village is pleasantly situated overlooking the valley. The 12C keep was provided in the 15C with machicolations and bartizans.

Return to Loudun by Ternay and the D 14.

Michelin map 🔢 fold 3 — Pop 4 495 — *Facilities pp 36-37*

Le Lude is a small town on the south bank of the Loir. Its principal activities are a dairy, furniture factory, stud farm and its famous fairs. The *Son et Lumière* is the town's main attraction and yet the château is also worth visiting.

"Son et Lumière"★★★. — *Performances (1 3/4 hours) Fridays and Saturdays 10.30pm June and July, Fridays, Saturdays and some Thursdays 10pm August, Fridays to Saturdays 9.30pm September; 25F to 45F. Fireworks Fridays and Saturdays : additional 15F.*

Entitled **Sumptuous Nights on the Banks of the Loir** (*les glorieuses et fastueuses soirées au bord du Loir),* this performance created in 1957, is an unforgettable experience. Five centuries of history unfold before you : admirable illuminations, sound, fountains, and a cast of 350 in period costumes help create a memorable evening.

Château★. — *Guided tours 1 April to 30 September 3 to 6pm ; time : 1/2 hour ; 15F. Gardens open 10am to noon and 2 to 6pm ; 10F.*

Strategically important Le Lude has seen a succession of fortified strongholds : 11C fortress for the Counts of Anjou, which during the 13 and 14C resisted attack by the English ; captured by the English in 1425 the fortress was, nevertheless, retaken in 1429 by the French.

In 1457 the château was acquired by Jean de Daillon, a childhood friend of Louis XI. The transformation of this feudal fortress into a stately home was started by Daillon's son who built the château on the foundations of the old fortress : square layout with massive towers at each corner ; however, the large windows and the carved decoration reflect the search for refined decor characteristic of that period.

Enter the U-shaped courtyard (early 17C), which was closed in the late 18C by an arched portico. Facing the park, to the right, lies the François I Wing. Its façade is a mixture of the fortress style, with its round mediaeval towers, and Renaissance refinement, with its windows framed by pilasters, pedimented dormer windows, medallions and carved ornamentation. Overlooking the river, the Louis XVI Wing in white tufa stone exemplifies the Classical style : it is severe and symmetrical and the façade's central projecting part is topped by a carved pediment, typical of that period. The north wing *(visible from the Rue du Pont, which skirts the château),* built during the Louis XII period, is the earliest wing (early 16C) it was rearranged in the 19C when the stone balconies and equestrian statue of Jean de Daillon were added.

The apartments have all the charm and interest of a lived in stately home. In the Louis XII Wing is the ballroom restored in the 15 and 16C style. The 18C building contains a fine suite of rooms, especially a splendid oval saloon in pure Louis XVI style with woodwork and mirrors. In the François I Wing the library has a 17C Gobelins tapestry ; in the dining room, where the window recesses reveal the thickness of the mediaeval walls, there is a vast chimneypiece with a carved salamander and ermine tufts *(p 18),* while on the walls hang three Flemish tapestries including a *Verdure* showing a red parrot.

Maison des Architectes. — *3 Rue du Marché au Fil, on the left side of the post office near the entrance to the château.*

Built in the 16C by the architects of the château, the Architects' House presents the ornamentation typical of the Renaissance period : mullioned windows, pilasters with Corinthian capitals and friezes running between the floors.

EXCURSION

Genneteil ; La Boissière. — *Round trip 28 km - 17 miles — about 1 1/2 hours. Leave Le Lude to the west by the D 306, then turn left on the D 305 towards Baugé. In Savigné-sous-le-Lude turn left again.*

Genneteil. — Pop 453. The Romanesque church has a splendid 11C **doorway** with sculptured splaying depicting the signs of the zodiac and human faces.

Continue along the D 138 towards Chigné.

Chigné. — Pop 296. The 12-15C fortified church presents an interesting façade flanked by a tower.

Above the doorway note the line of carved brackets and the primitive carvings.

Via Les 4 Chemins continue to La Boissière.

Former Abbey of La Boissière. — *Guided tours 1 to 15 April, July, August, 20 to 31 December, 9am to noon and 2 to 6pm ; closed Sundays ; time : 1/4 hour ; 5F.* This is renowned as the one time sanctuary of the True Cross of Anjou *(p 49).*

In the 18C the abbatial buildings were transformed into a château. The chancel with two recumbent figures and an altarpiece is all that remains of the 12C abbey church. In the 13C the Cistercian monks built a chapel, **Chapelle de la Vraie-Croix** *(on the road to Dénezé),* to shelter the precious relic. Several times during the Hundred Years War the relic was taken to the Château d'Angers for safekeeping and then in 1790 it was transferred to the chapel of a hospice in Baugé where it now remains.

Return towards Le Lude on the D 767 ; at La Croix-de-Beauchêne bear right on the D 138 to Broc.

Broc. — Pop 402. The Romanesque village church possesses a squat Romanesque bell tower ; its east end is decorated with medallions.

Inside, the nave is covered with lierne and tierceron vaulting *(p 21).*The small Romanesque apse has preserved some 13C frescoes : at the half dome is a Christ Enthroned ; on the left is an Annunciation ; on the right a Virgin Enthroned. On the nave wall is a handsome wooden Crucifix of the Louis XIII period.

Return to Le Lude by turning right at La Croix-de-Beauchêne on to the D 307.

Michelin map 🗺 fold 13 — Pop 150 331 — *See plan of built up area in the current Michelin Guide France*

A thriving provincial capital, Le Mans stands on the banks of the Sarthe at its confluence with the Huisne.

A business centre it is one of the more important insurance centres in France. Industrially, the automobile is the city's main activity — its construction and the famous races (Le Mans Twenty-four Hour Race, Circuit Bugatti). Numerous fairs or exhibitions add to the everyday bustle — to name only a few : the Spring Fair, the Quatre Jours or Four Day exhibition *(mid-September)* and the Onion Fair *(first Friday in September)*.

A meal in the town should include some of the local specialities such as *rillettes,* potted pork ; *poulardes dodues,* plump pullets ; *chapons,* capons in sparkling cider and the famous *reinette* apple.

HISTORICAL NOTES

The Plantagenet Dynasty. — The Plantagenet connections with this town are many and various. When **Geoffroy Plantagenet,** Count of Anjou, married Matilda, the granddaughter of William the Conqueror he added Normandy and Maine to his domains. Geoffroy often resided at Le Mans and on his death in 1151 he was buried in the cathedral. His son Henri Plantagenet who was to become **Henry II** of England, was the founder of the Coëffort Hospital and it was to Le Mans, his birthplace, that he retired in his old age only to be expelled by one of his rebellious sons **Richard Lionheart,** then in alliance with the French King.

While on the Third Crusade Richard married Queen Berengaria of Navarre and it was to her in her widowhood that Philippe-Auguste gave the county of Maine which he had reconquered from Richard's younger brother, John Lackland. Berengaria founded Epau Abbey *(p 113)* where she was buried.

A famous writer. — The 17C poet and satirical writer, **Paul Scarron** (1610-60) was a member of the Le Mans Chapter. He was provided with a prebend and a canonical house in the cathedral precincts. This rhymer and gay fellow — married in 1652 to Françoise d'Aubigné later Mme de Maintenon, Louis XIV's mistress — became an invalid before the age of thirty. The work for which he is best known is *Le Roman Comique (The Comic Novel)* based on people and scenes from 17C Le Mans.

In the vanguard of progress. — Already under the *Ancien Régime,* Le Mans had several flourishing industries including the production of a coarse, black woollen material used for clerics' and lawyers' gowns, candle making, tanneries and the making of sailcloth from locally grown hemp.

The Bollée family, father and two sons were innovators in the early development of the motor car. **Amédée Bollée** senior's (1844-1917) first steam propelled car *L'Obéissante* (1873) was a twelve seater vehicle with two motors and a maximum speed of over 40 km per hour. His later model, *La Mancelle,* was the first to have its single motor placed in front, under the bonnet. His son, **Amédée** (1867-1926) dealt mainly with racing cars, some of which approached the then incredible speed of 100 km per hour. It was the second brother Léon who in 1908 invited the American, **Wilbur Wright,** to attempt one of his first flights in an aeroplane at nearby Les Hunaudières. The family firm is still active in the production of piston rings.

Association with the car industry continued when in 1936 Louis Renault built the first of his decentralized factories to the south of Le Mans. It employs around 8 000 people.

Le Mans Twenty-four Hour Race. — This event, attracting thousands of spectators, takes place in a carnival-like atmosphere. Started in 1923, the race has become a sporting event of universal interest and a testing ground for car manufacturers. The difficulties of the circuit and duration of the race are a severe test for both the quality of the machines and the endurance of the two drivers who take it in turn to drive. The circuit has been considerably improved since the tragic accident of 1955 when several spectators died.

The scene is unforgettable with the revving and roaring of the engines, the whining and whizzing of vehicles hurtling past at more than 300 km per hour on the straight sections, the constant smell of petrol, the chasing searching headlights at night, all mingled in an atmosphere of great excitement and suspense.

■ ST JULIAN'S CATHEDRAL★★ (Cathédrale St-Julien) *time : 1 hour*

Organ music and special lighting on Saturday evenings 15 June to 31 August from 9.30 to 11 pm.

This magnificent edifice, dedicated to St Julian, the first Bishop of Le Mans, rises proudly above the impressive tiered arrangement of the Gothic **chevet★★★,** amazing for its system of Y shaped two tiered flying buttresses.

The present building comprises a Romanesque nave, Gothic chancel and Radiant or Middle Gothic transept flanked by a tower.

Exterior. — Overlooking the charming **Place St-Michel** the south porch has a superb 12C **doorway★★** contemporary with the Royal Doorway of Chartres. A comparison of the two doorways shows that they portray the same themes : Christ in Majesty, the Apostles and a series of statue columns. The doorway is flanked by statue columns : on the jambs are Sts Peter and Paul while the figures on the splay embrasures represent Solomon and the Queen of Sheba, a Prophet, a Sibyl and the ancestors of Christ. The Apostles in serried ranks occupy the niches of the lintel with Christ the King on the tympanum, surrounded by the symbols of the Evangelists, being sprinkled with incense by the angels of the first recessed arch. The other scenes on the arches are the Annunciation, Visitation, Nativity, Presentation in the Temple, Massacre of the Innocents, Baptism of Christ, Wedding Feast at Cana.

Le MANS★★

Looking to the right of the porch note the transept pierced by immense windows and the 12-14C tower (64 m - 210 ft high).

The west front, overlooking the **Place du Cardinal-Grente**, bordered by Renaissance dwellings, is in an archaic Romanesque style. One can clearly distinguish the original 11C gable embedded in the gable added the following century when the new vaulting was being built.

At the right hand corner of the west front is a pink veined sandstone menhir. Tradition has it that to have really visited Le Mans, visitors should insert a thumb into the hole in the stone.

Nave. – The Romanesque main building rests on great 11C round arches which were reinforced in the following century by pointed arches. The domical vaults or Plantagenet style vaulting *(p 21)* springs from majestic capitals which show great finesse of detail. In the side aisles are eight Romanesque stained glass windows, the most famous one represents the Ascension (1). The great window of the west front, heavily restored in the 19C, evokes the Legend of St Julian.

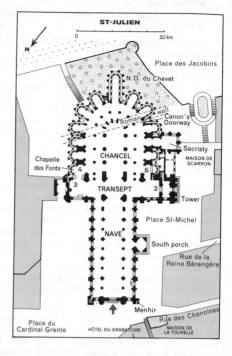

Transept. – The 14-15C transept, pierced by a small columned gallery and immense windows, is striking for its ethereal quality and its bold elevation.

The south arm is dominated by the 16C organ loft (2), while the north arm is suffused with light transmitted by the beautiful 15C stained glass. Three 16C tapestry hangings represent the Legend of St Julian.

At the entrance to the baptismal chapel (Chapelle des Fonts), which opens on to the north arm, facing one another are two remarkable Renaissance **tombs★★**. The one on the left (3), that of Charles I of Anjou, the brother of King René *(p 42)*, is the work of Francesco Laurana. The recumbent figure lies, in the Italian style, on an antique sarcophagus and the delicacy of the facial features recall Laurana's talents as a portraitist. On the right the magnificent monument (4) to the memory of Guillaume Du Bellay, cousin of the poet, shows the figure holding a sword and a book and reclining on one elbow in the antique manner on a sarcophagus which is adorned with an attractive frieze of aquatic divinities.

The tomb of Cardinal Grente was placed here in 1965.

Chancel. – This lofty and soaring Gothic chancel (13C) is one of the finest in France – 34 m - 112 ft high (compare Notre-Dame in Paris 35 m - 115 ft); it is encircled by a double ambulatory with a crown of apsidal chapels.

The serried ranks of the tall upward sweeping columns support lancet arches showing a definite Norman influence. Above the triforium level adorned with intricate stylized foliage, the 13C **stained glass★★** is a blaze of colour dominated by vivid blues and reds. Binoculars are needed to identify the rather rigid and wild figures of the Apostles, bishops, saints and donors.

(After photo: Archives Photographiques)

Cathedral: Stained glass window of Yolanda of Aragon

Hanging above the 16C choir stalls in the famous series of **tapestries** of the same period depicting the lives of Sts Gervase and Protase.

Chancel precincts. – In the first chapel on the right (5) is a 17C terracotta Entombment. The sacristy door beyond was formerly part of the 17C rood screen. The beautiful 16C woodwork, in the sacristy, originally formed the high backs of the choir stalls. The 14C Canon's Doorway which follows has a tympanum with an effigy of St Julian.

The 13C chapel Notre-Dame-du-Chevet, with its harmonious proportions, is closed by a delicate 17C wrought iron grille. The 13C stained glass windows depict the Tree of Jesse and the story of Adam and Eve.

The vaulting is covered with paintings dating from 1380. The scene illustrating an Angels' Concert, displays great delicacy of draughtsmanship.

Other outstanding collections of stained glass windows in the Loire country include:

Angers: St Maurice Cathedral

Champigny-sur-Veude: Sainte-Chapelle

Tours: St Gatien Cathedral

■ THE MEDIAEVAL TOWN★★ (Vieux Mans) *time: 1 hour*

Closely packed inside the Gallo-Roman ramparts (visible from the quays), the mediaeval town is built on a hill dominating the Sarthe. Restaurants and boutiques animate this picturesque ensemble of winding streets, cut by stepped alleys, bordered by 15C half timbered houses, Renaissance town houses and 18C *hôtels* graced with wrought iron balconies.

Starting from the Place des Jacobins follow on foot the itinerary indicated on the plan below.

Place St-Michel. – Standing in the cathedral precincts is the Renaissance house (**W**) where Paul Scarron lived during his period as a member of the Chapter. The presbytery, no 1*bis*, has retained a 15C staircase turret.

Take to the left the **Rue de la Reine-Bérengère** which is bordered by a variety of old houses. Nos 7 and 9 are both Renaissance – the latter is adorned with charming statues of St Catherine and St Barbara.

Maison de la Reine-Bérengère★ (**M²**). – *Nos 11-13.* Built for a rich Le Mans Alderman between 1490 and 1515 this elegant residence known by the name the House of Queen Berengaria, was never actually lived in by Richard the Lionheart's Queen as she lived during the 13C. The decoration consists of an ogee arch above the door and historiated brackets supporting the beams. The Museum of History and Ethnography is housed here *(p 113)*.

Maison des Deux-Amis (**Y**). – *Nos 18-20.* The two friends are shown supporting a coat of arms. Built in the 15C, a century later it was the home of Nicolas Denizot, the poet and painter and friend of Ronsard and Du Bellay.

Continue to the Rue Wilbur-Wright; across from this street, which has cut the hillside in two, is the **Maison du Pilier Rouge** (**B**) a half timbered house containing the tourist information centre *(open 1 July to 31 August)*; its corner post is decorated with a death's-head.

At the beginning of the Grande-Rue note to the right the Maison du Pilier Vert (**E**) and further on the former 17C Hôtel d'Arcy (**F**).

Assé (Cour d')	2	Pans-de-Gorron (R. des)	57
Boucheries (R.)	16	Pilier-Rouge (R. du)	61
Bouquet (R.)	18	Reine-Bérengère (R. de la)	64
Chanoines (R. des)	22	St-Honoré (R.)	72
Chapelains (R. des)	23	St-Pavin-de-la-Cité (R.)	75
Écrevisse (R. de l')	36	Truie-qui-file (R. de la)	79

Return to the Maison du Pilier Rouge and turn right on the street of the same name which ends on the Place St-Pierre lined with half timbered houses.

Hôtel de Ville (**H**). – Built in 1760, the town hall was formerly the palace of the Counts of Maine. Take the staircase to the right of the building down to the Rue des Filles-Dieu from where there is a view of the old town's southeast ramparts; on one side of the staircase is a 14C tower (**K**) and on the other the former Collegiate Church of St-Pierre-de-la-Cour (**L**).

Hôtel de Vignoles (**N**). – This late 16C mansion with tall French style roofs stands at the beginning of Rue de l'Écrevisse on the right.

Maison d'Adam et Ève (**R**). – *No 71 La Grande-Rue.* This superb Renaissance mansion was the home of Jean de l'Épine, an astrologer and physician.

At the corner of the **Rue St-Honoré** a columm shaft is decorated with three keys, the former coat of arms of Le Mans. The street is lined with half timbered houses. The picturesque Cour d'Assé opens opposite the Rue St-Honoré. From here onwards the Grande-Rue descends between noble Classical *hôtels*. Bear right on the more popular Rue St-Pavin-de-la-Cité; on the left is the Hôtel d'Argouges (**S**) which has a lovely 15C doorway in its courtyard.

Continue along the Rue St-Pavin-de-la-Cité; after a vaulted passageway turn left into the Rue Bouquet. At the corner of Rue de Vaux a 15C niche shelters a Mary Magdalene; at no 12 the Hôtel de Vaux (**V**), is late 16C. Further on to the left there is a view of the Great Postern staircase (**X**), part of the Gallo-Roman ramparts.

Retrace your steps on the Rue de Vaux to the Rue Wilbur-Wright; cross it and continue along the Rue des Chanoines. At no 26 stands the St-Jacques's canon's residence (**D**) built around 1560.

Maison de la Tourelle (**Q**). – This Renaissance dwelling, with its windows and dormers decorated with delicate scrollwork, has a turret at the corner of the Pans-de-Gorron alley.

Hôtel du Grabatoire (**Z**). – On the other side of the staircase, facing the Romanesque doorway of the cathedral, this 16C mansion was originally the infirmary for sick canons; it is, today, the episcopal palace. On its right note the Maison du Pèlerin (Pilgrim's House) decorated with cockleshells, the symbol adopted by the pilgrims who had visited the shrine of St James at Compostela *(see Michelin Green Guide to Spain)*.

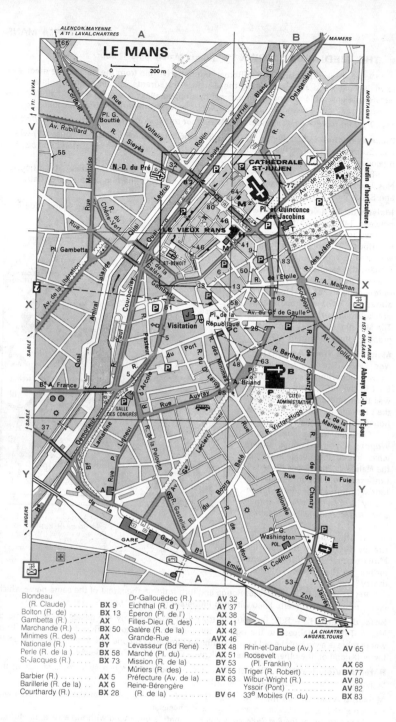

■ ADDITIONAL SIGHTS

Tessé Museum★ (BV M¹). − *Open 9am to noon and 2 to 6pm ; closed 1 May and some public holidays.*

Set in a fine park, the museum is housed in the former episcopal palace (19C) built where the mansion of the Tessé family once stood.

The rich collection of paintings are exhibited on a rotating basis. Italian painting is represented by a series of 14C primitives with the typical gold background, including works by Pietro Lorenzetti and Pesellino representing David's Penitence and the Death of Absalom.

There are several good portraits from the 16C French school : Henri III and Catherine de Medici and some 17 to 19C canvases. Classical painting includes the works of Vouet and Poussin ; Le Sueur, Philippe de Champaigne and Georges de la Tour are also represented. A very stately family portrait is attributed to David.

The Dutch and Flemish schools are represented by works of Van Balen and Kalf among others.

An entire room is devoted to Paul Scarron (portrait) and his work **The Comic Novel** (paintings and engravings illustrating the comical adventures recounted). *Exhibition July to September.*

In a small gallery on the ground floor is a 12C **enamelled plaque** representing Geoffroy Plantagenet *(p 109)* ; it was originally part of the tomb (no longer exists) in the cathedral.

Église de la Couture★ (BX B). – This was formerly the abbatial church of the monastery St-Pierre-de-la-Couture. It is in the centre of town and is contiguous to the Préfecture, which is located in the former conventual buildings (18C). The twin towered west front is 13C. The doorway is intricately sculptured ; the column statues on the jambs represent the Apostles ; the Last Judgement on the tympanum shows Christ between the Virgin and St John ; the recessed arches carry the heavenly court of angels, patriarchs and prophets (first arch), martyrs (second arch), and virgins (third arch).

The wide single nave, built in the late 12C in the Plantagenet style *(p 21)*, is lit by elegant twinned windows surmounted by oculi.

Note the forms of the Romanesque arches of the original nave on the blind walls of the great pointed arches which support a narrow ledge below the windows. To the left on entering is a curious 11C pilaster sculptured with a Christ in Benediction. The enchanting white marble **Virgin★★** (1571), on the pillar directly opposite the pulpit, is by Germain Pilon and originally came from the now vanished retable of the high altar. The blind arcades are hung with 17C **tapestries** and 16C painted panels.

The massive round 11C columns of the chancel with squat capitals showing Eastern influence in the decoration, support very narrow round arches. Above, the vaulting ribs spring from fine Plantagenet style statues.

The 11C crypt, altered in 1838, has pre-Romanesque or Gallo-Roman columns and capitals ; an inverted Antique capital serves as a base for one of the pillars. The 6-7C shroud of St Bertrand, Bishop of Le Mans and founder in 616 of the monastery, is exposed at the entrance *(automatic time switch for lighting)*. The presumed burial place of St Bertrand is marked by a reclining plaster figure in a wall alcove.

Ste-Jeanne-d'Arc★ (BY E). – This, the former Coëffort Hospital, was founded about 1180 by Henry II of England in atonement for the murder of his former Chancellor, Archbishop Thomas Becket in Canterbury Cathedral. The 12C great hall or ward for the sick is now the parish church. A similar institution, the former Hospital of St John in Angers was built by the same monarch. The plain façade, pierced by an arched doorway, above which are twinned windows, opens onto a vast room divided into three naves of equal

(After photo: Robert Château)

The Virgin

height. The elevation is elegant with slender columns with finely carved capitals, supporting Plantagenet vaulting. In the Middle Ages wide canopied beds for several patients at a time, were aligned down the side aisles with an altar in the central passage.

Jardin d'horticulture (BV). – This fine garden with artificial rocks and cascading streams was designed in 1851 by Alphand, the landscape gardener of the Paris parks, Buttes-Chaumont, Montsouris and Boulogne. The terraced mall affords a fine view over the cathedral.

Museum of History and Ethnography (M²). – *Open 9am to noon and 2 to 6pm ; closed Mondays, Tuesdays and public holidays.*

The museum is housed in the 15C Maison de la Reine Bérangère. The glazed pottery from the Sarthe (Ligron, Malicorne, Prévelles, etc.) is astonishing for the vigour of the design and freshness of the colours, especially the yellows, greens and browns.

The objects include statuettes, retables, jars and finials. There are paintings and sketches of mediaeval Le Mans and other local scenes.

Pont Yssoir (AV 82). – The bridge affords a view of the cathedral, the mediaeval town, the Gallo-Roman ramparts and, down beside the river, a walk passing remains of fortifications dating from the Middle Ages.

Notre-Dame-du-Pré (AV). – *To visit apply at the presbytery.* Standing in a square planted with magnolias, this former abbatial church belonging to the Benedictines has Romanesque capitals and chancel.

Place and Quinconce des Jacobins (BV). – Famous for its view of the cathedral chevet, the square, Place des Jacobins, is laid out on the site of a former convent of the same name. At the entrance to the tunnel which crosses the old town is a monument to the American aviator Wilbur Wright and a curious floral clock. Directly opposite is a modern concert hall with inside a tapestry by Picart Le Doux.

The gardens, Quinconce des Jacobins, are a series of terraced avenues of lime trees.

Église de la Visitation (AX). – *Open 9.30 am to 5pm, closed Sundays and holidays.*

Overlooking the Place de la République, the heart of the modern city, this church (1730) is the former chapel of the Convent of the Visitation. The ornate façade, on the Rue Gambetta, has a portico with four Corinthian columns sheltering a fine Rococo stone door ; the interior of the same period is Baroque.

EXCURSIONS

Notre-Dame-de-L'Epau Abbey★. – *4 km - 2 1/2 miles from Le Mans. Open 9.30am to noon and 2 to 6pm ; closed Thursdays 15 September to 15 April ; 5F.*

Located in a pastoral setting on the banks of the Huisne is the former Cistercian abbey, founded in 1229 by Queen Berengaria, Richard Lionheart's widow, which is now often used for exhibitions and concerts. It was here that she found her final resting place ; her recumbent figure lies in the church.

Standing in a large park the abbey buildings are grouped round the former cloisters, destroyed in 1365 by brigands.

To the right is the **refectory** wing with the wall arcades of the former laver or washbasin.

Facing it are the monks' quarters which include the **scriptorium** (on the right) and the **chapter house** (on the left) with elegant ogive vaulting; on the first floor is the **dormitory** with wood vaulting.

On the left is the **church** built in the 13 and early 14C and restored in the early 15C. The Cistercian plan was used with the characteristic square east end and chapels oriented eastwards opening on each arm of the transept.

The large yet delicate stained glass window (15C) in the chancel is lovely. In the south transept is the recumbent figure of Queen Berengaria and the entrance to the sacristy, its columns decorated with water lilies; in the north transept a spiral staircase *(closed during exhibitions)* leads up to an attractive 15C timber roof *(by prior appointment, ☏ 43 84 22 29).*

Motor racing circuits. – To the south of Le Mans between the N 138 and the D 139 are the racing circuits which are the venue for both motor and motorcycle Grand Prix races which have made Le Mans famous to the world.

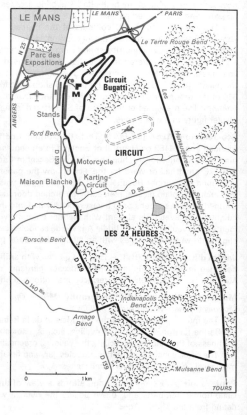

Circuit des 24 heures. – *13.64 km - 8 1/2 miles.* This road circuit is the scene of the Twenty-four Hour Race, a sporting event of universal interest. *See the historical notes on p 108.* Set amid pinewoods this 10 m - 33 ft wide circuit follows public roads for part of its layout. Coming from Le Mans pick up the track at the Tertre Rouge bend on the N 138. The S-bend of the private road and the hairpin bends of Mulsanne and Arnage are where the most exciting scenes of this twenty-four hour event occur. The course was realigned in 1972 to give the public a better view of the course and again in 1978. Inside this track is the Les Hunaudières Racecourse where Wilbur Wright attempted one of his early flights. A stele memorializes this achievement. The main entrance, a tunnel from the D 139, gives access to both the Bugatti racing circuit and the interesting Automobile Museum.

Circuit Bugatti. – *4.24 km - 2 1/2 miles. For further information apply to the Automobile-Club de l'Ouest-Circuit Bugatti. X 19, 72040 - Le Mans Cedex,* ☏ 43 72 50 25. This track, with a school for racing drivers, can be used by motorists *(excepting Mondays)* and motorcyclists *(excepting Monday mornings).*

Automobile Museum★ (M). – *Access by the D 139, north of the D 92 ; entrance across from the Automobile-Club (see above) ; continue on the road to the left and under the bridge. Open 9am to noon and 2 to 7pm (6pm 16 October to Easter) ; closed Tuesdays out of season and in the morning of 25 December and 1 January ; 16F. Exhibits are displayed on a rotating basis.*

With more than sixty bicycles and motorcycles and 150 vintage cars, the history of the automobile is vividly evoked from its earliest beginnings to 1949 : steam driven cars, De Dion Bouton 1885, Serpollet ; Krieger electric car ; petrol driven Bollée cars, racing and other models from 1920 to 1949..

Pont-de-Gennes. – Pop 1 452. *20 km - 12 miles east of Le Mans by the N 23, then bear left.*

Pont-de-Gennes near **Connerré** (pop 2 636), a small town famous for its *rillettes* or potted pork, forms a lovely picture with its small church of St-Gilles (13C), crumbling mill, and quaint 15C narrow hump backed **bridge** over the Huisne (Pont-de-Gennes was already a bridging point in Roman times).

To the west of Pont-de-Gennes, the D 119 follows a picturesque stretch on the south bank as far as St-Mars-la-Brière.

Loudon Woods (Bois de Loudon). – *18 km - 11 miles southeast of Le Mans by the N 223, D 304 then left on the D 145E and left again on the D 145.*

Forest paths branching off the D 145 drive through this coniferous forest which in September is carpeted with heather.

Castles, châteaux and churches will be more interesting
if you read the chapter on Art and Architecture on pp 20 to 27.

Michelin map ☒ fold 14 and 15 and ☒ fold 4

A tributary of the Vienne, the Manse cuts through a tranquil pastoral landscape.

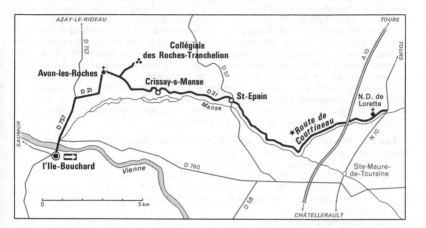

From L'Ile-Bouchard to the N 10 – 27 km - 17 miles – about 2 hours – local map above

Leave L'Ile-Bouchard north on the D757, turn right on the D21 and left on the D132 to Avon-les-Roches.

Avon-les-Roches. – Pop 688. This 12-13C **church** has a porch with three decorated arches; the doorway beside it is adorned with archivolts and delicately carved capitals.

Follow the Crissay road and after 1 km - ½ mile turn left towards Les Roches-Tranchelion.

Roches-Tranchelion Collegiate Church. – *Drive up the steep dirt path to the church's parvis.* Perched on a hill, the ruins of this Gothic collegiate church, founded in 1527, overlook the valley. The elegant façade is finely carved; note, in particular, the seated figure in the triumphal arch, above what once was a rose window, and the Renaissance decoration of the pilasters and the medallions representing the local lords.

Turn back on to the Crissay road.

Crissay-sur-Manse. – Pop 118. The ruins of the 15C castle (on the left), the stone spire of the village church (on the right) and the several 15C houses with square turrets compose a charming picture.

St-Epain. – Pop 1 409. The village **church** (12, 13 and 15C) is capped by a 13C square tower; the **fortified gate**, adjoining it, is all that remains of the 15C curtain wall. Note the **Hôtel de la Prévôté** with its mullioned window and overhanging upper storey.
Pass through the doorway to admire the hôtel's other façade, which is flanked by a round tower.
On the other side of the main street stands a house with a watch turret, indicating the bend in the road to Ste-Maure.

This road climbs up the verdant Manse valley. After passing under the railway, bear left.

Courtineau Road★. – This small picturesque road winds between the stream hidden amidst the trees and the cliff dotted with troglodyte dwellings. The chapel of **Notre-Dame-de-Lorette**, a small 15C oratory, has been carved into the cliff face beside a small troglodyte dwelling of the same period. *Pilgrimage in October.*

Les MAUGES

Michelin map ☒ fold 18 and 19 and ☒ folds 5 and 6

This green mysterious countryside is delimited by the valleys of the Divatte in the west, the Loire to the north, the Layon to the east and the Moine and town of Cholet in the south. The basic relief, a ridge of schist rocks, is dissected by small valleys and ravines and covered by *bocage,* the open woodland landscape so typical of the Armorican Massif.

A continuation of the massif, the region of Les Mauges culminates in the Puy de la Garde (210 m - 689 ft). Livestock rearing is the principal activity with the Durham-Mancelle breed being fattened on the rich pastures and sold in their thousands at the markets of Chemillé and Cholet.

On the heights stand lone sentinels, ruined windmills once used during the civil war to transmit signals while a network of sunken paths, resembling a labyrinth, leads to long, squat houses often roofed with Roman tiles. The straight main roads, often deserted, were built for strategic reasons during the Revolution and the Empire.

The Vendéen War (1793-96). – This silent hedge compartmented countryside, so suitable for ambushing, was the theatre of some of the most tragic events in the Vendéen War.

Long live God and the King. This civil war between Royalists (**Whites**, the colour of one of the monarchy's flags) and Republicans (**Blues,** colour of the Revolutionary infantry's uniform) takes its name from the province, Vendée, to the southwest of Les Mauges.

The execution of Louis XVI, the persecution of priests and military conscription were some of the causes of the first insurrections in March 1793 at Cholet and St-Florent. The counter revolt spread quickly and the peasants eagerly followed their leaders whether of noble birth like d'Elbée, Bonchamps and La Rochejaquelein or of their own background like the gamekeeper Stofflet and the pedlar Cathelineau, known as the "Saint of Anjou".

Cholet fell immediately into Royalist hands (after the Battle of Golleau Wood) followed by Chemillé, Vihiers, etc, and by May, Les Mauges was held by the Whites. The Convention, worried by the turn of events, sent the Mayence Army commanded by Westermann, Kléber and Marceau to deal with the Royal, Catholic army of Vendéens. After an initial victory at Torfou the Royalists suffered a massive defeat at Cholet on 17 October 1793. The Royalist campaign continued to the north of the Loire but in December 1793 following a defeat at Savenay all was lost. Royalists were executed by their thousands on the Place du Ralliement in Angers. Reprisals continued and the "infernal columns" commanded by Turreau were to sack Les Mauges and quell any sporadic resistance that was to arise from then on.

"Glorious" Reminders of the Vendéen War. – Scattered throughout the region are many poignant and "glorious" reminders of this civil war.

At **Maulévrier** a pyramidal monument in the park of the Château de Colbert commemorates the local Royalist leader Stofflet, nearby is the Martyrs' Cemetery *(see below)*.

Near **Torfou**, at the crossroads of the N 149 and D 753, a column evokes the Vendéen Victory of 19 September 1793 against the Mayence army sent by the Convention. At **St-Florent-le-Vieil**, is Bonchamps' tomb *(p 105)*.

Near **Cholet**, on the road to Nuaillé, a cross has been erected on the spot where La Rochejaquelein fell (29 January 1794).

■ TOWNS and SIGHTS

Beaupréau. – Pop 6195. Michelin map 🗺 fold 5. Sited in the heart of Les Mauges this small town with narrow winding streets was the Royalists headquarters in 1793. The leader d'Elbée had a home. The 15C **château** overlooking the Evre (there is a good view of it from the river's south bank) has been much altered since its construction. Set fire to by the Blues in 1793, it was restored in the early 19C. Two large towers flank a 17C pavilion, the pyramidal roof of which is framed by two slate covered cupolas.

Cholet. – Pop 56528. *Town plan in the current Michelin Red Guide France.* Since the 11C Cholet has been associated with the cultivation and weaving of hemp and flax and even today its production of cloth, handkerchiefs, table and household linen is world famous. The Rue Nationale and Avenue Gambetta are lined with shops selling linen and the traditional handkerchief, a small red handkerchief with a white border dear to the Vendéens. Other industries include footwear factories, electronic components, plastics, agricultural machinery and a Michelin tyre factory. There are also livestock markets.

The small **History Museum★** (Musée d'Histoire – *open 10am to noon and 2 to 5pm; closed Tuesdays and holidays)* exhibits on the ground floor the linen craft and its handiwork; the first floor recounts this violent period of local history, evoking local leaders and other Royalist memories.

An elegant 18C hôtel, surrounded by a park, houses the **Fine Arts Museum★** (Musée des Beaux-Arts, *same visiting times as the history museum*). It displays canvases by such artists as Toulouse-Lautrec, Vuillard, Braque, Matisse, Arp...

In the heart of the city the Rue du Devau and the **Rue du Commerce** now reserved for pedestrians, have preserved several elegant town houses graced with 18C wrought iron balconies. The street continues to the **Jardin du Mail**, a pleasant garden surrounding the Law Courts.

Le Fuilet. – Pop 1761. Michelin map 🗺 fold 5 – *8 km - 5 miles west of Montrevault.* Le Fuilet and its environs – Les Challonges, Bellevue, Les Recoins etc. – lie on clay soil, which explains the profusion of brick-kilns and pottery workshops in the area *(open during work week)*.

Maulévrier Forest. – Michelin map 🗺 fold 6 – *15 km - 9 miles east of Cholet.* Beside the D 196 between Yzernay and Chanteloup, the **Martyrs' Cemetery** is set in an oak forest. This forest during the Vendéen war hid Stofflet's headquarters and was where the Whites, wounded in battle, were taken care of. On 25 March 1794, the Blues penetrated this thick forest and massacred 1 200 Whites; two days later the Whites retaliated. A small commemorative chapel has been erected.

■ MAYENNE Valley ★
Michelin map 🗺 folds 10 and 20

Winding and deeply embanked, wending from north to south, the Mayenne follows a majestic course. Canalized in the 19C the river, has thirty-nine locks between Laval and Angers lending itself particularly to the navigation of pleasure craft *(boat rental see p 37)*.

Crossing the schists, a prolongation of the Armorican Massif, the river flows between steep slopes where broom and chestnut grow in abundance. The deep, narrow form of the valley has prevented the siting of villages on the valley floor.

The road described on the next page crosses a succession of tranquil villages, perched on hills in a verdant *bocage (p 10)* landscape, with charming slate roofed low houses; it offers views of the river either from a bridge or driving along small country lanes, which run along the river bank permitting discovery, along the way, of the isolated château with its landscaped park or windmill.

From Laval to Angers — *116 km - 72 miles — about 1 day — local map below*

Leave Laval *(p 88)* to the south by the D 1 which parallels the west bank of the Mayenne and then offers pleasant perspectives of the valley as it climbs towards L'Huisserie ; take the D 112 towards Entrammes ; 1 km - 1/2 mile further take to the left a road to l'Enclos and Bonne (Ecluse) which goes down to the Mayenne : very pretty **viewpoint★** of the river, lock, mill and château.

Return to the D 112. The D 103 branching off to the left leads to the **Trappe du Port-du-Salut.** The Trappist monks produced the famous Port-Salut cheese up until 1959, a cheese factory, now independent of the abbey, producing it at Entrammes.

The D 112 crosses tributary valleys ; cows graze in the meadows planted with apple trees ; views to the left over the valley. At Houssay cross to the east bank ; from the bridge there are views of the Mayenne.

Further on take to the right the N 162 which leads to Château-Gontier.

Château-Gontier. — *Description p 66.*
Leave Château-Gontier by ③ and the D 22 : views to the right over the valley.

Daon. — Pop 430. Well placed on the hillside, overlooking the Mayenne, Daon, the birthplace of the Abbot Bernier who negotiated the peace between the Chouans and Republicans, still has a 16C manor.

At Daon bear left on the D 213 towards St-Michel de Feins and again take the second road to the left. An alley of lime and plane trees leads to the **Manoir de l'Escoublère** (16C) encircled by a moat.

After Daon turn right on to the D 190.

Chenillé-Changé. — Pop 153. Well situated on the banks of the Mayenne.

Cross the river towards Chambellay, bear right on the D 187.

La Jaille-Yvon. — Pop 249. Village perched on the cliff dominating the river. To the left of the church is the path which leads to the east end from where there is a panoramic view of the wide, winding valley.

Continue to the N 162 towards Angers.

From the N 162, there are views to the left, a little after the road to Chambellay, of the **Château du Bois-Mauboucher** (15-17C), surrounded by woods and lawns and on the edge of a vast lake.

Le Lion d'Angers. — Pop 2775. This small town is set on the banks of the Oudon at the centre of a stock rearing region, specializing in half bred horses. **St-Martin Church** has a doorway, the upper part of which presents a pre-Romanesque delicate tracery pattern formed by the red cement ; the nave is Romanesque. Above the entrance doorway and on the left wall of the nave are 16C mural paintings representing the demon vomiting the Deadly Sins, a Crucifix and Saint Christopher. In a recess one can see a diptych of an Ecce Homo.

National Stud of Isle-Briand★ (Haras national de l'Isle-Briand). — *1 km - 1/2 mile east of Lion d'Angers via the D 770. Open 9am to noon and 2 to 6pm. The full complement of stallions is present only between 15 July and 15 February. Apply to the attendant.*
The National Stud, transferred in 1974 from the Angers Stud, holds some eighty stallions and has a personnel of forty-five. The visit of these ultra-modern buildings includes the barns, harness room, forge and riding stables ; there is even a maternity unit !

Take the D 770 to the right, then after the bridge over the Mayenne bear right on the D 187.

Grez-Neuville. — Pop 943. A lovely flowered village.

Continue along the D 191 which at times dominates and at other times overhangs the river ; the road passes at the foot of the imposing **Château du Sautret.** At Feneu, take the D 768 to the right which crosses the Mayenne and climbs towards Montreuil-Juigné. *Continue to Angers (p 41).*

Michelin map 🔲 fold 19 – Pop 938

This sleepy village kas kept its mediaeval aspect.

Ramparts. – *The visit can be done by car.* Built in the early 13C the ramparts have kept three of their five towers and three gates : Porte Bonne-Nouvelle, Porte d'En-Bas, Porte d'En-Haut.

Old Houses. – Lining the steep and windy Grande-Rue, from the Porte Bonne-Nouvelle to the Porte d'En-Haut, are old 13-16C houses. The church *(not open)* is all that remains of a Benedictine priory.

MEUNG-SUR-LOIRE ★

Michelin map 🔲 fold 8 – *Local map p 101* – Pop 5659

This picturesque fortified village lies between the Loire, lapping the mall (Mail) planted with tall trees and the N 152, running along the plateau away from the old town.

Pass in front of the **old marketplace** and go up the narrow **Rue Porte-d'Amont** which ends underneath an arch. Stroll along the small alleyways bordering the **Mauves,** a tributary of the Loire, which runs between the houses on Rue des Mauves and Rue du Trianon.

The town commemorates its most famous son, **Jean de Meung,** with a statue. It was he who, *c* 1280, added 18000 lines to the original 4000 lines of the *Roman de la Rose* or *Romance of the Rose,* written about fifty years earlier by Guillaume de Lorris *(p 106).* This allegorical narrative was the greatest literary achievement of a period in which patient readers abounded. Chaucer translated it in part and was much influenced by it throughout his poetic career.

St-Liphard★. – *Closed 11 November.* This is a fine building, erected from the 11 to 13C, including a plain and massive tower, a semicircular chevet and an original transept with rounded ends. From behind the chevet there is a good view of the church and the château.

Château. – *Guided tours Easter to All Saints' Day 8.30am to 6pm ; the rest of the year Saturdays and Sundays and holidays only ; time : 1 hour ; 7F château, 5F underground and oubliette.*

The château is a mixture of styles : feudal on the entrance side (13C) – the remains of the drawbridge and dried moat are visible ; on the other side the mediaeval entrance was replaced by the 16C entrance which was remodelled in the 18C. The interior (rooms are furnished) was restored in the 19C.

After visiting the château, the tour goes **underground** to the 12C chapel with palm tree vaulting and the dungeons. In the park is an **oubliette** discovered in 1973. It is a large underground tower with a well at the bottom ; the condemned were lowered on ropes ; each day they received one loaf of bread and a pitcher of water to divide among themselves. Only the poet François Villon *(p 28)* with the help of his numerous patrons was liberated.

Numerous camping sites
have : shops, licensed premises, laundries, games rooms, mini-golf,
play grounds, paddling and swimming pools.
*Consult the **Michelin Guide, Camping Caravaning France.***

MONDOUBLEAU

Michelin maps 🔲 south of folds 15 and 16 and 🔲 north of folds 5 and 6 – Pop 1694

On arriving from the west on the D 86, one discovers Mondoubleau clustered on the hillside. Standing on a knoll dominating the road to Cormenon, the ruins of the **keep,** made of local red sandstone, lean curiously. They are all that remain of the fortress built during the end of the 10C by Hugues Doubleau who gave his name to the town. The curtain wall, partly hidden among the houses and trees, also stands.

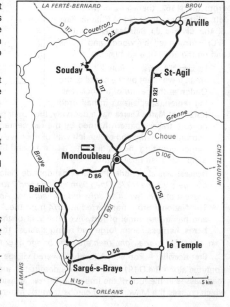

Old house. – This 15C house stands at the corner of the Rue de la Basse-Ville and the entrance ramp to the castle.

Grand Mail. – The Rue Gheerbrandt passes the post office (PTT) on the way to the Place St-Denis. Go behind the post office and cross the public gardens to reach the Grand Mail, a long shaded alley affording a fine view of the valley.

EXCURSIONS

Arville. – *Round tour of 26 km - 16 miles to the north by the D 921 – about 1 hour.*

Château de St-Agil. – *Only the exterior can be visited.* This interesting château is encircled with moats. The part of the building dating from the 13C was remodelled in 1720. The early 16C entrance pavilion is flanked by two towers decorated with patterns made by the red and black bricks. The white masonry of the machicolations follows the watchpath which is dominated by pepperpot roofs. The main building has a medallioned dormer window figuring the local lord, Antoine de la Vove. The park was landscaped by Jules Hardouin-Mansart and transformed in 1872 into the English style. There are still some splendid lime trees dating from 1720.

Arville. – Pop 152. This small village is known for the Templars' commandery situated slightly to the north, at the side of the D 921. This was one of the commanderies erected by the military and religious Order of the Templars (founded 1119) to protect the main pilgrimage routes. Fortified in the 13C they also served as banks and consequently the Order amassed considerable wealth, independence and influence which were to be its undoing in 1307 when the Order was disbanded by Philippe the Fair.

The commandery has a 12C chapel preceded by a bell gable which is linked to a flint tower, formerly part of the ramparts. The late 15C gateway through the wall has two brick turrets with curious roofs.

(After photo: C. Breteau, Éd. Delmas)

Arville — Commandery

Take the road to the left towards Oigny and Souday.

Souday. – Pop 688. The nave of the church is extended by a curious 16C two storeyed chancel. Two staircases with wrought iron railings (1838) climb to the upper chancel glazed with Renaissance stained glass (1540) representing the Passion and the Resurrection.

In the crypt the elegant ogive vaulting springs from columns without capitals. The south transept has 16C mural paintings of various saints; on the vaulting are the symbols of the Four Evangelists.

Return to Mondoubleau by the D 117.

Sargé. – *Round tour of 24 km - 15 miles.* Map **64** north of folds 5 and 6. *Leave Mondoubleau to the southeast by the D 151.*

Le Temple. – Pop 156. The Templars' commandery has now disappeared but a 12-16C church still remains.

Turn right on to the D 56.

Sargé-sur-Braye. – Pop 974. In the 11 and 15C Church of St-Martin *(to visit apply at the baker's - boulangerie except Thursdays)* with painted wainscoting dating from 1549, 16C wall paintings have been uncovered in the nave evoking the *Pietà* and St Martin and some from the 14C in the chancel showing Christ in Majesty and the Work of the Months : note in particular Janus with three faces symbolizing January.

Baillou. – Pop 250. The village is pleasantly grouped at the foot of a 16-17C château. Isolated on a mound the attractive **church** (early 16C) has a Renaissance doorway with pilasters adorned by foliated scrolls, the whole surmounted by the figures of Adam and Eve. Inside *(to visit apply to Mme Cornet, right of the church)*, note in the north transept a sculptured altarpiece (1618) evoking the Death of the Virgin with the Apostles and the donor.

(After photo: Arlette de la Moussaye)

Sargé Church — Janus' Feast

The D 86 takes you back to Mondoubleau; nice view on arrival.

MONTGEOFFROY, Château de ★

Michelin map **64** folds 11 and 12 – 24 km - 15 miles east of Angers

This fine building on a regular plan – an imposing main building joined to two large wings at right angles to it by terrace pavilions – was erected in the 18C for Marshal de Contades. The Marshal had, however, kept some of the 16C buildings : two round towers flanking the château, the moats, which delimit the small courtyard, and the chapel.

Guided tours late March to 30 October 9.30 am to noon and 2.30 to 6.30 pm ; time : 1/2 hour ; 18F.

It remained the property of this one family which explains why the original furniture signed by Gourdin, Garnier and Durand, and fine pictures by Rigaud, Drouais, Pourbus the Younger, Van Loo, Desportes, etc. have been preserved. The whole is a model of proportion and harmony. Every piece of furniture stands in the place for which it was designed. The hangings and tapestries appear as if they were just made.

The tour ends in the chapel, which has a fine 16C stained glass window, and in the harness room, which is well arranged ; in the stables are the different horse carriages used by the family.

Michelin map 👁️64 fold 5 – *Local map p 99* – Pop 4431 – *Facilities pp 36-37*

Former capital of Bas-Vendômois, Montoire attracts many anglers because of the good fishing provided by this stretch of the Loir.

Pilgrimage routes. – The 7C Priory of St-Gilles was followed by a fort in the 9C as defence against the Norman incursions.

In the Middle Ages several pilgrimage routes passed by Montoire, the first to the tomb of St Martin in Tours and the second to St James's shrine in Santiago de Compostela. Hospices and leper hospitals were built in both Montoire and Troo.

A momentous meeting. – Following an initial meeting with one of his Ministers of State it was here, at the station in Montoire, on the 24 October 1940 that Marshal Pétain, head of the Vichy Government, met Hitler in a specially built train. On this occasion Hitler tried in vain to convince the Marshal to take up arms against Britain.

■ SIGHTS

Bridge. – This bridge affords attractive **views**★ of the Loir flowing between banks lined with weeping willows and wistaria covered old houses. The numerous small rowing boats moored along the banks belong to the anglers and clubs of the region.

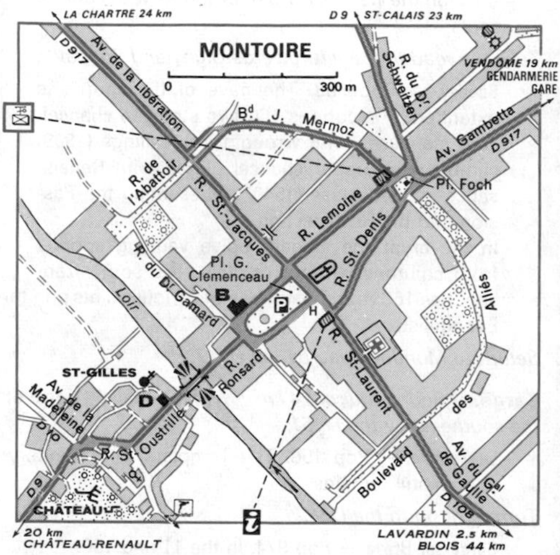

Chapel of St-Gilles★. – *Closed Wednesdays, 1 October to 28 February; 6F.* An attractive Renaissance house (**D**) adorned with a sign dedicated by a guild to one of its members *(p 157)* a native of Montoire, marks the entrance to the narrow lane which leads to the chapel.

On entering the gateway there is a view of the apse of a gracious Romanesque chapel, which once belonged to a Benedictine priory, of which Ronsard held the charge. It was from there that he left in October 1585 for his other priories of Ste-Madeleine de Croixval and St-Cosme near Tours, where he was to die two months later. A cypress, yew trees, a garden sloping down to the Loir and the Prior's lodging make a pleasant setting for the chapel.

Mural paintings★★. – These cover the three apses which arranged in the form of a clover make up the chancel and transept. Compare the two Christs of different periods on the oven vaults. The oldest on the main apse, dating from the first quarter of the 12C, shows a very majestic Christ of the Apocalypse, surrounded by angels. At the end of the south transept a 12C mural of Christ proffering the keys to St Peter (faint) shows a marked Byzantine influence with the tightly symmetrical folds. The mural in the north transept showing Christ and the Apostles recounts the story of Pentecost. The unnatural attitudes and colours are typical of the early works of the local school *(p 26)*. The arches of the transept crossing are also adorned with paintings : see the Battle of the Virtues and Vices on the western arch.

Château. – *To visit apply to Mr. Michel, ☎ 54 85 13 61 (except Tuesdays in July).*

Ruined but imposing this fortress, standing on a rocky spur comprises an 11C square keep preceded by a stone and flint wall. There is a fine view over the Loir Valley and the keep at Lavardin.

There is a model of the château as it was, in the entrance hall of the town hall *(closed Saturday afternoons).*

Renaissance houses (**B**). – Montoire-sur-le-Loir has preserved several fine examples of Renaissance houses. Two stand side by side on Place Clemenceau. The biggest with its mullioned and very high dormer windows is also the oldest. In Rue St-Oustrille note the house (**D**) with the curious chimney *(see above).*

The traveller's friends:
*The **Michelin Map series** at a scale of 1 : 200 000*
*and the **Michelin Red Guide France**.*

When choosing your lunchtime or overnight stop
use the above maps as all towns listed in the
Red Guide are underlined in red.

When driving into or through a town
use the map as it also indicates all places with
a town plan in the Red Guide. Common reference
numbers make the transfer from map to plan easier.

Michelin map 📖 south of folds 16 and 17 – Pop 499

Montrésor rises high above the right bank of the Indrois. In the village note the old timbered market and on the main street a 16C building with a corner turret now housing the police station.

Château★. – *Guided tours 1 June to 31 August 9am to noon and 2 to 7pm ; 1 April to 31 May and 1 September to 31 October, 10am to noon and 2 to 6pm ; time : 1/2 hour ; 15F.*

Still standing of the 11C fortress built by Foulques Nerra *(p 42)* are the curtain wall and crumbling towers. Enclosed within these strong walls, in a charming overgrown park, is the early 16C residence built by **Imbert de Bastarnay,** lord of Montrésor (as of 1493). The château's south façade, overlooking the river, is decorated with gabled dormer windows and two machicolated towers. In 1849 the château was restored by a Polish nobleman, **Count Branicki,** who was later to become a senator under Napoleon III.

The furnishings are as they were at the time of Branicki : his shooting trophies decorate the entrance hall ; military souvenirs and medals and pictures by Polish and French painters are exhibited throughout. Also worthy of note are bas-reliefs in wood representing the battles of John III Sobieski of Poland (17C), a boudoir containing Italian Primitives and gold and silver plate.

From the curtain wall, dominating the Indrois, there is a pleasant view of the valley and village.

Church. – Built from 1519-41 in the Gothic style (only the doorway is Renaissance), this collegiate church was founded by Imbert de Bastarnay *(see above)* to house his tomb. The **Bastarnay tomb★** is at the end of the nave : three recumbent figures (the lord, his wife and son) in white marble are supported by a base decorated with statues of the Twelve Apostles. The stalls carved with medallions and two stained glass windows are Renaissance. In the apsidal chapel (on the left) is an *Annunciation* (17C) painted by Philippe de Champaigne.

EXCURSION

Chartreuse du Liget. – *6 km - 4 miles west on the D 760.*

The road crosses orchards before arriving at the edge of the Loches Forest. To the right of the road behind some trees is **La Corroirie,** a former annexe of the monastery. To the west, the fortified gateway and square tower with machicolations date from the 15C when La Corroirie was fortified.

Also on the side of the road is the **charterhouse** (Carthusian monastery) ; pass through the monumental 18C **gateway★**. The number of its outbuildings gives an idea of the wealth and importance of this charterhouse founded by Henri II of England in expiation, it is said, for the murder of Thomas Becket.

Pass in front of the outbuildings (once the baker, locksmith, carpenter, etc.) go down the central path to the end of the courtyard ; apply to

(After photo : Éd. du Zodiaque)

Chapel of St-Jean-du-Liget

the house – door on the left – for the key to visit the chapel of St-Jean and for permission to visit the charterhouse.

In front of the house, on the left, are the ruins of the 12C church, behind it one side of the great cloisters, built in 1787 is still standing.

Chapel of St-Jean. – *After having received the key (see above) take the road to Loches for 1 km - 1/2 mile then take the first path on the left.*

This curious round 12C chapel, standing alone in an open field, is where the first monks of the charterhouse lived. Inside are some Romanesque frescoes.

Michelin map 📖 south of fold 12 – Pop 4 331 – *Facilities pp 36-37*

The little town of Montreuil-Bellay possesses a very lovely **site★** beside the Thouet on the border of the Poitou and Anjou regions. From the east bank of the river and bridge there are good views of the château and church. While the gardens along the west bank are an agreeable place to stroll, the picturesque Place des Ormeaux, in front of the château's entrance is also worth a stop.

Parts of the mediaeval wall are still standing : the **Porte St-Jean (D),** a 15C fortified gateway, is flanked by two large rusticated towers.

Recalcitrant vassals. – In 1025 Foulques Nerra count of Anjou, gave this stronghold to his vassal **Berlay** (distorted into Bellay), who made it a strong, powerful fortress. A century later these warlike feudal lords did not hesitate to plot and intrigue even against their overlord. It was only after a year of siege and the ensuing famine, that another Berlay finally capitulated to Geoffroy Plantagenet. The latter razed the castle's fortifications in 1150. When their overlords the Plantagenets, through Henry II, became kings of England and thus enemy to the king of France, the Berlays pledged allegiance to their overlord to the detriment of their king Philippe-Auguste.

■ SIGHTS

Château★★. – *Guided tours 1 April to 1 November 10 to 11.30am and 2 to 5.30pm; closed Tuesdays; time: 3/4 hour; 17F, 9F gardens only. At Easter, Whitsun and in summer, enter by the moats arranged as gardens, from where you can hear a recording of the château's history.*

This château is imposing, due to its fortifications, pleasant, thanks to its gardens, interesting for its history and remarkable for its furnishings.

Once past the fortified gateway, the stronghold aspect of the château disappears as the visitor is confronted by a gracious 15C residence built by the d'Harcourt family.

From the château's courtyard, which forms a terrace, there are pleasant views of the church, château and its park.

To the right of the gatehouse, or old castle, enter the small square edifice which opens onto the courtyard. This is the **mediaeval kitchen** with a central chimney inspired by the one at Fontevraud *(p 82);* it contains 19C furnishings and a set of copperware.

To the right of the kitchen is the **canons' dwelling** (15C), the four turreted staircases of which lead to four private dwellings – storeroom below, room upstairs. This unusual arrangement was reserved for the canons attached to the château's chapel *(see below).*

To the left is the **Château Neuf** or New Castle, which also dates from the 15C. The turreted staircase is lovely with its delicately carved panels underneath the mullioned windows. The loggia, however, is 19C with its ogee arch and beside it is a 12-13C tower. In the Plantagenet vaulted *(p 21)* **cellar** the Sacavins meet. This wine growers' brotherhood *(p 41)* was founded in 1904 by the owner of the château, at that time Georges de Grandmaison, to make Anjou wine known.

The château's rooms have ceilings 7m-23 ft high! The dining room has a painted ceiling; the small **oratory** is covered with late 15C frescoes, those on the vaulting depict angels as musicians playing a motet (written by a Scottish monk Walter Frye, while accompanying his master to Tours; *the guide plays it on tape).* The bedroom of the Duchess of Longueville (1619-79), Condé's sister, is shown. She was exiled to Montreuil by Louis XIV for her role during the Fronde. In the Grand Salon, above the German cupboard in marquetry hangs a Brussels tapestry. Chamber music entices the visitor into the music room; note the superb bureau by Boulle (1642-1732) inlaid in brass and tortoise shell.

ANGERS 53 km
D 761
SAUMUR 16 km
N 147

MONTREUIL-BELLAY

0   400 m

32 km
ARGENTON-
CHÂTEAU
D 77

CHÂTEAU

Av. Paul Painlevé

Thouet

B

E

Ardenne

Bellay

Nationale

FONTEVRAUD
20 km

Méron

D 160

D 766

Av. Duret

D

Bd

A

Briand

R. des Ormeaux

GARE

N 147

D 938   THOUARS 18 km   LOUDUN 25 km

Ardiller (Bd de l')	.....	1	
Ardiller (R. de l')	.....	2	Dr-Gaudrez (R. du) 5
Château (R. du)	.....	3	Douves (R. des) 6
		4	Ormeaux (Pl. des) 7

Notre-Dame (B). – This former seigneurial chapel was built from 1472 to 1484. It has a single nave with a painted litre *(p 77);* the lord's small oratory is on the north side.

Les Nobis (E). – In a charming verdant setting beside the Thouet, are the ruins of the church of St-Pierre burned by the Huguenots in the 16C; it has a Romanesque apse (11C) with carved capitals.

Beside it stand two wings of a 17C cloister which house a cultural centre.

EXCURSION

Asnières Abbey. – *7.5 km - 5 miles to the northwest by the D 761; after 5.5 km - 3 miles turn right. Open 1 July to 31 August 10am to noon and 2 to 6pm; time: 1/2 hour; 5F.*

The romantic ruins, lying north of the Cizay Forest, were once an important monastery. It was founded in the 12C. The graceful finely ribbed vaulting of the **chancel★**, with that of St-Serge at Angers, is the most perfect specimen extant of the Angevin style *(p 21).*

The south transept is the oldest part of the building. The north transept, like the chancel, dates from the early 13C.

The Abbot's chapel was added in the 15C. This charming little oratory is decorated with trefoils and festoons, and contains a 14C Crucifix.

MONTRICHARD ★

Michelin map **64** folds 16 and 17 – Pop 3 786 – *Facilities pp 36-37*

From the south bank of the river (bathing place) and the bridge over the Cher there are good views of the town and its mediaeval houses clustered around the church and the base of the crumbling keep.

The cliff upstream from the town is pitted with quarries (**Bourré** is a village 3 km - 2 miles to the east, its stone has been used for the construction of the nearby châteaux) which have now been transformed into **méthode champenoise cellars** *(open Easter to 1 November 9 – 10am Sundays and holidays – to 11.30am and 2 to 6pm; the rest of the year Mondays to Fridays only),* troglodyte houses or converted into caves for growing mushrooms.

■ SIGHTS

Keep★. – *Open mid-June to 15 September 9.30am to 12.15pm and 2.30 to 6.30pm; Palm Sunday to mid-June and 15 to 29 September, Sundays and public holidays only at the above times; 5F.*

The square keep overlooking the Cher from the edge of the plateau is surrounded by a curtain wall and rampart. It was built by Foulques Nerra *(p 42)* in around 1010, with two further sets of ramparts being added in the 12 and 13C and dismantled by Henri IV in 1589. From the top of the keep *(platform small; limited to 4 at a time)* there is an excellent **view★★** of the town and the Cher Valley.

Ste-Croix. – This former seigneurial chapel has a façade with elegant Romanesque arches, those of the porch are adorned with a twisted torus; the doorway is also Romanesque. The marriage of the future Louis XII with Jeanne de France, the daughter of Louis XI, was celebrated here in 1476.

Old Houses. – Picturesque houses can be found not far from the keep: **Hôtel d'Effiat** (now a hospice), Rue Porte au Roi, a late 15-early 16C house which is Gothic in decoration with some Renaissance details; on the Place Barthélemy-Gilbert stand two old half timbered houses; and at the corner of the Rue du Pont is the 16C **Maison de l'Ave Maria** or "house of the three gables" with finely carved beams. Across the street is the Petits Degrés Ste-Croix which leads to several troglodyte dwellings. Further on, at the corner of the Rue du Prêche, is the stone façade of the 11C **Maison du Prêche.**

Nanteuil Church. – *On the road to Amboise more than 1 km - 1/2 mile from the town centre.* This Gothic church with a Flamboyant doorway has a Romanesque apse decorated with elegantly carved capitals. Its narrow yet high nave is covered with Angevin vaulting. Left of the façade, stairs lead up to a chapel built by Louis XI *(access by the stairs inside the church).*

The Virgin of Nanteuil is the object of a very old pilgrimage on Whit Monday.

EXCURSIONS

Château de Montpoupon★. – *12 km - 7 1/2 miles southwest on the D764. Guided tours 15 June to 30 September 10am to noon and 2 to 7pm (Saturdays and Sundays 10am to 7pm); during the spring holidays, Saturdays, Sundays and holidays, 2 to 7pm; up to 14 June and in October, Saturdays and Sundays and holidays 10am to noon and 2 to 7pm; time: 1/2 hour; 10.50F.*

This imposing mass dominates the small wooded valley. The towers, once linked by a curtain wall are all that remain of the 13C fortress. The main building with mullioned windows and gables in the Gothic style was built in the 15C while the entrance gatehouse – which on one side is decorated in the Renaissance style – dates from the early 16C.

After visiting the interior of the château and gatehouse, the tour continues to the **outbuildings★**: kitchen (set of copperware), linen room (old dresses and lovely lace), a small hunting museum, stables (horse carriages) and harness room.

Château du Gué-Péan★. – *13 km - 8 miles east via Monthou-sur-Cher and a private alley. Guided tours (3/4 hour) 15 March to 15 November 9.30am to 6.30pm; the rest of the year 10.30am to 5pm; 18F.*

Isolated in a peaceful wooded valley the château houses a riding club in its outbuildings and has picnic grounds *(admission charge).*

The château (16, 17C) is built round a square inner courtyard and is really a country house, although there are still some traces of fortifications in the plan, notably the four angle towers and dried moats. The tallest tower (the three others were never completed) has a bell shaped roof and delicately carved machicolations. The main ranges of the building are given a flow of line by their arcades and the graceful pilaster flanked windows. Roofs in the French manner, high pitched, elegant and remarkable in their variety crown the whole.

The inside is furnished in the Louis XV and Louis XVI style and adorned with tapestries and pictures by master painters. The great saloon has a monumental fireplace designed by Germain Pilon; the library includes a rich collection of autographs and mementoes.

One can go up the tallest tower and walk along its watch path.

Thésée. – Pop 1 157. *10 km - 6 miles east on the D76.* 1 km - 1/2 mile to the north before the village are the remains of Roman Tasciaca, once a staging post and storehouse on the road between Bourges and Tours. East of Thésée, the cliff dominating the Cher is riddled with troglodyte dwellings and cellars.

MONTSOREAU ★

Michelin map **64** fold 13 – *Local map p 105* – Pop 454 – *Facilities pp 36-37*

The village, prettily situated a little downstream from the confluence of the Loire and the Vienne, is known for its château. *Boat trips, p 76.*

Château★. – *Guided tours 10am to noon and 2 to 7pm; closed Tuesdays; time: 1 hour; 6F.*

It was built in the 15C by a Chambes. This family produced bold warriors and enterprising women. A lady of Montsoreau attracted the Duc de Berry, brother of Louis XI, and through him formed the *Ligue du Bien Public* (League for Public Good) which the king defeated only by the assassination of the pretender and his mistress. A century later another Chambes was one of the most ferocious executioners in the massacre of the Huguenots on St Bartholemew's Day, 1572.

The château owes its renown to Alexandre Dumas's novel *La Dame de Montsoreau.* The heroine, the Countess of Montsoreau was compelled by her outraged husband to make a rendez-vous with her lover, Bussy d'Amboise, at the Château de la Coutancière (across the river) on which occasion the unsuspecting lover was assassinated. In spite of this affair the couple were seemingly reconciled and continued to live on excellent terms for many years to follow.

The imposing façade, which until 1820 plunged into the river, is military in aspect.

The château has a Goums Museum, illustrating the history of the *goums* or cavalry units recruited in Morocco. There are also souvenirs of the conquest of Morocco and of Marshal Lyautey and his campaign.

EXCURSIONS

Panorama★★. – *1 km - 1/2 mile by the road to the right of the château ; signposted.*

A cliff top belvedere in the heart of the vineyard affords a view downstream of the village, château and the Val and upstream of the confluence of the Loire and Vienne.

Moulin de la Herpinière. – *1.5 km - 1 mile south by the VC3. Open Easter to 30 September 9.30 to 11.30am and 2 to 6.30pm ; the rest of the year Sunday afternoons and school holidays only 2.30 to 6.30pm ; closed in January and Mondays except in July and August ; 10F.*

This 15C windmill is one of the few remaining ones once dotting the Anjou plateau. It is rather unique in that its millstone is "buried" in a tufa chalk cellar. The miller's house *(artist's studio : sculpture, weaving)* and its outbuildings (forge, press) are also troglodyte.

ORLÉANS ★

Michelin map 🔢 fold 19 – *Local map p 101* – Pop 105 589 – *See plan of built up area in the current Michelin Guide France*

Orléans has always been an active business centre. The wheat of the Beauce, the honey, poultry and potatoes of the Gâtinais, the game of the Sologne, the wine of the Val, together with local products – vinegar, trees, shrubs and flowers (Orléans roses are famous) – keep trade going. Industrial zones : Fleury-les-Aubrais, St-Jean-de-la-Ruelle and Chapelle-St-Mesmin – where Michelin erected a tyre factory in 1951 – surround the city.

Capital of the Loiret and of the Centre (an economic division) Orléans plays an important administrative role as well as being a major university centre. The related service industries are concentrated mostly 9 km - 5 1/2 miles south of Orléans in **Orléans-la-Source**, a new city built in the 1960's beside the Sologne Forest.

Orléans also played an important role in French history. It became the capital of France, with the first Capetians, when Robert the Pious, son of Hugh Capet, was crowned in Orléans in 996. Beginning in the 14C, the duchy of Orléans would traditionally go to the youngest branch of the reigning family.

Little of old Orléans is left to recount its prodigious past as the wars – Hundred Years War, Wars of Religion, and bombardments of 1940 – have left their mark ; and yet the old quarter has preserved some picturesque old mediaeval and Renaissance houses.

THE SIEGE OF 1428-29

The Adversaries. – On 12 October 1428, Lord Salisbury, with an English and Burgundian army, arrived before Orléans on the south bank of the Loire. The people of Orléans had razed the suburbs to a distance of 200 m - 219 yd beyond the walls to make the attack more difficult for the enemy. The English captured the fort, Les Tourelles, at the head of the bridge, but could not debouch from it. The defenders had blown up an arch and hastily erected a small wooden outwork in front of the Bastille St-Antoine. For their own protection the attackers destroyed another arch in front of Les Tourelles.

Divided into thirty-four companies, the 5000 citizens who were fit to bear arms, manned the thirty-four towers on the walls. Altogether about 10000 men defended Orléans. The English effectives were about the same, at least at the beginning.

Salisbury, being obliged to lay siege to the place, surrounded it with trenches overlooked by strongpoints. These were works made of earth and wood and protected by ditches. Each sheltered a garrison of 400 to 500 men and a few bombards. These works commanded only the Loire and the western part of the town, for the English had not enough men to close the circle and resist any sorties by the besieged garrison. The people of Orléans could communicate with the country to the northeast without too much risk.

The artillery. – Artillery already played an important role at this time. The bombards, made of a wooden tube bound with iron or of an iron tube, could throw a stone ball weighing 10 to 100 kg (22 to 220 lb) for a distance of up to 1000 m - 1 mile. The adversaries could, therefore, reach one another across the Loire. There were seventy-two bombards in Orléans, but the damage done by their missiles was limited, for they were not explosive. Their firing was also inaccurate in range, because the firing powders were unreliable.

Daily life. – After a few months, besiegers and besieged found time lay heavy on their hands. They would shout to one another, arrange small exchanges and watch single combats to relieve the tedium.

Salisbury was struck by a shot and died of his wounds. An astonishing version, which delighted the people of Orléans, made the rounds : a loaded bombard had been left for a moment by its gunner in the Tour Notre-Dame. A small boy, imitating what he had seen the gunner do, touched the gun with the red hot rod that served as a match. The gun fired, and the shot, guided by the Virgin who wished to punish Salisbury for having burnt the Basilica Notre-Dame de Cléry, decapitated the English nobleman just as one of his officers, pointing out Orléans to him, exclaimed : "My Lord, there is your town !"

Another subject of endless talk was the prowess and cunning of Master-Gunner Jean. With his two bombards, *Rifflart* and *Montargis,* he gave the English a hard time. Sometimes he pretended to be killed. He was carried away with every sign of grief and the enemy shouted for joy. But the next day Master Jean, hale and hearty, opened fire once more.

Five months passed. The morale of the defenders was getting low. The English became no more aggressive; some of their troops had been withdrawn and there were only two or three thousand rather tired men left.

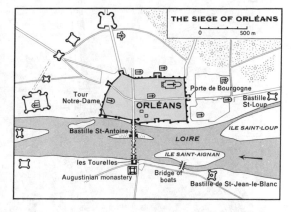

Arrival of Joan of Arc.
– Joan came from Blois via Olivet. The Domrémy shepherdess, unfamiliar with local topography and no doubt purposely deceived by her military advisers, was surprised, on reaching the Loire, to find Orléans on the far side of the river. To transfer her troops to the north bank she had to send them back to Blois, since the English held the bridge at Beaugency. Having crossed the bridge at Blois the troops avoided the English defences to the north and arrived at Orléans five days after Joan. The Maid, with a few companions, had gone 10 km - 6 miles upstream, and on 28 April 1429, she crossed the Loire in a boat at **Chécy**. She spent the night at the Château de Reuilly, which she left on 29 April to enter Orléans by the Porte de Bourgogne.

Joan of Arc was welcomed with enthusiasm by the people of Orléans. She also had a great effect on the troops. For love of the Maid they gave up their debaucheries, went to church and bit their lips to keep from swearing. They followed her with the good people who dogged her footsteps to kiss her sword or touch her horse.

Among the military leaders, however, with the exception of Dunois *(p 64),* Joan found only envy, deceit and ill will. The most hostile was **Gaucourt,** the Governor of the fortress.

The animator. – After four days of discussion and argument Joan obtained consent to an attack on the Bastille St-Loup.

Gaucourt attacked without warning her and was repulsed with losses. The heroine, hearing the noise of battle, hurried to the spot. Raising her banner, she charged the ditch of the fort, followed by soldiers shouting: "Hurrah for the Maid!" The English gave away, leaving 200 killed.

St-Loup having fallen, the warlike Joan proposed to attack the Bastille de St-Jean-Le-Blanc, on the opposite side of the river, the next day (5 May). The Captains' Council refused. It was not until 6 May that the Maid, with 4 000 men, crossed to the Ile St-Aignan and from there to the south bank over a bridge of boats.

As a tactical ruse, the English had evacuated St-Jean and retired to the Augustinian monastery, the ruins of which they had fortified. The French gave chase, but a counter attack threw them back to their boats in disorder. Joan was at first swept back with the retreating troops, but she rallied her men and faced the enemy. The English troops were impressed, withdrew in their turn, failed to hold the Augustinian monastery and took cover in the Boulevard des Tourelles. The heroine pitched her camp on the spot and returned to Orléans to arrange for the next day's attack. She proposed a feint towards Les Tourelles, starting from the Bastille St-Antoine. Gaucourt opposed this. When Joan tried to go out by the Porte de Bourgogne he barred her way, but the people swept the governor aside and Joan hurried to rejoin her troops.

Deliverance. – In her constant desire to spare the lives of her men and with her usual intuition Joan quickly understood the importance of artillery. Before attacking the Boulevard des Tourelles she had it pounded by the bombards in Orléans and those she had brought with her.

But the resistance of the English was desperate. To inspire her soldiers Joan jumped into the ditch and tried to set a ladder against the wall. She was struck by an arrow which pierced her flesh above her shoulder and projected six inches behind her neck, and she fell backwards. The English, thinking they had killed her, shouted for joy: "The witch is dead!"

Carried away by her companions, Joan pulled out the arrow herself, crying with pain. But the saints appeared to her and she overcame her weakness. A compress of fat and olive oil relieved her. She returned to the attack and the English, seized with panic at the approach of her standard, abandoned the ramparts and retreated to the fort. Meanwhile, on the bridge, the people of Orléans had thrown gangways over the broken arches and the feint began. The English, caught between the crossfire, capitulated. Two hundred were taken prisoner and 300 were killed or drowned in the river.

The next day, 8 May, the besiegers withdrew from the last forts, leaving behind their equipment, stores and sick. Joan of Arc re-entered Orléans in a storm of enthusiasm.

This deliverance is celebrated solemnly every year (especially on 29 April, 7 and 8 May) during the **Festival of Joan of Arc,** when the Saint of France accomplishes the final miracle of uniting citizens of all opinions in a common fervour.

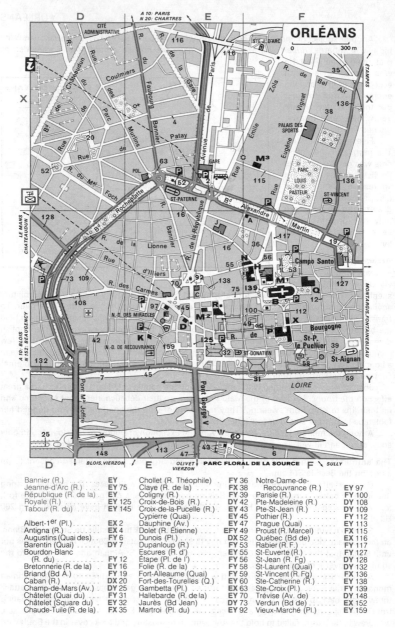

■ SIGHTS

Cathédrale Ste-Croix★ (FY B). — The Cathedral of the Holy Cross was begun in the 13C and its building went on until the 16C, but it was partly destroyed by the Protestants in 1568.

Henri IV, the first Bourbon King, being grateful to the town for having supported him, undertook to rebuild the cathedral, not in the style of the 17C, but in the Gothic manner. The work went on throughout the 18 and 19C ending under Charles X. The old Romanesque towers still standing before the Wars of Religion (1562-98), gave place to pseudo Gothic towers.

Façade. — The three large doorways with three rose windows above them are crowned by a gallery with openwork design. Note the fine workmanship — the stone becomes lacework at the uppermost level of the towers. At the base of the two towers admire the delicacy of the spiral staircases, also with openwork design, at each of the four corners.

It is only on reaching the vast **doorway** that one realizes that this is not a typical mediaeval façade; contrary to the very detailed carved scenes usually found covering a doorway, at Ste-Croix there are but four gigantic statues; they are the Evangelists.

Interior. — *Open 8.30am to noon and 2.30 to 7pm.* The vast main body of the cathedral comprises five naves enhanced by the pure lines of the elegant pillars. On the north side of the chancel, in the Chapel of St Joan of Arc, is the statue of Cardinal Touchet (1894-1926), who made incessant efforts to propagate the cult of the Maid. In the central chapel of the apse is a fine marble Virgin by Michel Bourdin (early 17C), a sculptor born in Orléans. In the side aisle of the central nave are late 19C stained glass windows, representing the life of Joan of Arc.

Splendid early 18C **woodwork★★** adorns the chancel. It was made to the designs of Mansart, Gabriel and Lebrun by Jules Degoullons, one of the decorators of Versailles and designer of the stalls in Notre-Dame, Paris. *Guided tours of the chancel to see the woodwork, of the crypt and the treasury in season only; apply in advance to the Tourist Centre.*

In the crypt may be seen traces of the three buildings which preceded the present cathedral. The **treasury** contains Byzantine enamels of the 11C, goldsmiths' work of the 13C, the Tree of Jesse (late 15C Flemish work) and interesting 17C paintings. Note in particular Zurbarán's *Christ's bearing of the Cross.*

North Side and East End. – Go round the cathedral. On the north side, note in the centre of the rose window the sun rays – Louis XIV's emblem. At the base are excavations, which have revealed the old Gallo-Roman walls and part of a tower. The **east end** is clearly visible from the gardens of the former episcopal palace (**FY Q**), an 18C building which now houses the municipal library. Admire the openwork of the flying buttresses and the pinnacles surmounting the piers.

Return to the north parvis.

Campo Santo (FY). – To the left of the ultra-modern Regional Fine Arts School *(École Régionale des Beaux-Arts)* is a graceful Renaissance portal and on the west side of this same building is a garden *(under rearrangement)* edged with an arcaded gallery. The garden was a cemetery in the 12C, the galleries were added in the 16C.

Fine Arts Museum★★ **(Musée des Beaux-Arts** – FY M^1). – *Open 10am to noon and 2 to 6pm ; closed Tuesdays, 1 January, 1 and 8 May, 1 November and 25 December ; 10F, free Wednesdays.*

The new museum's arcaded façade harmonises with that of the Préfecture building to the south of Place Ste-Croix. Start the visit from the second floor and walk down.

In the gallery devoted to the primitives is an outstanding 15C painting from the Sienese school, a Virgin and Child with two angels by Matteo di Giovanni. The 14-16C sculptures include a marble Virgin and Child (1370) from the Abbey of La Cour-Dieu and a fine bust by Germain Pilon. The Italian, Flemish and Dutch schools are represented by works by Correggio *(Holy Family),* Tintoretto *(Portrait of a Venetian),* A. Carracci *(Adoration of the Shepherds),* Pourbus the Younger *(Anne of Austria),* Van Goyen *(Skaters)* and Van de Velde *(Battle of the North Sea).* Velasquez's remarkable *St Thomas (c* 1620) dates from the period the artist spent in Seville.

On the first floor is displayed the 17-18C French school : vast religious paintings inspired by the Counter-Reformation, *St Charles Borromeo* by P. de Champaigne, *Triumph of St Ignatius* by Claude Vignon. The chiaroscuro technique is exemplified in *St Sebastian* from G. de La Tour's workshop. Among 17C canvases are *Bacchus and Ariadne,* a rare mythological work by Le Nain and a good portrait of *Le Nôtre* from Claude Lefevre's studio. Masterpieces from Richelieu's château *(p 132)* include the graceful *The Four Elements* by Deruet and *Louis XIV as a child.* The remarkable collection of 18C portraits shows the evolution of portraiture as formal likeness gradually gave way to character study : Mme de Pompadour by Drouais, Moyreau, the engraver by Nonotte. Paintings by H. Robert *(Landscape with ruined tower, The Wash House)* and Boucher *(The Dovecote)* are noteworthy. In the Pastel Gallery there are precious 18C portraits including works by Perroneau and Nattier as well as expressive busts by Pigalle and Houdon and French ceramics and medallions. The 19C is represented by artists such as Gros, Courbet *(The Wave),* Boudin and Gauguin *(Fête Gloanec).* 20C art is illustrated by works by Soutine, Gromaire, Max Jacob and sculptures by Bourdelle, Maillol, Zadkine.

Hôtel Groslot (FY H). – Built in 1530 by the bailiff Jacques Groslot, this large Renaissance mansion in red brick with diapering in black was subject to extensive remodelling in the 19C. Admire the delicate scrollwork on the staircase pillars and the two main entrances flanked by caryatids. This was the king's residence in Orléans : François II, who died here after opening in 1560 the States-General, Charles IX, Henri III and Henri IV all stayed here.

Cross the building. On the other side in the **garden** the façade of the former chapel of St-Jacques (15C) has been set up.

Across from the garden stand the elegant **Pavillons d'Escures** (EY N). These bourgeois town houses in brick with stone courses date from the early 17C.

Cross the **Place Ste-Croix** (FY 139). This vast symmetrical esplanade bordered by Classical façades was laid out in around 1840. The north and south sides were added in 1980s.

The 15C **Hôtel des Créneaux** (EY R) was the town hall from the 16C to 1790.

Historical Museum★ **(Musée Historique** - EY M^2). – *Open 10am to noon and 2 to 6pm ; closed Tuesdays, 1 January, 1 and 8 May, 1 November and 25 December ; 5F, free Wednesdays and Sunday mornings.*

The museum is in the small but elegant **Hôtel Caby** (1550). On the ground floor is the interesting **Gallo-Roman treasure**★ from Neuvy-en-Sullias (31 km - 19 miles east of Orléans). The treasure comprises a series of expressive statues, horses and wild boar in bronze and statuettes from a pagan temple. The first floor exhibits mediaeval objects : delicately carved **ivories**★ (12-16C), souvenirs recalling Joan of Arc (15C German tapestry, banner from the Festival of Joan of Arc in the 17C) and ceramics. The second floor is devoted to local folklore.

The inside courtyard has preserved its arcaded gallery and well.

Place du Martroi (EY 92). – This square can be considered the historical centre because of the statue of Joan of Arc (1855), by Foyatier, which stands in its centre. Martroi is derived from the Latin *Martyretum,* as the sites of Christian cemeteries were called in the 16C.

On the western corner of the Rue Royale is the **Pavillon de la Chancellerie,** built in 1759 by the Duke of Orléans to house his archives.

Rue Royale (EY 125). – This grand shopping avenue, lined with arcades was opened up in 1755 at the same time as the Pont Royal (**Pont George-V**) was being built.

Centre Charles Péguy (EY D). – *Open 9am to noon and 1.30 to 6pm ; closed Sundays and public holidays.*

The centre is housed in the former **Hôtel Euverte Hatte,** known as the House of Agnès Sorel, perhaps Charles VII's favourite had lived here in her youth.

The actual building, however, was built later under Louis XII. The windows are framed by Gothic friezes and in the courtyard the Renaissance gallery was added under François I.

This museum traces the life and career of **Charles Péguy** (1873-1914), a poet and philosopher, from Orléans. He combined Christianity, Socialism and patriotism into a deeply personal faith that he carried into action. In 1990 he published a journal, *Cahiers de la Quinzaine* (Fortnightly Notebooks), which exercised a profound cultural influence. He also wrote two important works on Joan of Arc; a Socialist play (1897) and a philosophic poem, *Mystère de la charité de Jeanne d'Arc* (1910). His last work *Eve* (1913), was a poem of 4000 alexandrines.

Centre Jeanne d'Arc★ (EY E). − *Open 10am to noon and 2 to 6pm; afternoons only 2 November to 30 April; closed Mondays, 1 January, 1 May, 1 November and 25 December; 4F. Bookstore.*

Known as Joan of Arc's house, this brick and half timbered construction stands on the modern Place Général de Gaulle. This was the house of Jacques Boucher, Chancellor to the Duke of Orléans and where Joan of Arc stayed in 1429.

On the first floor an audio-visual presentation is a good opportunity to learn through relief models, lighting and recorded commentary Joan of Arc's victories on 7 May 1429 and her entrance into the city on 8 May. There are also period costumes and assault weapons.

To the right of the Centre and the two Renaissance façades alongside, pass under the archway to the Square Jacques-Boucher. In a garden stands the **Pavillon Colas des Francs** an elegant Renaissance building. Belonging to Boucher's grandson it served as a trading house; the ground floor housed the archives and the first floor was where the silver was kept.

Hôtel Toutin (EY K). − *Visit by prior appointment, ☎ 38 62 70 61, 9am to 12.30pm and 2 to 6pm. Closed Mondays, holidays and in August.*

Built in 1540 for Toutin (manservant to François I's son), the *hôtel* is now a store specializing in interior decorating. Pass through the doorway. In the lovely small courtyard, bordered by a Renaissance arcaded gallery covered with Virginia creeper, stands the statue of François I leaning against a carpet of ivy.

Quai Fort-des-Tourelles (EY 60). − Opposite the small square, with its statue of Joan of Arc, a commemorative cross and inscriptions on the wall alongside the Loire record the position of Les Tourelles *(p 125)*. A good general **view★** of the town.

The **Quai du Châtelet** (FY 31) offers a pleasant stroll along the Loire.

Rue de Bourgogne (EFY). − This was the main street, running east to west, of the old Gallo-Roman city. For the most part a pedestrian street, it encourages window shopping. Note the façade of no 261, a 15C stone house with a half-timbered gable.

Pass in front of the **Préfecture** (FY P) formerly a 17C Benedictine monastery. Opposite on Rue Pothier is the **Salle des Thèses** (FY X). This 15C library is all that remains of the famous university which had 4000 to 5000 students in the Middle Ages. Calvin, the great Reformer, studied law there in 1528.

St-Pierre-le-Puellier (FY). − Located in the old quarter − pedestrian streets, old half-timbered houses − this 12C Romanesque church is now used for exhibitions and concerts.

St-Aignan (FY). − All that remains of this large Gothic church, consecrated in 1509, are the chancel and transept. The nave was burnt down during the Wars of Religion (1562-98). *To visit, apply at the Tourist Centre, ☎ 38 53 05 95.*

Museum of National Sciences (Musée des Sciences Naturelles − FX M³). − *Open Mondays, Tuesdays, Thursdays 2 to 6pm; Wednesdays and Sundays 10am to noon and 2 to 6pm; closed Saturdays, 1 January, 1 May, 1 November and 25 December.*

Dioramas present mounted animals in their habitat. The ground floor is devoted to aquariums while on the third floor plans explain the flow of the Loire and the birth of the Loiret.

■ OLIVET and FLORAL PARK OF LA SOURCE★★

Olivet. − Pop 14489. Most of Olivet is given over to market gardens, fields of flowers and nurseries. Just 4 km - 2 1/2 miles beyond the Pont Georges-V, Olivet presents a pleasant picture along the banks of the Loiret. In a charming setting with fine houses and old windmills, it attracts fishermen and rowers alike *(landing stage near the bridge over the Loiret)*.

Promenade des Moulins. − *Round tour of 5 km - 3 miles by car from the bridge via the country lane on the north bank of the Loiret going westwards; return on the D 14.* At the end of the walk, two old windmills reflect in the river composing a pastoral picture.

Floral Park of La Source★★ (Parc Floral de la Source). − *Open 1 April to 11 November 9am to 6pm; the rest of the year 2 to 5pm; 11F.*

Tour of the park by miniature train in service afternoons (except Fridays) from 1 May to 15 September, and in April and October on Wednesday, Saturday, and holidays afternoons only; 6F.

The Floral Park, 30 hectares - 74 acres with its fountains, shrubs and century old trees, is a constantly changing pleasure. Every season is a palette of colours: Spring − tulips, narcissi, irises; May − rhododendrons and azaleas; mid-June to mid-July − glorious roses; July and August − summer flowers; September − second blooming of roses, dahlias; the year ends with chrysanthemums *(in exhibition hall)*.

During the walk skirt the semi-circular basin called the **Miroir★** from where there is a nice view of the château and the lovely plant motif *(broderie Louis XIII)* on the lawn.

Not far is the **Source du Loiret★** (Spring of the Loiret), the resurgence of a branch of the Loire, which is formed near St-Benoît and reappears in the park. Intense bubbling marks the spot.

Flamingoes, cranes, emus and deer roam the park all the year round.

PLESSIS-BOURRÉ, Château du ★

Michelin map **63** east of fold 20 — 20 km - 12 miles to the north of Angers — *Local map p 117*

Le Plessis-Bourré stands far away at the end of a vista of meadowland, a white building beneath blue grey slate roofs, bringing to the mind's eye the seigneurial life of the 15C.

Jean Bourré (1424-1506). — Born in Château-Gontier Jean Bourré first entered royal service under the dauphin Louis, the son of Charles VII, whom he served faithfully. When Louis XI assumed the Crown in 1461, Bourré was appointed Financial Secretary and Treasurer of France. In addition to building several châteaux — Jarzé *(p 51)* and Vaux *(p 170)* among others — he bought the estate of Plessis-le-Vent and in 1468 ordered work to begin on the new château. The design was inspired by the château at Langeais and has a magnificent unity of style.

Among the many illustrious guests that Bourré welcomed to his new residence were Pierre de Rohan *(p 99)*, Louis XI and Charles VIII.

■ THE CHÂTEAU★ *time : 3/4 hour*

Guided tours 1 April to 30 September 10am to noon and 2 to 7pm (5pm the rest of the year); closed 15 November to 20 December and on Wednesday and Thursday mornings; time : 1 hour; 16F.

Le Plessis, isolated by a wide moat spanned by a many arched bridge 43 m - 47 yd long looks, from outside, like a fortress protected by a gatehouse with a double draw-bridge and four flanking towers. The largest of these is battlemented and served as a keep. A platform 3 m - 10 ft wide at the base of the wall provided for artillery crossfire.

Château du Plessis-Bourré

The chapel's slender spire rises above the roof to the left of the gatehouse.

Beyond the entrance archway, Le Plessis is transformed into a country mansion with a spacious courtyard, low wings, an arcaded gallery, turret staircases and high dormer windows of the seigneurial wing.

On the ground floor the visitor will see the Chapel Ste-Anne and the Hall of Justice before visiting the richly furnished and decorated state apartments.

The first floor has among other rooms a great vaulted chamber with a monumental fireplace. The guardroom has a coffered wooden **ceiling**★★ painted at the end of the 15C with such allegorical figures as Fortune, Truth, Chastity (a unicorn) and Lust, the Musician Ass, etc. Humorous and moral scenes depict the unskilled barber at work on a patient, the overweening man trying to wring the neck of an eel, a woman sewing up a chicken's crop, etc. There is a large collection of fans in the library.

PLESSIS-MACÉ, Château du

Michelin map **63** fold 20 — 13 km - 8 miles to the northwest of Angers — *Local map p 117*

Hidden amidst greenery this château is surrounded by a wide moat.

Started in the 11C by a certain Macé, the château became the property in the mid 15C of Louis de Beaumont, the Chamberlain and favourite of Louis XI, who transformed it into a residence fit to accommodate his royal master. The year 1510 saw the beginning of a 168 year old ownership by the Du Bellay family.

From the exterior Le Plessis still has the appearance of a fortress with its tower studded wall and rectangular keep defended by moats, dismantled but still battlemented.

Guided tours 10am to noon and 2 to 6.30pm July to September; 1.30 to 6pm, May and June; 1.30 to 5.30pm, March, April, October, November; closed on Tuesdays and 1 December to 28 February; time : 1 hour; 8F.

Once inside the great courtyard the country residence becomes apparent: the decorative elements in white tufa stone enhance the grey of the schists, while windows testify to the search for light.

(After photo: Chrétien, Angers)

Château du Plessis-Macé — Balcony

To the right are the outbuildings housing the stables and guardroom. To the left are the chapel, an unusual staircase turret, and the main dwelling surmounted by pointed gables. At the corner of the main dwelling is a charming **balcony** which served as a vantage point for the ladies during jousting tournaments and other entertainments. The balcony opposite, in the outbuildings, was reserved for the servants.

One can visit the dining room, the large banqueting hall, several bedrooms, one of which was the king's, and the **chapel**, which has kept its rare Gothic panelling of the 15C and forms two floors of galleries, the first reserved for the Lord and his Squires, the second for the servants.

PONCÉ-SUR-LE-LOIR

Michelin map 🔲 fold 5 – *Local map 99* – Pop 426

Poncé, as you leave it to the east by the D 917, has a beautiful Renaissance château, while on the road to the west are two **craft centres** facing each other on opposite sides of the road.

To the north the "Atelier de la Volonnière" has brought together leather handicrafts, painted silk, painted furniture and antiques *(open weekends and in summer Sunday afternoons only)*. To the south of the road and the railway line, the next centre signposted by "Centre Artisanal du Poncé" is installed in the large 18C buildings of the former Paillard paper mill, on the banks of the river; independent craftsmen have grouped their workshops together: pottery, glassware, ironwork, weaving, woodwork, candle making. *Open Mondays to Saturdays 9am to noon and 2 to 6pm; Sundays and holidays 2 to 6pm.*

Château★. – *Open 10am to noon and 2 to 6pm; Sundays and holidays 2 to 6pm; 11F.*

The château originally consisted of two pavilions flanking the central staircase tower, one of which was destroyed in the 18C and replaced by a characterless wing. Mullioned, pedimented windows and pronounced horizontal cornices give a balanced but geometrically severe aspect to the façade. The north front, formerly the main one, has at ground level an elegant Italian style arcade which forms a terrace at the first floor level.

The stone **Renaissance staircase★★** is one of the most remarkable in France. The coffered ceilings of the six flights are sumptuously sculptured, with a delicacy, fantasy and art of perspective rarely attained. Over 130 motifs portray realistic, allegorical and mythological subjects.

One can also stroll in the well kept **gardens★**, with their highly effective symmetrical layout: on the edge of the square lawn, the tree covered walk makes a long vaulted path on one side, and on the other is a labyrinth conducive to tranquillity and meditation; overlooking the entire scene runs a terrace with a mall of lime trees.

The dovecote remains with its 1 800 holes and revolving ladders for gathering the eggs.

The outbuildings house a museum of Sarthe folklore.

PONTLEVOY

Michelin map 🔲 fold 17 – Pop 1 700

A small town situated in the agricultural region to the north of Montrichard, Pontlevoy still has some charming old houses.

Former Abbey. – *Guided tours 1 June to 15 September 10.30am to noon and 2.30 to 6.30pm; closed Mondays; time: 3/4 hour; 15F.*

The former abbey is mainly interesting for its noble 18C buildings and a 15C Gothic church. It is true that the foundation of the abbey dates back to 1034, when Gelduin de Chaumont, vassal of the Comte de Blois, established a Benedictine community here as a token of gratitude to the Virgin for saving from shipwreck.

In the 17C, when a reform of monastic life became essential, the abbey was entrusted to the Benedictines of Saint-Maur and the Abbot Pierre de Bérule who opened an educational establishment in 1644 which made Pontlevoy famous until the 19C. Renowned for the quality of its teaching and discipline, the college was open to all social levels, aristocracy and gentry, lawyers and middle class. Crébillon, one of its pupils, subsequently became a well known playwright. In 1720 the college had 177 boarders.

Proclaimed the École Royale Militaire in 1776, the college added to its secular teaching, the military training of scholars chosen by the king from among the gentry.

In keeping with this scholastic tradition, the former abbey today undertakes technical teaching with respect to road transport.

Tour. – One first enters the former **abbey church**, rebuilt in the 2nd half of the 15C after destruction during the Hundred Years War, but which only has the chancel of the imposing edifice which was planned but never completed. Wide, lit by great openings, ringed by an ambulatory and radiating chapels, the chancel bears witness to the builder's ambition. In 1651 two large stone retables were added with marble columns to the high altar and to the axial chapel where Gelduin and his first descendants are buried.

In the 18C **conventual buildings** one can see the old refectory decorated with a monumental stove of Delftware, one of four which the Maréchal de Saxe had commissioned for heating Chambord *(p 61)*, the remarkable staircase leading to the next floor and the majestic façade giving on to the gardens, with emblazoned pediments at regular intervals.

The former riding school houses a road transport museum including some 20 vehicles dating between 1900 and 1960.

A local museum will open in part of the west wing.

La POSSONNIÈRE Manor ★

Michelin map 🔲 fold 5 – 1 km - 1/2 mile south of Couture-sur-Loir – *Local map p 99*

When Louis de Ronsard, soldier and man of letters, returned from Italy in the early 16C he undertook the building of a country seat in the new Italian style. Here at La Possonnière the decoration is undisguisedly Renaissance.

It was here in 1524 that **Pierre de Ronsard**, the famous poet and leader of the Pléiade group of poets, was born. He held a court appointment – accompanying Princess Madeleine, James V's future wife to Scotland – and undertook diplomatic missions but it was to the Church that he finally turned, holding several benefices. He then began his prolific poetry writing achieving, in his lifetime, fame and recognition as the poet of the Renaissance. He died in the Priory of St-Cosme *(p 161)*.

The white stone of the house against the green of the wooded hillside makes it visible from afar despite a surrounding wall.

Inscribed with Latin sayings, the walls of the garden façade are pierced at ground level by mullioned windows in the Louis XII style. Those higher up are flanked by medallioned pilasters which are undisguisedly Renaissance.

Projecting from the courtyard façade is a gracious staircase turret, pierced by a doorway, surmounted by a bust adorned pediment. Note the Ronsard arms on the pediment at the top of the tower, accompanied by the family motto – "the future belongs to the capable".

POUANCÉ

Michelin map 🔢 fold 8 – Pop 3 410

Pouancé surrounded by a ring of pools stands on the borders of Brittany and Anjou. Already a flourishing town in the Middle Ages it was of both strategic and economic importance, due to its iron foundries using the ore from the Segré Basin. The surrounding woods served as refuges for the Chouans (p 88) during the Vendéen War.

The N 171 which skirts the town passes alongside the ruins of the 12-14C château. Façades and towers of dark schist are imposing, and further intensified by a shelter for archers linked to the keep by a postern. *Guided tours July and August, 9am to noon and 2 to 6pm; the rest of the year, Sundays only; time: 1 hour.*

EXCURSIONS

Menhir de Pierre Frite. – *5 km - 3 miles south by the D 878 to La Prévière, then take the D 6 on the left, and a small signposted path.* This menhir is 6 m - 20 ft high.

Château de la Motte-Glain. – *17 km - 11 miles to the south by the D 878. Open 15 June to 15 September, 2.30 to 6.30pm; closed Tuesdays; time: 1/2 hour; 12F.*

Built at the end of the 15C by Pierre de Rohan, Counsellor to Louis XI, then one of the army commanding officers under Charles VIII and Louis XII in Italy, the château is mainly interesting from the outside, for its reddish brown stonework, powerful lines and its gatehouse flanked by two round towers. Note the decoration of the seigneurial dwelling on the courtyard: scallop shells and pilgrim staffs are reminders that the château was on the road to Santiago de Compostela originating from Mont-St-Michel.

If in doubt where to find a place name or historic reference
look in the index at the end of the guide.

Le PUY-NOTRE-DAME

Michelin map 🔢 southwest of fold 12 – 7 km - 4 miles west of Montreuil-Bellay – Pop 1 497

Church★. – Built in the 13C, it is a remarkable example of Angevin architecture. The bell tower, with a stone spire at the corner of the south transept, has a bay decorated with mouldings which form a niche in which there is a very beautiful statue of the Virgin (16C). On the north side of the church the well after which the town is named, still exists, now incorporated into a cylindrical building. During the Middle Ages people came from all over France to worship the Virgin's Girdle, a relic brought back from Jerusalem in the 12C, which is still there.

Its three naves of equal height, very gracefully shaped, give a majestic air to the interior architecture: in the chancel, with a square apse, the lierne and tierceron ribbing is extremely richly traced. Behind the high altar are 16C carved stalls.

RICHELIEU ★

Michelin map 🔢 southeast of fold 10 – Pop 2 496

Lying on the southern limits of Touraine, bordering on Poitou, Richelieu is what La Fontaine called "the finest village in the universe". A peaceful town it comes to life on market days. This rare example of Classical town planning was the project of one man, the statesman and churchman, **Richelieu**, who was eager to lodge his court near his château which was then under construction. The building of the town itself started in 1631 at a time when Versailles was still only an idea.

Cardinal de Richelieu. – In 1621 when **Armand du Plessis** (1585-1642) bought the property of Richelieu, it consisted of a village and manor on the banks of the Mable. Ten years later the estate was raised to the status of a duchy. On becoming Cardinal and First Minister of France he commissioned Jacques Le Mercier, the architect of the Sorbonne and Cardinal's Palace, now Palais-Royal in Paris, to prepare plans for a château and a wall enclosed town. Built under the supervision of the architect's brother, Pierre Le Mercier, the project was considered at the time to be a marvel of urban planning which Louis XIV was to visit at the age of twelve.

Determined not to have his creation oustripped in grandeur, Richelieu created a small principality around his masterpiece and jealously razed entirely or partially many other châteaux in the vicinity. He already owned Bois-le-Vicomte and was to add to his estates Champigny-sur-Veude, L'Ile-Bouchard, Cravant, Crissay, Mirebeau, Faye-la-Vineuse and even the royal residence of Chinon, which he was to allow to fall into disrepair. The great fortress of Loudon also suffered destruction but only after its owner, Urbain Grandier, an arch enemy of the Cardinal, had perished at the stake.

■ SIGHTS

The town. – Built to a rectangular plan 700 m - 766 yd long and 500 m - 547 yd wide, the site was to be surrounded by walls and a water filled moat. The entrance gatehouses still stand rusticated, pedimented and crowned with tall typically French style roofs.

Grande-Rue. – This the main artery crosses Richelieu from end to end. In addition to the gateways note the Louis XIII style hôtels with the decorative elements in white tufa stone, especially no 17, Hôtel du Sénéchal, which has retained its elegant courtyard decorated with busts of Roman emperors.

RICHELIEU	Collège (R. du)	3
	Marché (Pl. du)	5
Cardinal (Pl. du) ... 2	Religieuses (Pl. des)	6

On the Place du Marché opposite the Classical church is the fine 17C covered market roofed with slates. The nearby Palais de Justice now serves as town hall.

Richelieu museum. – *In the town hall (H). Open 1 July to 31 August, 10am to noon and 2 to 6pm (4pm, the rest of the year); closed Tuesdays, also Sundays out of season; 3.50F.*

Interesting exhibition of documents and works of art pertaining to both the Richelieu family and the château are kept here.

Notre-Dame. – Built in the Classical or Jesuit style, this edifice in white masonry has a certain harmony and nobleness.

The main façade has a series of niches which contain statues of the Evangelists and the chancel is flanked, in an unusual arrangement, by two towers surmounted with obelisks.

Inside the same architectural qualities are to be found; note the grandeur of the 18C high altar.

The park. – *Open 15 June to 30 October, 10am to noon and 2 to 7pm; 6 April to 14 June, Saturdays and Sundays, 2 to 7pm; the rest of the year, 8am to 7pm; closed Tuesdays; 8F; free out of season.*

At the southern end of the town the park, preceded by a majestic statue of Richelieu by Ramey, covers 475 hectares - 1 174 acres and is crossed by a number of straight, chestnut or plane tree-lined avenues. At one time the centrepiece was a marvellous palace filled with great works of art.

Two vast courtyards surrounded by outbuildings preceded the château proper, which was protected by moats, bastions and watch towers. The entrance porch was adorned with a statue of Louis XIII and surmounted by an allegorical figure of Fame, both the works of Guillaume Berthelot. The pavilion at the far end of the château's main courtyard was originally graced by obelisks, rostral columns (in the form of ships' prows) and Michelangelo's famous group, *The Slaves*, once intended for the tomb of Pope Julius II.

(After engraving: photo Combier, Mâcon)

Château de Richelieu in the 17C

The apartments, gallery and chapel were hung with works by Poussin, Claude, Champaigne, Mantegna, Perugino, Bassano, Caravaggio,Titian, Giulio Romano, Dürer, Rubens and Van Dyck.

The gardens were dotted with copies of antique statues and artificial grottoes which concealed the, then popular, water farces. It was in these gardens that the first poplar trees from Italy were planted.

The dispersal of the riches gathered here began in 1727 when the then Marshal de Richelieu, the Cardinal's great nephew, transported some back to his Parisian town house and sold others. Confiscated in 1792 the château was visited by Tallien a collector of silverware, and the Dufourni and Visconti who took all that was suitable for the Museum of French Monuments. The Revolution over, the descendants of Richelieu ceded the château to a certain Boutron who demolished it for the sale of the building materials.

Of the many splendid buildings there still exist a domed pavilion, canals and at the far end of the formal gardens two pavilions, the orangery and wine cellar. The entrance is on the D749.

The works of art were dispersed: the Louvre has *The Slaves* by Michelangelo, Perugino's paintings and a marble table encrusted with precious stones; the series of twelve paintings depicting the victories of Louis XIII are in Versailles; the local museums in Tours and Azay-le-Ferron have several paintings and sculptures; the museum in Poitiers has Berthelot's statue of Louis XIII. The Orléans Fine Arts Museum in its Richelieu Gallery has the works of Fréminet and Deruet. The obelisks are now at Malmaison and the rostral columns in the Maritime Museum, Paris.

EXCURSIONS

Faye-la-Vineuse. – Pop 409. *7 km - 4 miles to the south by the D 749 and the D 757 to the left.*

Situated on a formerly vine covered mound overlooking a tributary of the Veude, Faye was a prosperous city in the Middle Ages with a population of 11 000 with 5 parishes and enclosed with high walls. The Wars of Religion ruined the town and caused its decline; today it is only a small country town.

St-Georges. – This Romanesque church was formerly a collegiate served by monks, and enclosed by cloisters and conventual buildings instead of the roads and houses which encircle it today. A little over-restored it still has a few interesting features: a high transept crossing with a dome on pendentives; two lateral passages connecting the transept to the nave, as in the churches of the province of Berry; the very high chancel with an ambulatory; the sculptured capitals which are worth a close look, for battle scenes can be seen amongst the mass of foliage and fantastic animals.

The **crypt** *(closed temporarily)* is unusual for its large dimensions and height under the vault. Amongst the capitals of the pillars there are two which are very finely sculptured, depicting the Adoration of the Three Kings and a combat between horsemen.

Bois-Aubry Abbey. – *16 km - 10 miles to the east by the D 757 towards Tours, turn right on the D 58 towards Ste-Maure, then right on the D 114 towards Luzé, there take the D 110 towards Marigny-Marmande then a small road on the left.*

On nearing this 12C Benedictine abbey, the stone spire rises up as if standing on the horizon. Isolated in the countryside, the abbey is almost completely in ruins and surrounded by farm buildings. Only the 15C square bell tower is in good condition. In the vaulting of the 15C nave there is a keystone decorated with a sculptured coat of arms, and in the chapter house (early 12C) there are twelve beautifully sculptured capitals. *Guided tours (1/2 hour) 10am to noon and 2 to 6pm except Sunday mornings; apply to the community of Orthodox monks living in the farm on the opposite side of the road.*

Richelieu to Chinon by steam train. – *Every weekend between 25 May and 15 September with 3 departures in all; single: 39F; return 52F; children: 20F; return: 27F; time: 1 hour 30 minutes. Further information from the station at Richelieu on the days of trips only ☎ 47 58 36 29.*

Stops are made at Champigny-sur-Veude, Coutureau and Ligré-Rivière.

La ROCHE-RACAN, Château de

Michelin map 👊 fold 4 – 2 km - 1 mile to the southeast of St-Paterne-Racan

The Château de la Roche-Racan stands perched on a rock (*roche* in French) overlooking the Escotais Valley which together with the nearby Loir, were a constant source of inspiration to the first owner and poet, **Racan** (1589-1670).

Born at Champmarin near Aubigné, Honorat de Bueil, marquis de Racan, was a member of the well known local family, the Bueils *(p 169)*. Little inclined to the life of a soldier and unlucky in love, Racan retired to his country seat for the last forty years of his life, a period described in his work, *Stances à la retraite.*

Château. – *Guided tours 5 August to 15 September, 10am to noon and 3 to 5pm; 8F.*

In 1634 Racan commissioned a local master mason, Jacques Gabriel, a member of a long established family of architects to build this château. The main building was originally flanked by two pavilions only one of which remains standing today, pedimented and adorned with a corner turret and caryatids. Long balustrated terraces, above mask decorated arcades, overlook the park and Escotais Valley, the perfect bucolic setting for a pastoral poet.

ROMORANTIN-LANTHENAY ★

Michelin map 👊 fold 18 – Pop 18 187 – *Facilities pp 36-37*

This attractive town with several ancient houses, formerly the capital of the Sologne, grew up at a point where the Sauldre subdivided into several arms. Always an important Sologne market centre, various industries (electronics, refrigeration and ciné cameras) and other activities such as flour milling, sheet iron and steel plate rolling have given the town a new impetus. New suburbs have sprung up to the south of the town, while in the east a Matra plant has been producing plastic car bodies and assembling a medium range of touring cars since 1968.

Royal associations. – In the 15C Romorantin was the fief of the Valois-Angoulême *(p 17)* branch of the French royal family and it was here that François d'Angoulême, later **François I**, spent his turbulent childhood. Always a favourite place of residence with the cavalier king, in 1517 he was to prove his attachment by commissioning Leonardo da Vinci, then at Amboise *(p 39)*, to draw up plans for a palace destined for his mother Louise de Savoie. Leonardo envisaged a palace astride the Sauldre, to be built with prefabricated units, but the death of Louise put an end to the project. The genius also studied the possibility of creating a canal to link Romorantin to the Loire.

(After photo: Sologne Museum)

Romorantin
La Chancellerie, corner post

In France, the Epiphany *(la Fête des Rois)* is celebrated by eating the Twelfth cake *(la Galette des Rois)* which contains a bean. The finder of this bean is the bean king of Twelfth Night. On 6 January, Epiphany, 1521, François I led a mock attack on the Hôtel St-Pol, where a bean king reigned. The occupants of the hôtel were defending themselves by hurling snowballs, apples and eggs, when some ill advised person threw a glowing log out of a window which landed on the royal cranium. To dress the wound the doctors shaved his head; the King then grew a beard. His courtiers followed suit.

■ SIGHTS

Old Houses★ (Maisons anciennes – B). – The finest examples are to be found in the Rue de la Résistance. At the corner of the latter with Rue du Milieu, is **La Chancellerie**, a corbelled Renaissance house, of brick and half timber construction, where the royal seals were kept when the King sojourned in the town. The carved corner post portrays a coat of arms and a musician playing an instrument similar to the bagpipes. Opposite, the **Hôtel St-Pol**, built of stone and glazed bricks is pierced by charming windows with mouldings.

Standing where the Rue du Milieu and the Rue de la Pierre meet is the charming **Maison du Carroir d'Orée** (archaeological museum) with its remarkable carved corner posts showing, to the left, the Annunciation and to the right St George killing the Dragon.

ROMORANTIN-LANTHENAY

Clemenceau (R. Georges)	6
Trois-Rois (R. des)	34
Verdun (R. de)	35
Brault (R. Porte)	2
Bubes (R. des)	3
Capucins (R. des)	4
Écu (R. de l')	7
Four-à-Chaux (R. du)	8
Gaulle (Pl. Gén. de)	10
Haies (R. des)	12
Ile-Marin (Quai de l')	13
Lattre-de-Tassigny (Av. Mar. de)	14
Limousins (R. des)	15
Lyautey (Av. Mar.)	16
Mail de l'Hôtel-Dieu	18
Mail-des-Platanes	19
Milieu (R. du)	20
Orléans (Fg d')	22
Paix (Pl. de la)	23
Pierre (R. de la)	24
Prés. Wilson (R. du)	26
Résistance (R. de la)	28
St-Fiacre (R.)	29
St-Roch (Fg)	30
Salengro (Av. R.)	32
Sirène (R. de la)	33

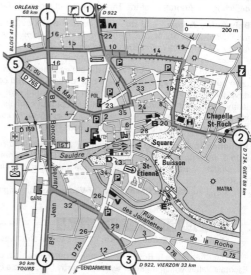

Sologne Museum★ (Musée de Sologne). – *Open 1 April to 30 September 9.30 (10am Thursdays to Sundays) to 11.30am and 2 to 5.30pm (6pm Sundays); the rest of the year 10 to 11.30am (11 am to noon on Sundays) and 2 to 5pm (5.30pm weekends); closed on Tuesdays and 1 January, 1 May and 25 December; 6F.*

Installed in the town hall (**H**) the collections are well presented in a modern setting. The natural geographical region of the Sologne *(p 150)* was for a long time a closed economy with its own particular way of life. The museum presents the Sologne in all its diversity: geology, soils, vegetation, fauna, people, occupations, crafts, tools, traditions and costumes.

The Sologne has retained crafts and cottage industries such as cartwrights and coopers, itinerant woodcutters and charcoal burners and the making of sabots, fire lighters and broom handles, which are fast disappearing elsewhere. Note also the low timber framed buildings with brick or cob infillings sometimes thatched but more often tiled. Two interiors have been recreated: the main room of a peasant's cottage and a sabot maker's workshop.

View from the bridges★. – The bridges over the Sauldre reveal some lovely views. On the north branch, there is a **view★** over the **Moulin du Châpitre (D)** and opposite over the former 15-16C **royal château (P)**, which is now the sub-prefecture.

Crossing over the narrow southern branch there are lovely half-timbered houses (**V**).

Public Gardens (Square Ferdinand Buisson). – A pleasant park with large trees and footbridges crossing the various branches and reaches of the river; it has picturesque views of the river banks and particularly of the fulling mill (**E**).

St-Étienne. – Note the Romanesque bell tower with delicate sculptures at the transept crossing. The nave, with Angevin vaulted roof, is extended by a dark chancel where the powerful Romanesque pillars support lighter and more recent Angevin vaulting. In the rounded part of the apse, against each rib of the vaulting leans the statue of an evangelist.

St-Roch. – Towards the east is the Chapel St-Roch, a gracious building. The west front is flanked by small turrets. The semicircular windows are typical of the neo-Renaissance.

Racing car museum (Musée de la course automobile – M). – *29-31 Faubourg d'Orléans. Open 1 April to 30 September 10am (11am the rest of the year) to noon and 2 to 7pm (5pm Mondays, 6pm Thursdays and Fridays); closed Tuesdays and Sunday mornings and 1 May, 25 December, 1 January; 6F.*

Various Matra cars are on display including the Formula One model which won the 1969 World Championship. A series of showcases illustrate the numerous innovations, especially technical, made in the world of Grand Prix racing. A specialist library *(free access)* covers all aspects of this sport.

Les ROSIERS

Michelin map 64 fold 12 – *Local map p 105* – Pop 1933

This small site on the right bank of the Loire, opposite Gennes, has a church with a Renaissance bell tower which is the work of the Angevin architect Jean de l'Espine; the adjoining staircase turret has lovely windows surrounded with pilasters.

On the church square there is a statue of Jeanne de Laval, second wife of King René of Anjou *(p 42)*.

EXCURSION

Le Prieuré. – *7.5 km - 5 miles to the west by the Gennes bridge, then to the right on the D 751 and in the locality of Sale-Village take a road on the left.*
This small hamlet in the commune of St-Georges-des-Sept-Voies is grouped round an attractive priory hidden in the middle of beautiful trees, cedars and elms said to be from Sully; the 12-13C church has a beautiful Romanesque square tower, and inside a lovely 17C altar of polychrome wood *(open on Sundays)*.

SABLÉ-SUR-SARTHE

Michelin map 64 fold 1 – *Local map p 143* – Pop 12721 – *Facilities pp 36-37* – *See town plan in the current Michelin Guide France.*

Situated at a point where two tributaries, the Vaige and Erve, flow into the Sarthe, Sablé is dominated by the austere façade of its château, which once belonged to the Colbert family and is now used by a department of the National Library. A biscuit factory has made the name of the town famous, that of a small shortbread biscuit.

Yesteryear to the present. – Originally the fief belonged to Laval-Boisdauphin, marquis de Sablé in the 17C. In 1711 Colbert de Torcy, the nephew of the great Jean Baptiste Colbert, Louis XIV's Minister, rebuilt the château and radically changed the aspect of the town: many houses and the hospital date from this period.

The town was once renowned for a black marble veined with white, which was extracted from the quarries on the north bank of the Sarthe, upstream from the town. It was much used at Versailles.

The small port on the canalized part of the Sarthe used to receive sand laden barges from the Loire.

Secondary metallurgical industries such as wire drawing, screw cutting, smelting, bolt and nut works and the production of foodstuffs (milk, cheese and biscuits) are the main sources of employment today.

EXCURSIONS

Solesmes Abbey. – *3 km - 2 miles to the northeast by the D 138. Description p 149.*

Auvers-le-Hamon. – Pop 1201. *8.5 km - 5 miles to the north by the D 24.* The church's nave is ornamented with 15-16C mural paintings depicting a series of local saints: to the right St Mémès holding his intestines, St Martin on horseback, St Cénéré as a Cardinal, St Eutropius, St Andrew with his cross, St Luke riding a bull, the Nativity and the Flight into Egypt. To the left a macabre dance, St Avertin, St Apollonia whose teeth were pulled out by her torturers, St James and the Sacrifice of Isaac.

These paintings have the same curious iconography as those in the church of the neighbouring town of Asnières-sur-Vègre.

Pincé. – *10 km - 6 miles to the southwest by the D 159, then opposite the gates of the Château de Beaufort, take an unsignposted road to the right.* This country lane has vistas over the Sarthe.

    Pincé. – Pop 173. This pretty village contains charming houses decked with flowers along the river.

La Chapelle-du-Chêne. – *6 km - 4 miles to the southeast by the D 306. At Les Nœuds turn left.* The basilica is the object of pilgrimages to Notre-Dame-du-Chêne (Our Lady of the Oak), represented by a 15C terracotta statue. In the park there is a small scale model of the Holy Sepulchre and the Stations of the Cross.

ST-AIGNAN ★

Michelin map 64 fold 17 – Pop 3690 – *Facilities pp 36-37*

St-Aignan on the banks of the Cher is in the heart of the forest and vineyard region: **Coteaux du Cher** around Seigny and Couffy, and **Blanc Foussy**, a sparkling wine, at Noyers.

There is a picturesque view to be seen from the bridge of this small town which rises in tiers above the Cher and further north of the D 675. The church and the château are interesting as is also the Rue Constant-Ragot which includes two Gothic houses and affords the best glimpses of the church's chevet.

It is also worth walking along the small streets and neighbouring squares where some old 15C half-timbered or sculptured stone houses can be seen.

St-Aignan★. – *Open 9am (11am on Sundays) to 7pm. Ascent to the bell-tower in season: 5F.* The building dates from the 11 and 12C. Passing through the Romanesque porchway with delicately sculptured capitals, one enters the high and well-lit nave with finely chiselled capitals depicting acanthus and fantastic animals; in the chancel and the ambulatory, amongst the historiated capitals there is one depicting the Flight into Egypt (to the north of the ambulatory), and Abraham's Sacrifice and King David (south side).

The Romanesque **crypt★** *(enter from the north transept)* has a similar plan to the chancel and is adorned with frescoes. The painting in the apsidal chapel which depicts Christ in Majesty goes back to the 12C, the others date from the 12 to the 15C.

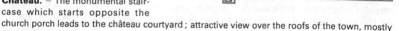

Château. — The monumental staircase which starts opposite the church porch leads to the château courtyard ; attractive view over the roofs of the town, mostly tiled, a few with slates.

The château consists of two buildings at right angles, mainly 16C, part of it built against the remains of the mediaeval fortifications which close the courtyard on the east side. Note the elegant Renaissance dwelling with windows surrounded by pilasters, dormer windows with sculptured gables, and above all the beautiful staircase in an octagonal turret in the shape of a lantern.

The terrace overlooks the bridge over the Cher with its turbulent water.

EXCURSIONS

St-Lazare Chapel. — *2 km - 1 ¼ miles to the northeast by the road to Noyers, N 76.* This chapel stands out on the left of the road, dominated by a gabled bell tower, which was part of a leper house.

Beauval Ornithological Park. — *4 km - 2 1/2 miles to the south by the D 675. Open 10am to sunset ; 25F, children 12F.*

After going down a hill with lovely views over the vineyards, the Beauval park appears, set amidst the undergrowth in the hollow of a small valley. The park is above all a bird breeding farm for the protection of species which are dying out. Around the duck lake there are mandarin ducks, Barbary ducks, Canadian geese, pink flamingos, crested cranes, etc. ; further on large aviaries shelter mainly parrots, budgerigars and toucans.

ST-BENOÎT-SUR-LOIRE ★★

Michelin map 🔢 fold 10 — 10 km - 6 miles southeast of Châteauneuf — Pop 1 925

The Basilica *(1)* of St-Benoît is one of the finest Romanesque buildings in France.

HISTORICAL NOTES *(2)*

Origins of the abbey (7C). — The religious role of this corner of the Loire country appeared early. In Gaulish times the Druids held a sort of council there every year. In the 7C a Benedictine abbey with the name of Fleury was built.

The founder of the Benedictine Order, St Benedict (St Benoît), who died in the 6C, was buried in the Monastery of Monte Cassino in Italy, which he had founded. About 672 the Abbot of Fleury learned that the monastery had been destroyed by the Barbarians ; St Benedict's body and that of his sister, St Scolastica, lay under the ruins. Distressed by this neglect he sent a few monks beyond the Alps. The bodies were exhumed and the precious relics were brought back to France. It was then that the Abbaye de Fleury took the name of St-Benoît.

The Middle Ages (beginning of 9C). — Under Charlemagne, the abbey had an exceptionally distinguished abbot in Theodulf, Bishop of Orléans *(p 84)* who founded the celebrated monastic schools of Fleury. The fame of these schools spread through all the Christian world — here were taught theology and the seven liberal arts : grammar, rhetoric, logic, arithmetic, geometry, music and astronomy. An army of copyists and illuminators piled up manuscripts. Pious writers collected histories of the saints ; chroniclers told the story of their time. The abbey employed masters of agriculture, industry, art and medicine. It was a great centre of culture and civilisation.

9th and 10th centuries. — The day of the Norman invasions dawned. When the Barbarians were reported approaching, the monks and their pupils took flight, carefully carrying the relics of their sainted patron. Orléans received them within its walls. When the pirates were gone they returned to their devastated home and repaired the damage as they waited for the next attack. Monastic discipline suffered under this régime. But in the 10C strict and pious abbots restored the Rule in all its rigour : rising at 2am, work between the services, total abstention from meat, corporal chastisement, etc. St-Benoît once more became prosperous. Pupils flocked to it again. The kings of France and great personages came to it often and loaded it with gifts. The opening of the 11C was marked by the building of a tower (the belfry porch) designed by Abbot Gauzlin, a future Archbishop of Bourges.

The present church (crypt, chancel and transept) was built from 1067 to 1108. The nave was completed only at the end of the 12C.

---

(1) A basilica is not a cathedral: the bishop does not preside there. The name is an honorary title given to a church for the importance of its relics.
(2) For further information, in English, read St-Benoît-sur-Loire *by J.M. Berland (Collection Art et Tourisme).*

Modern times. — St-Benoît passed *in commendam* in the 15C, when the revenues of the abbey were granted by the kings to "commendatory abbots", often laymen, who were simply beneficiaries and took no active part in the religious life of the community.

The monks did not always make them welcome. Under François I they refused to receive Cardinal Duprat and shut themselves up in the tower of the porch. The King had to come in person, at the head of an armed force, to make them submit.

During the Wars of Religion (1562-1598) one of these abbots, Odet de Châtillon-Coligny, the brother of the Protestant leader Admiral Coligny, was himself converted to Protestantism. He had St-Benoît looted by Condé's Huguenot troops. The treasure was melted down — the gold casket containing the relics of the Saint alone weighed 17.5 kg - 39 lb — the marvellous library was sold and its precious manuscripts, about 2000 in number, were scattered to the four corners of Europe. Some are now to be found in Berne, Rome, Leyden, Oxford and Moscow.

The celebrated Congregation of St-Maur, introduced to St-Benoît in 1627 by Cardinal Richelieu, restored its spiritual and intellectual life. The abbey was closed at the Revolution, its archives transferred to Orléans and its property dispersed. At the beginning of the First Empire the monastic buildings were destroyed *(1)* and the church fell into disrepair. In 1835 it was registered as an historical monument, and it was restored on various occasions between 1836 and 1923. Monastic life was revived there in 1944.

The poet and artist Max Jacob (1876-1944) retired to the abbey in St-Benoît-sur-Loire, before he was arrested in 1944.

■ THE BASILICA★★ *time : 3/4 hour*

Individuals may hire audio guides, apply at the Benedictine bookstall, to the right of the porch from Easter to 1 November 9 to 11am and 3 to 5pm ; for groups of more than 10 people guides are provided, apply in writing to the Frère chargé des visites, abbaye de St-Benoît-sur-Loire, 45730 St-Benoît-sur-Loire. The public is allowed to follow services (Gregorian Chant) : Conventual Mass at noon (11am on Sundays and holidays), Vespers at 6.15pm.

This imposing edifice was built between 1067 and 1218. The towers were originally much taller.

Belfry Porch★★. — The belfry originally stood by itself, and is one of the finest examples of Romanesque art. The richly carved capitals are particularly worthy of attention. The tourist can pick out for himself in the beautiful golden stone brought from Nivernais the delicately carved abaci and corbels. Stylised plants and, particularly, flowing acanthus leaves alternate with fantastic animals, scenes from the Apocalypse, and events in the life of Christ and the Virgin Mary. On the porch (second column from the left), one of the capitals is signed *Umbertus me fecit.*

(After photo: Éd. du Zodiaque)

The Basilica

Nave. — In the transitional Romanesque style, it was completed in 1218. It is very luminous with its white stonework and high vaulting which let in plenty of daylight. The organ loft was added about 1700 on the reverse side of the façade.

Transept. — Like the chancel, this was finished in 1108. The dome, built on superimposed squinches, carries the central bell tower. Under the dome are the stalls dated 1413, and the remains of a choir screen in carved wood presented in 1635 by Richelieu, when he was Commendatory Abbot of St-Benoît.

In the north transept is the precious 14C alabaster statue of Notre-Dame-de-Fleury. A plaque on the right recalls that the poet Max Jacob lies in the village cemetery.

Chancel★★. — The very deep Romanesque chancel was built between 1065 and 1108 ; note the decor of blind arcades with sculptured capitals forming a triforium. The ambulatory with radiating chapels *(not open to the public)* is typical of a church of high prestige, built for crowds and processions ; this plan can be found in most Benedictine churches.

The floor is paved with a Roman mosaic brought from Italy in 1531. The recumbent figure is that of Philippe I, the fourth Capet King, who died in 1108.

Crypt★. — An impressive masterpiece of the second half of the 11C, it has kept its original appearance. Large round columns form a double ambulatory with radiating chapels round the large central pillar containing the shrine of St Benedict, whose relics have been venerated here since the 8C.

---

(1) Only a small façade, belonging to the former students' chapel, remains. It is in the village on the Place de l'Université, opposite the war memorial.

The traveller's friends :

The Michelin Map series at a scale of 1 : 200 000
and the Michelin Red Guide France

ST-CALAIS

Michelin map 64 fold 5 – Pop 4779

St-Calais, an agricultural market town on the northwestern limits of the Vendômois, is dominated by the ruins of a feudal fortress. The narrow streets are occasionally bordered by old gabled dwellings.

Situated astride the Anille, five bridges connect the main thoroughfares on either bank. The western part of the town grew up under the St-Calais Benedictine Abbey founded by Calais, a cœnobite monk from Auvergne, during the reign of Childebert in the 6C. The monastery was destroyed during the Revolution, and those buildings that survived now serve as town hall, theatre and museum.

Every year since 1581 the town has commemorated the end of the Plague. The very popular *Fête du chausson aux pommes* (apple turnover festival) is held annually on the first Saturday and Sunday in September.

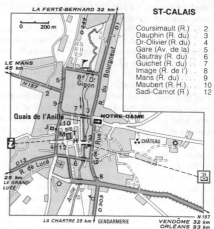

ST-CALAIS

Coursimault (R.)	2
Dauphin (R. du)	3
Dr-Olivier (R. du)	4
Gare (Av. de la)	5
Gautray (R. du)	6
Guichet (R. du)	7
Image (R. de l')	8
Mans (R. du)	9
Maubert (R. H.)	10
Sadi-Carnot (R.)	12

■ SIGHTS

Notre-Dame. – *To see the shroud apply at the town hall.* The building of this church was begun in 1425 with the chancel, and it is partly Flamboyant and partly Renaissance. The bell tower is surmounted by a stone steeple.

Finished in 1549 the Italian **façade★**, typical of the second Renaissance, is particularly remarkable for its rhythm and sculptured decoration. The carved panels of the twin doors portray scenes from the life of the Virgin with above two cornucopias framed in the semicircular arch. The whole is framed by Ionic pilasters. The charming side doorways are surmounted by curvilinear pediments and niches. A window with a pediment and occuli open on to the upper part of the gable.

The first three Renaissance bays have vaulting resting on pendentives and conical capitals in turn, the whole supported by majestic columns. The 17C organ loft originally came from the abbey and has an organ case of the same period.

A Baroque style retable adorns the high altar; a stout cupboard to the right of the chancel contains the shroud of St Calais made of Sassanian or 6C Persian material.

Quais de l'Anille. – This tree lined way offers attractive views of the riverside wash houses now disused and moss covered, and colourful gardens backed by a picturesque jumble of roof tops.

(After photo: Artaud, Nantes)

Notre-Dame Church — Main doorway

ST-GEORGES-SUR-LOIRE

Michelin map 63 folds 19 and 20 – *Local map p 104* – Pop 3015

St-Georges on the north bank of the Loire is situated not far from a famous vineyard, *La Coulée de Serrant,* where some of Anjou's finest white wines are produced.

Former abbey. – The village developed round an abbey founded in 1158 under the auspices of the Augustinian Order. Only a few buildings remain to remind us of this former establishment. One dating from 1684 houses both the town hall and the presbytery. Note the monumental staircase with its remarkable wrought iron railings, and the chapter house with its original wainscoting where are held temporary exhibitions.

EXCURSION

Château de Serrant★★. – *2 km - 1 mile by N 23 in the direction of Angers. Description p 149.*

EUROPE on a single sheet
Michelin map No. 920
(scale 1/3 000 000)

ST-PATERNE-RACAN

Michelin map 64 south of fold 4 — Pop 1 508

St-Paterne stretches out along the Escotais, which is bordered by riverside wash houses and weeping willows.

Church. — The church contains interesting works of art, some of which came from the nearby Abbey of La Clarté-Dieu. The 16C terracotta group to the left of the high altar portrays the Adoration of the Magi and in the centre is a charming **Virgin and Child★**.

In the nave, 18C polychrome statues represent the four great Latin Doctors of the Church — Ambrose, Augustine, Jerome and Gregory the Great — while in the south chapel a large retable (the Virgin of the Rosary) of the same period is accompanied by a 16C terracotta group of St Anne and the Virgin.

EXCURSIONS

Château de la Roche-Racan. — *2 km - 1 mile to the south by the D 28. Description p 133.*

St-Christophe-sur-le-Nais. — *Pop 877. 2.5 km - 1 1/2 miles to the north by the D 6.*
Also in the Escotais Valley this village is the scene of a pilgrimage to St Christopher, the patron saint of wayfarers and motorists today *(second last Sunday in July)*. The **church** is in reality composed of two separate buildings, a former 11-14C priory chapel and the parish church with its 16C nave and belfry.

At the threshold to the nave a gigantic St Christopher welcomes the visitor. To the right in a recess is a reliquary bust of the Saint.

To the left of the chancel, the door leading to the Prior's oratory is surmounted by a fine 14C statue of the Virgin and Child. Two curious medallions decorate the church's wooden roof.

Neuvy-le-Roi. — *Pop 1 052. 9 km - 6 miles to the east by the D 54.* The church *(closed on Saturday afternoons)* dating from the 12 and 16C has a Romanesque chancel and a nave covered with Angevin vaulting; note in the north aisle the complex pattern of vaulting with projecting keystones (16C), and to the south of the chancel the elegant seigneurial chapel, also with projecting keystones.

On the outside of the north aisle there are many lateral gable ends, frequently to be seen in the region.

STE-CATHERINE-DE-FIERBOIS

Michelin map 64 southwest of fold 15 — Pop 484

This village has many associations with Joan of Arc. Grouped round its church with its tapering steeple, the latter acts as a landmark from afar.

Church. — *Closed noon to 2pm.* Following directions given by Joan of Arc on 23 April 1428, a sword marked with five crosses was found here. It was said to have been placed there by Charles Martel after his victory against the Saracens at Poitiers (732).

Rebuilt in 1479 and finished during Charles VIII's reign, the building is emblazoned with the coats of arms of Charles and Anne of Brittany. Restored in 1859 this Flamboyant edifice dominated by its 41 m - 135 ft tall spire, has an interestingly sculptured doorway with pierced tympanum.

Inside the barrel vaulting springs directly from the piers. The north aisle has a small but very realistic 15C Entombment. The south transept contains a 15C altar surmounted by a statue of St Catherine, whose image is also portrayed on the front of the altar. Opposite is an unusual Flamboyant style confession box, very delicately carved.

Maison du Dauphin (1415). — This, the so called Dauphin's House, to the right after the church, is flanked by two statues of the sphinx and has a sculptured well wall in the courtyard.

STE-MAURE-DE-TOURAINE

Michelin map 68 north of folds 4 and 5 — Pop 4 130

This pleasant small town occupies a sunny site on a knoll commanding the Manse Valley and the Paris to Bordeaux road. Roman in origin, the settlement developed in the 6C round the tombs of St Bridget and St Maure, then round Foulques Nerra's keep. The Rohan-Montbazon family were the overlords from 1492 to the Revolution.

The town is known for its busy poultry markets and its local goats' milk cheeses. An annual Food Fair is held in June.

Church. — *To visit apply at the presbytery, 8 Rue de l'Église.* Dating back to the 11C, the original appearance was altered by a restoration in 1866. A chapel to the right of the chancel has an attractive 16C white marble Virgin by the Italian school. In the central apse there are two painted panels, one depicting the Last Supper (16C), and the other, Christ on a gold background; the relics of St Maure are venerated here. The crypt has a curious series of archaic Romanesque arcades and a small lapidary museum.

Covered market. — Standing well above the town, the 17C covered market was built by the Rohan family.

The aisles are still used for the weekly markets while the central or main aisle has been restored and serves as the village hall. The inscriptions and armorial bearings were destroyed during the Revolution.

THE STE-MAURE PLATEAU

Round tour of 56 km - 35 miles — about 1 hour — local map below

Dissected by the green valleys of the Manse and Esves, bounded by the Indre, Creuse and Vienne this plateau is composed of lacustrine limestone, easily eroded by running water. The plateau ends in the south with marl pits, bands of sand and shells, deposited during the Tertiary era by the Falun Sea. This rich mixture was formerly much used in the improvement of the soil.

Wheat is the primary crop with maize or fodder crops as the main alternatives, all interspersed with occasional fruit trees. Stock raising is increasing in popularity and cattle are to be found alongside the traditional goats, pigs, geese and famous small hen, the *géline noire de Touraine*. The folklore traditions of Touraine have been fiercely preserved by the local people.

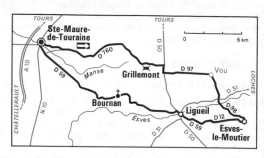

Leave Ste-Maure to the south-east by the D 59 taking the itinerary shown on the above map. The itinerary follows the deep, winding small valleys often marked out by poplars with the limestone evident along the sides. There are numerous good viewpoints.

Bournan. – Pop 231. The Romanesque church has a fine apse with a tower rising above the side chapel, terminated by a many sided spire. *Apply to Mme Pellevrault opposite the church.*

Ligueil. – Pop 2426. This small white stone town with several old houses has an important creamery and its markets are lively affairs attracting large crowds.

Esves-le-Moutier. – Pop 161. In a pleasantly green site on the banks of the Esves, this village takes its name from a wall encircled priory. The 10-12C church's square tower is flanked by bartizans *(open in the afternoon).*

Château de Grillemont. – This great white château stands midway up the slope of a small **valley★** whose crests are crowned with pines and oaks. During the reign of Charles VII it was equipped with large round towers with pepperpot roofs. In 1765 the 15C curtain walls were replaced by majestic Classical buildings.

Walkers, campers, smokers
please take care
Fire is the scourge of forests everywhere

SANCERRE ★

Michelin map 🟦 fold 12 – Pop 2286

Sancerre is perched on a hillock on the west bank of the Loire, overlooking the villages of St-Satur and St-Thibault. From this **elevation★** there is a wide panorama over the river and the Nivernais region to the east, and Berry to the west. The little town, with its narrow winding streets has considerable character.

As the chief town of a region famous for its vineyards and goats, Sancerre is well known for its delicious white wine with a gunflint flavour *(pierre à fusil)* and its little round cheeses made from goats' milk, bearing the unexpected name of *crottins* (goat droppings) and made at Chavignol.

Sancerre, the stronghold. – Sancerre, because of its strategic position, and as the key to the Berry region, played an important part in the Hundred Years War, opposing both the Burgundians and the English. It was here that Charles VII, King of Bourges amassed an army of 20 000 soldiers which he commanded in person for some time.

In 1534 Sancerre adopted Protestantism and became a Protestant citadel and the butt for the unavailing attacks of the Royal forces. The Treaty of St-Germain in 1570 and the Massacre of St Bartholomew in 1572 in no way affected those adhering to the "so called Reformed religion" who continued their unrest, with the result that on 3 January 1573, Marshal de la Châtre with 7 000 men laid siege to the town. After an intense period of preparatory artillery fire, the assault was launched by means of three gaps in the walls, but the people of Sancerre maintained their ground. Then La Châtre decided to starve them out by imposing a rigorous blockade. The besieged reduced to the most dire famine, were forced to eat powdered slates and all the leather and skins that the town could provide. Only after seven months of resistance did the town give in. They were awarded military honours along with the freedom to practise their chosen religion.

The wine of Sancerre. – "Wine", wrote Balzac in 1844 in the *Muse du Département,* " is the principal activity and provides the chief source of business for a countryside that has several generous vintages, with full bouquets ; it is like enough to the wines of Burgundy to deceive the vulgar palates in Paris. Thus the wine of Sancerre is much drunk in the Parisian cabarets, which after all is only right with wines that cannot be kept for more than seven or eight years". Vineyards are found on all slopes exposed to the sun. The "regional" name Sancerre is reserved for white wines from the *Sauvignon* vine as well as the red and rosé wines of the *Pinot* variety.

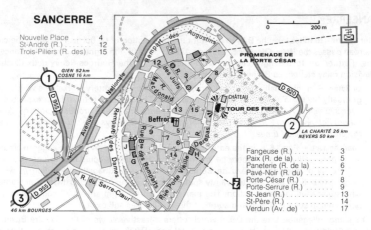

■ SIGHTS

Promenade de la porte César★★. – This affords a good view★★ of the vineyards, St-Satur with its viaduct, St-Thibault and the Loire Valley and the Morvan foothills on the horizon.

Tour des Fiefs. – This late 14C round keep is all that remains of the castle of the counts of Sancerre, a Huguenot fortress which was fiercely defended during the siege of 1573. *The tower is open 1 March to 1 November Sundays and holidays from 2 to 6pm.*
From the top there is a vast **panorama★** over the Loire Valley and the Sancerre Hills.

Belfry (Beffroi). – Dating from 1509 this former alarm tower now serves as the belfry to Notre-Dame de Sancerre.

Old town. – Stroll through the old quarter with its narrow streets and note the gables, doorways, turrets and sculptured decoration. Plaques indicate the interesting houses and other points of interest. Craft shops can be seen around the Nouvelle Place.

EXCURSIONS

St-Satur. – Pop 1961. *4 km - 2 1/2 miles by ①, the D955.* Only the chancel and the apse of the Church of St-Pierre, the abbey church begun in 1362, were completed, but their vastness, the purity of their soaring lines leave to the imagination the considerable project started by the Augustinian Canons.

Léré. – Pop 925. *20 km - 12 miles by ①, and the D955 and D751.* This once fortified village retains some ruined round towers and the curved layout of the Rue des Remparts. The **canal** leading to the Loire runs along the village. The **Collegiate Church of St-Martin** with its Romanesque nave and 15C chancel has a lectern and 16C statues. The crypt is 9C.

Chavignol. – *3 km - 2 miles by ①, the D955. At Fontenay turn left into the D183.* This picturesque wine growers' village has given its name to one of the best known wines of the Sancerre vineyards and also to a goats' milk cheese.

The Sancerrois★. – *Round tour of 79 km - 49 miles – about 3 hours – local map below. Leave Sancerre by ③ the D955.* The road affords far reaching views to the south of a hedge compartmented, undulating countryside dotted with elms and chestnuts. Flocks of sheep and goats pasture round isolated farmsteads.

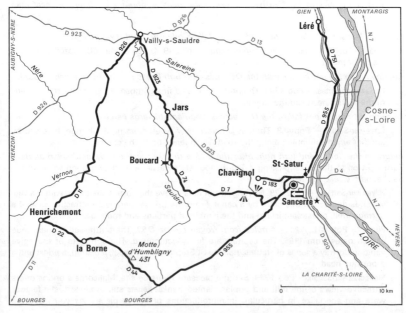

After 16 km - 10 miles take the D 44 to the right in the direction of La Borne. Following the crest this road passes the **Motte d'Humbligny** (altitude 431 m - 1414 ft), the highest point in the Sancerre Hills. Further on to the right can be seen the mast of the Bourges-Neuvy-deux-Clochers television relay station. La Borne is the next village.

La Borne. – In this small village, lost amidst the woods, are pottery workshops which have gradually been replaced by other craft industries. The local clays have been exploited for over 300 years. *An exhibition in the school presents the locally produced pottery, during school holidays from 3 to 7pm; the rest of the year on Sundays and public holidays only at the aforementioned times.*

Henrichemont. – Pop 1 826. In the early 17C Sully, Minister to Henri IV, was eager to create a small principality in Berry where he and his fellow Huguenots could take refuge. Although he already owned the Château de Béthune at nearby La Chapelle d'Angillon *(p 63)* he decided to build in this deserted sandy spot. Although never completed it was Sully himself who supervised the construction. The plan provided for eight streets all converging on a large central square. A well and some of the 17C houses still exist.

On reaching Villegenon take the D 926 which offers attractive views of the Sauldre Basin. At **Vailly-sur-Sauldre** (pop 875), in its riverside site, take the D 923 towards the south and then the D 74 which overlooks the Sauldre Valley.

Jars. – Pop 554. This charming village is dominated by a round tower flanked manor house. The 15-16C red sandstone and white limestone church is preceded by a belfry porch. The nave has lierne and tierceron vaulting. From behind the church there is a fine view of the Sancerre countryside.

Château de Boucard. – *Open 10am to noon and 2 to 7pm (6pm 1 October to 28 February; time: 3/4 hour; 13F.*

Still surrounded by its moat in front of which is a lovely group of outbuildings *(in summer: exhibitions, concerts)*, the château dates from the 14 and 16C. The north wing, built in 1560 formerly gave on to beautiful formal gardens, surrounded by canals which alone have resisted the passage of time. In the Renaissance wing there is the guardroom, the grand salon with a large fireplace, a desk of citrus-wood and Louis XIV furniture, the small salon, the dining room with beautiful pewterware, the bedroom of the Duke of Naveuil, and the kitchen where the rustic fireplace still has its mechanical spit. In the older part there is the chapel which has a slanting aperture made under the First Empire so that the Princesse de la Tremoille could be present at Divine Services without leaving her bedroom.
Near the outbuildings, the dovecote still has its revolving ladder.

At Sens-Beaujeu take the D 7. Just before the junction with the D 923 there is a remarkable **view★** to the right of the village of Bué and the Sancerre Hills. At the road junction itself the admirable **view★★** is of Sancerre, the vineyards, St-Satur and the Loire Valley beyond.

SARTHE Valley

Michelin map 🔢 folds 1 to 3 – *Cruising see p 37*

A northern tributary of the Loire, the Sarthe flows slowly across the rich smiling countryside of the Angevin Maine, meandering on the floor of the spacious valley carved out of the soft Upper Cretaceous rocks. In the vicinity of Sablé the river has forced a way across a granite outcrop. Navigable up to Le Mans, the Sarthe is paralleled in places by canals. Woodlands and prairies alternate with light agricultural soils, on which are cultivated cereals, potatoes and cabbages.

From Le Mans to Sablé – *71 km - 44 miles – about 2 1/2 hours – local map opposite*

Leave Le Mans (p 109) by ⑥, the N 23; at La Belle-Étoile turn right towards Fillé.

Fillé. – Pop 744. The village church, rebuilt since 1944, has a late 16C, glazed terracotta statue of the Virgin.

Continuing on the north bank with the D 51, pass through Roëze-sur-Sarthe to reach La Suze.

La Suze-sur-Sarthe. – Pop 3 709. The bridge affords a fine glimpse of the Sarthe, the remains of the 15C château and the church.

Once on the south bank follow the D 79 across woodland towards Fercé.

Fercé-sur-Sarthe. – Pop 458. There is a lovely view when crossing the bridge, followed by another when continuing along the road which leads up to the church.

Return to the Sarthe and turn right after the bridge to take the V 5 towards St-Jean-du-Bois. Turn right on to the D 229, passing a Troubadour style castle and offering good views of the Sarthe, before reaching Noyen.

Noyen-sur-Sarthe. – Pop 2 029. Noyen rises in tiers above the north bank of the wide Sarthe, which is doubled at this point by a canal. From the bridge there is an attractive **view** of a barrage, mill, midstream island and the jumble of gardens and rooftops.

Pirmil. – Pop 401. *7 km - 4 miles from Noyen by the D 69.* The buttressed Romanesque church dates from 1165. The capitals are finely sculptured. The springers of the ogive vaulting portray a series of statues, namely St Stephen, St Michael, a bishop, a priest and a grotesque head.

Malicorne-sur-Sarthe. – Pop 1 773. Set in a pleasant riverside site, Malicorne's bridge offers attractive views of the mill and poplar planted banks. **Potters** still produce rustic faience ware and specialize, in particular, in reproductions of period pieces. *As you leave the*

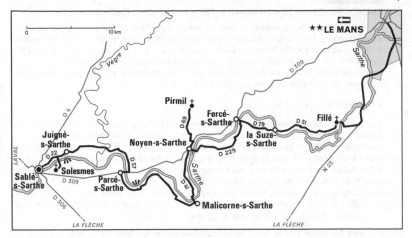

village to the east, where the D 133 starts towards Mézéray, guided tours of the workshops: Easter to 30 September, weekdays 9am to noon and 2 to 6pm; Sundays and holidays 3 to 6pm; closed Mondays and Sunday and holiday mornings; time: 1 1/4 hour; 10F.

The 11C **church** contains some interesting works of art: the recumbent figure of a local overlord (chapel to the right of the nave), a *Pietà* (south transept) and 16C piscina on the wall to the north of the nave.

Downstream and standing a little way back from the river in a fine park is a restored 17C **château** with small turrets and mansard roofs, encircled by moats, crossed by a charming 17C hump backed bridge.

Take the D 8 towards Parcé, then turn right into the V 1 towards Dureil; reach once again the D 8, the itinerary gives fine glimpses of the Sarthe.

Parcé-sur-Sarthe. — Pop 1 432. This charming village with its mill on the bank of the river, is grouped round its Romanesque belfry. At the entrance of the settlement the cypress shaded cemetery is the setting for a chapel surmounted by that unusual architectural feature, a bell gable.

Cross to the north bank and after the canal turn left into the D 57.
Beyond Avoise turn left into the V 4 towards Juigné, the road crosses the Vègre, then take the D 22 to the left.

Juigné-sur-Sarthe. — Pop 816. This pleasant village, situated on a promontory jutting across the valley, has several 16 and 17C houses and an 18C château, the seat of the marquis de Juigné. From the church square there are plunging views of the Sarthe and the great mass of the Abbey of Solesmes.

Solesmes. — *Description p 149.*

Continue along the D 22, which follows the canal and passes former marble quarries, to reach Sablé-sur-Sarthe *(p 135).*

SAULGES

Michelin map 🗺 south of fold 11 — Pop 348

This peaceful village overlooks the Erve Valley.

The region was converted to Christianity in the 7C by St Cénéré (or Sérénède), whose name was given to several sanctuaries.

Merovingian Church of St-Pierre. — It is opposite the parish church on the village square. One first enters the simple 16C **St-Sérénède Chapel** where his relics are venerated; the fresco on the right wall of the chapel depicts St-Cénéré on the left, and further to the right, St Anne teaching the Virgin to read.

Down a few steps is the **St-Pierre Chapel**, built in the middle of the 7C by St-Cénéré, a rare vestige of this remote period.

Caves. — *To visit the Grotte à Margot apply to the restaurant nearby (9am - 8am Sundays and holidays to 8pm; time: 3/4 h; 10F).*

The Saulges caves are in an attractive site to the north of the village of the same name. They have interesting geological formations and have provided varied evidence of early human habitation such as bones and flint tools.

Grotte à Margot. — This cave is interesting for its narrowness, fissures and erosional phenomena.

Grotte de Rochefort. — *Not open to the public.* The cave, cut out of dark coloured rocks, has an opening in the cliffs on the right bank.

St-Cénéré Oratory. — *1 km - 1/2 mile.* On leaving Saulges in the direction of Vaiges, follow to the left a gently rising road which leads to a car park.

Take the footbridge across the river to reach the hermitage, pleasantly surrounded by trees, at the foot of rocks. Nearby the Erve widens into a small lake which is very popular with anglers.

Michelin map 🔟 fold 12 – *Local map p 105* – Pop 33 953 – *Facilities pp 36-37*

Saumur is famous for its cavalry school, its wines, especially *mousseux* or sparkling wines and its mushrooms. The region's production of the latter represents 70 per cent of the national figure. Recent additions to the industrial sector include toymaking, hosiery, and mechanical and electrical firms. Saumur also has Europe's most important carnival mask factory.

Every year in the large Place du Chardonnet there are equestrian and motorized tatoos, and performances by the *Cadre Noir,* which attract the crowds.

HISTORICAL NOTES

Saumur was a bone of contention between the counts of Anjou and the counts of Blois and was sacked by the Normans. It became Crown property under Philippe-Auguste.

The town enjoyed its zenith at the end of the 16C and in the 17C. It was one of the great centres of Protestantism. Henri III gave it to the King of Navarre as a stronghold. The future Henri IV installed there as Governor one Duplessis-Mornay, a great soldier, a great scholar and a fervent Reformer. The Catholics called him "the Pope of the Huguenots"; in the town he founded a Protestant academy, which acquired great fame. The Revocation of the Edict of Nantes (1685), depriving French Protestants of their religious and civil liberties, was a great blow to Saumur. Many of the inhabitants emigrated.

Cavalry and Amoured Corps Academy (École d'application de l'Arme blindée et de la Cavalerie – Y). – It was in 1763 that the Carabiniers Regiment, a crack corps recruited from the best horsemen in the army, was stationed in Saumur and to garrison the regiment the central range was built from 1767 to 1770. It now serves as headquarters for the Cavalry Academy which trains the élite of the French cavalry, both mounted and armoured.

In 1940 the town was badly damaged, when the cavalry school made an heroic three day stand against superior German forces.

In 1972 the **National Riding School** was created with the aim of training civilian riding instructors. The famous **Cadre Noir** belongs to this school. The school has modern premises at St-Hilaire-St-Florent outside Saumur.

■ THE CHÂTEAU★★ (Z) *time:* 1 1/2 hours

Guided tours 1 April to 30 June 9 to 11.30am and 2 to 6pm; 1 July to 30 September 9am to 6.30pm; in October 9 to 11.30am and 2 to 6pm; 1 November to 31 March (closed Tuesdays) 9.30 to 11.30am and 2 to 5pm. In addition open 8.30 to 10.30pm on Easter and Whitsun Saturdays and Sundays, and July and August. Closed on 1 January and 25 December: 12F (museums and historical presentation included).

It is compact and massive, but has a graceful thrust due to the vertical lines of its arris towers. Although a fortress, it has been decorated with care like a country mansion, with sculptured machicolations and window balustrades in the interior courtyard. The château

(After photo: Yvon)

Château de Saumur

stands above the Loire Valley on a sort of pedestal formed by the 16C radial fortifications.

Several fortresses succeeded one another on this sheer promontory. The present building was erected at the end of the 14C by Louis I, Duke of Anjou, and finished by Louis II. The interior was re-modelled in the 15C by René of Anjou and fortified at the end of the 16C by Duplessis-Mornay *(see above).* It was the residence of the Governor of Saumur under Louis XIV and Louis XV, became a prison and then a barracks, and today houses two museums.

From the Guet Tower, there is a beautiful **panorama★** of the town and the valleys of the Thouet and the Loire.

Museum of Decorative Arts★★ (Musée d'Arts décoratifs). – Formed partly from the Lair Collection, this museum shows fine specimens of mediaeval and Renaissance work: Limoges enamels, sculptures in wood and alabaster, tapestries, furniture, paintings, church ornaments and a large collection of pottery and French porcelain of the 17 and 18C, together with furniture and tapestries of the same period.

Among the 15 and 16C tapestries note the series entitled *The History of Titus* and in particular the *Coronation of the Emperor Vespasianus* and the *Capture of Jerusalem.*

Equine Museum★ (Musée du Cheval). – The museum depicts the history of the horse throughout the ages and in all countries. Note especially the collection of saddles, bridle bits, stirrups and spurs and the series of fine engravings by George Stubbs.

■ ADDITIONAL SIGHTS

The old quarter★. – The small twisting streets which run between the château and the bridge have not changed over the years. Whereas some parts of the town have been rebuilt in mediaeval style or are resolutely modern and full of surprises (south of the Church of St-Pierre), others have kept and enhanced the old façades. It is worth walking along the shopping Rue St-Jean as far as the charming and irregular **Place St-Pierre,** where half-timbered façades and 18C houses with wrought iron balconies stand side by side.

St-Pierre (YD). – *Closed noon to 2.30pm.* A partly 12C Romanesque building. The west front collapsed but was rebuilt in the 17C. Enter by the fine Romanesque door *(illustration p 20)* in the south transept. You will see 15C stalls and two sets of **tapestries★** of the 16C, one representing the life of St Peter, the other the life of St Florentius *(start from the left of the nave).* Beautiful Baroque organ case.

Hôtel de Ville★ (YH). – Only the left part is old (16C). The building used to be washed by the Loire and was part of the town wall; this explains its military appearance. Seen from the courtyard the building is not at all warlike, it is Gothic and finely sculptured.

Notre-Dame-de-Nantilly★ (ZB). – Lovely Romanesque building. Louis XI who was greatly devoted to Notre-Dame, added the right aisle; the oratory is used as a baptismal chapel.

In the same aisle there is an epitaph on one of the pillars written by King René of Anjou for his nurse. Opposite, there is an enamelled copper cross by Gilles, Archbishop of Tyr, Keeper of the Seals under St Louis. The venerated 12C statue of Notre-Dame-de-Nantilly, in painted wood, is in the small apse on the right of the chancel.

Very beautiful **tapestries★★** decorate the church. They date from the 15 and 16C, except for eight in the central nave, made at Aubusson in the 17C, which depict scenes from the life of Christ. Note Jesse's tree in the left arm of the transept and the 18 very interesting capitals.

The organ case, supported by telamones, dates from 1690.

Cavalry Museum★ (YM[1]). – *Enter from Avenue Foch. Open 15 April to 15 October except Mondays and Fridays, 2 to 5pm; Sundays and holidays, 9 to 11.30am and 2 to 5pm; closed Easter weekend.*

There is a large collection of souvenirs, which tells the history of the Cavalry Academy and the armoured corps since the 18C.

Among the objects shown are elegant swords encrusted with mother of pearl, ebony or shell; sabres belonging to Egyptian mamelukes; military equipment belonging to famous field marshals and generals of the Empire. The uniforms of Napoleon's Army and the Garde Impériale are evoked by a collection of porcelain figures from Sèvres and Meissen. There are also Dragoon and Hussar helmets and breastplates.

Finally the history of the French cavalry is portrayed from 1870 through the two world wars and the Indo-Chinese and Algerian campaigns.

Museum of Armoured Cavalry (Musée des Blindés – XM[2]). – *At the north end of Place du Chardonnet. Open 9am to noon and 2 to 6pm; 15F.*

There are some 150 armoured vehicles showing the evolution of the armoured corps since 1918. The hall to the left is devoted to French equipment including the Renault tank of 1918. The hall to the right contains foreign equipment: Soviet T34s, several German "Panthers" and the imposing British "Conqueror".

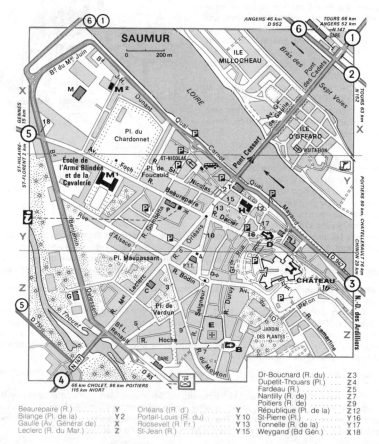

SAUMUR★★

St-Hilaire-St-Florent. – *2 km - 1 1/4 miles to the northwest by ⑤, the D 751.*
St-Hilaire is on the outskirts of Saumur, a straggling village built along a street which stretches into the hillside and left bank of the Thouet. All the great wine growers who make the famous mousseux by the champagne method are here, their cellars line the whole road *(all the well known makes offer a visit to their cellars to taste their wine).*

National Riding School★. – *Guided tours 9.15 to 11am and 2 to 4pm, apply in advance to the Tourist Centre.* ☏ 41 51 03 06; *time : 1 1/4 hours ; 10F.*
Created in 1972, this school has very modern premises and it is interesting, for example, to compare this installation with that of the National Stud at Isle-Briand *(p 117)*. The school is divided into several units, each with a granary where grain and fodder are stocked, a large and cool manege, and stables for 120 horses, with saddle rooms and showers. Automatic facilities are very advanced ; horse-dung is evacuated on a conveyor belt, and the grain, correctly measured for each horse is distributed automatically through piping at fixed hours.
The tour is very interesting with a good commentary.

Mushroom Museum (Musée du champignon). – *West of the village, 2 km - 1 1/4 miles after the cellars. Guided tours 15 March to 15 November, 10am to noon and 2 to 6pm ; 3/4 hour ; 11F.*
The old tufa quarries dug out of the hillsides in the vicinity of Saumur are mainly used for growing mushrooms, which benefit from the humidity and the unchanging temperature (between 11 and 14 ºC). Although cultivation in the quarries has taken place since Napoleon I, it has now been developed on an industrial scale and covers 800 km - 497 miles of galleries, with an annual production in the region of 120 000 tons.
The tour does not include a visit to the actual profit making installation, but the various cultivation methods are shown ; the old method of cultivation in stacks of straw is being replaced more and more by recent techniques, using wooden crates or plastic bags.

Notre-Dame-des-Ardilliers. – *Going east from the town on the Quai L-Mayaud, by ③, the D 947.* This beautiful 17C building (1635-9) a little isolated on the edge of the road was one of the most frequented pilgrim sanctuaries in France. Devotions at Notre-Dame-des-Ardilliers grew as from the reign of François I due to a miraculous statue found there by a labourer in the preceding century, but it was in the 17C that it had the greatest number of devotees, more than 10 000 pilgrims going there each year. *Closed noon to 2pm.*

EXCURSIONS

Château de Boumois★. – *7 km - 4 miles to the northwest by ⑥, the D 952 and then the first road on the right.*
Boumois Château lies hidden in the trees, 300 m - 328 yd from the D 952. Built at the beginning of the 16C it has a double aspect : the feudal exterior hides an inner dwelling house of graceful Flamboyant and Renaissance styles.
Guided tours Palm Sunday to 1 November 10am to noon and 2 to 6pm (6.30pm July and August) ; closed Tuesdays ; time : 3/4 hour ; 17F.
The drive leads to the main entrance, on the left of which stands a dovecote. A moat and fortified perimeter wall protect the seigneurial courtyard which is reached by a massive doorway.
The main building, which was built at the end of the 15C, is flanked on the left by two great machicolated towers. A turret staircase leads to the living quarters, and this is closed by a door embellished with an extraordinary wrought iron lock and detailed Renaissance motifs. The visitor may go

(After photo: Karquel)

Château de Boumois

through a great hall on the first floor (collection of 15-16C arms) and along the parapet walk. There is a beautiful Flamboyant chapel with a pointed roof. The 17C dovecote still has its revolving ladder for collecting the eggs.
Aristide Dupetit-Thouars was born at Boumois in 1760. He died gloriously on the quarterdeck of his ship, the *Tonnant,* in the Battle of Aboukir in 1798 rather than haul down his flag.

Dolmen de Bagneux. – *2 km - 1 mile to the south by ④, the N 147 ; opposite the church of Bagneux, turn left into the D 160.*
The great dolmen, or prehistoric tomb, is to be found in the town of Bagneux, near the café restaurant du Dolmen *(open to customers patronising the café)*. This is Anjou's most important megalithic monument : 20 m long by 7 m wide it is really a covered gallery grave or long rectangular burial chamber with sixteen upright stones supporting a roof of four horizontal stone slabs 3 m off the ground (66 ft × 23 ft × 10 ft).

St-Cyr-en-Bourg. – Pop 1 772. *8 km - 5 miles to the south by the Boulevard Louis-Renault and the D 93.*
The wine making enterprise, Les vignerons de Saumur, allows the visitor to follow the entire production process from grape to wine, while descending 25 m - 82 ft in all, within its plant at various underground levels. The underground galleries can be visited in a motorised vehicle. *Guided tours including wine tasting from May to the end of September ; 4.50F.*

SEGRÉ

Michelin map 📖 fold 9 — Pop 7 416

The schist houses of Segré rise in tiers above the river with its quays and picturesque bridges.

Segré is the capital of the Segréen, an area of *bocage* or wooded farmland, where mixed farming — both crops and livestock rear-
ing (pigs, cattle and horses), is common. The town has also given its name to a high grade (55 per cent) iron ore deposit, lying to the northwest near Pouancé and Renazé.

Old bridge. — This hump backed bridge of schist crosses the Oudon and offers attractive views of the older parts of the town.

St-Joseph. — From this chapel there are views of the old town and the Oudon Valley.

EXCURSIONS

Château de la Lorie★. — *2 km - 1 mile to the southeast. The château is sign-posted from the Cholet road. Open 1 July to 30 September, except Tuesdays, 3 to 6pm ; 14F.*

(After photo: R. Jacques)

Segré — The old bridge

This imposing 18C château, preceded by formal French gardens, is ap-
proached by a fine tree shaded avenue. The courtyard overlooked on three sides by buildings is protected on the fourth by a now empty moat. The formality of the design is enlivened by the contrasting colours and textures of the building materials, in particular the white tufa window surrounds and corner stones. The central range, adorned by a statue of Minerva, is the original 17C edifice built by René Le Pelletier, Provost General of Anjou. The imposing dimensions of the ensemble are due to the addition in the late 18C of symmetrical wings at right angles and outbuildings.

The same nobility of proportions and form is to be found inside, in particular in the great gallery adorned with fine pieces of Chinese porcelain, the late 18C marble Salon and adjoining chapel and 18C panelled dining room.

The château in the early 19C was the residence of James Duke of Alba and Berwick, a natural son of James II and able general in the French army.

Le Bourg-d'Iré ; Nyoiseau. — *21 km - 13 miles — about 3/4 hour. Leave Segré by the D 923 in the direction of Candé to the south and after a level crossing turn right into the D 181.*

Le Bourg-d'Iré. — Pop 911. Situated in the Verzée Valley the bridge affords a charming **view** of the river.

Return to the entrance of the village and follow the D 219 to reach the mining town of Noyant-la-Gravoyère. Turn right on to the D 775 and after 1 km - 1/2 mile turn left to Nyoiseau. This narrow road follows a gorge cut through schist rocks and forms the most picturesque part of the excursion.

Nyoiseau. — Pop 1 549. This village is perched on the slopes of the Oudon Valley. Note, in a riverside site, the remains of a Benedictine abbey for nuns.

Return to Segré by the D 71 and D 775.

SELLES-SUR-CHER

Michelin map 📖 fold 18 — Pop 5 020

Selles-sur-Cher is prettily situated in a bend of the Cher, the waters of which reflect the towers of its château.

The town owes its origins to St Eusice, who lived there as a hermit and founded an abbey on the spot. Only the abbey church remains of the former building.

■ SIGHTS

St-Eusice★. — *Closed noon to 2pm.* Built in the 12 and 15C and burnt out by Coligny in 1562, it was restored partly in the 17C and much more completely last century. The west front is almost entirely Romanesque and shows columns and capitals which come from a church destroyed by the Normans in 903.

The **chevet** is carefully built and adorned with two friezes of figures which are rough, naïve and heavy below the windows but better proportioned and more delicate above. The lower frieze depicts scenes from the New Testament ; the upper frieze, scenes from the life of St Eusice.

Near the north wall there are bas-reliefs of the Work of the Months and higher up on the right, a beautiful Visitation sheltered and protected by the transept chapel.

The north wall, which was built at the end of the 13C, has a delightful doorway with carved capitals supporting tori divided by a rope of flowers and wild rose leaves.

The 6C tomb of St Eusice is in the crypt.

Château. – *Guided tours 1 July to 15 September, 9am to noon and 2 to 6pm; during spring holidays 10 am to noon and 2 to 6pm; closed Sunday mornings; time: 1/2 hour; 15F.*

The remains of this grim 13C fortress with its rectangular wall lapped by wide moats full of water, crossed by four bridges, is hidden away on the banks of the Cher. In contrast, and surrounding the present access bridge are two bright and smiling 17C buildings on the east side, linked by a long wall with arcades pierced with small round windows and a parapet walk on top. These buildings are the work of **Philippe de Béthune,** brother of Sully *(p 152)* who bought the château of Selles in 1604.

Cross the small interior park shaded by a magnificent cedar and mulberry trees to visit first the **Pavillon Doré** (gilded pavilion) in the old part on the west side. It is an elegant building decorated in Italian Renaissance style which Philippe de Béthune made for himself in the old 13C fortress: magnificent fireplaces embellished with gilt work, murals, polychrome coffered ceilings; all have kept their lustre. There is also the Intendant's room, with mediaeval weapons, the study with a collection of souvenirs of the Comte de Chambord (1820-83), pretender to the throne of France after the death of Charles X, the small oratory and the bedroom.

While he was living in the Pavillon Doré, Philippe de Béthune built a new château for himself in the style of his time, in red brick outlined with white stone, which can be seen at the entrance. Here the grandeur and vastness of the proportions replace the intimate charm of the Pavillon Doré. One can also visit the guardroom with its large fireplace, the bedroom of Marie Sobieska, Queen of Poland, whose fourposter bed with wreathed columns stands on a dais, and the attractive games room.

Local History and Folklore Museum. – *Open 1 July to 30 September on Tuesdays and Thursdays 3 to 6pm; Saturdays, Sundays and public holidays 10am to noon and 2.30 to 6.30pm; 5F.*

It is installed in the cloisters of the former abbey, of which three galleries with sculptured keystones still exist on the right of the church. The museum has a description of Selles in former times, wine growers' implements, and an interesting room showing how gunflint was cut, a flourishing industry in the region in the middle of the 18C until the invention of the percussion cap *(see also Luçay-le-Mâle p 164).*

EXCURSIONS

Châtillon-sur-Cher. – *Pop 1 293. 5 km - 3 miles to the west by the N 76 towards St Aignan and a road to the left.*

In this small village built on the edge of the hillside overlooking the Cher is the **Church of St-Blaise,** in a very agreeable green setting, slightly on the edge of the village at the end of the Rue de l'Église *(open Sundays 11am to 1pm).*

Inside, on the left wall of the chancel there is a **panel**★ by the school of Leonardo da Vinci representing St Catherine between two cherubs: the outline of the hands, a little mannered but very beautiful, and her expression, are characteristic of the Master's style. A statue of St Vincent, patron of wine growers, is surrounded by batons of the brotherhood, used during processions.

Meusnes. – *Pop 1 017. 6.5 km - 4 miles to the southwest by the D 956 towards Valençay, then to the right on the D 17.*

The **church** is in pure Romanesque style. The interior has a triumphal arch in the transept surmounted by three openwork arcatures. Several fine 15 and 16C statues have been put back in place.

There is a small **gunflint museum** in the Mairie *(open Tuesdays to Saturdays 9am to 1pm; for afternoon visits apply in advance to the town hall; ☎ 54 71 00 23; closed holidays; 3F.)* It depicts this industry which flourished in the region for three centuries *(see also Luçay-le-Mâle p 164).*

Chabris. – *Pop 2 589. 8 km - 5 miles to the southeast by the D 51.*

Of Roman origin, Chabris is on the slopes of the left bank of the Cher and produces highly valued wines and goat cheese.

The **church,** dedicated to St-Phalier, a 5C recluse who died in Chabris, is the object of very ancient devotion. (Pilgrimage the 1st Sunday in September).

Walking round the chevet there are some very strange primitive sculptures to be seen, fantastic animals, an Annunciation, and sections of stones laid in a diamond pattern which come from a much older church. This one was rebuilt in the 15C: behind the porch with its double arcade and tribune, there is a lovely Gothic portal with sculptured leaves. In the chancel there are two naive style panels depicting the life and miracles of St Phalier who could make women fertile.

The **crypt** *(apply to the presbytery)* dates from the 11C. In the form of a "confessio" with a passage and openings to workship the relics, it contains the sarcophagus of the Saint.

The age of great Gothic cathedrals in France was heralded by the construction of

St-Denis (c 1136), Sens (c 1140) and Notre-Dame in Paris (1163);
followed by Strasbourg (c 1176),
Bourges (c 1185), Chartres (1194),
Rouen (1200), Reims (1211),
Amiens (1200) and Beauvais (1247).

Early English, the corresponding period in England, lasted until the end of the 13C and included in whole or in part the cathedrals of Wells (1174),

Lincoln (chancel and transept: 1186),
Salisbury (1220-1258),
Westminster Abbey (c 1250) and Durham (1242).

SERRANT, Château de ★★

This sumptuous mansion although built over a period of three centuries, 16-18C, has great unity of style. Massive round towers topped by cupolas, the dark schist and contrasting white tufa all go to give it considerable character.

The architect of the Tuileries in Paris and Fontainebleau, Philibert Delorme, worked on the plans for this château. The building is surrounded by a moat which becomes a lake on the park side.

Jacobite Connections. − Begun in 1546 by Charles de Brie, the château was bought in 1596 by Hercule de Rohan, duc de Montbazon, then in 1636 by Guillaume Bautru, whose granddaughter married the marquis de Vaubrun, Lieutenant General of the King's armies. On the death of her husband after the Battle of Altenheim in Alsace, the Marquise continued to supervise the work on the house till 1705. It was she who commisioned the architect Jules Hardouin-Mansart (The Invalides, Paris) to build the chapel in commemoration of her husband, and the sculptor Coysevox to create the white marble mausoleum.

Bought in 1749 by Walsh, Serrant was raised to the status of county by Louis XV as a reward to the Irishman Anthony Walsh for the support he had given to the Stuart cause in transporting Bonnie Prince Charlie to Moidart in 1745. Two generations earlier it had been another Walsh that carried the fleeing James II to exile in France.

The château is now owned by Jean-Charles de Ligne.

Château. − *Guided tours Saturday preceding Palm Sunday to last Sunday in October, 9 to 11.30am and 2 to 5.30pm; closed Tuesdays except in July and August; time : 3/4 hour; 18F.*

The **apartments** are magnificently furnished. Rich Flemish tapestries hang in the main dining room. Admire the main panelled staircase, the first floor apartments with their coffered ceilings and the library with its 10 000 volumes. Note in the latter the portrait of the Young Pretender and Anthony Walsh.

The state rooms were used by both Louis XIV and Napoleon. The art objects are many and various : Flemish and Brussels tapestries, a fine Italian cabinet, a bust of the Empress Marie-Louise by Canova and many portraits.

Join us in our never ending task of keeping up to date.
Send us your comments and suggestions, please.

Michelin Type PLC,
Tourism Department
Lyon Road, HARROW, Middlesex HA1 2 DQ.

SOLESMES

This village to the north of Sablé owes its fame to the presence of a Benedictine abbey. The north bank and the bridge both offer good **viewpoints★** of the impressive, towering mass of abbey buildings, built at the end of the 19C in a Romanesque-Gothic style. The massive ensemble, built close to the riverside, is extended by a more ordered 18C building, the original priory.

Under the Benedictine Order. − Founded in 1010 by a local lord the Benedictine Priory of Solesmes was served by monks from the Abbey of St-Pierre-de-la-Couture in Le Mans. It expanded rapidly and was extremely wealthy in the early 16C and decadent by the 17C − it was rescued by the Maurists.

Ruined by the Revolution, it was restored to its grandeur by a certain Dom Guéranger, a Sablé priest, and in 1837 became the mother house for the Benedictine Order in France. Dispersed again in 1901 it was more than twenty years before monastic life was to be resumed.

The name of Solesmes Abbey is closely associated with liturgical changes and in particular the revival of the Gregorian Chant.

The public is admitted to Mass, a unique opportunity to appreciate Latin liturgy as celebrated in a Benedictine abbey. *Mass at 10am Sundays, 9.45am weekdays, Vespers at 5pm (closing time on Thursdays varies), Compline 8.30pm.*

St Peter's Abbey (Abbaye St-Pierre). − *Time : 1/4 hour. Only the abbey church at the far end of the main courtyard is open to the public.*

The church is composed of an original nave and transept (11-15C) which were added to in 1865 with the construction of a domical vaulted chancel.

The famous groups of carvings known as the **Saints of Solesmes ★★** are to be found in the transepts. These are highly intricate monumental or even architectural pieces. The works in the south transept were commissioned by the Prior Guillaume Cheminart. They include an Entombment figuring an admirable Mary Magdalene dating from 1496 and to the left an earlier terracotta *Pietà*.

The group in the north transept dating from 1530 to 1556 is consecrated to the Virgin Mary and was commissioned by the Prior Jean Bougler. The composition is crowded but it is well worth trying to make out the different subjects. The main scene shows the Death of the Virgin Mary. Jean Bougler is portrayed holding one end of the shroud. Above are the Four Fathers of the Church and the Assumption. On the wall to the left Jesus is shown with the Four Doctors while opposite are scenes from the life of the Virgin.

The conventual buildings include the 18C priory and the great granite buildings dating from 1896 to 1901 which were added to in 1956.

The SOLOGNE

Michelin map 64 folds 8, 9, 18 and 19

The Sologne, immense and flat, stretching into infinity with its heaths, forests — occupying 40 per cent of the total surface — and solitary pools, is a paradise for shooters and anglers. Occupying the Orléans loop of the Loire, the Sologne is bordered to the south by the Loir and to the east by the Sancerre Hills.

History and development. — Formerly a desolate waste due to the fever ridden stagnant waters, the aspect of the region changed radically under Napoleon III. Having acquired the property of Lamotte-Beuvron he instigated improvements: the planting of pines and birch trees, the digging of canals, the building of roads, the clearing, dredging and draining of pools and improvement of the soils. The fevers vanquished, the population grew and living conditions became tolerable. In recent years with the selling and subsequent subdivising of the estates and the increasing number of residences, the ecological and economic balance of the Sologne has been put in jeopardy. In 1976 a plan was launched to safeguard the Sologne with, among other measures, the creation of an ecological reserve and research centre in addition to other facilities for the tourist (information centres, open air museums, etc.).

(After photo: Revue géographique et industrielle de France)

A Sologne landscape

The Sologne today. — Of the 200 000 hectares - 494 260 acres cultivated, those given over to cereals are diminishing in favour of fodder crops, while many farms are converting to pheasant rearing or the growing of fodder for the game. Vegetables and fruit are grown in the richer region of Contres and where man has mastered the waterlogged soil, as at the onetime Experimental Fruit Farm at Vernon-en-Sologne where the first experiments with irrigation were conducted. This area, with part of the Loire Valley, is France's main asparagus producing region.

The traditional local industries (sawmills, packaging materials) have witnessed the establishment of other factories: porcelain at Lamotte-Beuvron; armaments at La Ferté-St-Aubin and Salbris; sports cars at Romorantin; bee rearing at Theillay and cultivation of dahlias at Villeherviers. The increase in shooting means an added source of revenue for the landowners and a stimulus to the hotel and gunsmith trades. The shooting season provides the added attraction of great spectacles in the courtyards of often hidden châteaux. The region is well described by Maurice Genevoix in his novel *Raboliot* the story of a poacher.

■ TOWNS and SIGHTS

Attractive in spring and summer, the Sologne is at its best in autumn when the russets and greens vie with the purple carpet of heather to colour the melancholy landscape of pools.

The salvoes of shots do little to destroy the charm of the region.

The Sologne Tourist Road, the D 922 from La Ferté-St-Aubin to Romorantin, passes through some of the most typical Sologne countryside.

Argent-sur-Sauldre. — Pop 2 687. This small town has numerous enterprises: dress-making, pottery, dairy, furniture, hoisting machinery and printing. The 15C **château**, with its large round towers, has terraced gardens overlooking the Sauldre. **St-André**, the former chapel to the château preceded by a great belfry porch, contains a 16C group of the Trinity in the baptismal chapel.

Aubigny-sur-Nère★. — *Description p 47.*

Blancafort★ — Pop 1 070. The church of this Sologne village has an unusually shaped belfry porch. The 15C brick **château★** *(guided tours 10am to noon and 2 to 7pm - 5pm early October to early November; closed Tuesdays and early November to early April; 15F)* has a courtyard flanked by two 17C pavilions. The tour includes a visit to the library with woodwork of the Régence style and the dining room covered with embossed and gilt leather from Flanders; a nice collection of pewter is also on display. The gardens are in the French style.

Bracieux. — Pop 1 150. Lying in the Beuvron Valley on the borderland of the Sologne and the Blésois, Bracieux is a charming village grouped around its 18C covered market.

Cerdon. — Pop 1 005. This village has a 15C church which is reputed to have a painting by the school of Raphaël.

Château de Chambord★★★. — *Description p 61.*

La Chapelle-d'Angillon. — *Description p 63.*

Chaumont-sur-Tharonne. — Pop 905. The line of the former ramparts can still be traced in the layout of this village. Occupying an attractive site, Chaumont is dominated by its 15-16C church.

Château de Cheverny★★. — *Description p 72.*

Étang du Puits★. — *8 km - 5 miles to northwest of Argent-sur-Sauldre.* This vast stretch of water stands in a woodland setting. The road following the retaining causeway offers a good view of the lake. A venue for regattas, other facilities include beaches, pedal and rowing boats and children's amusements. The reservoir abounds with carp, bream and pike.

150

La Ferté-St-Aubin. – Pop 5 498. Strung out along the N 20 La Ferté-St-Aubin is contained to the west by the railway line. In the vicinity of the castle, the old quarter has some houses typical of the Sologne – squat brick and half timbered constructions they are covered with great flat tiled roofs. The 17C **château** of brick with stone string courses is a majestic building surrounded by moats. The 12-16C church with its belfy porch overlooks the Cosson.

A landscape typical of the Sologne - woodland, fields, streams and a solitary pool – can be found in the **Ciran Domain** *(7 km - 4 miles to the east ; signposted on the D 108 ; open 10am to noon and 2 to 6pm ; closed Tuesdays ; time : 1-2 hours ; 10F)*. In the house is a small local museum.

Fontaines-en-Sologne. – Pop 568. The church dating mainly from the 12C shows features typical of the Angevin style *(p 21) :* square east end, a single nave with remarkable domical vaulting. It was fortified in the 17C. Nearby are fine half timbered houses with flat tiled roofs.

Lanthenay Church. – *To visit apply to the presbytery or to Mme Firmain, Avenue de Paris, the house opposite the wayside cross.* Dating from the 12 to the 19C this church contains a painting (c 1523) of the Virgin attributed to Timoteo Viti from Urbino who greatly influenced Raphaël in his early days, in addition to various 16C statues, etc.

Lassay-sur-Croisne. – Pop 145. A typical Sologne village. The 15C **church** *(to visit apply to the town hall weekdays)* with its lovely rose window contains an early 16C **fresco** showing St Christopher and to the right Lassay Church with the Château du Moulin in the background. The tomb below belongs to the one time Lord of the Manor : Philippe du Moulin *(see below)*, who once saved the life of Charles VIII.

Château du Moulin*. – *Guided tours 1 March to 15 November 9 to 11.30am and 2 to 6.30pm ; time : 1/2 hour ; 14F.* This red brick building, marked at the angles by stone quoins, a decorative accessory frequently used in the 15C, is reflected in the moat. Built on a square fortress-like plan by **Philippe du Moulin** from 1480-1506, the structure had been surrounded by walls and defence towers – remains of which are still visible.

Enter the courtyard. To the right visit the keep or lord's manor pierced by mullioned windows. Inside the rooms are embellished with period furnishings : the dining room with its sideboard (15C) and chandelier typical of the Sologne ; the salon with its painted ceiling ; the bedrooms with their canopied beds and Flemish tapestries ; the vaulted kitchen with its enormous fireplace – the wheel on the side was used, with the help of a dog, to turn the spit.

Nançay. – Pop 790. This small village contains numerous artists' workshops – the **Grenier de Villâtre** *(open Saturdays and Sundays)* displays their works. To the north of this village on the right hand side of the D 29 is the **experimental research station in radio astronomy.** *A terrace at the entrance is open to the public and has explanatory noticeboards and a recorded commentary in English (2F) ; the station is open to visitors at 2.30pm on the second Saturday of each month (except July and August), apply in advance in writing to the station.* The powerful radio telescope has a large metal dish 40 m wide by 200 m long (131 ft by 656 ft) which captures the Hertzian waves and then reflects them to fixed points at a distance of 460 m - 503 yd.

Neuvy. – Pop 279. On the north bank of the Beuvron, Neuvy is on the edge of the Boulogne Forest. Its church is isolated on the opposite bank. The rood beam supports 15C statues. In the south arm a 17C canvas shows the Dead Christ being supported by two angels. *To visit apply to M. David André opposite the church.*

Romorantin-Lanthenay*. – *Description p 133.* Home of the Sologne Museum *(p 134)*.

St-Viâtre. – Pop 1 162. This pretty little town in the Sologne was formerly the site of a pilgrimage to the relics of St Viâtre, a hermit who withdrew here in the 6C, and according to legend, hollowed out his coffin in the trunk of an aspen (trembling poplar).

From the outside of the **church** *(closed on Sunday afternoons and public holidays)* note the 15C transept gable built in brick, decorated with black diapering and edged with spiral rosettes. A powerful bell tower porch covers the entrance to the building and its 14C portal.

The 15C **St Viâtre** wayside altar stands to the north of the town.

Salbris. – Pop 6 134. On the left bank of the Sauldre, Salbris has a 15 and 16C church with 17C furnishings. The retable of the high altar has a *Pietà.*

Selles-St-Denis. – Pop 1 172. This church (12-15C) with Flamboyant apsidal and lateral chapels has mural paintings dating from the 14C, retracing the life of St Genoulph.

Villeherviers. – Pop 342. Situated in the wide Sauldre Valley, planted with vines and asparagus. The 13C church possesses Angevin vaulting *(open for services)*.

Château de Villesavin. – *Description p 168.*

SUÈVRES

Michelin map 64 southeast of fold 7 – Pop 1 307

This small town, the ancient Gallo-Roman city of Sodobrium, hides its picturesque façades below the noisy N 152.

The **Church of St-Christophe** stands on the side of the road, preceded by a covered gallery or *caquetoire* (a place to chatter). The church has stonework with various fishbone and chevron patterns, characteristic of the Merovingian era.

Walk along the Rue Pierre Pouteau, opposite the church. No 9 and opposite, no 14 bis are 15C houses. Turn right into the picturesque cul-de-sac of the Rue des Moulins, which runs alongside the stream spanned by numerous footbridges, and where weeping willows and tamarisks are reflected in the water.

Turn back and cross the stone bridge. One passes in front of the washhouse on the corner of the Rue St-Simon ; on either side of the road there are traces of the old fortified gate. Further on the left, rising up from the verdure is the two-storied Romanesque bell tower of the **Church of St-Lubin**. This church has a fine 15C portal which opens on to the south aisle.

Michelin map 🔢 fold 1 — Pop 5825 — *Facilities pp 36-37*

The Château de Sully is interesting for its history, its picturesque site and its splendid timber roof. The best view of the château is from the D119, which skirts the Loire between Ouzouer and Sully. A shaded path follows the Sange which skirts the foot of the castle.

HISTORICAL NOTES

The early stronghold commanded a crossing of the Loire. Four great names stand out in its history: Maurice de Sully, Bishop of Paris when he commissioned the building of Notre-Dame, Joan of Arc, Sully and Voltaire.

The Ardent Life of Joan of Arc. — In 1429 Sully belonged to Georges de la Trémoille, a favourite of Charles VII. The King was living in the castle when Joan defeated the English at Patay and captured their leader, the famous Talbot, Earl of Shrewsbury. The Maid hurried to Sully and at last persuaded the indolent monarch to be crowned at Reims. She returned to the castle in 1430 after her check before Paris, and there felt the jealousy and hostility of La Trémoille gaining influence over the King. She was kept almost a prisoner but escaped to continue the struggle.

Sully's capacity for work. — In 1602 Maximilien de Béthune, the Lord of Rosny, bought the château and the barony for 330 000 *livres*. Henri IV made Maximilien the duc de Sully, and it was under this name that the great Minister passed into history.

Sully began to serve his King at the age of twelve. He was a great soldier, the best artilleryman of his time and a consummate administrator. He was active in all the departments of State: Finance, Agriculture, Industry and Public Works.

SULLY-SUR-LOIRE		
	Collégiale St-Ythier (Égl.)	**B**
	Épinettes (R.)	5
	Jeanne-d'Arc (Bd)	7
Grand-Sully (R. du)	Marronniers (rue des)	9
Porte-de-Sologne (R.) ... 12	Porte-Berry (R.)	10
	St-François (R. du Fg)	15
Champ-de-Foire (Bd du) . 2	St-Germain (R. du Fg)	16
Chemin-de-Fer (R. du) ... 3	St-Germain (Égl.)	**E**

Grand-Sully (R. du) 6

Sully made his fortune while he made that of France. He lived like a minor sovereign, with his own guard and court of retainers.

A glutton for work, Sully began his day at 3am and kept four secretaries busy writing his memoirs. He entitled them: *Wise and Royal Economies of State*. Fearing indiscretions, he had a printing press set up in one of the towers of the château and the work was printed on the spot, although it bore the address of a printer in Amsterdam. The old Duke had a mania for orderly accounts. Every tree to be planted, every table to be made, every ditch to be cleaned was the subject of a legal contract.

Sully had an awkward character, and he often went to law, especially with the Bishop of Orléans. Since the Middle Ages it had been the custom for the Lord of Sully to carry the Bishop's chair on the day of his entry into Orléans. The former Minister, very much the ducal peer and a Protestant into the bargain, refused to conform with this custom. Finally he obtained permission to be represented at the ceremony.

Sully embellished the feudal pile. The building originally stood on the Loire itself. He separated it from the river by an embankment, dug moats which he filled by deflecting a nearby river, laid out the park and enlarged the buildings.

The spirit of Voltaire (18C). — Exiled from Paris by the Regent for his too biting epigrams, Voltaire spent several seasons with the duc de Sully, who welcomed new ideas and surrounded himself with philosophers and "libertines". Voltaire was then only François-Marie-Arouet; he was twenty-two. His gaiety and wit made him the life and soul of the castle. A theatre was built for him in the château and there he had tragedies and comedies performed.

In the shade of the park among trees "carved upon", he said, "by urchins and lovers", young Arouet indulged in flirtations which he transferred to the stage, where the roles were played by his lady friends.

■ **THE CHÂTEAU** ★ *time: 3/4 hour*

Guided tours 1 May to 30 September 9 to 11.45am and 2 to 6pm; March and November 10 to 11.45am and 2 to 4.30pm; April and October 10am (9am Sundays and holidays) to 11.45am and 2 to 5pm (6pm Sundays and holidays); closed 1 December to 28 February; time: 1 hour; 10F.

The château or castle is an imposing feudal fortress dating largely from before 1360. The keep faces the Loire. It is rectangular, with round towers at the four corners. The wing added by Sully to the living quarters dates from the early 17C.

One can visit several apartments in the 14C keep, notably the large guardroom on the ground floor, another immense hall (portraits of the Dukes of Sully) on the first floor where Voltaire watched his plays being performed and the oratory in which there is an excellent copy of the funerary group showing Sully and his wife *(the original is at Nogent-le-Rotrou)*. Finally, on the second floor, there is the unique chamber with its famous timber roof. The apartment, unfortunately, is cut in two by the chimneystack. The visit ends with a tour of the watchpath.

The timber roof★★. – The upper hall of the keep has the finest timber roof that has come down to us from the Middle Ages. Dating from 1363 and keel shaped it is still like new. There are no worms in the wood, no rot to attract flies and, therefore, no cobwebs. This is due to the type of wood, chestnut, and the great care taken by the carpenters of the day. Trees aged fifty to a hundred years were chosen, barked standing and squared off, leaving only the heart. The beams were then weathered under water for several years to wash the sap out of the wood, dried in the open air for several years more, coated with disinfectant and finally assembled in such a way that air could circulate freely.

(After photo: Yvon)

Château de Sully

Renaissance pavilion. – This contains Sully's study and, on the first floor, the great saloon which was the Minister's bedroom. Both rooms with wall hangings and painted ceilings have been refurnished.

■ ADDITIONAL SIGHTS

Collegiate Church of St-Ythier (Collégiale de St-Ythier – B). – Built in 1529, the Chapel of Notre-Dame de Pitié was enlarged in 1605; it then became the Collegiate Church of St-Ythier. There are two 16C **stained glass windows**: the one at the end of the south aisle shows pilgrims on their way to St James's shrine in Santiago de Compostela; the second showing the Tree of Jesse with the Virgin and Baby Jesus is in the central apse. In the north aisle is a 16C *Pietà* above the high altar.

Renaissance House (D). – Above the façade decorated with medallions and pilasters, the dormer windows in the roof with twin bays are surrounded by caryatids.

St-Germain (E). – Remarkable for its fine spire, 38 m - 125 ft high, which can be seen from all around. The church itself is in ruins.

TALCY ★

Michelin map 🗺 fold 7 – Pop 241

The village standing isolated in the Beauce Plain, is linked to Mer by a road bordered at intervals with rose bushes.

Château de Talcy★. – *Guided tours 1 April to 30 September 9.30 to 11.15am and 2 to 6pm; the rest of the year 10 to 11.15am and 2 to 4.30pm; closed Tuesdays and 1 January, 1 May, 1 and 11 November, 25 December; time: 1/2 hour; 15F.*

Sold to the State in 1932, the château is severe in appearance, but interesting for its literary history, its furniture, and, on more familiar ground, for two little masterpieces: the dovecote and the wine press.

This 13C manorial dwelling was bought in 1571 by a rich Florentine, Bernardo Salviati, a cousin of Catherine de' Medici. This Salviati family so famous in literary history retained the estate until 1667. Bernardo was the father of Cassandra, to whom **Ronsard** dedicated so many sonnets, and of Giovanni Salviati, whose daughter, Diana, similarly inspired the young Agrippa d'Aubigné. Cassandra's daughter married Guillaume de Musset and one of her direct descendants was the great poet Alfred de Musset (1810-57).

Fine furniture (16-18C) and Gothic tapestries grace the severe setting of the feudal halls under the French style roofs with fine Renaissance beams. The 15C keep with two doorways, postern and carriage gate, has two corner turrets and a battlemented watchpath mediaeval looking but dating in fact from 1520. The fenestration at the first floor level was modified in the 18C.

(After photo : C. Breteau, Éd. Delmas)

Talcy – The well

The first courtyard owes its charm to a gracious gallery and an attractive well. In the second courtyard is a large 16C **dovecote** with its 1 500 pigeon holes which are admirably preserved.

An old **wine press** is still fit for use after 400 years of wear. A carefully balanced mechanism enables two men to obtain ten barrels of juice at a single pressing.

For maximum information from town plans:
consult the key, p 38.

Michelin map **67** fold 8 — Pop 11913 — *Facilities pp 36-37*

Approach Thouars from the south, crossing the River Thouet by the new bridge (le Pont Neuf), a perfect viewpoint from which to discover the town's **site★**: a rocky promontory, encircled by the river. On the borders of Poitou and Anjou, the rooftops of Thouars are a mixture of Romanesque tiles and Angevin slates.

The lords of Thouars. — The viscounts of Thouars were for a long time faithful to the Plantagenets and afterwards to the kings of England, but Du Guesclin seized the city in 1372 after a memorable siege. Having bought Thouars from the Amboise family, Louis XI stayed here several times. His first wife Margaret of Scotland had even expressed the wish to be buried here.

Charles VIII gave Thouars to the La Trémoille family, who remained the owners until the Revolution. Thouars, like Saumur, was one of the centres of the Reformation, but after the Revocation of the Edict of Nantes (1685) the town lost half its population.

■ SIGHTS

St-Médard Church
West front (detail)

St-Médard★. — Alongside a square 15C tower with a watch tower, St-Médard is a Romanesque building despite the Gothic rose window adorning the beautiful **west front★★** in the Poitou style.

The very ornamented central doorway is surmounted by Christ in Majesty adored by the angels; the recessed arches, the latter of which is broken by a Resurrected Christ fall on to historiated capitals showing the Chastisement of the Vices. Above the lateral doorways there are fine statues of St Peter and St Paul, the Prophets and the Sibyls. The curious Romanesque naves were altered in the 15C to a single nave with flattened vaulting.

Old houses★. — These are numerous in the Rues St-Médard and du Château, formerly Thouars' main street which ended at the old bridge. They include the brick and half timbered house, beside the Church of St-Médard, now occupied by the Tourist Information Centre, and the Hostellerie St-Médard (**D**) of the same period. Standing close together along the Rue du Château are several corbelled façades with pointed gables. It was in no 11, the 15C Hôtel des Trois Rois (**E**), that the Dauphin, the future Louis XI, is said to have passed the night. Passing by the former postern go down to the Thouet which is crossed by a **Gothic bridge**, defended by a fortified gateway.

Sainte-Chapelle (F). — Gabrielle de Bourbon had the chapel built over a series of crypts, one of which still serves as the La Trémoille family vault. The charming Flamboyant façade is surmounted by a Renaissance gallery.

Château (Collège Marie de la Tour d'Auvergne). — *The château is not open to the public but access is allowed to the porticoed gallery, apply to the caretaker for permission.* The present château replaced a mediaeval fortress and now serves as a school. This imposing group of buildings was started in 1635 by Marie de La Tour d'Auvergne, duchesse de La Trémoille and Turenne's eldest sister. The central wing has a projecting domed pavilion which houses the grand staircase.

Other pavilions flank the main wing. The path on the gallery affords a fine view of the façade of the Château.

The esplanade and small suspension bridge over the river, both afford good views of Thouars, in its exceptional site, and the Thouet Valley.

Bergeon (Bd) 2	Drouineau-de-Brie (R.) ... 6
Château (R. du) 3	Lavault (Pl.) 7
Curie (Bd Pierre) 5	Porte-au-Prévôt (R.) 9
	Porte-Maillot (R.) 10
	République (Bd de la) ... 13
	St-Médard (R.) 14

Tour du prince de Galles (K). — The Prince of Wales or Grénetière (corn chandler) Tower as it is sometimes known, was once the grain store and part of the city ramparts. Reinforced by small barbicans this massive round tower also served as a prison.

Porte au Prévôt (N). — It was by this gateway that Du Guesclin entered the town following its capitulation in 1372. It is flanked by two fine crescent shaped towers with octagonal bases.

Former Abbey (Ancienne abbaye St-Laon — H). — Formerly Benedictine and Augustinian from 1117, the abbey has a 12-15C church with a square Romanesque bell tower, founded by Margaret of Scotland wife of Louis XI, and it now serves as her resting place. The 17C conventual buildings serve now as the town hall.

Chemin du Panorama. — Leave by ⑤ and take to the left of the D759 a signposted steeply descending path which affords an attractive **view** of the town and Thouet Valley.

TOURS ★★

Michelin map 🔢 fold 15 — *Local map p 100* — Pop 136483

For many tourists Tours is the centre from which they will explore the whole châteaux country. The town itself offers visitors a fine cathedral, churches, monasteries, old houses, interesting museums and the luminous landscapes of the Loire.

Tours, now an urban agglomeration of more than 250000 inhabitants, has greatly outgrown its original site between the Loire and Cher, and urban development has followed the canalisation of the Loire along 7 km - 5 miles of its course. An industrial zone has been created in the north round St-Symphorien.

The industrial sector includes light ancillary industries in metallurgy, chemicals, plastics, electronics and textiles; pharmaceutical laboratories, Michelin tyre factory and printing works.

A communications crossroads, Tours is the economic focal point for the Centre-West and a regional agricultural and wine centre. The fairs *(ten days from the first Saturday in May and 18-21 September)* include the rather folkloric Garlic and Basil Fair *(in July on St Anne's Day)*.

A centre for higher education Tours has a University with 12000 students continuing the traditions of its illustrious mediaeval predecessor. The various faculties and departments cover the arts, science, medicine, pharmacy, law, economics, town and country planning, insurance and technology. In addition there is a School for Renaissance Studies, a Regional Music, Dance and Drama Conservatory, a Regional Fine Arts and three Nursing Schools, a foreign language institute for the training of interpreters and a Business School.

HISTORICAL NOTES

The Gallo-Roman metropolis. — During the *Pax Romana,* the area, Turons, consisting of more than 100 hectares - 250 acres, became a prosperous city and was named Caesarodunum or Caesar's Hill. However, constant pillaging forced the inhabitants to live in the administrative and economic centre, now the area surrounding the cathedral, which was also where the arenas and baths were located. This "city" was encircled by a wall which still remains in part.

In 375 the city took back its former name, Turones, and became the seat of government of the IIIrd Lyonnaise, a province that included the Touraine, The Maine, the Anjou and the Armorique.

The town of St Martin (4C). — From the 4C onwards Tours was the town of St Martin. The greatest bishop of the Gauls was first a legionary in the Roman army of occupation. At the gates of Amiens the young soldier saw a beggar shivering in the cold wind. He cut his cloak in two with his sword and gave half of it to the poor man. The following night the future St Martin had a dream — he saw Christ with half his cloak, and this decided his future; he was baptised and began his apostolate.

At Ligugé, in Poitou, he founded the first monastery on Gallic soil. His burning faith and boundless charity spread his renown far and wide. The people of Tours begged him to become their bishop.

Although Christianity had been introduced into Gaul a century before, paganism still flourished. St Martin fought it with pitiless zeal: idols, statues and old shrines were systematically destroyed; but, at the same time, he covered Touraine with churches and chapels. At the gates of Tours he founded the Monastery of Marmoutier.

St Martin died at Candes *(p 60)* in 397. Both the monks of Ligugé and those of Marmoutier claimed his body, but the men of Touraine carried it to a boat while those of Poitou slept, and rowed hard to their town. Then a miracle occurred: as the corpse passed, the trees grew green, plants burst into flower and the birds sang, even though it was November — so came about "St Martin's summer".

The Saint's tomb became a place of pilgrimage. In 470, a magnificent basilica was erected round the sarcophagus.

A popular pilgrimage. — In 573, the people of Tours brought from Clermont-Ferrand the heir of a great Gallo-Roman family, known for his scholarship and his piety, to be their bishop. He was Gregory of Tours, the forerunner of French historians. Under his direction the town made further progress. An abbey, to which was attached a large village, grew up round the basilica; to the west another borough, Châteauneuf sprang up; in 1354, during the Hundred Years War, the two areas amalgamated.

Pilgrims of all conditions and all countries, including the sick who hoped to be cured by touching the tomb of St Martin, succeeded one another in this mediaeval Lourdes. The basilica also afforded inviolable sanctuary to fugitives.

Propaganda maintained the popularity of the pilgrimage. A little history of the Saint's life and the miracles that had occurred at his tomb was composed. Copies of the text were distributed: they have been found at Carthage, Alexandria, Rome, the Thebaid (Upper Egypt) and Syria.

Kings and great men set an example of generosity in the cult of St Martin and immense riches were accumulated.

A great teacher : Alcuin (end of 8C). – In the Carolingian period (8C) Tours, while remaining a great religious centre, became a seat of art and learning under the direction of Alcuin. This monk of Anglo-Saxon origin, after fifty years in a cathedral school in York, was brought from Italy by Charlemagne. The Emperor, wishing to raise his people from their ignorance, installed a model educational centre in his palace at Aachen and placed Alcuin in charge of it. When the organization was complete Charlemagne sent the monk to Tours as Abbot of St Martin.

Alcuin also formed a school for copyists. A new calligraphy, clear and elegant, was designed. Illuminators joined the calligraphers. Masterpieces issued from this school, include the famous Bible of Charles the Bald as well as Charlemagne's Gospel Book.

Ups and downs (from the 9 to 14C). – The Norman invasions reached Tours. Its basilica, its abbeys and its twenty-eight churches were burnt down. Then rivalry developed between the counts of Blois and the counts of Anjou, whose domains were contiguous in Touraine. It ended in victory for the Angevins, who were supplanted in their turn by Philippe-Auguste (1204). The 13 and 14C were prosperous times.

The silk industry at Tours (15 and 16C). – Louis XI introduced the manufacture of silk and cloth of gold to Tours. At first the King set up this industry at Lyon, but as the people of that town were not enthusiastic the workers and looms were transferred to Tours. The industry reached its peak in the 16C.

It was in this world of artisans, intellectuals and artists that the Reformation found its first supporters, and Tours, like Lyon or La Rochelle, became one of the most active centres of the new religion. The Calvinists created great disorder which was pitilessly avenged by the Catholics. The town had its Massacre of St Bartholomew ten years before Paris (1572).

This was the beginning of a decline which was to continue until the opening of the 19C. By 1801 the 80 000 inhabitants were reduced to 20 000. But the railway revived the town by providing easy communications and by the installation of its vast railway workshops at St-Pierre-des-Corps.

The Wars. – Because of its advantageous position, Tours was chosen in September 1870 as the seat of the government for national defence ; but three months later as the Prussians approached, the government escaped to Bordeaux. During the Second World War, the centre and the parts of town bordering the Loire were heavily bombarded.

■ OLD TOURS★★ *time : about 1 1/2 hours*

The vast restoration work started about 1970 around the Place Plumereau has brought the old quarter to life ; its narrow streets, often pedestrian precincts, have attracted shops and craftsmen, and the whole quarter, near the university, with its numerous restaurants becomes one of the animated centres of the town at the end of the day. It is pleasant to wander along admiring a façade or a staircase turret standing at the end of a small courtyard.

Place Plumereau★. – This picturesque and animated square, the former *carroi aux Chapeaux* (hat market) is lined with fine 15C timber framed houses alternating with stone façades.

At the corner of the Rue du Change and the Rue de la Monnaie there is a lovely house with two gables hung with slates and posts decorated with sculptures ; at the corner post there is a 16C Virgin and Child. Continue to the corner of the Rue de la Rôtisserie where there is an old façade with wooden lattice work.

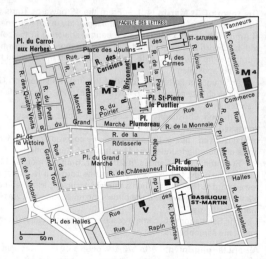

To the north of the square a vaulted passageway opens on to the attractive little **Place St-Pierre-le-Puellier,** with its pleasant gardens ; excavations have uncovered a Gallo-Roman and mediaeval cemetery and the foundations of the old church from which the square is named. Part of the nave is still visible on one side of the square and from the Rue Briçonnet. To the north, a large ogive vaulted porch opens on to a small square where four centuries of architecture are harmoniously represented together ; pass under the porch to reach the Rue de la Paix in order to see the façades of the houses.

Rue Briçonnet★. – This charming street is bordered by houses showing a rich variety of typically Tours styles : from the Romanesque façade to the 18C mansion. No 35 by the narrow Rue du Poirier has a Romanesque façade, no 31 has a late Gothic façade ; opposite no 32 is a Renaissance house with lovely wooden statues. Not far away an elegant staircase tower marks the entrance to the Place St-Pierre-le-Puellier. Further north on the left, nos 23 and 21 have Classical façades. Opposite no 16 is the **Maison de Tristan (K),** a remarkable brick and stone construction with a late 15C pierced gable, which houses the Language Study Centre ; in the courtyard *(open during school terms except Sundays and holidays),* one of the window lintels has the inscription *Priez Dieu Pur,* an anagram of Pierre du Puiz's name, who built the mansion.

Gemmail Museum (Musée du Gemmail — M³). – *Open Palm Sunday to 15 October 10am to noon and 2 to 6.30pm ; closed Mondays ; 10F.*

The **Hôtel Raimbault** (1835), a beautiful building with Restoration columns, displays gemmails, the name and aspect bringing to mind both the light of stained glass and the brillance of precious stones.

Rue Bretonneau. – No 33 is a 16C mansion with a fine decor of Renaissance foliage ; the north wing was added about 1875.

Rue des Cerisiers. – To the west of the Rue Bretonneau, no 21 is a 15C house with a Gothic façade.

Petit-St-Martin Quarter. – In this pedestrian quarter, round the Rue du Petit-St-Martin, there are numerous art and craft workshops, particularly around the charming **Place du Carroi aux herbes** (herb market).

Place de Châteauneuf. – Fine view over the **Tour Charlemagne (Q)**, remains of the **former Basilica of St-Martin** built in the 11 and 13C on the tomb of the Lord Bishop of Tours, after the Normans had destroyed the 5C sanctuary. The new building was as famous as the old for its size and splendour. Sacked by the Huguenots in 1562 it fell into disrepair during the Revolution and its vaulting collapsed. The nave was pulled down in 1802 to make way for the Rue des Halles.

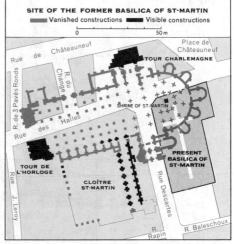

(After R. Ranjard - La Touraine archéologique)

The Tour Charlemagne which dominated the north transept, isolated since that time, partially collapsed in 1928, but carefully restored, still has its noble appearance.

From the Rue des Halles, note a fine sculptured capital dating from the 12C. At the top of the tower a bas-relief dating from the restoration work depicts St Martin sharing his mantle.

Further along the Rue des Halles the **Tour de l'Horloge (V)** rises up marking the façade of the basilica ; in the 19C it was crowned with a dome.

The **new Basilica of St-Martin,** built between 1887 and 1924, has the shrine of St Martin in the crypt ; it is still the object of pilgrimages *(mainly 11 November and the following Sunday).*

Hôtel Gouin★ (M⁴). – *Open 9am to noon and 2 to 6pm (5pm 1 October to 15 March) ; closed Fridays out of season and during December and January ; 8F.*

This mansion, a perfect example of living accommodation under the Renaissance, is one of the most interesting in Tours. Burnt out in 1940, the north façade with the staircase tower and the **south façade★** with finely sculpted Renaissance foliage scrolls were, however, spared. The **museum** includes a Gallo-Roman collection, mediaeval art and Renaissance works of art from Tours.

■ **ST-JULIEN QUARTER★** *time : about 1 1/2 hours*

This quarter is near the bridge over the Loire and greatly suffered in the last war ; but behind the straight façades of the modern Rue Nationale there are still small picturesque squares and interesting historical remains.

The **Wilson bridge** (BX), which is locally known as the stone bridge, was built in the 18C when the road from Paris to Spain went by way of Tours rather than Amboise. It spans the 434 m - 475 yd of the Loire. Partially fallen into disrepair in April 1978, this bridge was reopened to traffic in 1982.

St-Julien (CX X). – *Open from 3 to 5pm.*

The 11C belfry porch stands slightly back from the road, in front of the 13C church with its restrained Gothic interior lit by modern (1960) stained glass windows by Max Ingrand and Le Chevalier. It was formerly surrounded by a cloister (turned into a small garden) and conventual buildings.

There is still a Gothic chapter house *(temporary exhibitions)* and the 12C St Julien **wine cellars,** a great chamber with quadripartite vaulting which very appropriately houses the **Museum of Touraine Wines** (CX M¹) devoted to vines, wine and their rituals *(same opening times as for the Craft Guilds Museum).*

Craft Guilds Museum★★ (Musée du Compagnonnage — CX M⁵). – *8 Rue Nationale. Open from 9am to noon and from 2 to 6pm ; closed on Tuesdays and 1 January, 1 May, 14 July, 11 November, 25 December ; 4F.*

This museum in the 16C monks' **dormitory,** above the chapterhouse, traces the history, customs and skills of the various associations of craftsmen, or guilds. The trades of the past are

TOURS

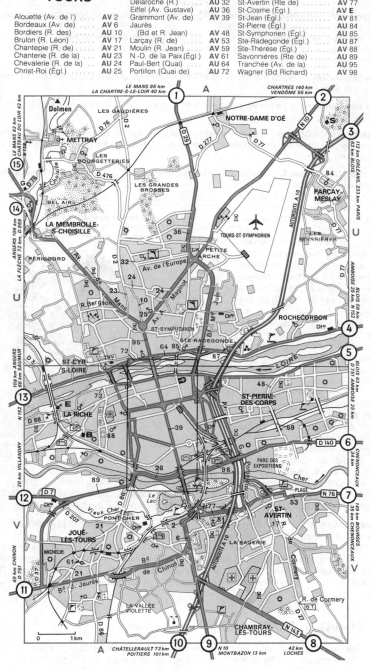

shown alongside those of the present, with their respective tools and **masterpieces** that the **compagnons** (*cum + panis* = the one with whom we share our bread) had to submit before becoming master craftsmen.

The variety of guilds shown, the exceptional quality of the work and the numerous historical and sociological documents make this museum of exceptional interest.

Beaune-Semblançay Gardens★ (CXYB). – *Enter by the porch at no 28 Rue Nationale.*

The Hôtel de Beaune-Semblançay belonged to François I's unfortunate Intendant of the Royal Finances, Jacques de Beaune-Semblançay.

This Renaissance hôtel was destroyed during the Second World War except for an arcaded gallery with a chapel above, a fine pilaster decorated façade and in the garden the beautiful, finely sculptured **Beaune fountain.**

On the opposite side of the Rue Jules-Favre is the sober but elegant façade of the **Palais du Commerce (CX C)**, which was built in the 18C for the merchants of Tours. Go into the more elaborately decorated courtyard.

Rue Colbert (CX). – Before the Wilson bridge was built this road was the continuation of the Rue du Commerce, the main road of the town.

At no 41, a half-timbered house, there is a sign "A la Pucelle armée" (to the armed Maid): in 1429 the craftsman who lived here made Joan of Arc's armour for her, before she went to confront the English at Orléans *(p 124).*

TOURS

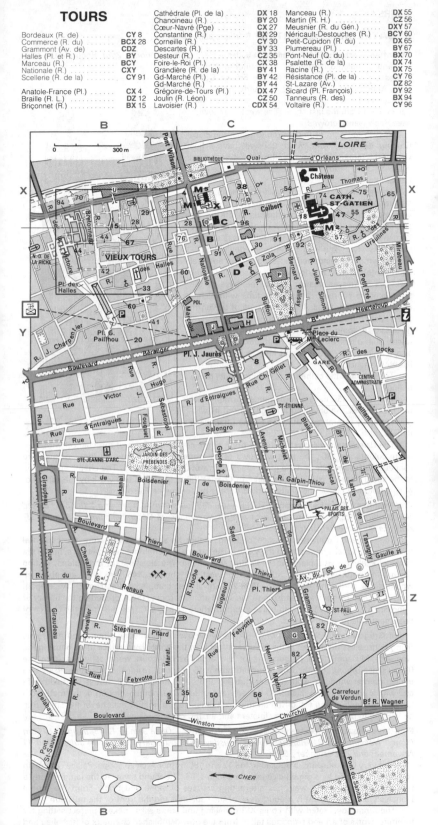

Place Foire-le-Roi (CX 38). – Mystery plays were performed in the square when the sovereign visited Tours.

On the north side are 15C gable houses. No 8, an elegant Renaissance mansion once belonged to Philibert Babou de la Bourdaisière, near Montlouis-sur-Loire. This famous 16C family in addition to Philibert, François I's Treasurer, included several royal mistresses.

On the right side coming from the quay, at the end of a small passageway, is the narrow and winding Passage du Cœur-Navré (Passage of the Broken-Hearted), a typical mediaeval thieves' alley.

■ **CATHEDRAL QUARTER**★★ *time: about 2 hours*

St Gatien Cathedral★★ **(Cathédrale St-Gatien – DX)**. – *Closed noon to 2pm.* Begun in the early
13C and completed in the 16C the building demon-
strates the complete evolution of the French Gothic
style. The chevet is typical of the early phase, the
transept and nave the development and the Flamboyant west front the last stage. The west front towers
have Renaissance crowns.

St-Gatien Cathedral — West front

Pass to the right of the church to reach the Place
Grégoire-de-Tours, from where you will have a fine
view of the remarkable **chevet**, in the pure style, typical
of the St Louis period *(p 22)*. Return to the Place de la
Cathédrale.

The soaring **west front** is attractive in spite of the
mixture of styles. Monotony is avoided by the delicate
asymmetry of details. The foundations of the towers
are set on the Gallo-Roman wall. The bases are
Romanesque, as are the solid side buttresses so typical of this style. The rich Flamboyant decoration –
pierced tympana, festooned recessed orders and leaf
adorned gables over the doorway – was added in the
15C. The buttresses soaring up to the base of the
steeples were adorned at the same time with niches
and crocketed pinnacles. The upper part of the north
tower, dating from the 15C, was crowned by an early
Renaissance dome with lantern. The 16C south bell
tower, built directly above the Romanesque tower, is
also terminated by a dome and lantern but from the
late Renaissance.

The **interior** of the cathedral is striking for its purity
of line.

The 14 and 15C nave complements harmoniously
the 13C **chancel**. The balanced arrangement of its windows strongly resembles that of the Sainte-Chapelle in
Paris.

The **stained glass windows**★★ are the pride of the cathedral. Those of the chancel with their
warm colours are 13C; the rose windows of the transepts are 14C; while those of the third
chapel of the south aisle and the great rose window of the nave are 15C. The chapel opening on
to the south transept contains the **tomb**★ of Charles VIII's children, a fine work by the school of
Michel Colombe (16C). The finely worked base is by Jerome de Fiesole.

The Psalette★ **(St-Gatien Cloisters – DX F)**. – *Guided tours 9am to noon and 2 to 5pm; closed
Sunday mornings, 1 January, 1 May, 1 and 11 November, 25 December; time: 20 mins; 5F.
Apply to the cathedral custodian.*

This elegant Gothic-Renaissance building cannot be seen properly from the cathedral
square, but gradually opens up to the visitor. The canons and choir masters met here, hence the
name of Psalette – the place where Psalms were sung. The cloisters are three-sided, resting
against the north wall of the cathedral; the west side, built in 1460 has a library above it,
whereas the north and east sides (1508-24) are almost completely flat roofed. An elegant
Renaissance spiral staircase leads up to the small archives room (1520), preceding the library or
"bookshop", a lovely room with ogive vaulting where 13 and 14C frescoes from the church of
Beaumont-Village are displayed.

Place Grégoire de Tours★ **(DX 47)**. – A fine view over the cathedral chevet and its Gothic
flying buttresses; on the left is the mediaeval gable of the **Archbishops' palace** (now housing the
Fine Arts Museum). The judgements of the ecclesiastical court were delivered from the
Renaissance tribune. On the Rue Manceau note a 15C canons' residence, surmounted by two
gabled dormer windows, and at the beginning of the Rue Racine, a 15C house built with tufa
and with a pointed roof, which held the Justice-les-Bains (seat of jurisdiction of the metropoli-
tan chapter, built on the Gallo-Roman thermal baths). To the right of the chevet the small Rue
de la Psalette passes between the cloisters and an 18C canons' residence.

Fine Arts Museum★★ **(Musée des Beaux-Arts – DXY M²)**. – *Open 9am to 12.45pm and 2 to 6pm
(5pm 1 November to 31 March); closed Tuesdays and 1 January, 1 May, 14 July, 1 and 11
November and 25 December; 5.50F.*

This very fine museum is housed in the 17 and 18C former Archiepiscopal Palace. The main
courtyard is shaded by a gigantic cedar, planted in 1804. The round tower to the left, formerly a
part of the Gallo-Roman wall, has alternating courses of stone and brick. From the formal
French style gardens there is a good **view** of the cathedral and the front of the museum.

The rooms, decorated with Louis XVI panelling and Tours silks, make a perfect setting for
furniture, works of art and paintings taken from the now demolished châteaux of Richelieu and
Chanteloup and some of the great Tourangelle abbeys: the duc de Choiseul's bureau, a
lacquered commode, paintings by Boucher, portraits by Largillière, Tocqué, Perronneau and
Vestier, as well as sculptures by Le Moyne and Houdon. The 17 and 18C North European
schools are well represented: Rembrandt's *Flight into Egypt* and Rubens's famous *ex-voto*.

The second floor displays works of the 19 and 20C: Delacroix, Degas and a portrait of
Balzac by Boulanger. Note the **faience** by the local craftsman Avisseau. On the ground floor are
the Italian primitives and the museum's masterpieces: **Mantegna's** *Christ in the Garden of Olives*
and the same artist's *Resurrection,* as well as a room with Greek and Etruscan pottery.

Château (DX). − Bordered by a beautiful shaded walk on the edge of the Loire, the château has heterogeneous buildings, remains of former days.

The **Tour de Guise** is almost all that remains of the fortress built in the first half of the 12C. It is crowned with machicolations and has a pepperpot tower; it takes its name from the young Duc de Guise imprisoned in the château after the assassination of his father *(pp 54-55)* but he subsequently escaped.

The **Pavillon de Mars** which adjoins it and was built under Louis XVI is flanked on the south by a 13C round tower.

Historical Museum★ (Historial de Touraine). − *Open 1 July to 30 September 9am to 9pm; 1 April to 30 June and in October 9am to 12.30pm and 2 to 7pm; the rest of the year 2 to 6pm; time: 3/4 hour; 20F.*

Housed in the Pavillon de Mars and the Tour de Guise the museum traces the highlights of the Touraine's history in some 30 tableaux with 165 wax figures in rich apparel. The most spectacular scenes depict the marriage of Charles VIII and Anne of Brittany, Jean Papillon and other goldsmiths' workshops, Ronsard at the St-Cosme Priory, a dance at the Valois court.

Along the quay is the 15C **Governors' Lodging,** with gabled dormer windows. At the base and in the extension towards the Tour de Guise, the Gallo-Roman wall can be seen, built with sections of small stones alternating with layers of brick, typical of this period.

■ ADDITIONAL SIGHTS

Hôtel Mame (CY D). − *Open 1 April to 15 August 2.30 to 6.30pm; 10F.*

This lovely mansion was built under Louis XV by a rich shipowner who imported raw silk from the Indies for Tours silk manufacturers. It was bought in the 18C by the Mame family, the king's printers, and subsequently pontifical printers, who also published many art books in the 19C.

In the lovely 18C salons of the mansion (note the beautiful wrought iron staircase **banister★**) samples of silks and passementerie are shown which were made in Tours in the 18C, and fine art books bound by Mame in the following century.

Rue de Bordeaux (CY 8). − Pedestrian and shopping street, it is tempting to wander along this very animated quarter between the station and the Avenue de Grammont.

It comes out not far from the **Place Jean-Jaurès** (or Place du Palais) which is bordered by the town hall, the law courts and numerous café terraces, and where the two main roads of the town cross: the north-south thoroughfare opened up in the 18C, 5 km - 3 miles long in a straight line spanning the Loire and the Cher, and the boulevards where the old elm trees were planted in 1796 on the former ramparts.

EXCURSIONS map p 158

Prieuré de St-Cosme★; Plessis-lès-Tours. − *3 km - 2 miles to the west by the Quai du Pont-Neuf and its continuation the Avenue Proudhon, before finally following the embankment to the priory.*

St-Cosme Priory★ (AV E). − *Open 15 March to 30 September, 9am to noon and 2 to 6pm (5pm out of season); 9am to 6pm July and August; closed Wednesdays and December and January; 10F.*

The priory, not much more than a ruin, is situated in a peaceful place in the middle of well cared for gardens; there remain a few traces of the church just above the ground, as well as the chevet wall, the chancel and the ambulatory (11 and 12C); the poet **Ronsard** was buried here in 1585. He was Prior of St-Cosme from 1565 until his death; a stone slab with a flowering rose tree covers his tomb.

In the monks' refectory, a large 12C building, note the reader's pulpit decorated with columns and sculptured capitals. The **Prior's lodging,** where Ronsard lived and died, is a charming small 15C house; in Ronsard's time an outside staircase led to the first floor of the residence, which only had one great room on each level; this staircase was pulled down in the 17C when the inside staircase was built. The "lodging" now houses a small lapidary museum and a collection of drawings, plans, photos and engravings evoking Ronsard's life.

Château de Plessis-lès-Tours (AV B). − *Guided tours 10am to noon and 2 to 6pm (5pm 1 October to 31 March); closed Tuesdays, January and certain public holidays; 3.10F.*

This modest brick building with stone piers is only a small part of the château built by Louis XI in the 15C and which consisted of three wings in an U-shape. In particular one can visit the room where Louis XI died, which is covered with linenfold panelling, frequent in the 15C; various other rooms evoke the memory of Louis XI.

Son of Charles VII and Marie of Anjou, **Louis XI** was born in Bourges in 1423 and acceded to the throne in 1461. He spent a lot of time at Plessis-lès-Tours. Historians sometimes depict him as deceitful, cruel, cynical and distrustful, sometimes as thoughtful, intelligent and clever. He was certainly not good-looking, and refused to compensate for this by wearing sumptuous costumes, preferring to dress simply, in thick cloth like ordinary people. Anxious to encourage the economic expansion of his kingdom after the ravages of the Hundred Years War, he developed industry and trade and deserved his nickname of "King of Merchants". His fights with the Duke of Burgundy, Charles the Bold, who dreamt of having the crown, ended in the defeat and death of the Duke in 1477, and annexation of part of the Duchy in 1482. The betrayal of Cardinal **Jean Balue** appeared in this context; a favourite of Louis XI who showered him with honours, the cardinal secretly conspired with the Duke of Burgundy; he was unmasked in 1469 and imprisoned at Loches until 1480, but lived another 11 years after his release.

Louis XI was very pious *(see Cléry-St-André)* and towards the end of his life he called to his side the Calabrian hermit **Francis of Paola**, founder of the severely ascetic Minim Order. He was present at his deathbed and subsequently established the first convents of his Order in France.

Mettray Dolmen (AU). – *12 km - 8 miles to the northwest by the N 138 and right on to the D 76 towards Mettray.* The beautiful "fairy Grotto" dolmen stands about 2 km - 1 mile north of Mettray, on the right bank of the Choisille in a small wood *(access by a stony, signposted path)*. The dolmen is one of the most skilfully worked megalithic monuments to be found in France – 11 m - 36 ft long and 3.70 m - 12 ft high it is composed of twelve very evenly cut stone slabs.

Meslay Tithe Barn★ (Grange de Meslay) (AU S). – *10 km - 7 miles to the northeast (by the N 10 and a road to the right). Guided tours Saturdays and Sundays 3 to 6.30pm ; closed All Saints' Day to Easter and 11 June to 11 July ; time : 1/2 hour ; 10F.*
This former fortified farm belonging to Marmoutier Abbey has a beautiful porch, the remains of a perimeter wall and a remarkable **tithe barn**. The latter is a very good example of a 13C agricultural building. The rounded main door is set in a pointed gable and the roof is 15C chestnut timberwork. Touraine music concerts *(p 32)* and art exhibitions are held in this barn.

Montlouis-sur-Loire. – Pop 7 003. *Facilities pp 36-37. 12 km - 8 miles to the east by* ⑤ *the D 751.* The village clings to the tufa slopes, riddled with cellars. Its vineyards between the Loire and the Cher produce a fine white wine from the *Pinot de la Loire* grape.
The Renaissance mansion (now the presbytery), next to the church, is enhanced by shell ornamented dormer windows. The Babou family from the nearby Château de la Bourdaisière, were the overlords of Montlouis in the 16C.

■ TROO ★

Michelin map 🔢 fold 5 – *Local map p 99* – Pop 337

The rather strange little town of Troo, perched on a steeply rising slope and distinguished from afar by its belfry tower, still has numerous troglodyte dwellings. The houses rising in tiers, one above the other, are linked by narrow alleys, stairways and mysterious passageways. An inextricable labyrinth of galleries, called *caforts* (short of *caves fortes)*, exists underground in the white tufa rock. In times of war these *caforts* served as hideouts.

■ SIGHTS

La "Butte". – This feudal motte or Gaulish burial mound, affords a splendid **panorama★** *(viewing table and telescope)* of the winding Loir and its valley and on the opposite bank the small Church of St-Jacques-des-Guérets.

Collegiate Church of St-Martin. – Founded in 1050 and altered a century later, the church is dominated by a remarkable square **tower** pierced by openings. The splays are ornamented with small columns so typically Angevin.

The Romanesque apse is lit by Gothic windows. The historiated capitals at the transept crossing are Romanesque. The choir stalls and communion table are 15C. The 16C wooden statue of St-Mamès is invoked for all stomach ailments.

Grand Puits. – Known as the talking well because of its excellent echo, this well is 45 m - 148 ft deep and is protected by a shingle board roof.

Maladrerie Ste-Catherine. – This 12C building standing on the D 917 at the eastern end of the town, has fine Romanesque blind arcades. It served as a lazar house (hospice) on the pilgrimage routes to St-Martin in Tours and St James's shrine in Santiago de Compostela.

Limestone Cave (Grotte pétrifiante). – *Open 1 April to 30 September from 8am to 8pm ; 3F.*
Stalactites and lime encrusted objects.

St-Jacques-des-Guérets. – *Time : 1/4 hour.* This church was ministered by the Augustinians from the Abbey of St-Georges-des-Bois. The **mural paintings★** dating from between 1130 and 1170, show a strong Byzantine influence. They are especially interesting for the draughtsmanship and the freshness of the colours, sky blue, jade, purple, etc. The finest paintings are in the apse : on the left the Crucifixion and the Resurrection of the Dead ; Christ in Majesty and the Last Supper to the right. St Augustine and St George are portrayed on the embrasures of the central window. Further to the right are the Martyrdom of St James and Paradise.
Continuing round to the south wall of the nave note above the Miracle of St Nicholas with the Saint throwing gold pieces to three girls to save them from prostitution as proposed by a profiteering father ; below is the Resurrection of Lazarus. Further on a vast composition represents Christ's descent into Limbo : a most majestic Jesus delivers Adam and Eve. The opposite wall has paintings of various periods from the 12 to the 15C : the Nativity and Massacre of the Innocents.

Michelin map **64** fold 13 — 14 km - 8 miles north of Chinon — *Local map p 100*

Overlooking the Indre and turning its back to the cliff where the Forest of Chinon ends, this castle stands above flowered terraces. Its massive shape and its fortified towers are rather grim, but the white stone and the number of its roofs, turrets, dormer windows and chimneys, bristling against the green background, are fascinating. Its poetic and slightly mysterious appearance has always appealed to the imagination.

It is said that Perrault, the great writer of fairy tales, looking for a worthy setting for his *Sleeping Beauty,* took Ussé as his model.

To get the best view the tourist should stand either on the bridge, 200 m - 220yd ft from the castle, or on the Loire embankment.

From the Bueils to the Blacas. — Ussé is an ancient fortress. In the second half of the 15C it became the property of a great family of Touraine, the Bueils. They had distinguished themselves in the Hundred Years War (1337-1453) and they wished to create a new dwelling worthy of their rank.

In 1485 Antoine de Bueil, the husband of a daughter of Charles VII and Agnès Sorel, sold Ussé to the Espinays, a Breton family who had supplied chamberlains and cup bearers to the Duke of Brittany, to Louis XI and to Charles VIII. To them we owe the living quarters overlooking the courtyard, and the pretty chapel in the park.

The castle often changed hands. Among its owners was Vauban's son-in-law. The great military engineer made frequent visits to Ussé.

Today the estate belongs to the marquis de Blacas, grandson of the founder of the Egyptian Department of the Louvre.

Château. — *Guided tours Easter to 30 September 9am to noon and 2 to 7pm; the rest of the year 10am to noon and 2 to 6pm; closed 4 November (except weekend of 11 November) to 14 March; time: 3/4 hour; 25F.*

The 15C outside walls look as though they were built as fortifications while the courtyard buildings are open and inviting to look at and some even have a Renaissance air. Three ranges, which have been much restored, stand round the courtyard: the east block is Gothic, the west is Renaissance and the south is partly Gothic and partly Classical. The north block was removed in the 17C to open up the view from the terraces of the valleys of the Loire and the Indre. The west wing is prolonged by a 17C pavilion.

On entering note the fine 17C *trompe l'œil* ceiling. The former kitchens now have a collection of Saracen arms brought back from his travels by a member of the Blacas family. Also worthy of note is the great staircase dating from the 17C, with its fine wrought iron balustrade. The antechamber to the State Bedroom has a very beautiful 16C Italian cabinet incrusted with ivory. The State or Royal Bedroom (chambre du roi) was obligatory in a château of this standing. The Bedroom with its great State Bed has fine 18C furniture and silk hangings.

Tapestries adorn the ground floor gallery and paintings that on the first floor.

The **chapel,** which stands alone in the park, was built between 1520 and 1538. It is in the purest Renaissance style and has remained almost intact with its sculptures and decorations. The west face is the best. The initials "C" and "L", which are to be found on this wall and elsewhere and are one of the decorative motifs of the chapel, are those of Charles d'Espinay, who built the chapel, and of his wife, Lucrèce de Pons. Inside the chancel is ornamented by a fine hanging keystone and magnificent stalls. An Aubusson tapestry traces the history of Joan of Arc. A graceful Virgin in enamelled clay by Luca della Robbia stands in the little ogive vaulted south chapel.

Michelin map **68** fold 18 — Pop 3 139

Valençay belongs geographically to the Berry district. The château dates from the 16C, the Golden Age of the Loire Valley. The great size of the château gives it a family resemblance to Chambord.

A financier's château. — Valençay was built about 1540 by Jacques d'Estampes, the owner of the feudal castle that already existed there. This lord, having married a financier's well dowried daughter, wished to have a seat worthy of his new fortune. The 12C castle was demolished and the present sumptuous building rose on its site.

Finance often mingled with the history of Valençay: among its successive owners were several Farmers-General and even the notorious John Law, whose dizzy financial adventure was an early and masterly example of inflation.

In 1803 Valençay was acquired by **Talleyrand,** that astonishing figure who began his career as Bishop of Autun under Louis XVI and supported the cause of the French Revolution. He died in 1838 after having occupied the highest posts in a whole series of régimes. Talleyrand gave princely receptions at the château.

■ THE CHÂTEAU★★ *time: 1 hour*

Guided tours 15 March to 15 November 9am to noon and 2 to 7pm (also open week-ends out of season 10am to noon and 1.30 to 4.30pm); 20F including park. Son et lumière performance see p 33.

The entrance pavilion is a huge structure designed like a keep, but a "pleasure keep" with many windows, harmless turrets and false machicolations. The pointed roof is pierced with high dormer windows and surmounted by monumental chimneys. This architecture is also found in the Renaissance châteaux of the Loire Valley, but in this case the first signs of the Classical style may be detected in the shape of pilasters above the Doric (ground floor), Ionic (first floor) and Corinthian capitals (second floor).

The Classical style is even more evident in the roofs of the large corner towers. Here domes take the place of the pepperpot roofs which were the rule on the banks of the Loire in the 16C.

Museum. – Installed in the outbuildings it contains historical souvenirs of Prince Talleyrand. The Prince's bedroom has been restored to its original aspect.

West Wing. – This was added in the 17C and remodelled in the following century. At roof level dormer windows alternate with *œils-de-bœuf* (ox eyes or rounded openings). On the ground floor you can see the gallery and two rooms containing many art objects and sumptuous Louis XVI, Regency and especially Empire furniture ; a room with fine Louis XVI wainscoting ; and the vestibule, the walls of which are hung with prints concerning Prince Talleyrand and his contemporaries. On the first floor is the room occupied by Ferdinand VII, King of Spain, when he was confined to Valençay from 1808 to 1814 on the orders of Napoleon. A glimpse of the gallery may be had from the antechamber.

Park. – *Open all year round except 25 December and 1 January ; 7F.* In this lovely formal garden in front of the château, black swans, ducks, peacocks etc. wander about freely and are living ornaments. Under the great trees of the park which stretches to the west of the château, there are deer, llamas, dromadaries and kangaroos kept in large enclosures.

Centre Automobile Museum (M). – Hidden in the park, it contains the collection of the Guignard brothers, grandsons of a coachbuilder in Vatan (Indre) ; this collection has more than 60 old motorcars (1898), perfectly maintained and in working order ; there are also road documents for the motorist of earlier days, old Michelin maps and Red guides from before 1914.

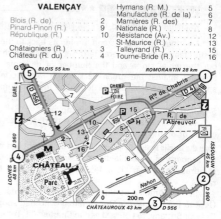

EXCURSION

Luçay-le-Mâle. – Pop 2 334. *10 km - 6 1/4 miles to the southwest by ④, the D 960.*

This quiet village has an interesting **Gunflint Museum** *(apply to Mr. Emy for a guided tour, 10am to noon and 2 to 6pm ; time : 1 hour)*. Like Selles-sur-Cher and Meusnes *(p 148)*, Luçay has long contributed to the large local production of gunflint, taken from a bed of high quality flint. In this museum the extraction of flint is shown in very concrete manner, how it is cut and its commercialisation from the 17 to 18C, up to the invention of the percussion cap. The way of life of the craftsmen is shown, their tools, their methods, the sale price and the export area of their products.

VENDÔME ★★

Michelin map **64** fold 6 – *Local maps pp 96 and 99* – Pop 18 218 – *Facilities pp 36-37*

At the foot of a steep, castle crowned hillside, the Loire subdivides into several narrow arms which pass under a series of multiple span bridges. Vendôme, centred on the islands thus created, is a huddled mass of belfries and gables with tall slated roofs, but urban development now reaches as far as the hillside. The traditional glove trade dates from the Renaissance. Other activities include the manufacture of car components, machine and aircraft control instruments, plastics, and an important printing works.

HISTORICAL NOTES

A much disputed place. – Although its origins date from Neolithic, Gaulish and Gallo-Roman times (Vindocenum), the town only really began to acquire importance under the Bouchard family, faithful supporters of the Capetian dynasty and in particular in the 11C under Foulques Nerra's son, Geoffroi Martel who founded the Abbey of La Trinité.

This seat of the counts of Vendôme, vassals of the Plantagenets, was caught up in the Hundred Years War due mainly to its border position between lands held by the rival camps of the English and the French. It was the theatre of many a battle. In 1371 the royal house of Bourbon inherited Vendôme and in 1515 François I raised it to the status of a duchy.

The town sided with the Catholic League but, in 1589, it was recaptured by its rightful feudal lord, Henri IV, suffering in the process a cruel sacking — only the Abbey Church of La Trinité was to remain standing.

César, the son of Henri IV. – The town was passed to **César de Vendôme**, Henri IV's son by Gabrielle d'Estrées, who often resided here during his lifetime of continual conspiring : firstly during the minority of Louis XIII and then against Richelieu. He spent four years imprisoned in the Château de Vincennes before being exiled. In the end he renounced his principles and threw in his lot with Cardinal Mazarin but he was to die in 1655.

Balzac's schooldays. – The register of the Oratorians' College in Vendôme has an entry on the 22 June 1807 recording the admission of an eight year old boy, Honoré de Balzac. The future novelist of prodigious output, proved to be an inattentive and undisciplined pupil. Discipline was strict and many were the times that the young Balzac had himself sent to the punishment cell, so as to be able to read in peace. When his health showed signs of suffering, Balzac's parents were quick to recall him to Tours.

■ FORMER TRINITÉ ABBEY★ (Ancienne Abbaye de la Trinité — A) time: 1 hour

One summer's night, Geoffroy Martel, the Count of Anjou having witnessed the spectacle of three swords of flame falling into a fountain, decided to found a monastery which was consecrated on 31 May 1040 to the Holy Trinity. Under the Benedictines the abbey experienced considerable growth to such an extent that the holder of the abbot's post was automatically nominated cardinal, as was the case of a 12C abbot who detained the famous Geoffroi de Vendôme, friend of Pope Urbain II, a native of Champagne. Up to the time of the Revolution La Trinité was the centre of a pilgrimage to the Holy Tear which Christ wept on the sepulchre of Lazarus and which Geoffroi Martel brought back from Constantinople. The Vendôme knights used to rally to the cries of "Holy Tear of Vendôme" and "Lazarus' Friday". The faithful come to venerate this relic which was invoked for eye diseases.

Abbey Church★★. — This a remarkable example of Flamboyant Gothic architecture.

Exterior. — Enter the abbey precincts from the Rue de l'Abbaye which cuts through the 12C visitor's hostel. To the right, standing on its own is the 12C **belfry**, 80 m — 262 ft high, which is said to have served as a model for the Clocher Vieux, one of the two spire towers of Chartres Cathedral. Note the increasing size of the arches, blind at the foot, which also become more recessed with an increase in height. The octagonal spire rises from the final storey of the belfry, which is also octagonal, being covered at the corners by pinnacled turrets. Marking off the base of the first floor are a series of grinning masks and animals.

(After photo: Arthaud, Grenoble)

La Trinité Abbey Church
Misericord

Built from east to west, the church has an astonishing Flamboyant façade, accentuated by a great openwork gable. It was built at the beginning of the 16C by Jean de Beauce, architect of the Clocher Neuf of Chartres cathedral ; delicately pierced like lace, it contrasts with the simplicity of the Romanesque tower.

The nave, begun near the transept in the middle of the 14C was only completed after the Hundred Years War ; the transept, all that remains of the 11C building, preceeds the apse with its radiating chapels.

Interior. — The nave is remarkable for the width of its triforium and the height of its windows. Note how the progression from the 14C to the 15C phase of construction is achieved without altering the unity of conception. There are no longer capitals, the design of the frieze and the decoration of the triforium and ribs all change.

The transept crossing has conserved its primitive capitals surmounted by 13C polychrome statues portraying the Archangel Gabriel and Virgin of the Annunciation, and St Peter with St Eutropius, who was venerated in this abbey church. The transept vaulting with its historiated keystones was transformed in the 14C to the Angevin style *(p 21)*. To the left of the high altar are statues of St John the Baptist (14C) and the Virgin (16C).

The 14C chancel, with stained glass of the same period, is adorned by fine late 15C choir stalls (1). Going round the ambulatory note the choir screen (2) which shows a decided Italian influence. On reaching the high altar note the base adorned with tears of the celebrated "monument of the Sainte-Larme", with an opening to allow the faithful to venerate the relic.

The windows of the chancel are glazed with much restored 16C stained glass : the best, representing the Meal at Simon's House after a German engraving, is found in the first chapel to the left of the axial one. The latter has the famous **Virgin and Child window** (3) dating from the 12C.

Conventual buildings. — For some time these have been occupied by the Rochambeau or Twentieth Light Cavalry regiment. Of the 14C cloisters only the gallery alongside the church remains intact. The chapter house has been uncovered and restored. The adjoining Classical buildings house a museum *(see opposite)*.

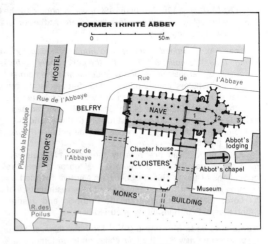

FORMER TRINITÉ ABBEY

0   50m

HOSTEL

Rue   de   l'Abbaye

Rue de l'Abbaye

BELFRY

NAVE

Place de la République

VISITOR'S

Cour de
l'Abbaye

Chapter house

CLOISTERS

Abbot's
lodging

Abbot's chapel

Museum

MONKS'

BUILDING

R. des
Poilus

From the cloisters take the passage leading under the monks' building, then turn round to admire the monumental façade built between 1732 and 1742. The pediment adorned with the royal fleur-de-lis, carries the motto *Pax* and the lamb emblem of the Benedictine Order.

Museum★ (A M). — *Open 10am to noon and 2 to 6pm ; closed on Tuesdays, 1 May, 25 December and 1 January ; 7.40F.*

Installed in the La Trinité Abbey monks' building, with its majestic staircase, the collections are well displayed. The rooms most worthy of attention on the **ground floor★** deal with mural painting in the Loir Valley and religious art in the Vendôme region during the Middle Ages and the Renaissance : fragments of the 16C tomb of François de Bourbon-Vendôme and of Marie de Luxembourg, vaulting keystones from the cloisters, abbey church holy water basin, etc.

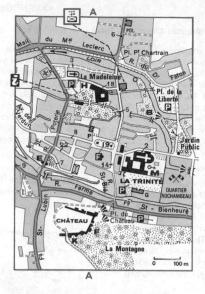

Upstairs are the prehistory and antiquity collections. Other rooms contain furniture and paintings of the French and Flemish schools of the 16-18Cs, including some good portraits and faiences. Note the harp by Naderman (1773-1835) Marie-Antoinette's instrument maker.

Another room shows the tools and instruments of once flourishing regional crafts and the reconstruction of a typical Vendômois rural interior.

■ ADDITIONAL SIGHTS

Public gardens (A). – Lapped by the waters of the Loir, these gardens have a pleasant view over Vendôme, La Trinité, and the 15C **Porte d'Eau**, also known as the Arche des Grands Près (B). The **Place de la Liberté** is a continuation of the gardens, with another picturesque view of the Porte d'Eau.

Former Lycée Ronsard (A H). – Previously the Oratorians' College (Ancien collège des Oratoriens) which Balzac attended at the beginning of the 19C. On the wall there is a plaque bearing the effigy of Ronsard (1524-85) showing where the house of the great Pléiade poet used to stand *(pp 130 and 153)*.

Church of the Madeleine (A). – 1474. It has a bell tower surmounted by a crocketed spire.

Porte St-Georges (A E). – Protecting the entrance to the town on the edge of the Loir, it is flanked by great towers, the massive stonework dating from the 14C. But from the bridge you can see the battlements and sculptured decoration of Renaissance gargoyles and medallions, added at the beginning of the 16C by Marie de Luxembourg, Duchess of Vendôme.

Place St-Martin (A 19). – Until the 19C it was occupied by the Church of St-Martin (15-16C) but now only the bell tower still stands in the square. At the corner of the Rue du Change there is an old 15C half timbered house.

Château (A). – *Guided tours 9am to noon, 2 to 6pm; closed Tuesdays and November to March; time: 1/2 hour; 5.30F; 2F for the park; apply to the keeper.*

Arrive by car via the Faubourg St-Lubin and the hamlet Le Temple which originally grew up round a Templars' commandery *(p 119)*. Situated at the top of what is known as "La Montagne" which dominates the Loir, this ruined château has an earth wall and ramparts marked out by round battlemented towers of the 13 and 14C; on the eastern side the great tower, Tour de Poitiers (F) was rebuilt in the 15C.

Enter the château precincts by the early 17C gateway, Porte de Beauce (K) laid out with a vast garden. Here the foundations of the St George Collegiate Church, founded by Geoffroy Martel can still be seen. This was the resting place of the Lords of Vendôme: Antoine de Bourbon and Jeanne d'Albret, parents of Henri IV were buried here.

Promenade de la Montagne (A). – From the terraces there are picturesque **views★** of the Loir Valley and Vendôme.

(After photo: Hurault)

Areines Church — Holy warrior

EXCURSIONS

Areines. – Pop 908. *3 km - 2 miles to the east by ②, the D 917 and the first road to the left.*

An important market town in Roman times, Areines is now one of the many small villages in the Loir plain.

The 12C church whose sober façade is adorned with a 14C Virgin contains an ensemble of **frescoes** interesting for the draughtsmanship and freshness of the colours.

In the oven vault of the apse a majestic Christ is surrounded by the symbols of the Evangelists: note St Mark's very stylised lion so typically Byzantine; below are the Apostles with their sky blue haloes, a colour typical of the Loir Valley frescoes; in the central openings are the warrior saints.

The chancel's vault shows the angels in adoration before the Lamb, with an elegant Annunciation and Visitation at the sides and a fairly faded Nativity. The frescoes on the chancel walls would appear to be more recent: on the right is the Marriage of the Virgin.

Nourray. – Pop 135. *11 km - 7 miles to the south by ④, the N 10 and the third road on the left.*

Isolated on the square, the small village church has a chevet decorated with a row of Romanesque arcadings under sculptured modillions; note the multifoil arch which decorates the central window.

Inside *(if the church is closed, the key is opposite at Mr. Geyer's house)*, the apse with its hemispherical vaulting over the circular plan is surrounded by arcading with sculptured capitals.

Rhodon. – Pop 98. *19 km - 12 miles to the southeast by ②, the D 917. At Villetrun turn right towards Selommes and there left into the D 161.*

On the walls of the church *(to visit apply to Mme Rentien)* and on the Gothic vaulting important traces of mural paintings remain, of the 14 and 15C. In particular, in the apse there is a Christ in Majesty, and on one of the transverse arches of the nave, the months of the year are depicted.

If you are looking for a pleasant hotel or camp site
in peaceful surroundings
you couldn't do better than look in the current Michelin Guides
FRANCE and CAMPING CARAVANING FRANCE.

VILLANDRY, Château de ★★

Michelin map **64** fold 14 – *Local map p 100*

Villandry is one of the most original châteaux in Touraine for the arrangement of its esplanade, terraces, moats and canals, and especially of its famous gardens.

■ THE GARDENS★★★

Open 8.30 or 9am to sunset; 14F.

In the 19C, when the landscaped English garden was all the rage, the owners of the château redesigned the grounds. When Dr. Carvallo, founder of Demeure Historique, the French Historic Houses Association, bought Villandry he patiently recon-structed the formal French gardens of the 16C; there is no other example of such gardens.

Three tiers of terraces are superimposed. On the highest is the water garden, with its fine sheet of water, below this is the ornamental garden, and then the kitchen garden. The geometrically shaped flower-beds are emphasised by yew trees and box borders. Each border represents a different arrangement of hearts, the symbol of Love. Canals, foun-tains, and vine bearing pergo-las add various effects. This architectural design is due to the influence of the first Italian gardeners brought to France by Charles VIII, but French influence appears in many de-tails. In the 16C, flowers, shrubs and fruit trees were practically the same that we

(After photo: Burthe d'Annelet)

Château de Villandry — The Gardens

know today. Among vegetables, the potato was missing – Parmentier, who brought it to France, lived in the 18C. The gardener's art was already advanced: he pruned and grafted and knew how to use the greenhouse and raise early vegetables.

The best view is from the terraces behind the château.

The small Romanesque Church of Villandry is a charming feature of the whole scene. It contains a 16C stained glass window.

The orchard, laid out in accordance with plans made by Du Cerceau, lies on the southern slope of the hill, separated from the rest of the property by a path, and overlooking both the property and the valley.

VILLANDRY, Château de★★

■ THE CHÂTEAU

Guided tours 1 May to 30 September 9am to 6.30pm; 15 March to 30 April, 9.30am to 5.30pm; 14 October to 11 November, 9.30am to 5pm; time: 1/2 hour; 16F.

Of the original fortress only the keep remains. It is a great tower embedded in the present edifice, which was built in the 16C by Jean Le Breton, Secretary of State to François I. Three ranges enclose a courtyard opening north on to the valley through which flow the Loire and the Cher.

The Spaniard Joachim de Carvallo filled the château with Spanish furniture and an interesting collection of paintings (mainly 16, 17 and 18C Spanish school). On the ground floor there is the main salon and dining room with Louis XV panelling, and then the great staircase with wrought iron banisters which leads to the picture gallery and the room with a 13C **Mudéjar ceiling** which came from Toledo; it is a coffered ceiling painted and gilded with typically Moorish designs, an unexpected sight under the Loire skies; there are two 16C Italian paintings on wood (St Paul and St John), with very luminous colours, and a portrait of the Infanta of the Velazquez school.

VILLESAVIN, Château de

Michelin map **64** fold 18 — 3 km - 2 miles north of Bracieux

The name of Villesavin comes from an old Roman villa (Villa Sabinus) built beside Hadrian's Roman road which runs alongside the present road from Ponts d'Arian (Arian = Adrien or Hadrian).

This charming Renaissance building, erected in 1537 by Jean Le Breton, Lord of Villandry, who was in charge of the work on the Château de Chambord, shows certain tendencies of the Classical style.

Guided tours 10am to 7pm; 1 October to 15 November 10am to 5pm; 16 November to 20 December 2 to 4pm; closed 21 December to 28 February; time: 3/4 hour; 14F; esplanade: 6F.

It consists of a central block on the ground level, framed between symmetrical pavilions. The attics with their fine dormer windows and the inscriptions on the rear façade give the building beautiful proportions. A very beautiful 16C Italian **basin** in marble adorns the main courtyard.

A few furnished apartments are open to view. They contain pewter serving dishes, jugs, pitchers and plates. Old carriages stand in the coach house.

To the left of the château is a large 16C **dovecote** with a well preserved revolving ladder.

OTHER PLACES OR INTERESTING SIGHTS

AIGRE Valley 60 fold 17 — 9 km - 6 miles from Cloyes-sur-le Loir.

The D 8, running along the north bank of this tributary of the Loir, affords good views of the peaceful rural Aigre valley. The tranquil village of **Romilly-sur-Aigre** (Pop 360) is the Rognes of Zola's novel *Earth*. In the small village of **La Ferté-Villeneuil** (Pop 361), in a pastoral setting beside the Aigre, stands the forceful tower of a fortified Romanesque church.

BEAUFORT-EN-VALLÉE 64 fold 12 — Pop 4 775 — 27 km - 17 miles east of Angers.

Lying in the rich alluvial plains to the north of the Loire, this town (14C) once had a thriving sail cloth industry. From the hilltop, with the ruins of a **castle** (14C), there is a wide **panorama** of the surrounding countryside. The **church** has a fine bell tower built by Jean de Lespine. Inside are two altars a 17C wood one and a second in marble.

BLOU 64 fold 12 — Pop 853 — 16 km - 10 miles from Beaufort-en-Vallée *(see above)* via the N 147. Longué and the D 206.

The Romanesque **church** with its massive buttresses has curious 11C diapering on its north transept. A 13C bell tower rises above the transept crossing. *To visit apply at the grocer's opposite except Thursdays and Sunday afternoons.*

BREIL 64 fold 13 — Pop 303 — 6 km - 4 miles to the southeast of Noyant.

The Romanesque **church** dominated by a tall stone spire has fine Plantagenet vaulting in the chancel. The pleasant 17C park *(apply to visit)* of the **Château du Lathan** offers a remarkable vista terminated by an elegant 18C pavilion.

BROU 60 east of fold 16 — Pop 3 844 — 22 km - 14 miles northwest of Châteaudun.

This market town (especially poultry), characteristic of the Beauce, is grouped round its market place, Place des Halles. Half timbered houses and sculptured woodwork are common features.

BUEIL-EN-TOURAINE 64 fold 4 — Pop 452 — 15 km - 9 miles northeast of St Paterne-Racan via Neuvy-le-Roi.

This was the home of the Bueil family, which included an Admiral, two Marshals and the poet Honorat de Bueil *(p 133)*. A curious agglomeration of buildings, atop the hill, have been formed by the juxtaposition of the **Church of St-Pierre-aux-Liens** (to the left) and the **Collegiate Church of Sts-Innocents-St-Michel**. Inside the church, adjoining an incomplete square tower, are early 16C frescoes, statues and a remarkable Renaissance **baptistery**. A door gives on to the collegiate church which the Bueil's had built to serve as a family vault. Recumbent figures of the Bueil family can be seen.

CHAMPTOCÉ-SUR-LOIRE 63 fold 19 — Pop 1 233 — 6 km - 4 miles to the east of Ingrandes by the N 23.

As you leave the village eastwards note the ruins of the château of Gilles de Rais (1404-40), the sinister personality who inspired Charles Perrault to create his character, **Bluebeard**.

DANGEAU 60 fold 17 — Pop 752 — 9 km - 6 miles west of Bonneval.

The **church** *(time: 1/4 hour)* in a very pure Romanesque style was built by monks from Marmoutier in the 12C. The south doorway has intricately sculptured carvings. The wooden ceiling of the nave is supported by archaic pillars. The aisles have statues, two of which are equestrian, typical of 15-17C local religious work; the baptismal chapel displays a marble triptych.

GIZEUX 64 centre of fold 13 — Pop 577.

The **church** *(east of the village on the D 15 — open 10am to 5.30pm in summer)* is the resting place of the elder branch of the Du Bellay family *(p 106)*. The white marble figures (17C) are interesting for the costumes portrayed.

ILLIERS-COMBRAY 60 fold 17 — Pop 3 453 — 29 km - 18 miles north of Châteaudun via Dangeau.

This market town, on the headstream of the Loir, serves both the Beauce and Perche regions. It was here in his father's native town that the novelist **Marcel Proust** (1871-1922) spent his childhood holidays providing many of the memories for his famous novel *Remembrance of Things Past*, in which Iliers is portrayed under the name of Combray. His **aunt's house** at 4 Rue du Docteur-Proust contains mementoes of the writer *(guided tours 3pm to 5pm; closed Tuesdays, 1 January, 1 May, 14 July and 25 December; 10F)*. Also evoked in the novel are the pleasant landscaped gardens, the **Pré-Catelan**, which border the D 149 to the south of the town.

LINIÈRES-BOUTON 64 fold 13 — Pop 97 — 5 km - 3 miles east of Mouliherne *(p 170)*.

The village church *(to visit apply at the grocer's-épicerie — Place de l'Église)* has a fine **chancel** with Plantagenet vaulting.

MIRÉ ⓖ4 fold 1 – Pop 1 035 – 10 km - 16 miles north of Châteauneuf-sur-Sarthe.

The **church** has wooden keel vaulting decorated with forty-three painted panels dating from the late 15C. Depicted are the Four Evangelists, the Angels carrying Instruments of the Passion and the Apostles presenting the Creed.

MONTBAZON ⓖ4 fold 15 – Pop 3 011 – 9 km - 5 1/2 miles – south of Tours – *Facilities pp 36-37.*

This is one of the twenty strongholds built by Foulques Nerra *(p 42)*. The dismantled **keep** *(open 1 June to 15 September 10am to 10pm ; 1 March to 31 May and 15 October to 31 January 10am to 2pm weekdays except Wednesdays and 10am to 6pm Saturdays, Sundays and holidays ; 10F)* provides a good vantage point. Take the road to the left of the town hall, the Rue des Moulins, go through a former town gate, then take a path to the right.

MOULIHERNE ⓖ4 folds 12 and 13 – Pop 1 079 – 13.5 km - 8 miles southeast of Baugé.

The **church** *(to visit apply at the grocer's-épicerie, near the church)* has a 13C bell tower crowned by a twisting spire typical of the Baugeois *(p 50)*. Inside the vaulting demonstrates the development of the Angevin style. Chancel with groined vaulting ; south transept : an early example of quadripartite vaulting with a more elaborate version in the north arm ; nave : 12-13C Gothic vaulting, wide and soaring.

ST-LAURENT-EN-GÂTINES ⓖ4 fold 6 – Pop 546 – 11 km - 7 miles to the west of Château-Renault by the D 766.

On the D 766 stands the former home of the abbots of Marmoutier, a massive edifice in brick and stone. This 15C building was transformed into a church in the 19C : the turreted polygonal staircase became a spire and two large Flamboyant windows were added on one of its side.

ST-OUEN (Château de) ⓖ3 fold 10 – 7 km - 4 miles southwest of Château-Gontier by the D 20.

Before reaching Chemazé notice on the right this 15-16C château with its pedimented dormer windows and large square staircase tower topped by a crown structure. *Not open to the public.*

VAUX (Château de) – 3.5 km - 2 miles northwest of Miré *(see above)*.

Standing back from the road this château now partly in ruins was built in the late 15C by Jean Bourré *(p 129)*. It was this same lord who introduced the *Bon Chrétien* variety of pear into Anjou. Covered with Virginia creeper, the château has preserved part of its ramparts and the elegant main building with its turreted staircase and mullioned windows.

VERNANTES ⓖ4 fold 13 – Pop 1 743 – 12 km - 8 miles west of Gizeux *(p 169)*.

The handsome 12C bell tower, topped by a slim stone spire, and the chancel are all that remains of the former church struck by lightning in the 19C *(to visit apply at the town hall)*. A new church has been built on the other side of the square.

VERNOIL ⓖ4 fold 13 – Pop 1 368 – 10 km - 6 miles west of Gizeux *(p 169)*.

The church is attractive with its massive bell tower and pure lines. The Prior's lodging has mullioned windows and an octagonal turret.

YÈVRES ⓖ0 folds 16 and 17 – Pop 1 458 – 1.5 km - 1 mile east of Brou *(p 169)*.

The 15-16C **church** has an elegant Renaissance doorway. Inside there is some remarkable Classical **woodwork★** : pulpit, altarpiece, lectern, church warden's pew and door to the baptismal chapel. Note the chest with fine 17 and 18C church vestments. The sacristy has Louis XIII style woodwork and a collection of sacred vases (17 and 18C).

YRON (Chapelle d') ⓖ0 fold 7 – 1 km - 1/2 mile from Cloyes-sur-le-Loir. Take the N 10, then the D 8[1] to the right.

Enter the garden of the old people's home. This Romanesque chapel is decorated with **mural paintings** in ochre and red tones. In the nave they are of the 12C and depict (on the left) the Flagellation and the Offering of the Magi ; (on the right) Judas's Kiss and an abbot (St Bernard). Overlooking the Apostles, in the apse, is a 14C Christ Enthroned.

INDEX

Loir (Valley) .... Towns, sights and tourist regions
Foulques Nerra, Tuffeau ..... Historical events, persons and local terms explained
in the text

The department is given in brackets after the town, see abbreviations below :

Indre-et-Loire (I.-et-L.)   Maine-et-Loire (M.-et-L.)
Loir-et-Cher (L.-et-C.)   Loire-Atlantique (Loire-Atl.)

NOTES

175

Ch. de Menars
Musée

MANUFACTURE FRANÇAISE DES PNEUMATIQUES MICHELIN
Société en commandite par actions au capital de 700 000 000 de francs
Place des Carmes-Déchaux - 63 Clermont-Ferrand (France)
R.C.S. Clermont-Fd B 855 200 507
© Michelin et Cie, Propriétaires-Éditeurs 1986
Dépôt légal 11-85 - ISBN 2 06 013 213-4 - ISSN 0763-1383

Printed in France - 9-85-30
Photocomposition : BLANCHARD, Le Plessis-Robinson - Impression : ISTRA, Strasbourg n° 509300